Melting the Venusberg

Melting the Venusberg

A Feminist Theology of Music

Heidi Epstein

2004

The Continuum International Publishing Group Inc
15 East 26 Street, New York, NY 10010

The Continuum International Publishing Group Ltd
The Tower Building, 11 York Road, London SE1 7NX

Printed in the United States of America

Library of Congress Cataloging-in-Publication Data

Epstein, Heidi.
    Melting the Venusberg : a feminist theology of music / Heidi Epstein.
        p. cm.
    Includes bibliographical references (p.   ) and index.
    ISBN 0-8264-1647-0 (hardcover : alk. paper)—ISBN 0-8264-1648-9 (pbk. :
alk. paper)
        1. Feminist and music. 2. Music—Religious aspects. 3. Feminism—Religious
    aspects. 4. Theology. I. Title.
    ML82.E67 2004
    780'.72—dc22

                                                        2004006963

for Tom,

    l'inoubliable

Contents

Preface

As a preliminary research project in graduate school, I explored and articulated the nature of the relationship between music and theology. My initial formulation of their rapport was shaped by two authoritative sources, namely, Oskar Söhngen's systematic theology of music (1962), and Olivier Messiaen's synthesis of religious aspirations and compositional practices. My more "neutral" findings, however, took a political turn when I asked what different conclusions I might have drawn had I made the same inquiry from a feminist perspective (a viewpoint acquired during doctoral boot camp). The theology of music that follows constitutes an initial, by no means definitive, reconceptualisation of music's theological significance in feminist terms. As such, this book contributes to the ongoing conversation among religionists and theologians about music's sacred uses and meanings. Given this discursive scope, the project does not directly address musicologists, yet it is hoped that they might also learn from the nascent interconnections that this essay makes between Christian musical ethics and aesthetics, on the one hand, and New Musicology's multivalent studies of gender "in" music, on the other.

Part One constitutes a critical survey of extant theologies of music, their classical sources and norms, and the polemical Christian rhetoric about music that these more traditional approaches have not interrogated. At times, the tone in Part One is sharp as recurring patterns of sexist thought in musico-theological discourse, as well as contemporary blindness toward the same, impair some of the finest theologians' discussions of music's meaning. The sharpness intensifies as desire mounts for "corrections" of these aporia. Such trenchant critique is also used to unsettle the most deeply entrenched biases. As one possible alternative to such classical models, part 2 offers a very modest, gender-sensitive rearticulation of music's theological import. Like other feminist theological reappraisals, it represents a relatively novel approach, given that feminism has altered academic theory and social practices only in the last century. The present book's contribution to this discursive forum, therefore, is situated as tentative and partial, yet constructively critical.

Both parts are broadly chronological in form and content. Consequently, given that my search for reconstructive raw materials spans several millennia, serious omissions are bound to occur. But the project was never meant to be an exhaustive survey and critique of theologians,' church leaders,' and composers' discussions of music; rather, the book's historical and contemporary samplings have been chosen as building blocks for constructing an alternative theology of music. Mining both center and margins of the Christian tradition, I consult those thinkers whose methods of inquiry and ideas about music have become normative for understanding music's religious significance, and also those whose astute insights have been overlooked.

Three editorial notes to the reader are in order. First, admittedly, the endnotes for each chapter are copious, yet, I would argue, necessarily so; they serve as probative evidence that mandates this feminist rereading of standard, authoritative musico-theological sources. Additionally, many of the notes contain extra citations from primary sources as well as those of secondary commentators, and further deliberations by the author, all of which are included to strengthen and further legitimate feminist critique of quasi-canonical theologies of music. More importantly, these notes allow readers to judge for themselves the persuasiveness of the implications that the author draws from particular ideas, rhetoric, and historical events. It is entirely possible, nonetheless, for readers to follow the critical and reconstructive projects without reading any or all of the additional notes. Second, when discussing specific theological or philosophical concepts of woman in the abstract, the word "Woman" will be capitalised to distinguish its theoretical valences from its more practical designations of living, breathing females.

Finally, a note about the title, *Melting the Venusberg*. It refers of course to Venus's lair in German mythology—a lavish sex parlour whose whoring queen nearly devoured Tannhäuser. Kierkegaard deemed the Venusberg a veritable "kingdom": "In this kingdom language has no home, nor thought's sobriety, nor the laborious business of reflection. All one hears is the elemental voice of passion, the play of the appetites, the wild din of intoxication; indulgence, only, in an eternal tumult."[1] To devout Christians, therefore, this medieval mythological space is the church's antithesis. Church and love-cave should remain miles apart. The music serenading Venus's captives must never infect Christian hymnody. As we shall see, however, the very course of music history and the very nature of music itself make of this mountain an irrigating stream.

Some have objected to the title's (tacitly) mixed metaphor: we melt tips of icebergs, yet the Venusberg is hardly frigid. For some reason, dissolution by heat, that is, by lava, does not automatically come to mind. Literally, lava kills, but figuratively, music's vesuvial powers merit resurrection.

Note

1. Kierkegaard, "The Immediate Erotic Stages or the Musical Erotic," 97.

Acknowledgments

Many people have provided invaluable assistance during the course of my research and writing. For their wise scholarly counsel, I thank my numerous associates during "the McGill years": Professors Mitchell B. Morris, Ian Henderson, Maurice Boutin, Gregory Baum, Katherine K. Young, Kathleen Roberts Skerrett, John Simons, Torrance Kirby, Eric Beresford, Douglas John Hall, Karen LeBacqz, Tamara Levitz, Natalie Polzer, and Maggie Kilgour.

For feminist lifelines thrown to me by both our correspondence and our panel discussions at the AAR, I thank Amy Hollywood, Ellen Armour, and Susan St. Ville.

For their revivifying collegiality as I raced to finish the project, I would also thank my new colleague-friends at St.Thomas More College: Myroslaw and Maruscia Tataryn, Mary Ann Beavis, Ivan and Zandra Wilson, Natalia Shostak, Darrell and Floranne McLaughlin, Ed Heidt, John and Patty Thompson, Brian Chartier, and the Regnier family.

For their superb technical assistance, I thank Steve Muranyi, Jim Harris, Alain Dorais, the Rev. Alan Perry, Sue Winn, Erin McConomy, Cynthia Hawkins, Suzanne Elizabeth Stewart, McGill librarians Norma Johnson, Gail Youster, and David Curtis, as well as graphic designer Jason Symington. Special thanks to Justus George Lawler at Continuum for his inimitable editorial brio.

My heartfelt thanks to Jim Kanaris, whose superlative intellect and wit saved innumerable dark days, and also to other treasured *montréalais* for their rare conviviality: Nancy and Marc Gold, Kelly Rice, Cynthia Taylor, David Jones, Paul Jennings, and Dave Turpie. For intellectual spice and side-splitting laughter, I thank Fiona Black, Andrew Wilson, Kate Wadds, and Lisbeth Dalgaard. For vital musings—both sonic and philosophical—at a time when this tome was just coffee-talk on Messiaen, I thank Will Spat and Thomas Annand. Infinite thanks to Adeline Gray whose animating sustenance defies articulation.

Finally, I sing praise for the inestimable love of family: to Bonnie and Hans, Edward and Pat, Peter, and Susan.

Musing the Obscure[1]

The Problem of Music and Meaning

To the skeptic's ear, only curious, auditory leaps of faith would translate bundled pitches spinning through time into divine revelations. The composer Olivier Messiaen claimed to reveal the eternal truths of the Catholic faith in every note he wrote.[2] Zoltan Kodaly intoned "the speech of the soul" in his works. Friedrich Schleiermacher believed that music's essence and our experiences of it provide near-perfect mirrors of their religious counterparts: "the infinite multiplicity of combinations in the realm of ordered tones is nothing other than the outward representative of the infinity of relations in self-consciousness."[3] Coincident with these lofty programmes, other voices hallow music's freedom from ideology. Sublimely apolitical, music speaks a "universal language." With such accolades, composers, theologians, philosophers, and music-lovers make music both diplomat and beast of burden. On the one hand, well-crafted melodies and chord progressions deliver secret messages from God; on the other, music transcends every human agenda.

This book contests the validity of such paradoxical *double entendres*. For since its inception, I remain unconvinced that we can have it both ways or, if we can, something very precious—a vital, self-critical candour—is lost in translation. This book challenges, therefore, the universality and timelessness of previous articulations of music's meaning: its symbolic function, for example, as microcosm of divine harmony and cosmic order; as proleptic exemplar of discords resolved. It problematises theologians' praise of music's powers for spiritual transport, its ability to unify warring hearts and minds, whatever their creed, colour, and social location. These tenets must be questioned, because their dystopic backdrop violently contradicts such happy endings. Furthermore, the sublime musicospiritual transcendence endemic to these discursive trajectories is swamped by its own gendered undertow. The sexist and escapist subtexts that have produced music's elite status as a divine, harmonising emissary require thorough diagnosis. From this re-examination, as we shall see, musico-theological discourse, as much as any other, confirms Gayatri Chakratovy Spivak's assertion that "the discourse of man lies in the metaphor of woman."[4]

This analysis of the politics of meaning-making in musico-theological discourse is a project of both critique and reconstruction. It will not be a systematic theology of music that sequentially develops, for example, a musically informed Christology, ecclesiology, and eschatology. Several dogmatic theologies of music already exist, and, as implied above, they become musical apologetics for bolstering doctrinal truths, usually rooted in music's symbolic/sonic reiteration of Christian harmonies—its redemptions, for example, of time and space. Systematic theology's prerequisites want theology, like music, to begin and end a certain way—classically, euphoniously, with emphatic final cadences. Obligations to follow systematic suit have constrained our musico-theological imaginations enough, overprescribing the normative themes and types of music without which legitimate or genuine theological models cannot take shape. Instead, what follows will be an exploratory "metaphorical theology," an approach formulated and practiced by Sallie McFague. McFague characterises theologies as "'houses' to live in for a while, with windows partly open and doors ajar," structures that quickly "become prisons when they no longer allow us to come and go."[5] Methodologically, this approach continually emphasises the inadequacy and impropriety of all language for God. Given that metaphors by their very nature cannot "be univocally applied," this method refuses to conflate human models with "divine reality."[6] Stylistically, it pursues the *via negativa*.[7] For the project at hand, this experimental mode is doubly appropriate given that *musical* God-talk adds a second semantically elusive variable to the hermeneutic equation.

Where McFague imaginatively reconstructs "metaphors and models of the God-world relationship appropriate for an ecological nuclear age," an ambitious project that produces various reconceptualisations within Christology, soteriology, and theology proper (for example, new trinitarian formulae),[8] the following inquiry seeks only to furnish one room within such larger constructions. It theologically reimagines music's metaphorical valences such that these then dramatically shift music's role and place within the "God–world relationship," and in terms relevant to a post-Christian context. Like McFague's model, it is pointedly heuristic, for it "experiments and tests," choosing its sources and content not in deference to doctrinaire authorities but on the basis of their contextual persuasiveness. To that end, it purposely enlists myriad sources "outside religious traditions."[9] It incorporates a wide range of non-theological (feminist) materials: literary criticism, new historicism, deconstruction, musicology, and, of course, the actual music of female composer/performers. This variety is meant to "break the hold of androcentric texts"[10] over our musico-theological imaginations, pitching the latter in new keys. Its ways and means may spark charges of eclecticism from those who circumscribe God-talk within the bounds of credal, scriptural, liturgical, and ecclesial canons.[11] While, for some, the modulations of this feminist theology of music breach methodological rigour *(mortis)*, for others, it may enrich and facilitate the "polyglot discourse"[12] that our pluralistic context requires.

Despite its less orthodox style and content, this inquiry still abides by and elucidates what McFague describes as Christian theology's "material norm":[13] This theology of music reconfigures God, Christ, and humanity in ways that amplify how Jesus the Christ is "paradigmatic" for comprehending the nature and purpose of divine-human interactions—in this case, describing these relational dynamics within human musicality itself, that is, within the musical activities of composition, performance, and reception. This feminist, metaphorical counterpoint is further christically attuned insofar as its findings disrupt conservative norms, upend standard dichotomies, integrate previously marginalised voices, and challenge triumphalist, hierarchical thought.[14]

I do, however, temper McFague's more positive thematic foci—remodeling God so as "to express the trustworthiness and graciousness of the power of the universe *for our time*"—with what religionist Kathleen Sands terms a "tragic sensibility."[15] In her groundbreaking critique of Christian theodicies, Sands urges theologians to adopt a tragic heuristic: "In the tragic heuristic I propose, moral judgment is wrenched beyond its conventional limits and dislodged from any secure metaphysical or transcendental grounds."[16] Her critique is pertinent to the present project because so often music is situated as concrete evidence of God's Truth, Beauty, and Goodness, "metaphysical authorities" that today's epistemologies now expose as largely human constructs.[17] Such monoliths, moreover, generate a plethora of violently "conflicting truths and [moral] goods."[18] These terminal illnesses Sands names tragedy; they reside "[i]n the angry, implacable ghosts of Auschwitz and Hiroshima, in the struggle among vital goods such as environmental and economic concerns, in the confrontation of irreconcilable definitions of moral responsibility."[19] Analogous to Christian dualist and rationalist strategies for "explaining" these social "evils," theologians have similarly harnessed the musical system of Western tonality, with its prerequisite of final harmonic resolutions, "to defend an unequivocal good by erasing loss and negation."[20] Tempered by a tragic heuristic, this feminist theology of music will attend to previous models' erasures, particularly the gendered ones, and to the theological meanings of music's nagging dissonances. It will also exhume musico-metaphorical resonances that previous theologians buried in the name of "clean or peaceful resurrections."[21]

According to Sands, now it is only the "power of living community" that adjudicates the credibility of our "moral dreams and mystical visions,"[22] and communal dissent invariably problematises such collective ideals. The task at hand, then, if theology constitutes critical thought about religion, is to absorb a community's shifts and "fissures," to scavenge viable precepts from within these rifts, and thus creatively short-circuit what has become the "blinding light of absolute transcendence."[23] Indeed, music has been made to translate into sound glimpses of this blinding light. In what follows, music—now less messenger than composer—

defects from its corseted subservience to conservative theological parties. Admittedly, many readers may still crave and christen those musics that deliver comforting promises and beauteous symbols of harmony's victory, ultimately preferring the traditional models discussed below over the feminist theological alternative proposed in part 2. For particular tastes and social locations, these "old-faithfuls" may still afford tried and true refutations of global darkness. McFague's call for tolerance is well taken: "[S]ince no metaphor or model refers properly or directly to God, many are necessary. All are inappropriate, partial, and inadequate."[24] At best, each model will elucidate a particular facet of "the God-world relationship" in helpful terms for a given historical context.[25] Nevertheless, clearing new metaphorical space[26] remains necessary to feed other imaginations—those of auditors whose musical libraries are more shocking and non-eurocentric, often because the latter are consonant with more "atonal" experiences and perceptions of a tragic world.

Having set these theological parameters, it is necessary to return to Messiaen's sonic revelations, Kodaly's soul-speech, and Schleiermacher's musical intuitions. As critical antiphon to these mystifications, a new model needs first to inspect the infrastructure, the politics of meaning-making beneath such lofty formulations. Fortunately, critical interrogatives for tracing their genesis have recently emerged within the field of musicology. Since the late 1980s, New Musicologists, and among them, feminist musicologists, have challenged formalistic, "value-free" approaches to musical analysis. Instead, feminist musicologists such as Rose Rosengard Subotnik, Suzanne Cusick, Marcia Citron, Elizabeth Wood, Ruth Solie, Ellen Koskoff, and Susan McClary reread musical works as indelibly shaped by their environs. For example, in *Feminine Endings: Music, Gender, and Sexuality,* pioneer McClary analyses works by a vast array of composers—Monteverdi, Bach, Mozart, Beethoven, Berlioz, Brahms, Schubert, Tschaikovsky, Schoenberg, Laurie Anderson, Madonna, and Diamanda Galas—to illustrate that historical changes in musical styles can often be understood by investigating changes in extramusical "cultural priorities."[27] McClary shows ways in which wider "social agreements" inflect musical composition and reception. Her far-ranging musicological analyses indicate that very often the puzzling intricacies of the "purely musical" are more pointedly deciphered in terms of a specific culture's "discontents, and its competing modes of representation."[28] This dialectic is not surprising, given that music is a formative participant in our "social world."[29] As a musicological detective, McClary wants to expose the *social* basis of those musical codes and conventions that listeners think of as "natural," this because listeners have thoroughly internalised a certain set of musical norms for each style. By identifying socio-political impulses that actively determine which musical forms and content develop and predominate during particular historical periods, McClary can also assess their veiled influence upon the construction of gendered identity.[30] Moreover, she and other feminist musicologist have documented ways in which gender stereotypes actually inflect musical form and content.

Like feminist interrogations of the Bible, this new musicological interpretive framework no longer treats musical works as seal-tight, sacrosanct totalities, but as products of cultural and political forces. This corrective lens accentuates the reality that music is a "cultural activity" whose codes only become significant on the basis of "social interaction."[31] On the other side of formalism, music becomes a "living code," which, like any other cultural code, undergoes continual renegotiations as new and extant meanings are accepted, rejected, revised, "neutralized or reactivated."[32] New Musicologists owe much to Theodor Adorno, one of the first critical theorists to reject the treatment of classical music as a "set of icons."[33] Adorno rereads music as a series of wrestling matches between various "bourgeois contradictions," more specifically, between the assertion of "individual free will and social pressures to conform."[34] Composers' development of narratively structured musical forms are shaped by, even as they mirror, a culture's "anxieties," "priorities and blind spots."[35] Following Adorno's lead, musicologists began describing compositional themes metaphorically as "beleaguered individuals."[36] Romantic and atonal works, in particular, were reread as reflecting *and* contributing to the gradual erosion of both human and even musical selfhood.[37] Today, McClary and others make case after case for reading music's meaning as "model[s] of the self performed—that is, brought tangibly into existence."[38]

Additionally, this thoroughly historicised semiotics of music serves to demystify the composer's art, the latter traditionally shrouded by the rhetoric of ("supernatural") "genius." Rather, composition is reconstrued as a social practice. No longer divinely charged amanuenses, composers' mysterious powers instead participate in wider manipulations of social codes. For example, while a composer's individual musical choices define the different sets of tension in a piece, as well as their prescribed resolutions, these staged, even textless dilemmas take shape within a culturally endorsed and desired narrative framework. Composers can, therefore, promote or undermine a particular set of cultural priorities according to their works' form and content, where the latter set up, satisfy, or frustrate culturally valued expectations.[39] From such interanimation, one sees just how powerful composers can be in shaping a culture's definitions of pleasure and beauty. And here, McClary reminds us that, far from being neutral or "natural," mainstream pleasures actually help maintain the status quo with great efficacy.[40] And musical foretastes of soothing, paradisial harmonies constitute one such pleasure.

Music's theological symbolism stands to shift dramatically if music is reread as a cultural document, if its metaphoricity gestates from a dialectic sense that musical works participate in, and are themselves, "forcefields" of competing ideologies.[41] More specifically, a new presupposition for theologising about music in feminist terms is the awareness that music shapes human subjectivity and sexual identity. The project of critique and reconstruction that follows builds upon this new cornerstone and seeks above all else to detail ways in which feminist musicology, the latter barely consulted by theologians to date, can inform a new theology of music. If music is culturally determined, its previous symbolic roles as repository of eternal truths, as speech of the soul, as fraternal twin to humanity's religious intuition, no longer ring true. Additionally, the demystification of composers' genius problematises many articulations of Western composers' theological significance. As we shall see, with the exception of Priscilla Stuckey's rereading of Mozart's *Magic Flute*,[42] extant theologians' portraits of Bach, Palestrina, and Mozart's theological meanings border on hagiography and uphold in specifically theological terms previous secular ordinations of these composers' works as "icons" of "Father knows best."[43] In light of feminist/new musicology, our allegedly universal language, our celestial ambassador for peace, becomes a laboratory, a "public forum"[44] for sculpting subjectivity, a "technique of the self" governed by the same "structures of thought" that found the verbal and the social.[45]

Soliciting a range of feminist theorists as muses, I shall consequently treat music not as an ideologically immune, self-contained system, but as a "social barometer," a "product" of struggles over cultural meaning.[46] Music's theological meaning will emerge from its implication within specific historical struggles; more precisely, certain musical ethics and taboos will be reread as sites where Christians individually and collectively negotiate distinctive, *gendered* identities within antagonistic contexts. These symptomatic readings respond more appositely to the "timeless" reality that music is a powerful social and political practice that causes listeners to experience, or, if musical censorship abounds, not to experience their bodies in new ways.[47]

In sum, this book seeks to reconstruct music's theological significance by implicating it in the "politics of representation,"[48] by delineating the very concrete processes through which we ascribe music symbolic or metaphorical value, in short by treating it as a discursive practice, one socializing force among many. Such "radical" theological critiques and rearticulations of extramusical meanings will seem problematic only to those for whom music provides a transcendent oasis, who need music to remain hermetically sealed, unstained by the *mundane—virginal.* In part 1, I shall first attend to the now almost unconscious assumptions that have directed the "creative metaphor-making" processes in traditional and contemporary articulations of music's theological meaning.[49] As stated above, while a wide range of theologies of music is always justifiable, including each of those with which I take issue, the main objective in part 1 is to carefully anatomise the theological readings of music that have gradually taken shape, and then assess their persuasiveness for our context.[50] To these ends, this critical overview of antecedent sources for Christian theologies of music (chapter 1), Christian rhetoric about musical decorum (chapter 2), and twentieth-century masculinist musico-theological discourse (chapter 3) will reveal a tacitly sexist subtext in extant theologies of music, one that has buried a goldmine of musico-theological riches. By exhuming the latter in part 2 of this project, I will retrieve materials with which to construct a new model, namely, a neglected trope from the tradition, and insights derived from the musical activities of women-musician/composers: Hildegard of Bingen, Lucrezia Vizzana, Sister Rosetta Tharpe, and Diamanda Galas. As indicated earlier, in order to reformulate music's symbolic content and shift its locus within divine–human relations, we shall converse with a number of other feminist theorists. I do so not only to illustrate the valuable yet neglected contributions that theological discussions of music can make to other feminist discourses, but also to construct a more genuinely dialogical theology of music. By its very nature, this topic mandates a rigorous interdisciplinarity.

Finally, it must be emphasised that this is a theological project, not a historical one. The historical sources that are engaged are in no way construed as proto-feminist. Rather, reflection upon previously neglected insights from the past guides the construction of a conceptual framework that responds more compellingly to our current musical (and theological) contexts. In other words, alternative readings of particular moments within past tradition will unearth lost themes and concepts that will stimulate and redirect contemporary theological reflection. Through this recuperative synthesis of lost tradition and revisionist music history, this feminist initiative (in sharp contrast to its metaphysical antecedents) can set a precedent that will inspire other politicised, hence more ingenuous, theologies of music.

Notes

1. From a poem by Wallace Stevens, "To the One of Fictive Music," *Harmonium* in *Collected Poems*, 87.

2. Messiaen in Samuel, *Conversations with Olivier Messiaen*, 2.

3. Schleiermacher, *Aesthetik*, (ed. Lommatzsch) 394, and discussed in Blackwell, "Schleiermacher on Musical Experience and Religious Experience: 'What Hath Vienna to do with Jerusalem?,'" 131-38.

4. Spivak, "It would be possible to assemble here a collection of 'great passages' from literature and philosophy to show how, unobtrusively but crucially, a certain metaphor of woman has produced (rather than merely illustrated) a discourse that we are obliged 'historically' to call the discourse of man. Given the accepted charge of the notions of production and constitution, one might reformulate this: the discourse of man is in the metaphor of woman."

5. McFague, *Models of God*, 27.

6. Ibid., 22.

7. Ibid.

8. Ibid., 36.

9. Ibid., 37.

10. Schüssler Fiorenza, *In Memory of Her*, 61.

11. McFague, *Models of God*, 35.

12. Schüssler Fiorenza, *Jesus: Miriam's Son, Sophia's Prophet*, 28.

13. McFague, *Models of God*, 45.

14. McFague emphasises these criteria as characteristic of Christianity's material norm (*Models of God*, 45ff.).

15. McFague, *Models of God*, 57; author's emphasis, and Sands, *Escape from Paradise*, 13. The designated "tragic sensibility" is Kathleen Sands's preferred hermeneutic.

16. Sands, *Escape from Paradise*, 16.

17. Ibid., 110.

18. Ibid., 10f. and 63f.

19. Ibid., 36. Sands elaborates: "Not every human lifeboat is in a raging storm just now, but we are always, all of us, unmoored. . . . If society is torn by profound conflicts, and if character and consciousness are socially constructed, then human desire, affectivity, creativity, and intelligence are all subject to damage and defacement due to circumstances that, at least in the present, remain beyond

our individual or even collective control. Not only are these distinct powers and good separately vulnerable; so is our ability to weave them into some integral whole that does more good than harm. Not even the rudiments of morality—our powers to value, choose, and integrate goods—can root securely in the rocky peaks and precipices of history. . . . Tragedy speaks to extreme circumstances, but in practice extreme circumstances are not rare (11).

20. Ibid., 36.

21. Ibid., l.

22. Ibid.

23. Ibid., 110. On the "cracks," "fractures," and "borders" of both "intelligibility" and communal consensus, cf. ibid., chapter 1, especially 10-16.

24. McFague, *Models of God,* 38f.

25. Ibid., 39.

26. Elisabeth Schüssler Fiorenza calls for the creation of such new "metaphoric space" in *Jesus: Miriam's Son,* 28, and also in *But She Said,* 125-32.

27. McClary, "Paradigm Dissonances," 70.

28. Ibid., 73.

29. Ibid., 70.

30. Ibid., 77ff..

31. McClary, "A Musical Dialectic from the Enlightenment," 132.

32. Ibid.

33. McClary, *Feminine Endings,* 28.

34. Ibid.

35. McClary, "Paradigm Dissonances," 78 and 77 respectively.

36. Ibid., 77. Here McClary refers the reader to documentation in Mark Evan Bonds, *Wordless Rhetoric: Musical Form and the Metaphor of the Oration,* as well as in Leonard B. Meyer's *Style in Music,* and Richard Littlefield and David Neumeyer's "Rewriting Schenker: Narrative—History—Ideology," *Music Theory Spectrum* 14, no.1 (Spring, 1992): 38-65, 85 n. 25.

37. Ibid., 76f.

38. Ibid., 77.

39. McClary, "A Musical Dialectic from the Enlightenment," 139. See, for example, McClary's analyses of "6th degree interruptions," and deceptive "excursions to the submediant" in the following works: Mozart's Piano Concerto in G Major, K. 453, mvt. 2 ("A Musical Dialectic"); Schubert's Impromptu in C Minor, Op. 90. no. 1 ("Pitches, Expression, Ideology," 80); Beethoven's 9th Symphony, and his A Minor Quarter, Op.132 ("Pitches, Expression, Ideology," 81); Schubert's Unfinished Symphony and Quartet in E-flat Major, Op.127 ("Pitches, Expression, Ideology," 81f.).

40. Cf. McClary (via Foucault), *Feminine Endings,* 29.

41. Ibid., 28f.

42. Stuckey, "Light Dispels Darkness: Gender, Ritual and Society in Mozart's *Magic Flute.*"

43. McClary, *Feminine Endings,* 79.

44. Ibid., 8.

45. McClary, "Paradigm Dissonances, 77.

46. McClary, *Feminine Endings,* 28.

47. Ibid., 25.

48. Thus McClary: "As a cultural historian, I am drawn irresistibly to this medium in which various models of subjectivity were hammered out over the course of a century, the medium that we still take to represent our ideal selves, that teaches us about our inner emotions and public aspirations" ("Paradigm Dissonances," 77f.).

49. Two surveys of the problem of music and meaning that have helped me immeasurably, and which will be useful to other theologians, are Anthony Newcomb's article "Sound and Feeling," and Stephen Davies's book *Musical Meaning and Expression.* Main ideas from each are summarized here.

50. Newcomb clarifies: "[T]he important matter is not so much the expressive patterns suggested by the words chosen but the demonstration of how the processes of the music itself might be heard to have suggested the patterns suggested by the words" (Newcomb, "Sound and Feeling," 633). This anatomising is, after all, the project of all interpretive criticism.

Part One: Critique
Masculinist Theologies of Music

The laws of nature are as impersonal and free of human values as the rules of arithmetic. We didn't want it to come out that way, but it did.
Steve Weinberg, "Reflections of
a Working Scientist," *Daedalus*

Certainly nature seems to exult in abounding radicality, extremism, anarchy. If we were to judge nature by its common sense or likelihood, we wouldn't believe the world existed. In nature, improbabilities are the one stock in trade. The whole creation is one lunatic fringe.
Annie Dillard, *Pilgrim at Tinker Creek*

Phallic Rage for Order

Traditional Theologies of Music

MUSIC, "THE ART OF COMBINING vocal and instrumental sounds to produce beauty" (*OED*), has been drenched with deeper, soulful meanings since antiquity. Let us trace the more general process of such extramusical meaning construction by way of a specific example. The most enduring symbolic valence ascribed to music is its microcosmic reflection of cosmic and divine harmony. Because music revealed the laws of number and proportion governing the cosmos, it also disclosed the activity and purposes of divinity. Pythagoras's legendary acoustic experimentation with different lengths of vibrating string rendered musical harmony the most sublime yet concrete heuristic for understanding the internal logic, the fitting together of opposites (*harmonia*) at work everywhere else in the cosmos and on earth. His discernment of the numerical properties that compose musical sound established harmony as the *fundamentum* of all existence.[1] The ability to translate musical and physical truths into mathematical ratios that use only four numbers reveals for Pythagoras and his predecessors the elegant simplicity and literal integrity (from "integer") unifying all of life. Numerico-structural parallels in these philosophers' various experiments and speculations in mathematics, geometry, and astronomy reciprocally validated music's revelatory message.[2]

This classical example of music's theological significance foregrounds the interpretive key that is pivotal to all articulations of music's meaning, namely, that most pragmatic of linguistic and theological building blocks: metaphor. To give music meaning, one establishes "metaphorical resonances or analogies" between the musical works' internal properties, and components from other myriad fields of human experience.[3] Whatever one's interpretive stance (philosophical, social scientific, semiotic, acoustic, musicological, or theological), auditors ground music's extramusical significance in its internal properties—its formal elements, melodic details, rhythmic patterns, recurring motifs, even a work's orchestration. More specifically, the music's meaning is derived from the idiosyncratic 'behaviours' of these compositional elements. Like theologians who reflect upon human

11

experience to comprehend divinity, to articulate what music expresses, listeners invariably bring the structural patterns of music into relation with "other aspects of our experience."[4] In the case of the Presocratics and Plato, very sophisticated metaphorical transfers circulated among their musical, spiritual, and mathematical experiences.

The wondrously unified system of cosmos and creation expressed the triumph of order over chaos. Music's *numerositas* simultaneously reveals and confirms human intuition of the harmonic essence sustaining all life. Thus, the tuning ratios that Pythagoras formulated became an epistemological tool that justified by example the actual and ideal dynamics within society and the material world. The result is quite literally a thoroughgoing, musical worldview. On the basis of this musico-philosophical revelation, the Pythagoreans insist that humans must emulate, communicate, and instil this divine imperative. (Number itself, moreover, was the force that enabled humans to perceive, comprehend, and interpret these attributes.[5]) Centuries later, Aristotle and the Peripatetics, while they do not make harmony a preexistent first principle, retain it nonetheless as a pivotal organising principle of thought. Aristotle's model is more biological and physical than metaphysical and mathematical, but he still promotes a harmonic imperative, the divinely ordained joining or blending of contraries.

An important terminological nuance, which has political implications for assessing the adequacy of such traditional musico-theological formulations, is required here. Metaphor is sometimes defined as a subspecies of *symbol*—one image or quality (i.e., a sign) standing for another but without complete identity. Music has historically functioned as a revelatory symbol in theological discourse. Unlike metaphors, symbols participate in the transcendent reality to which they point. In Part One below, I prefer to ascribe to music specifically *metaphorical* resonances. Such theologising differs from that of the ancients for they regarded music as a full participant in the cosmic harmony it symbolised. Numbers actually constituted reality. *Numerositas* generated musical, cosmic, and existential purity, proportion, integrity, truth, and perfection. Harmony and number subsequently became inseparable ontological corollaries.[6]

There are also political reasons for maintaining this distinction: to rectify ideological abuses that religious symbols and meaning-making have undergirded throughout history, abuses similar to those I perceive in masculinist musico-theological meaning-systems. Sallie McFague argues that, in traditional usage, symbols operative in religious discourse have frequently been reified metaphors such that "this is *a part* of that." Such symbols constitute the "sedimentation and solidification of metaphor." Consequently, "the tension of metaphor is absorbed by the harmony of symbol."[7] Where metaphors hinge upon dissimilarity, connecting two disparate objects with but "a vein" of similarity, symbols are less subtle in the similarities highlighted; they are "already present and assumed."[8] Moreover, like the initially incongruous parables of Jesus, "good metaphors shock," jarring conventional sensibility and expectations with "revolutionary" overtones.[9] Additionally,

I value McFague's emphasis upon the "is-not" disclaimer intrinsic to metaphors, and upon which she subsequently erects this conceptual, symbol-metaphor dichotomy: "One critical difference between symbolic and metaphorical statements is that the latter always contain the whisper, 'it is *and it is not.*'"[10] This qualifying nuance is equally apposite to extramusical meaning-making since all our expressive predicates will similarly fail to articulate completely the meaning or unfolding of a particular musical event. When we lose our awe and humility toward the impenetrable mystery "surrounding all existence," and our concomitant sense of the failure of ideas and words to articulate divinity, the qualitative gap between human language and divine ineffability collapses. God then erroneously "*becomes* father, mother, lover, friend."[11]

By extension I suggest that, as God *becomes* Father and Ruler, Music *becomes* Harmonic Dictator. A certain rage for order reifies music's raison d'être. Harmony is not random but *right* order—the alignment of elements in their proper place and proportion. Music therefore possesses an innate ethicality; natural, cosmic, and material harmony and order had to be preserved as originally designed. *Harmonia* presupposes and demands propriety. Disruptions to this order constitute dissonances—discordant ethical breaches. *Unity as harmonic conformity* thus becomes a normative criterion in aesthetics and ethics. The most well-known example of this dialectical confluence lies in Plato's republican music. It must embody (as best any materiality can) simplicity, virtue, and truth, so that paideutically it will foster harmony and order in the souls of both performer and auditor. Music itself is true, good, and beautiful only if it "reveals harmonic Forms."[12] Thus Plato: "And gracelessness and arrhythmia and disharmony are akin to evil speaking and the evil temper, but the opposites are the symbols and the kin of the opposites, the sober and good disposition."[13] Music must imitate good objects which—as imperfect imitations—then inspire purer (because disembodied) contemplation.[14] Even with Aristotle's epistemological shift, virtue-as-harmony remains normative. For although Aristotle assigns a more positive role to musical *practice* and to artistic *mimesis* in his philosophy of music,[15] the preservation of inter- and intrapersonal harmony still shapes his perception of music's socio-ethical functions.[16] (Parallel shifts mark the thought of Augustine and Aquinas.)

Unfortunately, neither the politics of assigning music such symbolic resonances, nor of course, the latter's implication in "divine harmonic command theory," have been critically questioned. Instead, these classical symbols are decontextualised and universalized in contemporary theologies of music, this despite the former's genesis within an anachronistically sacramentalist worldview. Indeed, McFague further justifies her approach by arguing that, if religious symbols are studied with greater attention to their historical contexts, it becomes obvious that they have their roots in a sacramentalist worldview which people today would be hard pressed to adopt.[17] (Hence metaphorical theology is far more appropriate for postmodern religious reflection.) Unless we retain a sacramentalist worldview, it would hardly seem accurate to say that music's primary function or nature is symbolic. As we shall see, however, not only ancient but even some contemporary philosophers and theologians have located music's quintessence therein.

Critics may argue that this tendency is by no means all-pervasive, and that the required distance between the symbolic object or property and the signified does not always collapse in contemporary theologies of music. McFague further nuances her critique by acknowledging that "a genuine symbolical sensibility" is not idolatrous (cf. Dante's *Divine Comedy*).[18] Despite this qualification, however, McFague maintains that, in modern and postmodern times, medieval perceptions of an overarching unity, not to mention their attendant symbol-systems, are met with skepticism. (To adapt tradition to this secularized context, fundamentalists literalise symbols while liberals[19] spiritualise them. Both represent polarised responses to the rejection of a sacramentalist worldview.[20]) It is precisely in order to maintain a distinct identity from such masculinist antecedents that I have adopted McFague's semantic strategy of upholding this distinction between metaphor and symbol as pivotal to the hermeneutic of suspicion one needs for evaluating extant musico-theological metaphors (and/or symbols). While I cannot—according to McFague's strategy—unilaterally reject the masculinist models I shall present and critique in the chapters ahead, like McFague, I do contest their hegemony. Like the parables' jarring metaphorical configurations for the Kingdom of God, and like Christ's unorthodox life as a metaphor for divine nature,[21] I shall engage in creative metaphor-making to articulate music's theological significance beyond its traditional symbolisation of harmony and order. The metaphorical meanings that feminist musicologists, for example, have already ascribed to music will "shock" us (as good metaphors should) into reconceptualising music's theological significance with greater relevance and less idolatrous (or ideological) reification.

Musical Baptisms:
Christian Variations on a Theme

The Presocratics' philosophical "calculus" with its cool, elegant simplicity and its categorical imperative of music's mathematical obedience must have seemed undeniably reassuring. The Greeks' harmonic resolutions and imperatives were converted and recast within Christian salvation history with great enthusiasm by the church fathers. The former's detailed articulations of earthly and cosmic harmony became the touchstones for musical theorising and practices in the early church.[22] However, the elaboration of this symbol's ethical content and the rhetoric deployed to preserve music's "natural" order and, by extension, social harmony would have grave repercussions. The examination of such spicy rhetoric in this chapter and the next might seem an amusing historical excursus, but more is at stake in this hermeneutical study. It is necessary to chronicle this trajectory to reveal the gendered silences that extant theologies of music unwittingly perpetuate and subsequently to question their interpretive adequacy for today. Music's numerical integrity reverberates with other, till now unacknowledged, theological meanings, not to mention devotionally oppressive, double standards. The earliest theologies of music elaborated, as it were, their own musically domesticating, "household codes."[23] Questioning the adequacy of traditional (and contemporary) theological symbolic/metaphorical resonances like Music as Number, Harmony, and Order precedes and inspires my own act of imaginative construction. As we trace the trajectory that these confluences precipitated, we will discover that at this correlative nexus, not only rhetorical descriptions of music, but even music's internal properties transmogrify—the latter exuding not so much number and order as unholy "terrors." At the same time, by tracing the tacit politics of representation at work beneath allegedly neutral symbolic conflations of music, harmony, and virtue, we shall turn stones previously refused and retrieve thereby theological building blocks long since buried beneath the exclusionary trappings of prior musico-theological frameworks.

Logocentrism as Musical Chastity Belt: A Rhetorical Trajectory

As mentioned earlier, like so many other branches of theology, the thought of Pythagoras, Plato, and Aristotle indelibly shaped Christian theologies of music. Homologising harmony and virtue implies a system of chain reactions: excessive or improper sensory stimulation provokes emotional turbulence in human beings, which could actually disrupt the movement of the planets and the music of the spheres. Particularly immoral was musical virtuosity, which, because musically complex, distracts. Virtue by inference is quintessentially simple. By extension, "virtuous" music concentrates the mind and consolidates human comportment rather than generating psychic disorder of any sort. Conversely, modal, rhythmic or timbral complexity, dissonance from the mixture of modes, rhythms, and instrumental timbres, provokes moral degeneracy. The by-product of such conflations is a rhetoric of musical purity and danger. Both Greek and Christian authorities describe musical harmony and order metaphorically in terms of purity and impurity, virtue and sin, carnality and spirituality. The classification of sacred and profane music takes its cues accordingly. To sustain cosmic, human, and social harmony, a system of taboos in the realm of musical practices develops. One disciplinary measure at composers' and auditors' disposal would be to assert the primacy of the text. This musico-theological imperative is another hangover from the classical treatment of music and text as an inseparable unity. Text bridles music's "body," sublimating its erotic pull to higher intellectual ends. Lactantius offers one of the most graphic examples of the tyranny of the text in the early church:

> But we have already spoken of spectacles: there remains one thing which is to be overcome by us, that we be not captivated by those things which penetrate to the

innermost perception. For all those things which are unconnected with words, that is, pleasant sounds of the air and of strings, may be easily disregarded, because they do not adhere to us, and cannot be written. . . . Therefore he who is anxious for the truth, who does not wish to deceive himself, must lay aside hurtful and injurious pleasures, which would bind the mind to themselves [including "well-composed poems" and "beguiling speeches"] . . . [L]et nothing be agreeable to the hearing but that which nourishes the soul and makes you a better man. And especially this sense ought not to be distorted to vice, since it is given to us for this purpose, that we might gain the knowledge of God. Therefore, if it be a pleasure to hear melodies and songs, let it be pleasant to sing and hear the praises of God. This is true pleasure, which is the attendant and companion of virtue.[24]

Similarly, Augustine confesses to this sin of distraction despite the sacred musical medium he absorbs: "Now I confess that I repose just a little in those sounds to which your words give life, when they are sung by a sweet and skilled voices. . . . [W]hen it happens to me that the song moves me more than the thing which is sung, I confess that I have sinned blamefully and then prefer not to hear the singer."[25]

In the Middle Ages, Bernard of Clairvaux sharply condemns music's obscuring of sacred texts, ranting as Boethius did against composers' innovative excess:

If there is to be singing, the melody should be grave and not flippant or uncouth. It should be sweet but not frivolous; it should both enchant the ears and move the heart; it should lighten sad hearts and soften angry passions; and it should never obscure but enhance the sense of the words. Not a little spiritual profit is lost when minds are distracted from the sense of the words by frivolity of the melody, when more is conveyed by the modulations of the voice than by the variations of the meaning.[26]

In England, John of Salisbury deplores singers' "glibness in running up and down the scale . . . their cutting apart or their conjoining of notes . . . their repetition or their elision of single phrases of the text," precisely because from these "the ears are almost completely divested of their critical power, and the intellect . . . is impotent to judge the merits of the things heard."[27] Likewise Erasmus strongly insists upon preserving textual clarity and denounces its absence in the sacred music he heard while visiting England—a "distorted music," "clamorous," and sung by "dolts":

Those who are more doltish than really learned in music are not content on feast days unless they use a distorted kind of music called *Fauburdum* [*sic*]. This neither gives forth the pre-existing melody nor observes the harmonies of the art. . . . [It] also seems a fine thing to some if one or other part, intermingled with the rest, produces a tremendous tonal clamor, so that not a single word is understood. Thus the whims of the foolish are indulged and their baser appetites are satisfied. . . . Let us sing vocally, but let us sing as Christians; let us sing sparingly, but let us sing more in our hearts.[28]

And despite the devotional freedom that Martin Luther initiates, the Reformers' championing of the Word only reinforces musical logocentrism (with some surprising exceptions).[29] While Luther, in contrast to the more ascetic Reformers, asserts music's divine *ontos*, he still requires music to serve the Word: "Thus it was not without reason that the fathers and prophets wanted nothing else to be associated as closely with the Word of God as music. . . . After all, the gift of language combined with the gift of song was only given to man to let him know that he should praise God with both word and music, namely, by proclaiming the Word through music and by providing sweet melodies with words."[30]

During the Counter-Reformation, clergy (echoing their humanist contemporaries) appeal to classical antiquity to justify a return to simpler, nonimitative, sacred styles so as to recover textual clarity. In a letter of 1549, Roman Bishop Cirillo Franco remarks that the polyphony of his day has become positively bestial: "In our times they have put all their industry and effort into the compositions of fugues . . . so that while one voice says 'Sanctus,' another says 'Sabaoth,' still another 'Gloria tua,' with howling, bellowing, and stammering, so that they seem at times like cats in January than flowers in May."[31] Franco cannot abide any such compromise to the text's meaning: "I should like, in short, when a mass is to be sung in church, the music to be framed to the fundamental meaning of the words, in certain intervals and numbers apt to move our affections to religion and piety, and likewise in psalms, hymns, and other praises that are offered to the Lord."[32] More subdued, Pope Gregory XIII merely deems such musical excesses "barbarisms and obscurities" which prevent full absorption of the divinely inspired textual messages. He therefore begs Palestrina and Zoilo to "purge" these "contrarieties" and "superfluities" from the Roman Antiphoners, Graduals, and Psalters.[33]

This tug of war between mind and body in both musical devotion and aesthetics persisted even after the Enlightenment. Rousseau protests against the rise of "Absolute Music," which began during the Enlightenment, as an "unnatural" human "taste";[34] he insists that music can only aspire to higher art forms via the mediating, imitative power of words. As we shall see in chapter 3, a different yet equally stifling form of logocentrism pervades twentieth-century musico-theological models; excessively text-based analyses function today not so much as a prescriptive means of social control but as the myopic locus of almost all theological insights into music's theological value. With the advent of atonal music in the wake of wars and genocide, more sophisticated though less "comforting" versions of number and order prevailed. (If these seemed less divinely revelatory, theologians like Karl Barth, for example, would look to Mozart, others to Bach or Palestrina, to preserve music's traditional theological meanings.)

A specifically Christian identity hinges on the exclusion of certain social and musical practices, engagement in which would require confessions and purification. Such purgative exhortations intensified during periods of musical reform (e.g., Cistercian and Tridentine). As evidenced above, calls for a return to former times of purity and order in musical practices are couched in reactionary idioms that construe new practices as "unclean" and "illicit" "profanities."[35] Composers of such "filthy" music are charged with disorderly conduct. Hence, without being "sociologically" defined as such, music is treated as a socialising force or technique of the self, charged with tremendous power to shape character. Immoral or unethical music could corrupt while virtuous music shaped virile warriors and obedient wives. Modal, rhythmic, or textural complexity, dissonance from the mixture of modes, rhythms, and instrumental textures, provoked moral degeneracy.

For philosophers and theologians since Pythagoras, decoding music's meanings owed much to Eros. Given that Eros drove Socrates' ardent "love of learning and desire for God,"[36] the metaphors he and his predecessors chose were, despite appearances, erotically inspired. But Eros got lost in top-heavy constructions of music's logocentric meanings, and, consequently, "the tension of metaphor [was] absorbed by the harmony of symbol" (McFague). The legacy within the Christian musico-theological tradition was a profound ambivalence, if not contempt for, music's sensual charm. Indeed, once music was tied to morality, the most basic criterion for evaluating good vs. bad music was its engagement of human sexuality. Construed as innately ethical (because harmonious), even *music's* behaviour could be moral or corrupt. In the name of socio-spiritual order, calls for propriety in musical practice were urged. Musical "foreplay" of any kind was anathema. A hermeneutic of suspicion has never been applied to this (theological) value judgment.

Let us follow the trajectory of this masculinist homology one step further. Symptomatic readings of famous passages from Augustine and Boethius expose music's extended metaphoricity: its harmony and virtue are always threatened by the loss of its virginity, and the fathers seem to demand impossible proofs of music's chastity.

Augustine's Musical Seduction:
Confessions, Book X

With his own sexual imagery, Augustine laments the fragility of music's goodness (Nussbaum).[37] In book 10 of the *Confessions,* as part of his catalogue of the pleasures and perils of sensual experience and their proper place in Christian devotion, Augustine recounts his struggle with music's sensual wiles. He describes his musical entanglements as a form of bondage from which God faithfully releases him. He begins:

> The delight of the ear drew me and held me more firmly, but you unbound and liberated me. Now I confess that I repose just a little in those sounds to which your words give life, when they are sung by a sweet and skilled voice; not such that I cling to them, but that I can rise out of them when I wish. . . . Sometimes I seem to myself to grant them more respect than is fitting, when I sense that our souls are more piously and earnestly moved to the ardor of devotion by these sacred words when they are thus sung than when not thus sung, and that all the affec-

tions of our soul, by their own diversity, have their voice and song, which are stimulated by I know not what secret correspondence.[38]

In rhetoric akin to that used to lament his sexual sins (but without making music explicitly "Woman" as he does in his prior portrait of ocular delights),[39] the chief patristic voice in Western Christendom expresses his sharply polarised ambivalence toward music's seductive power:

> Sometimes, however, in avoiding this deception too vigorously, I err by excessive severity, and sometimes so much so that I wish every melody of the sweet songs to which the Davidic Psalter is usually set, to be banished from my ears and from the church itself. And safer to me seem what I remember was often told me concerning Athanasius, Bishop of Alexandria, who required the reader of the Psalm to perform it with so little inflection (*flex*) of voice that it was closer to speaking (*pronuntianti*) than to singing (*canenti*).
>
> However, when I recall the tears which I shed at the song of the Church in the first days of my recovered faith, and even now as I am moved not by the song but by the things which are sung, when sung with fluent voice and music that is most appropriate (*conuenientissima modulatione*), I acknowledge again the great benefit of this practice.[40]

It is as if (like Light—the seductive "Queen of Colours") sonic sirens ("sweet skilled voices") lure him to musical bed, gratifying his flesh.[41] As with former mistresses, Augustine fantasises about "banishing" this temptress, but realises that—like proper sexual relations—"she" too, as part of Creation, and if kept in her proper place, can lead believers (especially weaker souls) to God. With God's help, and with a hyper (though not always efficacious) vigilance, Augustine navigates this musical Scylla and Charybdis, resisting aural concupiscence more easily than his former sexual enslavement:

> Thus I vacillate between the peril of pleasure and the value of the experience, and I am led more—while advocating no irrevocable position—to endorse the custom of singing in church so that by the pleasure of hearing the weaker soul might be elevated to an attitude of devotion. Yet when it happens to me that the song moves me more than the thing which is sung, I confess that I have sinned blamefully and then prefer not to hear the singer. Look at my condition! Weep with me and weep for me. . . . You however, O Lord my God, give ear, look and see, have pity and heal me in whose sight I have become an enigma unto myself; and this itself is my weakness. [42]

Read in the wake of Foucault's hermeneutics, Augustine's specifically confessional rhetoric also becomes musico-theologically symptomatic. Musical immersion is a sin that has little if any redemptive value. Music distracts Augustine's attention, preventing him from devoting his undivided attention to "seeing" God, dis-ordering the integrity of his mind-body-soul. More specifically, to sin musically is to forsake the text—the music's raison d'être—and savour music's body instead, her "sweet melody." Thus in one's anagogic ascent toward God, a disciple must discern and relish the true pleasure beneath the false, superficial joys of musical sound. The irony here is that the weaker souls which music converts to God must be ascetically savvy enough not to be distracted by the sweet tones, even in hymns that are "*connunenientissima modulatione*."[43] Only the text, by steering the mind toward God and thereby taming music's erotic pull, assures continence. Ironically, continence is personified as the sane, chaste voice of a woman who counters those of his former mistresses.[44] But even the purest musical tones cannot be univocally virgin.[45]

Margaret Miles's description of Augustine's anatomy of desire and delight further justifies this identification of an erotic tenor in Augustine's ambivalence toward music, and his subsequent need to spiritualise music's theological import. Miles contends that the male model of sexuality shapes Augustine's construction of the spiritual life.[46] By extension, this model of male sexual continence informs (and literally engenders) his musical asceticism: milder than sex, musical intercourse is still a potential threat to continence, a tempting mode of "distraction" and "dispersal." Thus in each musical *rencontre*, Augustine must exercise a similar "energetic resistance" to remain spiritually composed.[47]

It is noteworthy that, if Augustine stays within the confines of textual analysis, he remains unscattered by musical concupiscence. In its purest form, this sanitized disclosure of God's harmonic imperative through disembodied music appreciation proffers the purest, safest musical pleasure that an embodied creature can experience—an intellectual theophany that concrete musical practices always threaten to eclipse. If the song moves more than that which is sung, Augustine falls into sin. Thus Augustine's plight becomes the *locus classicus* of musicotheological purity and danger. Music minus text constitutes—or, at the very least, invites—sin. For Christians, music becomes "problem" the moment it takes flesh. (Miles does not point out in her book the possibility of such, for Augustine, purely mental musical pleasure. But she does discuss at length Augustine's inevitable polarisation of "true" and "false" Christian pleasures.)[48] Musical continence via ascetic stylistic practices or textual contemplation effectively neutralises her sway and denotes male self-control. Little wonder then that silent, cerebral speculation of musical texts is made the most sublime musical love-object. (In this most spectral of forms, perhaps "she" "becomes male."[49])

Boethius: Musical Chastity
and Perversion

The implied musical woman in Augustine's saga grows more defined in the rhetoric of Boethius. In the latter's day, music has lost "her" virginity and/or effeminates auditors. Boethius uses an extended sexual analogy to depict music's Fall: "Since the human race has become lascivious and impressionable, it is taken up totally by representational and theatrical modes. Music was indeed chaste and modest when it was performed on simpler instruments. But since it has been squandered in various promiscuous ways, it has lost its measure of dignity and virtue; and, having almost fallen into a state of disgrace, it preserves nothing of its ancient splendor."[50] In another passage, Boethius portrays musical "corruption" as seduction *or* hostage-taking. Musical "abduction" sparks spiritual recidivism, turning converts into pagans. Here, the listeners' backsliding is described in terms of sexual submission:

> Thus Plato holds that the greatest care should be exercised lest something be altered in music of good character. He states that there is no greater ruin of morals in a republic than the gradual perversion of chaste and temperate music, for the minds of those listening at first acquiesce. Then they gradually submit, preserving no trace of honesty or justice—whether lascivious modes bring something immodest into the dispositions of the people or rougher ones implant something warlike and savage.[51]

The conflation of mental and musical degradation is noteworthy here; music's own internal perversion is infectious. Also significant is the logic of identity-thinking at work in Boethius's model. In the following passage, for example, like can only be attracted to like such that similitude-as-predestined-conformity separates Christian wheat from pagan tares. Musicologist Calvin Bower confirms, moreover, the phallic connotations of "soft" and "hard" in this same excerpt:[52] "A lascivious disposition takes pleasure in more lascivious modes or is often made soft and corrupted upon hearing them. . . . A people finds pleasure in modes because of likeness to its own character, for it is not possible for gentle things to be joined with or find pleasure in rough things, nor rough things in gentle. Rather, as has been said, similitude brings about love and pleasure."[53] Oddly enough, Boethius then polarises music's infusion of good and bad character such that effeminacy and warrior violence become partners in crime. These two ne'er-do-wells, however, represent opposite ends on a musico-ethical continuum, yet they share nonetheless a wicked volatility; both "behaviours" destabilise both musical and social order: "Plato holds music of the highest moral character, modestly composed, to be a great guardian of the republic; thus it should be temperate, simple, and masculine, rather than effeminate, violent, or fickle."[54]

These Boethian musical "Others" are pejoratively construed as either sexual deviants or crass heathens. For the (post)modern reader, music's originally "pure essence" is perverted by its metaphorical sex, race, and class differences, an observation that has escaped modern commentary. (Historically, the masses loved popular music, dancing, and theatre music.) This is of course an anachronistic reading, but it underlines the historical contingency which Boethius's framework cannot escape and which should challenge its perduring authority in contemporary theological discourse.

Following the directives of Adorno and New Musicologists, if one rereads the above as cultural historians (rather than as metaphysicians), one should identify the "cultural priorities" that impelled such metaphysical models. Immersed in these numerically sophisticated, classical theologies of music, one easily forgets what prompted their construction. In his recent study of the positive and negative effects of multifarious erotic forces (divine and human) in Greek civilisation, Bruce Thornton reminds us that Plato, in modern parlance, was devising a "technology" with which to rationalise, and therefore manage, the world around him—epistemically to grasp and control it as best he could. Thornton's analysis explains by extension the genesis of Pythagoras's, Plato's, and Aristotle's philosophies of music, *and* their allure for Christian theologians. Christianity's uncritical assimilation of hellenistic philosophies of music irrevocably affected the thematic focus and organising principles of extant theologies of music. New theologies of music could be more critical of this metaphysical legacy for it by no means reflects the actual diversity of either pagan or Christian musical attitudes and practices.[55] Thornton's emphasis upon the chaotic underbelly that must have fueled the earliest notions of harmony and order also implies that, given nature's propensity for erotic volatility, one might just as easily have investigated and celebrated musically erotic dissonance, heterogeneity, and chaos rather than its unity, number, and order. But, in the phallic rage for order, music (like Woman) was negatively framed as either a harbinger of erotic fury or, if properly composed, the gateway to contemplation; these polarised musical practices would produce either dissident rebels or law-abiding citizens respectively. (In her own discipline, and with consummate poetic élan, Anne Carson also elucidates the persistently duplicitous "sweet-bitter" miens of eros in Greek literature and philosophy.)[56]

The very existence, however, of such barbed rants against improper musical decorum indicates that secular music's wiles must have proven irresistible to some if not many Christians. Belief in an overarching, instinctively harmonious cosmic order is a philosophical worldview that was not necessarily shared by the populus or even the artists of the day. *Hoi polloi* frequently indulged in musical erotica, as evidenced by the reactionary polemics against these bad habits. The sharpness of Christian exhortations against the latter also implies widespread Christian participation in such disorderly musical pleasures. Historian Peter Brown testifies to Christians' shameless immersion in the supposedly disruptive pagan recreations (including music) during Roman times. It has been falsely assumed that the early church embodied an otherworldly religious alternative. This was only the case for but "a minority of monks and, with far greater difficulty, some clergymen and a few quite exceptional laymen who had opted to follow the teachings of Christ in their entirety."[57] The majority of Christians—"*kosmikoi, saeculaeres*"— received no strict supervision regarding "a more Christian version of worldly life" and were accepted nonetheless.[58] Monks and bishops modeled otherworldly ideals precisely as a *via negativa*: "Thus, the perfectionism of the few full adherents to the Christian message left behind them a moral vacuum that the majority of average Christians filled with gusto from the traditions that lay at hand. The secularity of large areas of the society of the Christian Roman Empire, therefore, stood massively intact."[59] According to Brown, Christian appeals to Greek philosophy flew in the face of actual Christian excesses. Only pockets of Christians experienced late antiquity as an "age of spirituality."[60] As evidence, Brown quotes Joshua the Stylite's comments on fellow Christians attending a festival:

> Whilst these things were taking place, there came round again the time of that festival at which the heathen tales were sung; and the citizens took even more pains about it than usual. For seven days previously they were going up in crowds to the theatre at eventide, clad in linen garments, and wearing turbans, with their loins ungirt. Lamps were lighted before them, and *they were burning incense, and holding vigils the whole night, walking about the city and praising the dancers until morning, with singing and shouting and lewd behavior.*[61]

Thus, both historical and contemporary appeals to Plato and Pythagoras as prototypes for Christian theologies of music reveal an elitist legacy which does not necessarily resurrect all things musical in Greek antiquity. Pythagoras, Plato, and Aristotle were hardly representative of hellenistic attitudes toward music or actual musical practices. If anything they called for its rehabilitation.[63] Philosophical and/or ascetic disciplines were Plato's and Pythagoras's "technologies" for organising their otherwise unruly surroundings. For these two philosophers, the "really real" lay behind the deceptively chaotic cosmos. Thankfully then, for a humanity hungry for reassurance, earthly music revealed this otherwise imperceptible order and harmony.

Socially decorous music—the language of perfect fourths, fifths, and unisons—domesticated musical eros for a supposedly greater Good, namely, disembodied Order. Faced with such legislated 'sterility,' music's 'chastity' invites transgression by those who were and are invigorated (rather than emasculated) by her black-market vernacular. Indeed, today's textbook surveys of music in the Christian tradition rarely mention that these celebrated metaphysical models were not the only approaches to the music of the time. Nature, the cosmos, and the gods, were perceived as disorderly and unpredictable as much as harmonious and beneficent.

This is not to say that Christian thinkers never allowed the senses an important role in perceiving music's theological significance. Aquinas did not object to the making of music for sheer pleasure, so long as the music remained contextually appropriate. Nicholas of Cusa endorsed the passions—a consequence of human embodiment— as the gateway to spiritual ecstasy and revalorised music's symbolic meaning accordingly.[64] Ironically enough, even Boethius was particularly cognizant of the a priori musicality of human Being: "[m]usic is so naturally united with us that we cannot be free from it even if we so desired."[65] He agreed with Pythagoras that "[t]he whole structure of our soul and body has been joined by means of musical coalescence."[66] But this perspicacity produced a disappointing conclusion nonetheless:

For this reason the power of the intellect ought to be summoned, so that this art, innate through nature, may also be mastered, comprehended through knowledge. For just as in seeing it does not suffice for the learned to perceive colours and forms without also searching out their properties, so it does not suffice for musicians to find pleasure in melodies without also coming to know how they are structured internally by means of ratio of pitches.[67]

This sense of our innate musicality might have led us in the very different musico-theological direction that I shall take in part 2.

In his erudite synthesis *Music, Desire and the Body in Medieval Culture: From Boethius to Chaucer*, Bruce Wood Holsinger has taken exception to general portraits of patristic theologies of music as number-centered, speculative, and antipathetic toward the body.[68] While he does not deny the fathers' ambivalence toward music's corporeal effects, he impressively documents their simultaneous fascination with musical bodies, especially the latter's incarnationally symbolic content, hence its centrality to their musico-theological musings. But this more generous rereading of patristic theology requires even further qualification than acknowledgement of the fathers' ambivalence. For, while the patristic theologians might have found human, more specifically, the body's, musicality a richly *imagistic* site from which to wax eloquent rhetorically, connecting it theologically in all sorts of clever ways to the incarnation in their sermons and treatises, the messy tangents that actual music-making took were not positively embraced as equally edifying, evocative, or inspiring, as I shall demonstrate in chapter 2. Thus, ironically enough, patristic appreciation of musical bodies remains safely disembodied, reincarnated more palatably in tropes and allegory, hence in imaginary fancy and tame speculation. Furthermore, as Peter Brown suggests, the popular Christian fascination with musical bodies had little to do with its symbolic value as a christological interpretive key. The rhetoric in this chapter and the next might encourage contemporary scholars to affix a more narrowly circumscribed, patristic valorisation of the body in musical experience (or, perhaps more accurately, musical speculation). On a more specific note, with regard to Augustine's ambivalence toward music (again, an ineradicable tension that Holsinger acknowledges but "redeems"), a purposely feminist reframing of the former's musical confessions (as above) contextualises his suspicion of musical *practice* within broader readings of Augustine's attitudes toward sexuality, women, and the flesh. Only then does Augustine's place within the patriarchal trajectory of Music-as-Problem that I have begun to elucidate become evident.

Re-Defining Music's Theological Significance: Music as Erotic Mapping

Music-as-harmony has a silent accomplice here. Its virtuous mien is defined over against its alternative symbolic valence: proper music generates the rhetoric of purity and danger. Following the rhetorical trajectory of musical meanings discussed above, from music's incarnation of numbered order to divine exemplar/harbinger of a mandatory harmony and virtue, one must ask, in fact, if music is, *pace* the fathers, Reformers, and Elizabethans, innately "lascivious," and, moreover, infectiously degenerate. Here then, perhaps like so many other branches of theology, the thought of Pythagoras, Plato, and Aristotle indelibly shaped Christian theologies of music. The philosophers' detailed articulations of earthly and cosmic harmony became the touchstones for musical theorising and practices in the early church. New Musicologists, by contrast, leave the *quadrivium* behind and assign metaphorically "expressive predicates" to music, especially those that convey the "similarity of kinetic shapes" between music and erotic experience.[69] Music's meanings become bodily based, culled from actual musical experiences. In her survey of Western music's designated "erotic" repertoire, Susan McClary purposely attends to and revalorizes these affinities with kinetics.[70] Particularly noteworthy is her transfer of terms from the realms of cartography, corporeality, and sexuality to articulate metaphorically the channelling and arousing of human desire that "erotic" (or lascivious) music effects and expresses: erotic music consists of melodic, harmonic, and rhythmic "gestures," and sonic "contours" actively "mapping patterns through the medium of sound that resemble those of sexuality."[71] McClary's metaphors make sense to us precisely because of our musico-cultural conditioning, our corporeal absorption of such mapped patterns: "Even though such pieces may seem extraordinarily erotic—as though they have managed to bypass cultural mediation to resonate directly with one's own most private experiences—they are in fact constructions."[72]

In today's terms, music not only "structure[s] cognition," but also inscribes porous flesh with culturally defined kinetic and affective social codes, teaching proper or improper ways to experience the body, thereby shaping human consciousness. Sympotic drinking songs, French courtly dances, rock n' roll—musical innovations across the centuries "unleash [new] forms of physicality," which literally transform human embodiment.[73] Music "organises" bodily movement, and, therefore, one's corporeal sense of self. McClary's transhistorical study of (Western) erotic music testifies to the thoroughgoing "circular historicity" of music and the body.[74] Implied here, and overlooked in many musico-theological frameworks, is that music informs the very fields of human experience that we use to articulate its meaning. Unlike other, more traditional musicologists, McClary enlists Mark Johnson's epistemological precept that bodily experience is a primary source and norm for knowledge and the construction of meaning. She adapts Johnson's metaphorical approach to cognition to understand the politics of meaning making in music.[75] Johnson insists upon "the embodied origins of imaginative structures of understanding."[76] He demonstrates that via metaphor, human beings adopt patterns obtained from physical experience "to organize our more abstract understanding."[77] Johnson's linguistic research confirms that metaphors are not "mere figures of speech, . . . but rather . . . the fundamental means through which we as embodied beings orient ourselves with respect to the

world and thereby structure our discourses and our cognition."[78] McClary consequently accentuates the fact that musical experience is bodily based and urges
musicologists to shift their attention and interpretations accordingly.

Today, given that musical speculation is no longer a superior, more truthful
source for understanding music, listeners and performers (even composers)
ascribe meaning to music by culling "expressive predicates" from the kinetic,
erotic, and emotional affinities that they experience from their contact with
music's "body."[79] Yet, the sexualized epithets in this chapter reflect that, even during premodern times, auditors transferred and imposed shared erotic codes onto
music's internal properties. These "metaphorical resonances,"[80] however, were
pejorative—the marks of "dangerous" musics. The church fathers sensed that
wanton music in their time *especially without a text* might infuse "a vocabulary of
physical gestures" that would "infect" human comportment and teach new ways
of experiencing the body.[81] "Wanton" music mimed in space and time an
unwieldy plethora of erotic impulses. Thus, music's erotic resonances had to be
contained, sterilised, and if nothing else, redirected toward God.

From a feminist perspective, music's mandatory subservience to the Logos
(metaphorically) places it in the inferior, much maligned position of "body" in
traditional patriarchal meaning systems. As Body, music's erotic powers must be
spiritually sublimated. Contemporary theologies of music continue to rely uncritically upon classical formulations of music's theological significance without
questioning how the latter functioned as regulative ideals that occasioned very
harmful forms of musical and social censorship. And, as we shall see presently, the
rhetorical trajectory chronicled above takes another nasty turn, one that contemporary theologies of music omit at their own peril. In proportion to the perceived
threat of musical and personal virtue, the seemingly neutral rhetoric of purity and
danger, or community as unison and symphony, escalates into portraits of music
as dangerously effeminizing. The more explicit gynemorphic imagery of other
church fathers and educators, as well as its musico-theological significance, will be
the subject of the next chapter.

Notes

1. Musical intervals incarnate the tetractys of the decad to which Pythagoreans assigned sacred
status. That is, the first four whole numbers which, when added, yield the number ten, also translate
the proportional relationships between octave, fifth, and fourth.

2. Thus, via the tetractys, the decimal system in arithmetic was established.

3. Thus Newcomb: "As I see it, expressiveness results from the metaphorical resonances or
analogies that a viewer-listener-reader finds between properties that an object possesses and properties of experience outside the object itself (Newcomb, "Sound and Feeling," 625). "Expressive interpretation" is the study of this process. Here Newcomb adopts Jan L. Broeckx's definition: "'Expressive
interpretation as I understand it is concerned with *how the properties are connected to the resonances* for
a class of listeners—with the *conventions* of 'creative metaphor-making of a class of listeners'" (ibid.;
emphasis mine).

4. Ibid.

5. For example, Philolaus, a later Pythagorean writes: "And indeed all things that are known have

number. For without this nothing whatever could possibly be thought of or known" (Stobaeus, *Selections* in *Presocratics Reader*, #21, 23).

6. Musicologist and historian Edward Lippman summarises: "[For the Pythagoreans] number belongs to everything that can be known; its very nature is such as to give knowledge. Like knowledge, truth is inherent in number and specific to it, while falsehood is hostile to number and irreconcilable with it, belonging instead to the nature of the boundless, the senseless, and the unreasonable" (Lippman, *Musical Thought in Ancient Greece*, 14).

7. McFague, *Metaphorical Theology*, 16.

8. Ibid., 17.

9. Ibid.

10. Ibid., 13. McFague regards David Tracy's *The Analogical Imagination* as one exceptionally "sophisticated," "Catholic" "revitalisation of the symbolic." It succeeds precisely by emphasising the metaphoricity of this tradition—stressing "the negativities," keeping critical distance between image and its referent, rejecting "easy harmonies." While a radically "Protestant sensibility" would reject intimate "connections or unity between God and the world, tending toward agnosticism, McFague's metaphorical worldview perceives "connections" which remain, however, "tensive, discontinuous, and surprising" (McFague, *Metaphorical Theology*, 13).

11. McFague, ibid., 2.

12. Lippman, *Musical Thought*, 107.

13. Plato, *The Republic*, 3.11 in Strunk/Treitler, *Source Readings in Music History*, 14.

14. Thus later in *The Republic*, 3.12: "for surely the end and consummation of all musical things is the love of the beautiful" (ibid., 16).

15. Aristotle does not frown upon imitation as inferior modality; art as imitation is no "valueless copy of reality" (Lippman, *Musical Thought*, 138). Melody, rhythm, and dance are "natural imitations of character, emotion, and action" respectively (ibid., 137). His rejection of ideal Forms permits a freer, more physical understanding of imitation, one which allows a broader range of acceptable musical functions: "For first, inasmuch as it is necessary to take part in the performances for the sake of judging them, it is therefore proper for the pupils when young actually to engage in the performances, though when they get older they should be released from performing, but be able to judge what is beautiful and enjoy it rightly because of the study in which they engaged in their youth" (*Politics* 8.6, in Strunk/Treitler, *Source Readings*, 30).

While for Aristotle music can cultivate virtue and higher knowledge, it can also amuse and thereby refresh and relax as preparation for a return to work (Lippman, *Musical Thought*, 125f.). "Our first inquiry is whether music ought not or ought to be included in education, and what is its efficacy among the three uses of it that have been discussed—does it serve for education or amusement or entertainment? It is reasonable to reckon it under all of these heads, and it appears to participate in them all. Amusement is for the sake of relaxation, and relaxation must necessarily be pleasant, for it is a way of curing the pain due to laborious work; also entertainment ought admittedly to be not only honorable but also pleasant, for happiness is derived from both honor and pleasure" (Aristotle, *Politics* 8.5 in Strunk/Treitler, *Source Readings*, 27). Thus, Aristotle argues that "music makes virtue pleasurable" (Lippman, *Musical Thought*, 126). (Note the complementarity of previously antagonistic interests.) That is, it serves virtue by forming minds such that we recognise and pursue "true pleasures" (ibid., 126). Here is the original: "And since it is the case that music is one of the things that gives pleasure, and that virtue has to do with feeling delight and love and hatred rightly, there is obviously nothing that is more needful to learn and become habituated to than to judge correctly and to delight in virtuous ethoses and noble actions" (Aristotle, *Politics* 8.5; Strunk/Treitler, *Source Readings*, 28).

16. Thus Aristotle: "The young . . . must participate in such among the useful arts as will not render the person who participates in them vulgar. A task and also an art or a science must be deemed vulgar if it renders the body or soul or mind of free men useless for the employments and actions of virtue. Hence we entitle vulgar all such arts as deteriorate the condition of the body, and also the industries that earn wages; for they make the mind preoccupied and degraded" (*Politics*, 8.2 in ibid., 24).

"[T]hat the study of music must not place a hindrance in the way of subsequent activities, nor vulgarize the bodily frame and make it useless for the exercises of the soldier and the citizen, either for their practical pursuit now or for their scientific study later on (*Politics*, 8.6 in ibid., 30).

"It is clear therefore that we should lay down these three canons to guide education—moderation, possibility, and suitability" (*Politics*, 8.7 in ibid., 34).

17. Here is McFague's rationale: "The analogical way, the symbolic way, rests on a profound *similarity* beneath the surface dissimilarities; what we see and speak of must be the differences, but we rest

in the faith that all is empowered by the breath of God, Being-Itself. The vision of God, the goal of all creation, is the belief that one day all of creation shall be one. . . .

"Now, try as we might, many if not most of us cannot work ourselves back into this sacramentalist mentality. If the destiny of religious language rests on a return to the traditional sacramental universe, if the significance of imagistic language depends on a belief that symbols participate in a transcendent reality, the future for religious language is grim. I do not believe either is the case—that we must or can return to such a sacramental universe or that the significance of images rests on symbolic participationism" (*Metaphorical Theology*, 12).

18. In his *Divine Comedy*, for example, Dante did not "literalise" or "spiritualise" the "finite object" symbolised in the infinite through its own participation therein. It was not inflated as an idol nor reduced to "a mere sign" (McFague, ibid., 6).

19. Here McFague cites Feuerbach and Protestant liberalism (ibid.).

20. Ibid.

21. Cf. McFague on Jesus as "a parable for God" in *Metaphorical Theology*, 42-54.

22. For excellent surveys of Greek philosophies of music, see Warren D. Anderson, *Ethos and Education in Greek Music: The Evidence of Poetry and Philosophy* (Cambridge MA: Harvard University Press, 1966) as well as his *Music and Musicians in Ancient Greece* (Ithaca: Cornell University Press, 1994); cf. also Edward A. Lippman, *Musical Thought in Ancient Greece*.

23. For a feminist critique of the original household codes to which I am alluding, and the latter's sexist prescriptions for maintaining intrafamilial order among husbands, wives, children, and slaves, see Elisabeth Schüssler Fiorenza, *In Memory of Her*, chs. 7 and 8.

24. Lactantius, *Divine Institutions* 6.21 in Skeris, *Chroma Theou*, 52.

25. Augustine, *Confessions*, 10.33.49-50.

26. Bernard of Clairvaux, *Sermons on the Song of Songs*, 9-10.

27. Policraticus in Dalglish, "The Origin of the Hocket," 7.

28. Erasmus in Miller, "Erasmus on Music," 339.

29. Joyce Irwin discusses this non-logocentric turn among certain Protestant circles, one which stemmed from Georg Motz's full development of an "*opus operatum* theology." This "cantor and school music director at Tilse believed that spiritual impurity is not innate in particular musical styles, but in individual performers and auditors" (Irwin, "Shifting Alliances," 64). This attitude spawned a musical liberalism: "Nothing could better symbolize the completion of the barrier between musician and congregation than this. A new elite had been spawned within the priesthood of all believers. The professional musician, supported by the unqualified affirmation of the sacred nature of music, offered his re-creation of the harmonious universe for those who were prepared to receive it. The primacy of the text was denied. A half century later this was explicitly confirmed by the Lübeck cantor Caspar Ruetz (or Rüetz), who drew many of his ideas from Motz: 'But there is this dissimilarity between speech and music: namely, in speech one uses the sound of the voice for the sake of the words which are to be recognized and heard; but in music the words are for the sake of the sounds because here one speaks more through sounds than words.' Given this development, it was virtually inevitable that sacred art music would begin to make its way out of the church and into the concert hall. *It was a form of devotion unto itself, a means of experiencing the sacred as Beauty, not as Word*" (Irwin, ibid., 65; emphasis mine).

30. Luther, "Preface to *Symphoniae jucundae*, in Weiss and Taruskin, *Music in the Western World*, 102.

31. Bishop Franco in Weiss and Taruskin, *Music in the Western World*, 136f. (No original source is given save that of Gustave Reese, *Music in the Renaissance*, rev. ed. (New York: W.W. Norton, 1959) 449.

32. Bishop Franco, in Strunk, *Source Readings in Music History*, 1st ed., 371.

33. Pope Gregory XIII explains: "[T]he Breviary and Missal ordered by the Council of Trent have been filled to overflowing with barbarisms, obscurities, contrarieties, and superfluities as a result of the clumsiness or negligence or even wickedness of the composers, scribes, and printers." The Pope requests that these be "shorn away . . . that through their agency God's name may be reverently, distinctly, and devoutly praised" ("Brief on the Reform of the Chant" [October 25, 1577] in Strunk, *Source Readings*, 1st ed., 358-59).

34. Thus Rousseau: "We have adopted this poor taste from those who, wishing to introduce the manner of Italian music in a language alien to it, have forced us to try to do with instruments what we cannot accomplish with our voices. I dare predict that so unnatural a taste will not last. Purely harmonic music [i.e., without text] is short on substance; in order to be continually pleasing and avoid

boredom, music must raise itself to the level of the imitative arts; but its imitation is not always immediate like that of poetry or painting; *the word is the means through which music most frequently determines the object whose image it offers us*, and it is by means of sounds in conjunction with the human
voice that this image awakens at the bottom of our hearts the sentiment it is its purpose to produce
(Rousseau, *Dictionnaire de musique*, 451-52, in Weiss and Taruskin, *Music in the Western World*, 288;
emphasis mine).

35. Pope Gregory XIII in Strunk, *Source Readings*, 1st ed., 358f.

36. This is the title of Jean LeClercq's classic work. For the central role of eros in Plato's philosophical inquiries, see Anne Carson, *Eros the Bittersweet*, 117-73.

37. Here I have adapted the title of Martha Nussbaum's classic, *The Fragility of Goodness: Luck
and Ethics in Greek Tragedy and Philosophy* (Cambridge/New York: Cambridge University Press,
1986).

38. Augustine, *Confessions*, 10.33.49.

39. Augustine portrays Light as a Woman *after* his discussion of the "pleasures of the ear" in
10.34.51: "[Colours and other] pleasures of the eye . . . touch me, wide awake, throughout the day, nor
do they give me a moment's respite, in the way the voices of singers, sometimes the entire choir, keep
silence. *The very queen of colours*, which bathes with light all that we see, wherever I may be during the
day, comes down upon me with gentle subtlety through many media, while I am doing something else
and not noticing it. but the light makes its way with such power that, if suddenly it is withdrawn, it is
sought for with longing" (tr. Chadwick, 209; emphasis mine).

40. Augustine, *Confessions*, 10.33.50.

41. On Light as the "Queen of Colours," cf. *Confessions*, 10.34.51.

42. Ibid.

43. This is Augustine's original denomination of the "appropriate music" that accompanies
sacred texts (*Confessions*, 10.33.50).

44. Cf. ibid., 8.9.

45. In her book, Miles emphasises and offers an excellent critique of Augustine's different rhetorical treatment of female figures (e.g., the "good mother" and "tempting seductress") and of the "actual
women" in his life (cf. *Desire and Delight*, chapter 3, "The Erotic Text," 67-99, esp. 90-92). Ultimately,
"there are no seductive women. . . . [H]is understanding and literary treatment of actual women is limited by the female figures that inhabit his psyche: the good mother and the sexual object. A gendered
reading of the Confessions reveals that it contains no depictions of women who, like Augustine, suffer and struggle to define and achieve their own goals" (Miles, ibid., 92).

46. Miles elaborates: "Augustine's metaphors of tumescence contribute to the cumulative connotations by which he establishes male sexuality as his model of scattered and wasted strength. He con-
sistently used the verbs *turgeo* and *tumeo* to describe the "swelling" or "swollen" condition of prideful
arrogance that was his settled style [3.3, 7.7, 2.3.] (ibid., 94f.). Consequently, as a remedy for this sinful state: "Gathering, containing, recollecting: these are the activities that must replace dissipation—
both literally and symbolically. Continence was, for Augustine, the essential pivot on which he
turned—returned—to God" (ibid., 95).

47. Ibid., 97.

48. Augustine has "managed both to find maximal pleasure that is permanent, and to 'save' sensory delights by embedding them in the great beauty. He has dismantled or unraveled 'false' pleasure—pleasure diluted with pain, undermined by evanescence, constructed by lack. And he has
identified 'true' pleasure, pleasure that is secure, guaranteed, undiluted, everlasting. He feels that he
has recovered the 'true' senses, salvaging their transitory delights by placing them in a permanent
object" (Miles, ibid., 131; cf. Augustine, *Confessions*, 10.6).

49. On the varied enlistments of this standard andromorphic metaphor for Christian women's
attempts to "live an uncompromising Christian faith," see Miles, "'Becoming Male': Women Martyrs
and Ascetics," *Carnal Knowing*, chapter 2 (55).

50. Boethius, *De musica*, 1.1, 181 (Palisca), 3.

51. Ibid., 1.1, 180, (Palisca), 3.

52. Bower explains: "The terms *mollis* and *durus* (translated from *malakos* and *skleros*) are technical terms in ancient theory. At the more general level of discussion, *mollis* describes music that is soft,
tender, and effeminate in character, whereas *durus* describes music that is firm, austere, and masculine." Bower also directs readers to Carl Dahlhaus, "Di Termini Dur und Moll," *Archiv für Musik-
wissenschaft* 12 (1955): 280-96 (Bower, in Boethius, [Palisca], 3 n. 7).

53. Boethius, *De musica*, 2f.

54. Ibid., 4.

55. Cf. Bruce Thornton, *Eros: The Myth of Ancient Greek Sexuality*. Thornton describes the various physical manifestations of eros—forces of nature which undoubtedly impinged upon the construction of Greek philosophies of music as well as their cosmologies: "Like fire and storm, disease and death, the Greeks' eros is a force of nature, indiscriminate, chaotic, relentlessly attacking civilization and its orders—the mind and its projections onto the world, the political and social structures that clear the space for human identity" (120).

Eros is also located in human sexuality: "Embodied in golden, laughter-loving Aphrodite, the sexual drive deceives with its joy and beauty that, like a calm sea, veil its destructive powers" (ibid.). More specifically, woman personifies Eros: "Like the goddess, woman too is deceptively beautiful and lurks on the earth and its primal forces, yet her procreative power is necessary for the survival of the city and its institutions" (ibid.).

And finally, Eros governs the even more suspect *kinaidos*: "the creature of sterile pleasure—anal penetration—that abandons to the vortex of desire not just his own rational control over his passions but also the masculine order enshrined in the political and social institutions of the city, subjecting them to the corrosive acid of all appetites, all lusts" (ibid.). In the face of such unwieldy impulses, technologies and social hierarchies for control are developed, and eros itself is constructively channelled in the process; these consist of contemplation, agriculture, civic religion, marriage, and pederasty (ibid., 212).

Thornton ironically observes: "Plato represents the most extreme attempt to conquer a material world of change, decay, and death whose disorder is so frightening—and yet his yearning is betrayed by the central role eros must play in the soul's liberation, the way our blood must be the blood of paradise. . . . Only in death do we escape the dialectic of mind and body, culture and nature, reason and eros" (ibid.).

56. Cf. Carson, *Eros the Bittersweet*.

57. Brown, "Art and Society in Late Antiquity," 23.

58. Ibid.

59. Ibid.

60. Ibid.

61. Ibid.; emphasis mine.

62. There is also an ironic paradox at the heart of this vilification of music's appeal to human sexuality. It was precisely the erotics of *sexual* desire that spawned Plato's idealism, his politics of transcendence. Metaphysics begins in bodily experience. The rhetoric of transcendence so often used to articulate music's theological significance and function can never be disembodied, given the absolute necessity of flesh and blood to transmit musical "data." Thornton's anatomy of erotic technologies culminates in the following observation: "Here we see Plato's remarkable gambit, one that has profoundly influenced Western idealizations of sexuality: A reality defined as immaterial, rational, eternal, and absolute—that is, everything the natural world of matter and sex is not—will be *rationally* apprehended using the energy of sexual desire, which is an *irrational* function of a material, time- and space-bound physical body" (Thornton, *Eros*, 210). Given the strong taboos instituted to keep music and the erotic safely separated from each other, it is indeed ironic to realise that human sexuality originally grounded Plato's abstract, rationalised doctrine of eros. For example, "eros in the *Phaedrus* is still saturated with the physical reality of sexual passion" even though it is meant to allow the soul to commune with a disembodied version of the Good (ibid.). In the *Symposium,* conversely, Diotima's speech reflects a more sterilised, disembodied eros (ibid.). Surely Plato's displacement of eros and the subsequent disembodiment of musical pleasure themselves reflect a certain destructive power.

63. Scholars have concluded that the aim of Pythagoras was the creation of "a cultural aristocracy and a religion based upon moral principles." His musical hermeneutic simultaneously reflects, verifies, and defends these ideals (cf. Lampropoulou, "Some Pythagorean Female Virtues," *Women in Antiquity: New Assessments*, ed. Richard Hanley and Barbara Levick [New York: Routledge, 1995] 122-34).

64. Thus Nicholas of Cusa: "Enthusiasm is a moving force," and, therefore, "motion in music is an image, a symbol, a metaphor of our passions" (Nicholas of Cusa, in Meyer-Baer, "Nicholas of Cusa on the Meaning of Music," 308). Meyer-Baer therefore argues that Cusa posits "another resource for the relevant apprehension of moving sound. This is feeling, feeling that can rise to transport and that commands symbols; for the flow, the motion in music is an image, a symbol, a metaphor of our passions" (ibid.).

65. Boethius, 1.186 (Palisca), 8. Boethius unequivocally asserts: "So there can be no doubt that

the order of our soul and body seems to be related somehow through those same ratios by which subsequent argument will demonstrate sets of pitches, suitable for melody, are joined together and united" (ibid., 7).

66. Boethius, 1.186 (Palisca), 7.

67. Ibid. 1.187 (Palisca), 8.

68. See Holsinger, *Music, Body, and Desire*, part 1, 1-86.

69. Newcomb's terminology in "Sound and Feeling."

70. Such "erotica" in Western classical and popular music include Wagner's *Tristan und Isolde*, Debussy's *Prelude à l'après-midi d'un faune*, and Madonna and Prince's duet, "This is Not a Love Song." See McClary's discussion of the same in *Feminine Endings*, 7-9.

71. McClary, *Feminine Endings*, 8.

72. Ibid., 8f. Nor are those bodily experiences and musical gestures that are conventionally labelled "erotic" stable or immutable: "any living code is in constant flux" (McClary, "A Musical Dialectic of Enlightenment," 132).

73. McClary, "Music, Pythagoreans, and the Body," 86-93. Here McClary relies upon research done by Meredith Ellis Little, "Dance under Louis XIV and XV: Some Implications for the Musician," *Early Music* 3 (1975): 331-40, and Christopher Isherwood, *Music in Service of the King* (Ithaca: Cornell University Press, 1973). McClary summarises: "As part of his absolutist agenda, for instance, Louis XIV employed dance and its supporting music to regulate—indeed, literally to *synchronize*—the bodies and behaviors of his courtiers. In accordance with Louis's priorities (motivated at least as much by political as aesthetic considerations), French musicians maintained dance at the center of their activities" ("Music, Pythagoreans, and the Body," 90).

74. McClary, "Music, Pythagoreans, and the Body," 84.

75. Cf. Johnson, *The Body in the Mind.*

76. Johnson, *The Body in the Mind*, xv.

77. Ibid. Johnson gives examples of such "imaginative structures of understanding": "image schemata and their metaphorical elaborations"; an "image schema" is "a recurring, dynamic pattern of our perceptual interactions and motor programs that gives coherence and structure to our experience" (Johnson, xiv). He gives an example of the basic abstract, comparative "more" which we usually represent metaphorically in terms of the vertical "up" (p. xv). Johnson argues that "concrete bodily experience not only constrains the 'input' to the metaphorical projections, but also the nature of the projections themselves, that is, the kinds of mappings that can occur across domains" (Johnson, xv). Thus Johnson explores "*how* the body is in the mind"; that is, he traces the origins and development of abstract meanings, reason, and imagination from human embodiment (p. xvi). McClary discusses Johnson's work in her introduction to *Feminine Endings*, 23f.

78. McClary, *Feminine Endings*, 23.

79. "Expressive predicates" is Newcomb's term. See "Sound and Feeling," 618.

80. This is also Newcomb's term, "Sound and Feeling," 625.

81. McClary, *Feminine Endings*, 25.

Sexing the Semitone:
Music's Historical Engendering

A S WE HAVE SEEN, although enchanted by music's numerical properties Boethius and Augustine are troubled by its ability to wander from the harmonic straight and narrow and take auditors hostage in the process. Augustine's discussions of music's power to distract and Boethius's denunciation of musical decadence offer two examples of musico-theological rhetoric that implicitly conflate music's "body" with that of Woman. Augustine likens her to a siren, while Boethius mourns her loss of virginity, her edenic purity. Lest their lamentations remain unconvincing, because atypical, this chapter further documents this rhetorical trajectory as well as the disturbing socio-cultural side effect that these metaphorical transfers and conflations effected. We begin with the following complaints about music's mutinous potential from church fathers and later theologians.

I. Music of Spirit and Flesh

The combined influence of the Greek emphasis upon transcendent metaphysical unity, number, and order in music, and the Pauline elaborations of life in the flesh or spirit leads Christian authorities to classify music as either fleshly or spiritual. Indeed, Paul's minimalist prescription of "psalms, hymns, and spiritual songs" institutes a buck-stopping devotional canon. Theologians in the early church believe that pagan music literally dis-integrates the harmonious alignment of body-soul, individual-society, nature-cosmos. Cyprian describes the Music-problem thus: "We quickly get accustomed to what we hear and what we see. For since man's mind is itself drawn toward vice, what will it do if it should have inducements of a bodily nature as well as a downward tendency in its slippery will?"[1] Given this innate predisposition to fleshly temptation, directives for proper musical decorum protect nascent communities from the disorderly musical conduct of pagans and gnostics, against whom Christians fought to define themselves. Fleshly music is said to emasculate—eroding rational self-control, and softening, that is, effeminising, male character. Christian exhortations frequently characterize such music as "lascivious," "frivolous," "wanton," and "lewd." Here again, precedents for such rhetoric were set by Plato and others. Modes, instruments, and musical styles had already been deemed feminine —"sweet, soft, warbling and weak"—or masculine. Aristotle retains these binary oppositions: "And all agree that the Dorian harmonia is more sedate and of a specially manly ethos."[2] Aristotle also polarises virtue and "vulgarity," such that the latter is clearly an unmanly trait. Any activities that induce vulgarity (including music-making) are to be avoided by the free man. Such equations render professional musicians archly effeminate: "But professional musicians we speak of as vulgar people, and indeed we think it not manly to perform music, except when drunk or for fun."[3]

According to John Chrysostom, music actually penetrates the soul and exerts a palpable, illicit (i.e., "contrary to the law") force, leaving the soul "weak and soft."[4] He believes that chronic exposure to party music renders mind and spirit flaccid and assailable: "This is a sign of ultimate insensibility and a dissolute soul, to make a theater of one's own house and to give oneself up to such songs. And what drunkenness accomplishes by obscuring, the same does music as it slackens the tautness of the mind, enfeebles the vigor of the spirit, and leads it to greater licentiousness."[5] Thus, by rendering reason impotent, music makes women out of men.[6]

The chief musical fleshpots are (pagan) theatre, weddings, funerals, banquets, and any use of musical instruments. Both aulos and flute are vilified because of their erotically feminine connotations. The use of flutes in the cult of Cybele leads Gregory of Nazianzus to liken their "madness" to the sound of castrated men. Like Aristotle long before him,[7] Arnobius cannot countenance the ugly mien that flute-playing induced. His more general disgust for dance, and for instrumental music's engagement of human sexuality, is vehement:

> Was it for this He sent souls, that beings (*res*) of a sacred and august race should here practise singing and piping; that they should swell out their cheeks in blowing the flute; that they should take the lead in singing impure songs, and raising loud din of the castanets, by which another crowd of souls should be led in their wantonness to abandon themselves to clumsy motions, to dance and sing, form rings of dancers, and finally, raising their haunches and hips, float along with a tremulous motion of the loins? Was it for this that He sent souls, that in men they should become impure, in women harlots, players on the triangle and psaltery; that they should prostitute their bodies for hire, should make public their vileness, ready in the brothels, to be met with in the stews, ready to submit to anything, prepared to do violence to their mouth even?[8]

Cyprian dismisses instrumental grotesquerie as lust's most unlawful partner in crime. Like Arnobius's disdain for the flute—and this will be important later—the *visual* charms of musical performance erode Christian character as much as aural ones.[9] Lucian of Samosata deplores the emasculating evils of pantomime (and by inference, love songs sung by women) as follows: "My dear fellow, can a man who has had the benefit of an education as well as a little traffic with philosophy, who strives after better things and has familiarity with the ancients—can such a man sit down and listen to flute music and watch an effeminate man strutting about in women's clothes, imitating amorous females with his lewd singing?"[10] (Also of note in the above passage is the conviction that philosophical training will steel the mind from such temptations.) Cyril of Jerusalem also sanctions the "frantic dances of effeminate men" in the theatre; he ranks them among the *pompa diaboli* that Christians must renounce at baptism.[11] With typical incendiary élan, Tertullian denounces the contagious effeminacy of pagan spectacles. The music has an innately emasculating power, and the spectacles divert body, soul, and mind from their proper object of desire: "When a tragic actor is declaiming, will one be giving thought to prophetic appeals? Amid the measures of the effeminate player/tibicinist,[12] will he call up to himself a psalm?"[13] Tatian also deplores the "unnatural" behaviour of male actors, singers, and mimes: "I have no mind to stand agape at a number of singers, nor do I desire to be affected in sympathy with a man when he is winking and gesticulating in an unnatural manner."[14]

John Chrysostom rebukes those who would risk a kind of sexual perversion by "fluttering after Satan's pomp" in their wedding ceremonies, thereby "spoil[ing] the modesty of the maiden and mak[ing] the groom more wanton."[15] Church authorities deemed even grieving as "womanish," because women were the prime exponents of ritual mourning in Greek culture. In pagan customs this liturgical role for women becomes a source of social prestige, but Christian men were discouraged from such excessive emotional display. John Chrysostom calls it "the disease of females," and this contaminant could precipitate socio-harmonic decline.[16] Proper grieving by contrast preserves inter- and intrapersonal harmony, unity, and order.[17] (It seems some allowances were made; Eastern Patriarch John III forbade women to dance and play the tambourine at the grave site, but "professed sisters" were allowed to sing the "*madrashe* in procession behind the coffin."[18] And rationally restrained grieving was always acceptable.[19])

A long passage from Clement is representative of Christian disdain for pagan banquets, the consummate site of all appetitive, effeminising excess (sexual, musical, comestible):

> Let revelry keep away from our rational entertainments, and foolish vigils, too, that revel in intemperance, for revelry is an inebriating pipe, the chain of an amatory bridge, that is, of sorrow. And let love, and intoxication, and senseless passions, be removed from our choir. . . . Let the pipe be resigned to the shepherds, and the flute to the superstitious who are engrossed in idolatry. For, in truth, such instruments are to be banished from the temperate banquet, being more suitable to beasts than men, and the more irrational portion of mankind. . . . *[A]nd we must be on our guard against whatever pleasure titillates eye and ear, and effeminates.* For the various spells of the broken strains and plaintive numbers of the Carian muse corrupt men's morals, drawing to perturbation of mind, by the licentious and mischievous art of music.[20]

Interestingly enough, Bruce Holsinger overlooks this passage from Clement, preferring instead to recuperate and thematise the latter's christologically symbolic celebrations of musical bodies as proof positive that patristic theologians did not ignore the body, nor resort solely to Greek metaphysics, to convey music's theological meanings.[21]

In fairness to the fathers, one concedes that these freer pagan styles, rife with drums, dancing, and raunchy reeds, might impede orderly worship, their modern day analogue being, according to one scholar, vaudeville.[22] Steeped in our own socio-culturally determined aesthetic of musical holiness, one can understand that such music might not inspire prayerful quiescence. And yet, the untapped theological value of such fleshly tones and, more basically, sexist denigrations of them are not addressed in contemporary musico-theological discourse. To deny these "lascivious" media any positive musico-theological value, as even today's musico-theological discourse does, squelches a rich vein for contemporary theological transfusions.

In contrast to such fleshly musical venues and modalities, *music of the spirit* is chaste and pure. Gaudentius of Brecia sets in opposition the chaos of pagan banquets with their noisy instruments and dancing girls and the austere simplicity of Christian gatherings:

> You will at last be able to preserve this (your faith) if you avoid drunkenness and shameful banquets, where the serpentine movements of lewd women stir one to illicit desire, where the lyre and tibia sound, and where, finally, every sort of musician makes noise amid the cymbals of the dancers. Those are wretched homes which differ in nothing from theatres. Let the house of the Christian and the baptized man be free of the devil's choir; let it simply be human, let it be hospitable; let it be sanctified with continuous prayer; let it be filled with psalms, hymns and spiritual songs.[23]

Christian symposia shape spiritual heroes. Military rhetoric and images are used to describe holy musical practices—a manly alternative to the wanton musical habits of "actors, dancers, and lewd women." Christian music is a strategic defence, a psalmodic "fortress" against the collapse of—dare I say—family values.[24]

Not surprisingly, the most spiritual, distraction-free musical medium was *a capella* singing. Here, again, warrior imagery promotes this purest style. Singing, because uncluttered and wed to the Word, can increase Christian virility:

> Singing of itself is not to be considered as fit only for the unclean, but rather singing to the accompaniment of soulless instruments and dancing and the noise of the krotala. Therefore use of such instruments with singing in church must be shunned, as well as everything else that is proper only for fools. Simple singing alone remains. . . . Paul calls it a sword of the spirit with which it outfits pious fighters for God against the invisible enemy. For it is and remains God's word, whether it is contemplated, sung or listened to, a protection against the demon.[25]

This eroticised, musical dichotomy between spirit and flesh endured in Christian musico-theological discourse for centuries. The psalmodic virility described above is threatened in the Middle Ages when the rise and reign of Gregorian chant falls prey to certain allegedly feminising innovations. Cistercian musical reform is meant to restore its potency. Thus, a Cistercian statute of 1134 decrees: "It befits men to sing with a manly voice, and not in a womanish manner with tinkling, or, as it is said in the vernacular, with 'false' voices, as if imitating the wantonness of minstrels. We have therefore stipulated that the mean should be adhered to in chant, so that it may exude seriousness and devotion may be preserved."[26] Bernard of Clairvaux admonishes monks to sing "correctly and vigorously ... not wheezing through the nose with an effeminate stammering, in a weak and broken tone, but pronouncing the words of the Holy Spirit with becoming manliness and resonance and affection."[27] Similarly, Aelred of Rievaulx scorns the vocal and corporeal secular song style wherein the voice is "forced into whinnying of a horse, and sometimes it lays aside its manly power, and puts on the shrillness of a woman's voice. . . . The whole body is agitated by theatrical gestures, the lips are twisted, the eyes roll, the shoulders are shrugged, and the fingers bent responsive to every note."[28] The Carthusians are to abstain from the musically sensuous delights of "ornamental melismas" or the "breaking up" and "repetition of notes" because these "belong more to *curiositas* than to chaste song."[29] Even the, today seemingly innocuous, Christmas carol is initially vilified as "lascivious,"[30] this because some carol tunes were borrowed from (and thus, when sung, summoned to mind) the pagan *carole* dance-song rituals.[31] In England, John of Salisbury decides that music's ineradicable fleshliness made it totally unfit for use in worship—which he justifies in strikingly phallic imagery:

> Music sullies the Divine Service, for in the very sight of God . . . [the singers] attempt, with the lewdness of a lascivious singing voice and a singularly foppish manner, to feminize all their spellbound little fans with the girlish way they render the notes and end the phrases. Could you but hear the effete emotings of their before-singing and their after-singing . . . you would think it an ensemble of sirens, not of men. . . . [T]he intellect, which the pleasurableness of so much sweetness has caressed insensate is impotent to judge the merits of the things heard. Indeed, when such practices go too far, they can more easily occasion titillation between the legs than a sense of devotion in the brain.[32]

Similarly, in his *Opus tertium* (1267), Roger Bacon uses phallic rhetoric to lament musical decadence in the church:

> At present, the abuse of singing has increased steadily throughout the Church to the extent that the chant has fallen away from its ancient sobriety and strength. . . . [I]t has lapsed into a shameless flaccidity. It now manifests a faddish propensity for new harmonies, a prurient inventiveness in proses, and a tasteless delight in a multiplicity of *cantilenae*. More than anything else, this decline of the chant is manifested in those voices, adolescent in their effusiveness and feminine in their

dissoluteness, which counterfeit in falsetto the sacred and manly harmony almost everywhere throughout the Church.[33]

During the Renaissance, the progressive-minded Erasmus nonetheless reviles the insidious invasion of fleshly idioms into sacred compositions: "We have brought into sacred edifices a certain elaborate and theatrical music, a confused interplay of diverse sounds, such as I do not believe was ever heard in Greek or Roman theaters. Straight trumpets, curved trumpets, pipes and sambucas resound everywhere, and vie with human voices. Amorous and shameful songs are heard, the kind to which harlots and mimes dance. People flock to church as to a theater for aural delight."[34]

Later in the sixteenth century, Archbishop Artusi deplores the development of the *seconda prattica*, labelling it (and even its progenitor Monteverdi), a "painted whore."[35] Artusi lambastes both with epithets, calling the new style "wet," and "an unnatural, monstrous birth," in contrast to the traditional style which was "dry," "hot," "beautiful," and "healthy."[36] The emasculation of sacred music by such fleshly madrigalisms becomes a chief target of Tridentine musical reform. (I shall develop more positive theological implications from this famous debate in chapter 5.) The Reformers and their Pietist descendants, as we saw in chapter 1, also condemn fleshly, and promoted spiritual, music. (Intimations of this can already be glimpsed in Calvin's calls for order cited in chapter 1.) Carlstadt urges the expulsion of erotically suggestive musical instruments from worship: "Relegate trumpets, and flutes to the theatre. Better are heartfelt prayers than a thousand cantatas of the psalms. The *lascivious* notes of the organ awaken thoughts of the world. When we should be meditating on the sufferings of Christ, we are reminded of Pyramus and Thisbe. Or if there is to be singing, let it be no more than a solo."[37] And, despite his endorsement of secular art music and instrumental music in church, Luther's sacred-secular delineations are sexually charged. Musico-"erotic rantings" are deviant aberrations of music's divine *ontos*, and composers thereof pimps to music's body:

> And you, my young friends, let this noble, wholesome, and cheerful creation of God be commended to you. By it you may escape shameful desires and bad company. At the same time you may by this creation accustom yourselves to recognize the Creator. Take special care to shun *perverted minds who prostitute this lovely gift of nature and of art with their erotic rantings*; and be quite assured that none but the devil goads them on to defy their very nature which would and should praise God its Maker with this gift, so that these bastards purloin the gift of God and use it to worship the foe of God, the enemy of nature and of this lovely art. Farewell in the Lord.[38]

In his own purist apologetic, Calvin appeals to Plato and the fathers to scorn music's voluptuousness and its "dissipative," "emasculating" effects.[39]

In the seventeenth century, the development of the stylistically lavish oratorio (born moreover of the"whorish" *seconda prattica)* further erodes the separation of sacred and secular music and sparks great debate among pre-Pietists and Pietists such as Grossgebauer, Arnold, Spener, Muscovius, Vockerodt, and Müller, including prominent musicians Werckmeister and Georg Motz. For Heinrich Müller (echoing Augustine's fears), musical "frivolity" (historically, a "feminine" vice) sinfully distracts: "Externals, such as frivolous people or frivolous music, are a distraction; to avoid these one would do better to build a little church in one's house."[40] Such "frivolity" precipitates both external and interior chaos.[41] The only remedy of course is Paul's minimalist aesthetic. Grossgebauer continues: "But they could be well instructed by the spiritual songs of the congregation, which Paul exhorts. Some would like to pray but are so captivated and disoriented by the roaring and ringing that they can't. . . . [O]ccasionally everything breaks loose, and if an unbeliever should come into our gathering, would he not say that we were putting on a spectacle and that we were partly mad?" (1 Cor. 14:23)."[42]

Sometimes, however, there are curious fault lines in these Protestant delineations of spiritual and fleshly styles. Though disdainful of "erotic rantings," Luther seemingly "lusts" after the richness of secular tunes and defends their baptism as hymns: "How is it that *in Carnalibus* we have so many refined poems and beautiful songs yet *in Spiritualibus* we have but cold and miserly ones. . . . I submit that the cause is, as St. Paul says, 'I see a different law in the members of my body' [waging war against the law of my mind]."[43] The oddity in this logic is that Luther blames human *fleshliness* ("the law in our members") for the *sterility* of much sacred music. The musical barrenness caused by the law in our members must be remedied by importing fleshly tunes. Luther thus contends that true life in the spirit would inspire equally gorgeous music to rival the "carnal" strains that he finds so captivating. There is a similar erosion of spirit/flesh dichotomies within later Pietist discourse when theologians shift their fleshly/spiritual evaluative criterion from the music's curves to the composers' intent. By this new standard of intentionality, the same musical styles and gestures could be *both* carnal and spiritual, sparking a difficult-to-monitor, salvific crap-shoot for auditor and composer alike. Thus Gottfried Vockerodt determines: "A faithful musician by the same instrument which has driven others mad, can make those who hear him clear-headed and thus entice and allure pious souls to the fear and love of God with that which a godless musician uses as a Satanic panpipe."[44]

Nowhere is music more gendered than in the educational and theological treatises of Elizabethan England. Their musical gynemorphisms have been amply documented by Renaissance scholar Linda Phyllis Austern. Especially for Puritans, effeminacy in boys and "whoorishnesse" [*sic*] in girls are constant environmental hazards for performers and auditors alike. Music incarnates the "perils of femininity" *tout court.*[45] Partly because of its female gender in Latin and partly because of its cognate power "to move the affections and delight the senses," music is often "personified" or allegorised as a woman.[46] Thomas Ravenscroft, therefore, depicted music as a "fragile virtuous wife and mother in need of defence against the base-born common practitioners who batter her."[47] In the treatise *The Praise of Musicke* (authorship disputed), "she" is likened to a nubile virgin "fit to wedde men's hearts and minds unto her."[48]

Many Elizabethans regards exposure to love songs (now in the form of the madrigal) and instrumental music as immersion in a feckless sensuality that rendered men's minds flaccidly passive, that is, effeminate. To avoid such debauchery, proper Christian musical education is promoted in no uncertain terms.[49] Roger Ascham, in his *Toxophilus, the Schole, or partitions of Shooting,* contends that music "marreth mens manners" and "make[s] a mans wittes so soft and smothe, so tender and quaisye, that they be lesse able to broke stronge & tough studye."[50] To prove his point he offers historical examples of such emasculation, and this moreover, couched in unmistakably phallic imagery: Music has "quicklye of men made women and thus lutinge and singinge take aweay a manlye stomacke, which should enter and peerce deepe and harde studye."[51] Similarly, Puritan Philip Stubbes warns: "If you would have your sonne softe, womannishe, uncleane, smothe mouthed, affected to *baudie, scurrilitie, filthy Rimes,* and unsemely talkying: briefly, if you would have hym, as it were transnatured into a Woman, or worse, and inclined to all kinde of Whoredome and abomination, sett hym . . . to learne Musicke, and then shall you not faile your purpose."[52] Puritan extremist William Prynne reluctantly condones *a capella* hymn and psalm singing in public and private worship but denounces "public minstrelsy" because it could "enervate the virility of men's bodies."[53] Godly men must shun all "enticements of the eares or eyes from whence the vigor of the minde may be thought to be effeminated."[54] (It should be noted here that a wide range of conflicting attitudes toward music exists among Puritan writers and clergy—the term 'Puritan' itself misleadingly generic.[55])

Descriptions of the madrigal, particularly its stock "rhetorical" gestures, are equally gendered in Elizabethan discourse.[56] Prynne contrasts love songs' "effeminate, delicate, lust-provoking Musicke" to the manly (i.e., "sober, godly, chaste") settings of psalms.[57] Madrigals are effeminate because they are laced with "artifice, ornamentation, rhetorical excess and sensory delight."[58] In the words of Thomas Wright, they exude a "manifest loose effeminateness," which effects "a certain kind of tickling symphonie [that] maketh men effeminate and delicat."[59] Both Morley and Charles Butler attribute this effeminacy to the music's "varied delicacy," its virtuosic "artifice," and the musico-textual collusion in expressing the "delights of love."[60] Surprisingly enough, as a composer of madrigals, Morley does not seem concerned about the erosion of his own manliness. He still deems motets the manly, "grave and sober" genre.[61] Perhaps immune via his own rhetorical maturity, Morley even offers compositional strategies for good madrigal writing: "If therefore you will compose in this kind you must possesse your self with an amorous humor . . . so that you must in your musicke be wavering like the wind, sometime wanton, sometime drooping, sometime grave and staide, otherwhile effeminat, you must maintaine points and revert them, use triplaes, and shew the verie uttermost of your varietie, and the more varietie you shew the better shall you please."[62] Such compositional posturing, perhaps because controlled and self-induced, poses no threat to a composer's virility. (Austern finds Morley's description of madrigal compositional technique reminiscent of Shakespeare's characterisation of "feminine sexual teasing,"[63] something harmless which men can enact without emasculation—though actors in classical and medieval culture, as we have seen, and *pace* today's Hollywood norms, are never regarded as manly men.)

From her survey of Elizabethan literature, Austern concludes that the emblematically effeminate musical device in madrigals (and other genres) is chromaticism, that crafty manipulation of "inordinate half-notes":

> because as pictures are beautifyed with trim lively coollors, to pleaz the wanton ey; so this kinde is as it were coollored with delicate lively sounds to pleaz the wanton ear. . . . [W]oords of effeminate lamentations, sorrowful passions, and complaints are fitly expressed by the inordinate half-notes (such as the small keys of the Virginals) which change the direct order of the Scale, flattening the Notes naturally sharp, and sharpening them which are naturally flat: and those in longer time; with slow bindings and discording Cadences.[64]

Madrigals are musical Eves; their ultimate feminine vice is ornamental license. This already seductive musical cocktail can be made even more toxic by the performer's use of *falsetto* (the name says it all) and improvisation. Thus Prynne complains: "Sometimes the masculine vigor [of the voice] being laid aside, it is sharpened into the shrilnesse of a woman's voyce: now and then it is wrethed, and retorted with a certaine artificiall circumvolution."[65] All these excesses and affectations violate the ascetic masculinist ideal of musical beauty—"a manlye, roughe and stoute sound."[66]

II. Music-as-Woman in the Modern Era

Having identified in chapter 1 the real criterion of music's beauty and holiness as its engagement or transcendence of human sexuality, the symptomatic readings of Christian musical proscriptions in the present chapter now allow even more specificity: the more urgent preoccupation of church authorities (and their Greek antecedents) is "lewd" music's power to effeminise or emasculate. Highly charged sexual rhetoric develops to control Christian disciples' musical activities, thereby suppressing music's erotic powers, as well as any threats to "her" integrity. This rhetorical trajectory, moreover, precipitates the circumscription of acceptable musical practices, with sexist results, as we shall see in section 3 below. Lest one dismiss the above examples as archaic, long since purged from the more critically informed theological and musicological discourse today, consider the following examples from the eighteenth, nineteenth, and twentieth centuries. No matter how characterisations of masculinity and effeminacy might shift over time, it would seem that, at least in polemical rhetoric, such sweeping generalisations engraved virgin–whore stereotypes of music-as-woman in the popular imagination. Indeed, even in the late twentieth century, music's engendering power still infects both musicological discourse and at least one survey of church music. Contemporary works, while devoid of such slurs, are strangely silent about this historical trajectory, and the latter's impact upon the sources and norms, not only of classical musico-theological models, but also of current ones (as I shall show in chapter 3). As a result, contemporary theologians simply develop more sophisticated elaborations of music's logocentric, harmonically-driven thematics.

In the eighteenth century, German music theorist Georg Andreas Sorge regarded the hierarchical, gendered homology of the male/major and female/minor triads in tonal harmony as "natural" and "God-given." The female/minor is incomplete and lacking authenticity without the male/major: "And just as the womanly sex without the man would be quite bad, thus with music it would be in a bad way if we had no other harmony than that which the minor triad gives. We could not once make an authentic cadence."[67] In England, with the operatic/theatrically inspired oratorio on the rise, detractors of Italian opera and its pollution of British sacred repertoire were numerous. In 1706, remarks from John Dennis evidence the perdurance of past era's preoccupations: music should remain "subservient to Reason," but, unfortunately, Italian stylistic innovations have caused music "to set up for it self, and to grow independent," such that "it becomes a mere sensual Delight, utterly incapable of informing our Understanding.... [S]oft and delicious Music, by soothing the Senses ... by emasculating and dissolving the Mind ... shakes the very Foundation of Fortitude."[68] Despite his broader tolerance for sacred musical innovations, the Reverend George Lavington (later bishop of Exeter) uses female metaphors to decry this latest blurring of sacred and secular musics. He cautions against "robbing the Playhouse, only to dress up the Spouse of Christ in the attire of a harlot."[69]

Regarding the more specifically Italian aspect of such "harlotry" in her social history of Handel's oratorios, Ruth Smith explains that the English language was widely perceived as an essentially "manly" tongue over against Italian's "slithery softness."[70] Consequently, only English libretti would rehabilitate such musical exotica, if at all.[71] In the 1730s, James Miller, one of Handel's librettists, voices this patriotic dichotomy with poetic sexual imagery. He contrasts the "days of old when Englishmen were—men," and drawn to "a grave and plain" music supported with "the manly trumpet and the simple reed" with Englishmen's current passion for music and instruments that "give us sound, and show, instead of sense / In unknown tongues mysterious dullness chant / make love in tune, or thro' the gamut rant."[72] Librettist Aaron Hill concurs; Italian music is a decadent "softening syren":

Music, when purpose points her not the road,
Charms, to betray, and softens, to corrode.

> Empty of sense, the soul-seducing art
> Thrills a slow poison to the sick'ning heart ...[73]

Clergyman Arthur Bedford is similarly scandalised by the Italianate "exhibition-ism" infiltrating organ music (considered by most "the instrument of God") that he hears in church, expressing his disgust with sexual metaphors: "I know not any sober person, who can understand any thing in it, except a jargon of confusion ... including all the keys of the Gamut in a promiscuous Manner ... intermix'd some-times with a wanton airy fancy and at others with a heavy sordid performance."[74] Hill deems Italian opera the "Mother" of English opera, but hopes that its daugh-ter will eventually be released from "Italian bondage," a liberation effected by her English tongue (which would reconcile "reason and dignity") and, of course, by Handel's salvific musical powers.[75]

Decades later, Methodist icon Charles Wesley, with refreshing insouciance for sacred/secular divisions, chooses to "plunder the carnal lover" for tunes to accom-pany his sacred hymn texts.[76] Meanwhile, in France, parallel debates because of similar Italianate incursions erupt over operatic aesthetics. Pioneering naturalist and music theorist Bernard Germain Lacépède resolved such compositional con-fusion over vocal styles by reinscribing music-as-woman in her proper place—within five audibly distinct, functionally determined dispositions. Thus, upon "entering the sanctuary of vocal music,"

> she will show us the children who owe to her their life. At their head the *Tragédie lyrique*. . . . [H]er stride is lordly and animated; her hair is disheveled; often she sheds tears. At her side the *Comédie lyrique*. . . . [H]er stride is noble, but lively, her manner affable and familiar. . . . [T]he *Pastorale*. . . she sings only shepherds; she portrays only rustic scenes. . . . [T]he *Heroic Pastorale*. . . the trumpet and the pipe are in her hands. . . .
>
> Further away, one perceives the Music uniquely consecrated to sing the praises of the Eternal. . . . [T]he celestial chords of the saintly harp that sounds under her fingers accompany the soft, noble, and touching melody that she makes use of to send forth her affections. Sometimes she sighs; sometimes, hold-ing up her majestic head, she celebrates the Most High and his saints; nearly always in a tender voice and in a meditative air, she addresses to Heaven the prayers of the multitudes. . . .
>
> Finally there appears the Music whose use is to diffuse a thousand charms in our dwellings. . . . Let us approach all these daughters of vocal music, the better to receive their lessons and their sweet presents.[77]

In the nineteenth century, Søren Kierkegaard's and Friedrich Nietzsche's musical gynemorphisms arguably rival those of the Elizabethans. (While he was no Christian theologian, the powerful impact of Nietzsche's feminisation of music merits theologians' attention.) Both these masters of irony and cultural critique depict music as an emasculating seductress. Scholarly debate continues as to whether they subvert or reinforce gender stereotypes with their strategic deployments of "Woman," but evidence for the latter in their conflations of music and woman has been overlooked, and warrants a brief excursus here.

Søren Kierkegaard: Don Giovanni's Effeminised Auditors

Kierkegaard's pseudonymous celebration of the erotic in music—its "immediate" (unmediated) embodiment of "the spirit of sensuality"—seemingly promises to articulate the theological import of music's relation to sexuality.[78] However, the ontology of music that unfolds in this first part of *Either/Or* is actually "concept"-driven: music's underlying "concept" is defined over against that of language, and this opposition sets the dichotomizing tone for all that follows. Thus, according to the narrator named simply "A," language's "concept" is thought, man's "concept" is spirit, and music's "concept" is pure, immediate sensuality.[79] Music translates far better than language the spirit of sensuality.[80] Where the sensual is incidental to language, it is essential to music.[81] And yet, despite these specifications, A's desire to *know* music, to grasp its Truth, requires excavations of its concept from its body. The aesthete A therefore emphasizes: "The important thing in this respect is to be able to see the concept in each art, and not let oneself be put off by what it can do besides."[82] Moreover, the idea's penetration of the material is for Kierkegaard the measure of artistic virility.[83] Hence, although Kierkegaard rejects metaphysical worldviews, his own logocentric ontology of music hardly recuperates and revalorises music's concrete, erotic nature as yet another philosophical episteme must mediate music's truest meaning over and above the "other things" that it is capable of expressing (namely, the "spirit of sensuality").

As in previous theological discussions of music's meaning, Kierkegaard's neutral metaphysical framework of music vs. language, and thought vs. sensuality, triggers a conflation of music and woman. In the narrator A's analysis of Mozart's *Don Giovanni*, music's gynemorphic silhouette takes shape, more graphically if A's portrait is read in light of Kierkegaard's previous conflations of woman, dread, and sensuality.[84] In his explanation of this opera's sensual eroticism, A begins by instituting another metaphysical dichotomy (sensual vs. spiritual love), one which effectively connects music and woman. Both share an innate and ever-fleeting sensuality: "Love from the soul moves precisely in the rich multiplicity of the individual life, where the nuances are what are really significant. Sensual love, on the other hand, can lump everything together. What is essential for it is woman quite in the abstract, and at most distinctions of the more sensual kind. Love from the soul is a continuation in time, sensual love a disappearance in time, but the medium which expresses this is precisely music.[85] Given that music conveys the spirit of sensuality writ large, a *musically* conceived (rather than literary) Don Giovanni doubly allegorises this unstable and grasping sensual love.[86] Composed and existing in sheer sound, born from the overture's untexted (and thus *even more* sensual strains), the Don proceeds to consume "woman in the abstract," that

is, any and all available women. As the opera's tragic hero, Don Giovanni will live
and die trapped in this aesthetic realm, devoid of the self-consciousness so crucial
to living an ethical or religious existence. Musically conjured, he will later burn to
death in/behind 'her' closing bars: "Not until reflection enters does it [the kingdom of sensuality] present itself as the realm of sin, but then Don Juan is slain, the
music comes to an end, one sees only the despairing defiance which impotently
casts its negative vote but can find no constituency, not even in musical sounds."[87]
Music/Woman are the real governesses of this captivating realm.

Caveat auditor, fortunately for whom the musical sirens die away. Listeners are
thus spared from existential hellfires, and depart the concert hall edified by a musical life lesson. Recast within Kierkegaard's threefold existential plan Mozart's
tragedy of seduction becomes a morality play—Don Juan personifying that which
real (Christian) men, unseduced by pseudo/sexual virility, will transcend by leaving the sensual realm and painstakingly ascending into the religious. Don Giovanni
teaches by example that unreflective aesthetes allow the Venusberg to consume
them, prisoners of "pagan" excess.[88] They die of aesthetic consumption for they
never consciously choose their love-objects. (In fact, they cannot for they lack the
self-reflexivity that authentic individuality affords.) Aesthetic junkies are incapable
of spiritual love. Their desire is brute instinct. (Elsewhere in *Either/Or* Kierkegaard
ironically implies that even those who develop enough consciousness to ethically
particularize their relations with women by committing to marriage are still
settling for an ethical existence rather than leaping celibate into the religious.[89])

For further edification, a closer reading reveals that Don Giovanni is not the
opera's only casualty. The aesthete A is utterly infatuated with the opera's overture
and protagonist. He too has been "castrated," for when he listens to this opera, he
confesses quite shamelessly that he "loves like a woman." Ravished by the music,
he succumbs unreflectively to the Don's pseudo-machismo, and thus, Kierkegaard
has his narrator impersonate woman:

> It takes an attentive, an erotic ear to catch the first hint given in the overture of
> the light play of this desire, [embodied in Don Giovanni], which is later
> expressed so richly in all its extravagant abundance. I cannot say exactly to the
> dot where this place is because I am no expert in music, but then I am writing
> only for those in love, and they will surely understand me, some of them better
> than I understand myself. Still, I am content with my appointed lot, with this
> enigmatic infatuation, and although I usually thank the gods that I was born a
> man and not a woman, Mozart's music has taught me that it is beautiful and
> restorative and rich to love like a woman.[90]

Even earlier, A swoons, "I am like a young girl in love with Mozart and must have
him placed highest whatever the cost."[91] But this pseudonymous paean is ironic.
A's love affair with Mozart's music furthers by example Kierkegaard's broader
maieutic project—*Either/Or*'s enactment of the three stages of Man (*sic*)—aesthetic, ethical, and religious. The irony modulates with the realization that the

hyper-masculine Don has been seduced, not just by woman, but by seduction itself—lured unthinkingly as he is into crass, unreflective sensual indulgence. Unlike these impotent lost souls—Don Giovanni's lovers, the Don himself, and the aesthete A—readers will resist music and woman's terminally sensual wiles, and journey out of aesthetic solipsism toward a truer religious selfhood. One can also speculate as to whether Mozart was in manly control of music's sensual immediacy, and therefore immune to music's emasculating dangers.

With this ironic, double-edged tribute to Mozart's *Don Giovanni*, the original disembodied ontology of music with which "The Immediate Erotic Stages or The Musical Erotic" begins acquires a gendered corollary within Kierkegaard's theological anthropology. In the latter, women, music-as-siren, and effete Don Juans populate a fallen, unsalvageable realm. By contrast, creaturely redemption lies in the successful ascent of the (male) Christian disciple from the aesthetic, through the ethical, and into the religious existential modality. Embedded in this schema, music remains a Venusian flytrap which turns deluded heroes into tragic figures. The authentic human being (alias the Man of Faith) will renounce the erotic to embrace a manly, religious consciousness. But for Kierkegaard this will require disintegration and self-annihilation, processes for which music and woman, at best, can be aesthetic midwives (or house-bound Sarahs), to "dissolute" leaps of faith.

Scholars remain divided as to whether Kierkegaard thinks that any or all women can transcend this realm and its false consciousness. Some perceive back-handed revalorisations of woman, the feminine, and a religiously reformed aestheticism in Kierkegaard's thought.[92] (Perhaps, for example, baptised women may aspire to "become male" and evacuate their innate sensuality through similar leaps of faith). Even if these counterarguments persuade, it remains troubling that music, woman, and the feminine always begin as intrinsically cruder resources—raw materials in dire need of conversion (if such redemption is even possible). Either way, for the purposes of this project, the more pressing matter is that Kierkegaard's essay implicitly conflates music with woman. Toying or sincere, his writings evidence the continued currency of suspicion toward both music and woman's derailing powers over those who should transcend all things sensual for loftier existential gains. Thus a post-Enlightenment, albeit iconoclastic, theologian construes music as seductive distraction, emasculating quicksand. At the same time, it is also important to note that Kierkegaard has enlisted Mozart to teach a timeless theological lesson. In doing so, this nineteenth-century deployment of Mozart sets a musico-theological precedent: as we shall see in chapter 3, twentieth-century theologians continually christen Mozart an invaluable, didactic source of revelation. While Kierkegaard's successors will laud Mozart's powers of harmonizing opposites, however, the aesthete A's praise reinforces a different yet parallel strain within the tradition—music's dangerous, gendered, engendering powers. The erotic sensuality oozing from *Don Giovanni* validates the predictions of church authorities across history—listening to sensual music leaves one soft, weak, womanish. Sympathetic or critical, feminist rereadings of Kierkegaard's polyvocity do not erase his implication within this discursive trajectory of music as polluting seductress. Pseudonyms, irony, and intratextual contradictions cannot negate the gynemorphic musico-theological energies circulating intertextually among Kierkegaard's rants and his socio-cultural matrices. Virulent critic of Christian hypocrisy, Kierkegaard nevertheless aids and abets the sexing of the semitone.

The aesthete's *soi-disant* negative theology of music is plagued by another grave inconsistency. As a second, masculinist pillar in his musico-theological hermeneutic, Kierkegaard's A cannot penetrate music's meaning, cannot grasp its alleged immediacy, without (of all frameworks) the archly macho myth of Don Juan. Even though A contends that the music speaks for itself, unmediated by reflection, he needs Mozart's enfleshment of a mythic figure to articulate music's existential import. As with most hyperbole that theologians use to describe music's "mystical" communication of all that is "beyond language," Kierkegaard contradicts his own insistence upon music's unmediated message of sensuality by failing to recognize that both the culturally constructed myth of Don Juan, and his own three-tiered scaffolding, *produce* music's alleged immediacy.

Nietzsche and Wagnerian Effeminacy

Nietzsche conflates music and woman more explicitly than Kierkegaard and is even more ambiguous about both of their redemptive capacities. At first, Nietzsche's musical woman is construed as both cause and symptom of Wagner's steep fall from artistic grace. As a composer, Wagner has been completely "transgendered," because in fact he is no composer at all but a consummate actor and painter,[93] two artistic vocations which women pursue instinctively and definitively: "If we consider the whole history of women, are they not obliged first of all, and above all to be actresses? If we listen to doctors who have hypnotized women, or finally if we love them—and let ourselves be 'hypnotized' by them—what is divulged thereby? That they 'give themselves airs,' even when they 'give themselves.' . . . Woman is so artistic."[94] The effeminate Wagner can rival women's artistry for he "was in his old days by all means *femini generis.*"[95] Like birthing like, his "stage-consecrating festival play" (*Bühnenweihfestspiel*) *Parsifal* is the *ne plus ultra* of emasculating seductresses:

> In the art of seduction, *Parsifal* will always retain its rank—as *the stroke of genius* in seduction. . . . Never was there a greater master in dim, hieratic aromas—never was there a man equally expert in all *small* infinities, all that trembles and is effusive, all the feminism from the *idioticon* of happiness?—Drink, O my friends, the philters of this art! Nowhere will you find a more agreeable way of enervating your spirit, of forgetting your manhood under a rosebush. . . . How he indulges every cowardice of the modern soul with the tones of magic maidens.[96]

In an unpublished letter to Malwida von Meyensberg, Nietzsche actually conflates music and sex, maligning "the disgusting sexuality in [Wagner's] music." According to historian Joachim Köhler (and *contra* Nietzsche's own "free-love" ethos), the letter goes on to disdain *Parsifal*'s sirenic histrionics; the music's body simulates *and* aurally stimulates sexual orgasm "with panting and irregular breathing, flushes of blood, extreme passion followed by a sudden coma."[97]

In light of the above passages, the steady stream of epithets that Nietzsche hurls at Wagner identifies the latter's temperament, ideals, and musical translations thereof with those of woman. *Femini generis*, Wagner personifies all of the following: "a typical decadent in whom there is no trace of 'free will'";[98] "our greatest melancholiac in music, full of glances, tendernesses, and comforting words";[99] a tyrannizing "actor" whose pathos "topples every taste, every resistance"; an "incomparable *histrio*"; a "hypnotist";[100] a "neurosis";[101] an artist mired in the "decadent" virtue of "pity"; a "seducer on a large scale." His musical pathos "threatens to strangle"; its tones are named *Circe*.[102]

This explicit contempt for music-as-woman, however, is not unequivocal (though the conflation perdures nonetheless). In a later compilation, *Nietzsche contra Wagner*, Nietzsche *seems* more appreciative of Wagner's womanish compositions. Situating Wagner's oeuvre among other musical high points of Western music that share the dubious honour of heralding a culture's decline,[103] Nietzsche writes that, like these antecedents, Wagner's "musical woman" may well be true and original, given that music as woman is by nature polysemic:

> All true, all original music, is a swan song [for a decadent age].
>
> Perhaps our latest music too, however dominant and domineering it is, has but a short span of time ahead of it: for it developed out of a culture whose soil is rapidly sinking—a culture which will soon have sunk out of sight. A certain Catholicism of feeling and a delight in some old indigenous, so-called "national" sense and nonsense are its presuppositions. Wagner's appropriation of old sagas and songs . . . his reanimation of those Scandinavian monsters with a thirst for ecstatic sensuality and desensualization—this whole give-and-take of Wagner concerning materials, figures, passions, and nerves clearly expresses the *spirit of his music* too, supposing that this, like any music, could not speak of itself except ambiguously: for music is a *woman*.[104]

If this passage and the earlier critique of Wagner's effeminacy are contextualised within Nietzsche's more general endorsement of feminine ambiguity as an antidote to metaphysical notions of Truth, Nietzsche is implying that, like its sister Truth, it is good that music-as-woman speaks ambiguously; for "she" too can thereby mock modern philosophy's onerous impositions upon Truth/Music. Read more affirmatively, then, Nietzsche seems to accept Wagner's operatic "give-and-take" as one such appropriately duplicitous musical woman; in this case, she mocks Germany's grandiosity with a symptomatically telling overkill. If Nietzsche admires this Cassandra, perhaps he is an ally for theologising about music in feminist terms.

However, after implicitly praising music-as-woman above, Nietzsche confuses the reader further when he insists that "Wagner's music is never true. *But it is taken for true.*"[105] In this addendum, Nietzsche scorns Wagner's popular appeal. The operative semantic of truth here is a Nietzschean one, where the latter is an admirably duplicitous actress that Wagner's music fails to engage. At this level, Wagner's music is a bad actress. As "swansong" to a decadent German age, Wagner's musical innovations are as "true" and "original" as those in German philosophy, which, of course, Nietzsche despises. Wagner's music feeds, reflects, and colludes with the surrounding culture's decrepit inauthenticity. (It bears mentioning that, though they are estranged, Nietzsche still admires Wagner's craftsmanship. He reframes his—and now Germany's—love affair with Wagner as necessary growing pains.[106]) Further confirmation of this reading lies in Nietzsche's constant complaints that Wagner's operatic allegories nauseate him (whence the project itself *Nietzsche contra Wagner*). The *maestro* has betrayed his former "acolyte"[107] by embracing the same truths and values as metaphysicians, and Christians striving for redemption. Truest, non-Wagnerian music must shun representation and/or the embodiment of ideas, never becoming a means to an end, but always an end in itself. Exhibiting the effeminate gullibility of the aesthete A (though clearly reversing Kierkegaard's value system), Wagner has been seduced by Schopenhauer ("that Indian *Circe*"),[108] as well as by Hegel and Schelling, whose philosophies all played a part in transgendering Wagner's music into representational painting and posing.[109]

Kelly Oliver's discussion of "Woman as Truth in Nietzsche's Writing" clarifies Nietzsche's ambivalence about music-as-woman, precisely by not resolving, but nuancing, his equivocity. Crucial to determining the positive or negative value that Nietzsche assigns to Wagner's musical effeminacy is whether Wagner's (or woman's) masks and deception serve "ascending or descending life."[110] In Nietzsche's estimation, Wagner's serve the latter. Like the feminists and old-school philosophers of his day, Wagner's brilliance derails when he reifies illusion into "apodictic" truths.[111] So Wagner conveys in his music and "lays claim to objective truth," slips into descending life, and is castrated thereby.[112] Conversely, when illusion and deception serve ascending life, they are indeed valuable existential currencies; their "authors" never forget that these constructed truths are always illusion.[113] Indeed, Nietzsche has the highest esteem for all those who bravely compose life from masks and lies—actors, artists, and women. In fact, he contends that all of the arts (gendered female), by serving the will to illusion, are vital to human survival: "In this supreme jeopardy of the will, art, the sorceress expert in healing, approaches us, only she can turn our fits of nausea into imaginations with which it is possible to live."[114] Oliver comments: "The castrating [and therefore admirably virile] woman is the survivor, the artist, the actor. . . . She is the eternal dialectic of masks which perpetuates life. Nietzsche too is a dialectic of masks; he castrates the metaphysic of truth through his creative illusions and metaphors."[115]

Here again, as with Kierkegaard's puzzling ironies, regardless of whether

Nietzsche's musical woman is born from admiration or contempt, what matters most for the present inquiry is that in her we recognize the stubbornly persistent myth that dangerous musical seductresses can erode manly character. As *Nietzsche contra Wagner* progresses, this becomes unambiguously clear when Nietzsche elevates Bizet's musical woman over against Wagner's. Bizet's opera *Carmen* envigorates Nietzsche, while Wagner's music "wears him out" and galvanizes an entire nation's emasculation. We glean from Nietzsche's comparative exercise that, if *all* music is woman, then one composes either good or bad women:

> Really, every time I heard *Carmen* I seemed to myself more of a philosopher, a better philosopher, than I generally consider myself: so patient do I become, so happy, so Indian, so settled. . . .
>
> I become a better human being when this Bizet speaks to me. Also a better musician, a better *listener*. . . .
>
> Has it been noticed that music liberates the spirit? Gives wings to thought? That one becomes more of a philosopher the more one becomes a musician? The gray sky of abstraction rent as if by lightning; . . . the great problems near enough to grasp; . . . And unexpectedly answers drop into my lap, a little hail of ice and wisdom, of *solved* problems.—Where am I?—Bizet makes me fertile. Whatever is good makes me fertile. . . .
>
> You begin to see how much this music improves me? . . . The return to nature, health, cheerfulness, youth, *virtue*![116]

Nietzsche contrasts this good female stock with Wagner's "music-as-Circe," who does nothing to "liberate the spirit":

> One pays heavily for being one of Wagner's disciples. What does it do to the spirit? *Does Wagner liberate the spirit?* . . . There is nothing weary, nothing decrepit, nothing fatal and hostile to life in matters of the spirit that his art does not secretly safeguard: it is the blackest obscurantism that he conceals in the ideal's shrouds of light. . . . [E]verything that ever grew on the soil of *impoverished* life, all of the counterfeiting of transcendence and beyond, has found its most sublime advocate in Wagner's art—*not* by means of formulas: Wagner is too shrewd for formulas—but by means of a persuasion of sensuousness which in turn makes the spirit weary and worn-out. Music as Circe.[117]

Furthermore, in a transvaluation of traditional values, Bizet's opera *Carmen*—a tragic love story about an exotic, sensual peasant girl—actually increases Nietzsche's (intellectual) virility while Wagner's "selfless" Christian virgins deplete his philosophic energies. Only the former models "true" love: "Finally, love—love translated back into nature. Not the love of a 'higher virgin'! No Senta- sentimentality! But love as *fatum* as fatality, cynical, innocent, cruel. . . . Such a conception of love (the only one worthy of a philosopher) is rare: it raises a work of art above thousands. For on the average, artists do what all the world does, even worse— they misunderstand love. Wagner, too, misunderstood it."[118] With this Bizet–

Wagner duel, one can be even more specific in characterizing Nietzsche's musical women: I detect in Nietzsche's gynemorphic equivocations traces of the traditionalists' virgin–whore split. In Nietzsche's schema, however, the desirable tones are not the virgin's but the whore's. Of the latter muse, he gushes:

> This work [*Carmen*], too, redeems; Wagner is not the only "redeemer." . . . I envy Bizet for having had the courage for this sensibility which had hitherto had no language in the cultivated music of Europe—for this more southern, brown, burnt sensibility. . . . How the yellow afternoons of its happiness do us good! . . . [D]id we ever find the sea smoother?—And how soothingly the Moorish dance speaks to us? How even our insatiability for once gets to know satiety in this lascivious melancholy![119]

Nietzsche's polarised tirades resemble Archbishop Artusi's vivid denunciations of Monteverdi (the "painted whore") and his equally whorish musical innovations in the seventeenth century (rhetoric I shall investigate further in chapter 5). Artusi, we recall, characterized Monteverdi's music as "sick," "wet," "stinking," and "restless," and virtuous music as "dry," "hot," "healthy," and "beautiful." Nietzsche similarly deplores Wagner's music as "damp," "steamy." It is "bad weather" that makes him sweat.[120] More specifically, Wagner's musical innovation of infinite melody is equally "sick"; Nietzsche diagnoses it as "a polyp" in music:[121]

> Wagner increases exhaustion: that is why he attracts the weak and exhausted. . . . Wagner's art is sick. The problems he presents on the stage—all of them problems of hysterics—the convulsive nature of his affects, his overexcited sensibility . . . his instability which he dressed up as principles, not least of all the choice of his heroes and heroines . . . —all of this taken together represents a profile of sickness that permits no further doubt. *Wagner est une névrose.*[122]

Bizet's oeuvre by contrast is a picture of health: "light, supple, polite, pleasant, cheerful." Its libretto and the music that it inspires imbue the air with dryness and clarity ("*limpidezza*").[123]

Wagner's musical Eves have flesh-and-blood accomplices; his "parasitic" female entourage is partly to blame for his "sickness," his tainted compositional skills. Drawn by nature to melodrama and Christian happy endings, these female Wagnerians have polluted Wagner's musical palette and ethos. Thus, in a passage criticising Wagner's musical solutions to "the problem of redemption" (and the central roles women play therein), Nietzsche opines:

> Translated into reality: the danger for artists, for geniuses . . . is woman: adoring women confront them with corruption. Hardly any of them have character enough not to be corrupted—or "redeemed"—when they find themselves treated like gods: soon they condescend to the level of the women. —Man is a coward, confronted with the Eternal Feminine—and the females know it. —In many cases of feminine love, perhaps including the most famous ones above all,

> love is merely a more refined form of parasitism, a form of nestling down in
> another soul, sometimes even in the flesh of another—alas, always decided at the
> expense of "the host"![124]

Not surprisingly, given this toxic environment, Wagner's male fans are also effeminate—"pale, rigid, breathless."[125] The epidemic spreads beyond this male and
female entourage, for the German masses are easily seduced by Wagner's ersatz-
music given that they consist of "cultural cretins, petty snobs, eternally feminine."[126]

In sum, after his "Fall," Wagner's sonic woman becomes an ailing nation's
tawdry pin-up girl; she has seduced the masses, corrupting youth and women,
shattering any hope for lasting *übermenschlich* transcendence. Wagner's *femini
generis,* exacerbated by his poisonous female patrons, pollutes his compositional
techniques; all these forces in turn create effeminate male and hysterical female
characters such that this composite musical and extramusical femininity seduces
the masses, who themselves are by nature "eternally feminine."[127] Nietzsche himself has narrowly escaped castration by this *weiblich* onslaught.

Or has he? Nietzsche's manic, decades-long obsession with Wagner's demise
leads one to wonder whether in fact he has reified his own originally tactical mas-
querades, his fabricated gynemorphic illusions, into metaphysical truths. If so, he
feeds "descending life" in spite of himself. Kelly Oliver believes that such sedimentation befell Nietzsche's initially ironic contempt for women's duplicity. Consequently, Wagner's music-as-woman *is* in essence dangerously emasculating, a
hateful creature. If so, in the absence of relentless, playful deconstruction, Nietzsche courts misogyny and loses his own "castrating" virility. Here again, whether
or not Nietzsche himself has successfully escaped castration (by always responding playfully to others' misguided musical "truths") remains beside the point. In
this genealogy of Wagner's and Germany's feminisation, we hear a now familiar,
*un*equivocal refrain—a gynophobic dirge on music's character-eroding powers;
tears spilt this time, not for warriors, philosopher-kings, or Christian soldiers, but
for aborted *Übermenschen.*

Titillations and Castrations in the Twentieth Century

Moving now to the twentieth century, an otherwise innocuous introduction
to church music written by Russell N. Squire (b. 1908), former professor of music
at California State University (Long Beach), indicates that the rhetoric of effeminacy still circulates in musico-theological discourse. As late as 1962, Squire
denounces what he perceives to be the flaws in Eastern Orthodox music:

> But with the separation of the Eastern and the Western churches over the icono-
> clastic struggles there came upon the Eastern church a softening, a spiritual
> decay, an effeminacy, a formalism, a stagnation, and a bigotry that stopped the
> growth of the Eastern music. But in the Western church this was not the case.

> From the beginning, the growth and developing vigor of the Western music kept
> pace with the resolving of the Roman Empire's tempestuous inner struggles,
> from which evolved the feudal system and the centralized doctrinal systems of
> the papacy.[128]

A product of his prefeminist times, Squire cannot be expected to apply a hermeneutic of suspicion when he makes the following observations about women in music history. We, however, especially in light of chapters 1 and 2, cannot be so unassuming: "It is of special interest to note that women singers are thought never to have participated in the temple worship; references to women's singing in the Old Testament are always to occasions of singing other than in temple services."[129] (What "special interest" has he in mind?) Certainly women's silence in the liturgy is of special interest to feminists, and will be discussed presently.[130]

Two further jarring conflations of music and effeminacy surface in musicological discourse. Susan McClary accuses Edward T. Cone of trying to "butch up" a polonaise by Chopin; its "feminine endings" (this is an actual musicological term, based on classical poetic metrics) are "problematic," and must be explained away, lest Chopin lose his compositional integrity: "Even in the case of movements that seem to remain *incorrigibly feminine,* some differentiation can still be made. In the case of Chopin's Polonaise in A major, for example, a clever emphasis on one of the concealed cross-rhythms at the cadence can make the last chord sound, *if not precisely masculine,* at least like a strong tonic postponed by a suspension of the entire dominant."[131]

As for such "feminine endings," they are defined in the *Harvard Dictionary of Music* (1970 ed.) as follows: "Masculine, feminine cadence. A cadence or ending is called 'masculine' if the final chord of a phrase or section occurs on the strong beat and 'feminine' if it is postponed to fall on a weak beat. The masculine ending must be considered the normal one, while the feminine is preferred in more romantic styles." (The masculine ending's "normative" status has been deleted from the 1986 revised edition of the dictionary.[132]) And while avant-garde composer Arnold Schoenberg metaphorically transfers such gender stereotypes into more equitable pairings, he reinscribes them nonetheless: "The dualism presented by major and minor has the power of a symbol suggesting higher forms of order: it reminds us of male and female and delimits the spheres of expression according to attraction and repulsion. . . . The will of nature is supposedly fulfilled in them."[133]

Where Squire locates a certain effeminacy in sacred Eastern aesthetics, Theodor Adorno is more troubled by its crasser secular eruptions. He scathingly condemns jazz in terms reminiscent (at least in their graphic intensity) of John of Salisbury's "titillation between the legs": "The aim of jazz is the mechanical reproduction of a regressive moment, a castration symbolism. 'Give up your masculinity, let yourself be castrated.'"[134] Masculine virility is also threatened simply by choosing to become a musician or composer. Maynard Solomon's interview with

Charles Ives[135] reveals the persistence of the equation of musical professions with effeminate character in men:

> [Ives] is both drawn to music and repelled by it. "As a boy [I was] partially ashamed of music," he recalled, —an entirely wrong attitude but it was strong— most boys in American country towns, I think felt the same. . . . And there may be something in it. Hasn't music always been too much an emasculated art?" To ward off such feelings, Ives would eradicate the traces of the "soft-bodied" and "decadent" in his own work, perhaps employing the techniques of modernism to conceal the atmospheric, lyrical, yielding strata which often underlie his first ideas.[136]

This historical survey of gendered rhetoric in masculinist musico-theological (and musicological) discourse unveils a rather base subtext beneath the loftier metaphysical rhetoric of harmony and order documented in chapter 1. In effect, musico-theological prescriptions function to preserve a precariously established manhood, couching male insecurities about identity and male ambivalence toward women and the body in a politics of transcendence. Thus, a male preoccupation with virility fuels an aesthetic fantasy of disembodied, musically induced transcendence. Theologians discussing music in the twentieth and twenty-first centuries have not considered the musico-theological significance of music's historical engendering; nor that of its "objective correlative": if music is a dangerous seductress, women making music pose a doubly sirenic threat to male virility and self-control.

III. Double Jeopardy: Women Making Music

The musical prowess that women displayed in secular and sacred pagan contexts was a source of seductive power that Christian women were not to emulate. Pagan women's emasculating virility is described in lurid detail by Pseudo-Basil:

> "Woe," it is written, "unto them who drink wine to the accompaniment of cithara, aulos, tympanum and song" (Is. 5.11-12). You place a lyre ornamented with gold and ivory upon a high pedestal as if it were a statue or devilish idol, and some miserable woman, rather than being taught to place her hands upon the spindle, is taught by you, bound as she is in servitude, to stretch them out upon the lyre. [137]

Those who expose women to such corrupting *paideia* are targets of the author's venom:

> Perhaps you pay her wages or perhaps you turn her over to some female pimp, who after exhausting the licentious potential of her body, presides over young

women as the teacher of similar deeds. Because of her you will meet with a double punishment on the day of judgment, since you are yourself immoral, and since you have estranged this poor soul from God through evil teaching. So she stands at the lyre and lays her hands upon the strings, her arms bare and her expression impudent. The entire symposium is then transformed, as the eyes of all are focused upon her and the ears upon her strumming; the crowd noise dies down, as the laughter and the din of ribald talk are quieted. All in the house are silenced, charmed by the lascivious song. (While he who is silent here is not silent in the church of God, nor does he listen quietly to the words of the gospel. Not surprisingly! For that enemy who enjoins quiet there, advocates a disturbance here.) What a sorry sight for sober eyes that a woman weaves not but rather plays the lyre.[138]

A variety of rhetorical and practical counterstrategies were devised. Depending on the intensity of the threat from pagan and gnostic influences surrounding them, Christian bishops cite Paul's exhortation that women should be silent in church to justify women's total exclusion from communal singing. With the uncensored musical opportunities for women in gnostic circles (similar to those of prophesy and leadership), orthodox authorities distance themselves unequivocally from these sects by strictly controlling or altogether banning female musical activities. Cyril of Jerusalem, Isidore of Pelusium, and Jerome are strong proponents of this ban.[139] Thus begins the marginalisation of female musicality: "Women are ordered not to speak in church, not even softly, nor may they sing along or take part in the responses, but they should only be silent and pray to God."[140]

For Jerome, such heretical liberties imbue women's singing with a very un-Christian "arrogance."[141] In private it would seem, women are allowed to sing psalms for their personal edification. Within Jerome's sphere of influence, women are "to avoid playing musical instruments and singing 'worldly songs,'" feeding solely on "sweet psalms."[142] Thus in his letter to Laeta and Furia: "Let her be deaf to musical instruments (*organa*); let her not know why the tibia, lyre and cithara are made."[143] Elsewhere, for added rhetorical punch, Jerome contrasts the saintly woman's musical *habitus* with the sirenically wanton, "long-haired" male singers and female citharists and harpists: "Avoid the company of young men. Let long-haired fellows, ornamented and wanton, not be seen under your roof. Let the male singer (*cantor*) be repelled as a bane, banish from your house female citharists (*fidicinis*) and harpists (*psaltrias*) and that devil's choir whose songs lead to death like those of the sirens."[144] Thus any instrumental prowess evokes whorish proclivities. Apparently there is also an immediate association of women's singing with pagan courtesans.[145] Arnobius therefore admonishes: "Has God created souls for this, that women should become harlots, sambucists and harpists in order to surrender their bodies to lust?"[146] Jerome does, however, praise one Christian woman for being a harpist for Christ, teaching citharists for the saviour. Perhaps, immersed in psalmody, this extraordinary woman was inoculated against the fleshly sway of musical instruments.[147] To Laeta, he exhorts: "Thus must be educated the soul, whose future is to be a temple of the Lord. It must learn to hear nothing, to say nothing, which has no bearing on the fear of God. It must not comprehend foul words, nor have knowledge of worldly songs, and while still tender its tongue must be imbued with sweet psalms."[148]

Further justification was provided by the allegedly "sensuous quality" attributed to women's singing, a natural aberration which impeded the *"compunctio cordis"* (*katanyxis*) that singing was meant to effectuate.[149] To wit, Gregory of Nazianzus euphemised that women should sing "with their hearts" and leave vocal psalm singing to men.[150] In the fifth century, Isidore of Pelusium portrayed women's singing as the lesser of two evils—at least it prevented them from gossiping. Also of note in the following passage is the strictly penitential role he assigns to music in worship: "[P]erhaps women were originally permitted by the Apostles and presbyters to join in singing so as to prevent their gossiping in church. But later this permission was withdrawn since it was learned that they did not gain any salutory fruits of penance (*katanyxis*) from divine song, but used the sweetness of melody for disturbances of every kind, since they looked on it in exactly the same way as theater music."[151] Ephraem the Syrian was more tactical; rather than lose women to the gnostics, he preferred to lure them into Christian circles by conceding to them certain musical freedoms.[152] Strictly supervised, "virtuous" Christian *music* could, moreover, buttress female *chastity*—like enhancing like, so to speak. Hence, he established women's choirs to rival those of Paul of Samosata.[153]

Pagan boys' singing, on the other hand, posed no grave threat to Christian communities: "the institutions of the heretics were not able to dilute the joy which the faithful took in boys' singing, and what happened here was quite other than it was with the singing of women," speculates Quasten.[154] Boys' voices embodied innocence and were "perfectly delicate, not so deep as to be called masculine nor so fine as to be effeminate and lacking in power, but falling soft, mild and lovely upon the ear," says Lucian of Samosata.[155] Presumably, they were unequivocally spiritual while women's and girls' voices always risked slippage into the connotatively fleshly. Thus while boys' choirs and musical schooling proliferated, women's musical activity became increasingly circumscribed.[156]

The rhetorical intensity of this musico-theological censorship peaked in Elizabethan treatises on musical decorum where the effects of women's music-making became most sharply polarised. According to the Neoplatonism that shaped Renaissance and Elizabethan thought, the combination of observing feminine beauty while listening to music could lure men's "souls and bodies into a love so intense that it was considered almost sorcerous."[157] During public performance, music's aural curves, combined with women's visible ones, could destroy men. Elizabethans, therefore, adopted Castiglione's regulative ideal that women's music-making should exude a "soft," "sweete mildness," not only aurally, but also visually.[158] For everyone's safety, therefore, gentlewomen were instructed to make music only in private, for their personal spiritual edification.[159] Some exceptions were made, however. Women were allowed to harness some of that natural vocal sensuality to charm potential suitor-husbands.[160]

And, in spite of such censure, more liberal Renaissance educators still regarded music as a vital component in the education of both boys and girls.[161] Pedagogical double standards allowed this: the controlled use of music for fostering well-tempered souls in both sexes was acknowledged. Girls, however, were not to study composition or music theory, nor to seek professional employment as musicians in church, theater, or court.[162] Puritans censored even further the few educational opportunities for women that the humanists promoted.[163] More neutral, Thomas Powell discouraged women's musical pursuits as simply an impractical waste of time.[164] (It bears mentioning that formal musical training required time and money, and therefore only rich and middle-class women could develop such genteel skills.)

Musico-Spiritual "Rehab": The Convent

One sacred musical forum did allow women to make morally and aesthetically appropriate music: in pure, non-emotive tones, safely screened within convents. Behind these walls, and in this socio-culturally symbolic context, women transcended their fleshly musicality. Cloistered women's singing and playing could and did simulate that of the angels. Indeed, the convent became one secure creative space for women's musical agency and for what is now called "self-expression." As early as the fourth century, women received exceptional musical training in convents.[165] Between 500 and 1500 CE, singing eight offices and a mass each day made music central to nuns' "communal lives."[166] Nevertheless, it remains significant that nuns' musical practices were more strictly controlled than monks' were.[167] Archival research into convent life highlights the more frequent intervention by male authorities in the excesses of nuns' musical activity.[168] (The musico-theological importance of nuns' music will be developed at length in part 2 below.) The following excerpt from an official complaint about nuns' singing in sixteenth-century Bologna illustrates this gendered censorship. Even more significantly, the author's objections flesh out *in extremis* Augustine's fear of music's distractive powers discussed in chapter 1; it seems that musical excesses at Santa Cristina instilled a very dangerous (albeit disembodied) *wanderlust*:

> Experience demonstrates that the excessive study that the nuns devote these days to their songs not only fails to serve the end to which music was permitted them (which is) to praise God and be aroused themselves to the contemplation of celestial harmony; but (rather) it impedes them from greater goods and encumbers their souls in perpetual distraction it causes them vainly to expend precious time that they could use more fruitfully. *And, while they stand with their bodies within the sacred cloisters, it causes them to wander outside in their hearts, nourishing within themselves an ambitious desire to please the world with their songs.*[169]

In other words, even a purely spiritual or fantasised displacement within nuns' imaginations could erode communal order. Clerics feared that such "fancied sway" might lead the nuns to resist physical claustration. Historian Craig Monson frames these clerical complaints within the then popular conviction that women's truest eloquence lay in "well-considered and dignified silence." In the words of Nicolo Barbo, "An eloquent woman is never chaste."[170]

The strict vigilance over the nuns' musical chastity may also stem from a musical version of the virgin–whore dichotomy ingrained in the hegemonic imagination of the time; the antithesis of nuns' singing took flesh in the musical virtuosity of the famed (Venetian) courtesan.[171] Within this imagined polarity, nuns must be kept (literally and symbolically) in their proper place.[172] This "problem"—the preservation of nuns' musical "chastity"—in fact proffers ample opportunity for musico-theological revisions, as we shall see in part 2.

IV. Re-Defining Music's Theological Metaphoricity

From a feminist perspective, it would seem that music and women provoke almost interchangeable attitudes and responses from church authorities. Keeping women in their place becomes analogous to keeping music in its proper place—subservient (to a text) and virtuously pure (free from the stain of dissonance); ideally, both must be chaste love-objects who inspire disembodied union with God. Thus music's theological significance was derived from metaphorical transfers made between music's internal properties and gendered conventions and behaviours. Though never consciously construed as such by its censors in the gendered, often gynemorphic, rhetoric above, *music becomes a "metaphor for sexual relations"*;[173] this quite apart from, and in seeming contradiction to, its metaphysical expression of divine unity, number, and order—cosmic or psychic.

The engendering of musico-theological discourse surveyed above supports Ellen Koskoff's research that both crossculturally and transhistorically women's socio-sexual identities and their degree of musical freedom are dialectically determined. The interplay of several variables increases or decreases these liberties. One central variable is the "exclusive heterosexual activity" that men assign women as "mates, lovers, concubines, courtesans, and/or prostitutes."[174] According to Koskoff, a change in women's sexual active-ness, whether "actual" or "perceived," often effects parallel shifts in their musical "roles and/or statuses."[175] Culturally specific "beliefs in women's inherent sexuality" (as seen above) often result in the censorship of women's musical practices. Obviously, expectations surrounding particular "performance environments" further allow or restrict "sexually explicit behaviour" for men and women, thereby dictating appropriate musical practices for the latter.[176] The censorship of women's musical behaviour within the Christian tradition and its curtailment of what might have (and had) been a source of social agency and prestige (though lower-class women's musical virility, we recall, was intransigently vulgar) have not informed masculinist readings of music's theological significance, but have been of primary importance in establishing the sources and norms of a feminist theology of music.

Koskoff uses the expression "metaphor for sexual relations" more narrowly to describe music's translation or symbolisation of sexual explicitly behaviour. But I think that it is also a good general rubric for articulating music's basic metaphorical relationship to human sexuality. Susan McClary has described music as erotic mappings. Musical works are very often "fabrications of sexuality,"[177] and music itself thus becomes a sonic composer of human sexual identity. The composer's art can be similarly demystified: formerly gifted with mysterious powers, composers should be assessed/understood more pragmatically as steeped and versed in stylistic musical languages that they harness to arouse, manipulate, and channel our desires, reinforcing (and sometimes transgressing) cultural norms of sexuality and gender construction. Historically, theologians and clerics vilified music's preeminent worth as a source of sensual pleasure, condemning its "erotic mappings," and promoting instead its exemplary embodiment of ontic harmony and order. Thus they clearly recognised its socialising power but circumscribed this force to serve their ideals of otherworldly union with God. It bears mentioning, however, that many people may have enjoyed 'lascivious' music and dancing without becoming effeminate or morally derelict. (Perhaps the threat of effeminacy was like the threat of blindness from premarital sex.) Nevertheless, even if its listeners were not effeminised, those in power were determined to domesticate music's unruly wiles, its circulation of dangerous energies. Even if not emasculating, music—when uncensored—dangerously aroused the passions and libido. The devil's music, when not effeminate, is at the very least "lascivious."

In light of these two chapters, can anyone really slake her musico-theological thirst by blandly defining music's religious significance as some ahistorical, divinely inspired gift or medium of spiritual transcendence? The sexualised, often gynemorphic, rhetoric and the music it vilified belie utopian appeals to these standard musico-theological tropes. The musical *is* political; negative rhetoric and the censorship it enforced *were* disciplinary tools that preserved the patriarchal status quo. Yet, as we shall see in chapter 3, these "cultural priorities" still wield enormous influence over normative values. Correlatively, contemporary theologians have yet to reframe music as a technique of the self, even though the Presocratics and others intuitively recognised that music shaped personal and social identity.

To counterbalance the hegemony of these musico-theological antecedents, I shall explore the possibility that music's "quintessence" is not veiled *numerositas*, but its full-bodied eros, a volatile, yet fecund (because sexually driven), chthonic force. This conceptual shift prompts other discursive ones. Music will be treated as a culturally determined "technique of the self"; a socializing force that organizes our perception—corporeal, emotional, and cognitive; a circulator of social energies;[178] a semiotics of pleasure and desire. Before constructing one possible feminist theology of music that treats *and* revalorises music as a metaphor for sexual relations, in the following chapter I critically survey and—in light of the above documentation— question the adequacy of twentieth-century musico-theological discourse. Most of the contemporary models available to us continue to perpetuate the phallic rage for order in similarly conventional terms of harmony and transcendence, sidestepping once again the messy yet creative potential that music's erotic metaphoricity might afford.

Notes

1. Cyprian, *De spectaculis* VIII, in Skeris, *Chroma theou*, 49.

2. Aristotle, *Politics*, 8.8 [tr. Rackham], in Strunk and Treitler, *Source Readings in Music History*, 34.

3. Aristotle, *Politics*, 8.3, in Strunk and Treitler, *Source Readings in Music History*, 27.

4. Thus John Chrysostom: "Since this sort of pleasure is natural to our soul, and lest the demons introduce licentious songs and upset everything, God erected the barrier of the psalms, so that they would be a matter of both pleasure and profit. For from strange songs, harm and destruction enter in along with many a dread thing, since what is wanton and contrary to the law in these songs settles in the various parts of the soul, rendering it weak and soft. But from the spiritual psalms can come considerable pleasure, much that is useful, much that is holy, and the foundation of all philosophy, as these texts cleanse the soul and the Holy Spirit flies swiftly to the soul who sings such songs" (John Chrysostom, *In psalmum xli*, 1, in MacKinnon, *Music in Early Christian Literature*, # 165, 80).

5. John Chrysostom, *In Isaiam*, v.5, in MacKinnon, *Music in Early Christian Literature*, #177, 84.

6. Gregory of Nazianzus describes this mental impotence as "philosophy overcome by passion" in his description of the lamentation at the funeral of Basil of Caesarea (*PG* 36.601 in Alexiou, *The Ritual Lament in Greek Tradition*, 30).

7. In Aristotle's *Politics*, *auloi* must "not be introduced into education, nor any other professional instrument, such as the kithara or any other of that sort, but such instruments as will make them attentive pupils either at their musical education or in their other lessons. Moreover the aulos is not an ethical but rather an exciting instrument, so that it ought to be used for occasions of the kind at which attendance has the effect of purification rather than instruction. . . . And indeed there is a reasonable foundation for the story that was told by the ancients about the auloi. The tale goes that Athena found a pair of auloi and threw them away. Now it is not a bad point in the story that the goddess did this out of annoyance because of the ugly distortion of her features; but as a matter of fact it is more likely that it was because education in aulos-music has no effect on the intelligence, whereas we attribute science and art to Athena" (Aristotle, in Strunk and Treitler, *Source Readings*, 31f.).

8. Arnobius, *Adversus nationes*, 2.42 in Skeris, *Chroma theou*, 49.

9. Thus Tertullian: "It is not sufficient for lust to make use of its present means of mischief, unless by the exhibition it makes its own that which in a former age had also gone wrong. It is not lawful, I say, for faithful Christians to be present; it is not lawful, I say, at all, even for those whom for the delight of their ears Greece sends everywhere to all who are instructed in her vain arts. One imitates the hoarse warlike clangours of the trumpet; another with his breath blowing into a pipe regulates its mournful sounds; another with dances, and with the musical voice of a man, strives with his body, to play upon the stops of pipes; now letting forth the sound, and now closing it up inside, and forcing it into the air by certain openings of the stops; now breaking the sound in measure, he endeavours to speak with his fingers, ungrateful to the Artificer who gave him a tongue. Why should I speak of comic and useless efforts? Why of those great tragic vocal ravings? Why of strings set vibrating with noise? These things, even if they were not dedicated to idols, ought not to be approached and gazed upon by faithful Christians; because, even if they were not criminal, they are characterised by a worthlessness which is extreme, and which is little suited to believers" (Tertullian, *De spectaculis* VII 1/3 in Skeris, *Chroma theou*, 48).

10. Lucian of Samosata, *De saltatione* 2, in Quasten, *Music and Worship in Pagan and Christian Antiquity*, 126. Basil, John Chrysostom, and Ambrose all believed that the psaltery and cithara produced the same evil effects as wine. Basil, for example, pointed out that Nebuchadnezzar had seduced the Jews with trumpet, psaltery, sambuca, cithara, and syrinx (Quasten, *Music and Worship*, 129).

11. Cyril of Jerusalem, *Catacheses* 19.6, in Quasten, *Music and Worship*, 135.

12. MacKinnon translates *tibicinis* as tibicinist whereas Skeris uses the more generic "player."

13. Tertullian continues: "And when the athletes are hard at struggle, will he be ready to proclaim there must be not striking again? And with his eye fixed on the bites of bears, and the sponge-nets of the net-fighters, can he be moved by compassion? May God avert from His people any such passionate eagerness after a cruel enjoyment! For how monstrous it is to go from God's church to the devil's— from the sky to the stye, as they say; to raise your hands to God, and then to weary them in the applause of an actor; out of the mouth, from which you uttered Amen over the Holy Thing, to give witness in a gladiator's favour; to cry 'for ever' to anyone else but God and Christ!" (Tertullian, *De spectaculis* XXV 3/5 in Skeris, *Chroma theou*, 39).

14. Tatian, *Address to the Greeks* 22/4, in Skeris, *Chroma theou*, 30.

15. John Chrysostom, *In caput XXIX Genesim*, Hom. LVI, 1, in MacKinnon, *Music in Early Christian Literature*, #176, 84. He describes the bestial and irrational "musical abuses" of other Christian weddings: "those present become brutes rather than men; they neigh like horses and kick like asses. There is much dissipation, much dissolution, but nothing earnest, nothing high-minded; there is much pomp of the devil here—cymbals, auloi and songs full of fornication and adultery" (*In Acta Apostolorum*, Hom. XLII, 3, in MacKinnon, *Music in Early Christian Literature*, #182, 85).

16. Chrysostom does so "in no less than eight homilies and commentaries" (Alexiou, *Ritual Lament*, 28).

17. At Makrina's funeral, Gregory of Nyssa therefore enforced a proper reserve: "I took care that the chants should be sung with due rhythm and harmony, by arranging the two groups of singers on opposite sides, as in the liturgy, so that the chanting was properly blended with the sound of all the people joining in" (*PG* 46.993A, in Alexiou, *Ritual Lament*, 29). He could not, however, prevent a post-burial bout of hysteria: "That prayer caused the people to break out into fresh lamentation. The chants had died down . . . then one of the holy sisters cried out in disorderly fashion that never again from that hour should we set eyes on this divine face, whereupon the other sisters cried out likewise, and disorder and confusion spoiled that orderly and sacred chanting, with everyone breaking down at the lament of the holy sisters" (*PG* 46.993D, in Alexiou, ibid., 31).

Gregory of Nazianzus praised a Christian woman who resisted such histrionics, vowing instead: "I will not tear my hair, nor will I rend my cloak, nor will I scratch my flesh with my nails, nor will I start up the dirge, nor will I call up the mourning women, nor will I shut myself in darkness that the air might lament with me, nor will I await the comforters, nor will I prepare the funeral bread. For such things belong to vulgar mothers, who are mothers only in the flesh" (*PG* 35.928.A-B, in Alexiou, *Ritual Lament*, 33). Elsewhere John Chrysostom similarly chides women who do not mourn with proper Christian decorum: "What are you doing, woman? Tell me, would you shamelessly strip yourself naked in the middle of the market-place, you, who are a part of Christ, in the presence of men and in the very market-place? And would you tear your hair, rend your garments and wail loudly, dancing and preserving the image of Bacchic women, without regard for your offence to God?" (*PG* 59.346, in Alexiou, *Ritual Lament*, 29). Here again Plato's reforms served to set a precedent (ibid.).

18. Quasten, *Music and Worship*, 87.

19. Thus Basil of Caesarea's prescription: "Therefore neither men nor women should be permitted too much lamentation and mourning. They should show moderate distress in their affliction, with only a few tears, shed quietly and without moaning, wailing, tearing of clothes and grovelling in the dust, or committing any other indecency commonly practised by the ungodly" (*PG* 31.229C in Alexiou, *Ritual Lament*, 28).

20. Clement, *Paidagogos*, II 4, 40, 1/2-41, 1/3 in Skeris, *Chroma theou*, 68; emphasis mine.

21. Cf. Holsinger's discussion of Clement's musical imagery in *Music, Body and Desire in Medieval Culture*, 31-46.

22. According to theologian Gerardus van der Leeuw: "When Christianity conquered the ancient world, it did not find there tragedy or comedy, but only the least elevated dramatic forms, indeed the oldest, but certainly not the most venerable: mime and pantomime. Today we would call it vaudeville. Not only the ancient forms of the fertility play, but also unavoidable objections to the lighthearted way of life of the actors, *and, above all, of the actresses*, were bound to bring down upon the theater of dis-

integrating antiquity the implacable hatred of Christianity" (*Sacred and Profane Beauty*, 98; emphasis mine).

23. Gaudentius of Brecia, *Sermo* VIII in MacKinnon, #392, *Music in Early Christian Literature*, 169.

24. Thus John Chrysostom instructs the *Paterfamilias* in his exegesis of Ps. 41:2: "I say this not so that you may sing praise alone, but that you may also teach your children and your wives such songs, to sing not only while weaving and doing other work, but especially at table. For at the banquets the devil is waiting in ambush, since there he has drunkenness and gluttony, laughter, idleness and licentiousness as companions. Thus it is particularly necessary before and after eating to erect a fortress of psalms, so to speak, against him, and when leaving the table to sing to God together with your wife and children. For just as those who invite actors, dancers, and lewd women to their banquets also invite demons and the devil and fill their house with numberless enemies, so those who invite David with the cithara through him invite Christ into their home" (*Homilia in Ps.* 41 in Quasten, *Music and Worship*, 130).

25. *Quaestiones et responsiones ad orthodoxos*, #107, in Quasten, *Music and Worship*, 74f.

26. Page, *The Owl and the Nightingale*, 156. Bruce Wood Holsinger describes these reform measures as "polemics against the 'feminization' of chant." He discusses Hildegard of Bingen's deviation from this conservative censorship in his "The Flesh of the Voice: Embodiment and the Homoerotics of Devotion in the Music of Hildegard of Bingen (1078-1179)," 106, and in chapter 3 of his *Music, Body and Desire in Medieval Culture*.

27. Bernard of Clairvaux, *Sermon 47 on the Song of Songs*, vol. 3, 1979, 9-10. Holsinger comments: "For the Cistercians and other twelfth-century reformers of the chant, musical excess is associated with bodily display and effeminacy" (Holsinger, "The Flesh of the Voice," 106).

28. Aelred of Rievaulx, *Speculum caritatis*, bk. 2, ch. 23 in *PL* 199:402.

29. *Statuta antiqua* (before 1259) in Dalglish, 8.

30. McClary, "Music, Pythagoreans, and the Body," 102 n. 13.

31. Stevens and Libby in *New Grove Dictionary*, 803f. What is more interesting, however, is that carols in church were used not only for liturgical processions on feast days, but also to accompany clerical dancing. Here again, ties with the raucously secular and often erotic *carole* challenge today's impression of Christmas carols as otherwise pure, Christian inventions. Cf. Stevens, and also chapter 5 of Page, *The Owl and the Nightingale*, 110-33.

32. John of Salisbury, *Policraticus* [tr. Webb], in Dalglish, "The Origin of the Hocket," 70.

33. Bacon, *Opus tertium*, in Dalglish, "The Origin of the Hocket," 9.

34. Erasmus, *Omnia opera* VI.731C, in Miller, "Erasmus on Music," 339. To Erasmus, organists and professional church singers are "the dregs of humanity [*Dionysiaci*] . . . vile and unreliable (as a great many are drunken revelers)" whose musical offerings are little more than tawdry "warblings," at great expense to the church no less (ibid.). Not surprisingly, secular composers and musicians were even more reprehensible: "If laws were enforced, composers of such common ditties would be flogged for singing these doleful songs to the licentious. Men who publicly corrupt youth are making a living from crime, yet parents are found who think it a mark of good breeding if their daughters know such songs" (Erasmus *Omnia opera*, V.717F, in Miller, "Erasmus on Music," 348).

35. *L'Artusi, overo delle imperfettioni della moderna musica*, 1600, in Cusick, "Gendering Modern Music," 8.

36. Ibid. These and other Artusian epithets have been catalogued and listed in opposing categories in table 2, "Gendered Oppositions in Artusi," in Cusick, "Gendering Modern Music," 8.

37. Carlstadt, in Horne, "A *Civitas* of Sound," 25.

38. Luther, Preface to *Symphoniae jucundae* [1538], 103; emphasis mine. In his preface to the *Wittenberg Gesangbuch* (1524), Luther also discourages corruption of youth by "wanton songs": "These, further, are set for four voices for no other reason than that I wished that the young (who, apart from this, should and must be trained in music and in other proper arts) might have something to rid them of their love ditties and wanton songs and might, instead of these, learn wholesome things and thus yield willingly, as becomes them, to the good; also, because I am not of the opinion that all the arts shall be crushed to earth and perish through the Gospel, as some bigoted persons pretend, but would willingly see them all, and especially music, servants of him who gave and created them" (Strunk and Treitler, *Source Readings*, 362).

39. Thus Calvin: "[A]nd we must consider it [music] a gift from God expressly made for that purpose. And for this reason we must be all the more careful not to abuse it, for fear of defiling or con-

taminating it, converting to our damnation what is intended for our profit and salvation. If even for this reason alone, we might well be moved to restrict the use of music to make it serve only what is respectable and never use if for unbridled dissipations or for emasculating ourselves with immoderate pleasure. Nor should it lead us to lasciviousness or shamelessness. But more than this, there is hardly anything in the world that has greater powers to bend the morals of men this way or that, as Plato has wisely observed. And in fact we find from experience that it has an insidious and well-nigh incredible power to move us whither it will. And for this reason we must be all the more diligent to control music in such a way that it will serve us for good and in no way harm us. This is why the early doctors of the Church used to complain that the people of their time were addicted to illicit and shameless songs, which they were right to call, a mortal world-corrupting poison of Satan" (Preface to the *Geneva Psalter* [1543], Weiss and Taruskin, *Music in the Western World*, 108).

40. The most outspoken opponent of musical fleshliness was Theophilus Grossgebauer. "Unspiritual" church musicians pollute worship with their virtuosity and instrumental flamboyance: "But because at one time the Pope gave only the clerics the power to sing and make music it seems to us difficult to throw out such a human trinket through the command of God. Therefore unfortunately organists, cantors, town pipers, and musicians—for the most part unspiritual people—have control in the city churches. They play, sing, bow, and ring according to their pleasure. You hear the rushing, ringing, and roaring, but you don't know what it is, whether you should arm yourself for battle or whether you should withdraw. One chases after the other in concertizing and some contend with one another over which can do it most skillfully or which can most subtly imitate a nightingale" (*Wächter-Stimme aus dem verwüstern Zion*, [1661] 208f. in Irwin, "German Pietists and Church Music," 31f.).

41. "And just as the world now is not serious but frivolous and has lost the old quiet devotion, so songs have been sent to us in Germany from Italy in which the biblical texts are torn apart and chopped up into little pieces through swift runs of the throat; those are the warblers (Amos 6:5) who can stretch and break the voice like singing birds. Then it becomes an ambitious collective screaming to see who sings most like the birds. Now it's Latin, now German, only a few can understand the words; and even if they are understood they go in one ear and out the other. There the organist sits, plays, and shows his art; in order that the art of one person be shown, the whole congregation of Jesus Christ is supposed to sit and hear the sound of pipes. This makes the congregation sleepy and lazy: some sleep; some gossip; some look where it isn't fitting; some would like to read but can't because they haven't learned how" (Grossgebauer, *Wächter-Stimme aus dem verwüstern Zion*, [1661], 208f., cited in Irwin, "German Pietists and Church Music," 31f.).

42. Irwin, "German Pietists."

43. Luther, *WATR* 5:274, 9 ss, Nr 5603, in Kraege, "Luther, Théologien de la Musique."

44. Vockerodt, *Missbrauch der freyen Künste* [1697], in Irwin, "German Pietists," 37. Irwin comments: "The problem for the musicians of the late seventeenth and early eighteenth centuries was that too few of them were able to persuade ministers and congregations that either their lives or their music were guided by the Holy Spirit. Not only Pietists, but church musicians themselves were dismayed by the hypocrisy and quackery evident among musicians of their time" (Irwin, "German Pietists," 40).

45. Austern, "Alluring the Auditorie," 354. Austern explains: "Because of perceived affective similarities between music and femininity, many English writers of the late 16th and early 17th centuries discussed one in terms of the other; applied the technical vocabularies of music theory and performance to descriptions of woman; or categorised both women and music as potential inflamers of the passions that could, through similarly strict masculine control, serve as earthly reminders of divine love and providence" (343).

46. Austern, "Alluring the Auditorie," 347.

47. Ibid.

48. Ibid.

49. Ibid., 349. Elsewhere, Stubbes cites Plutarch: "*Plutarchus* complineth of *Musicke*, & saith, that it doeth rather feminine the mynde as prickes unto vice, then conduce to godliness as spurres unto Vertue" (349).

50. Austern, "Alluring the Auditorie," 351.

51. Ibid.

52. Stubbes, *Anatomie of Abuses*, in Austern, "Alluring the Auditorie," 350.

53. *Histriomastix* [1633], in Austern, "Alluring the Auditorie," 349.

54. Austern, "Alluring the Auditorie," 351. In rhetoric very similar to Augustine's, Elizabethan educator Richard Mulcaster elaborates upon music's sirenic sway as follows: "The scie[n]ce [of music] it selfe hath naturally a verie forcible strength to trie and touche the inclination of the minde, to this

or that affection. . . . For which cause *Musick* moveth great misliking in men, as to[o] great a provoker of vain deites, still laying baite, to drawe on pleasure . . . bycause it carrieth away the eare with the sweetnesse of the melodie, and bewitcheth the minde, with a *Syrenes* sounde, pulling it from the delite, wherein of duetie it ought to dwell, unto harmonicall fantasies, and with drawing it from the best meditations and most vertuous thoughtes to forreine conceites and wandring devises" (*Positions wherein those primitive circumstances be examined, which are necessary for the training up of children* [1581], in ibid., 348).

55. My thanks to Dr. Maggie Kilgour for helpful clarifications about Puritan attitudes toward the arts. Percy A. Scholes contends that often Puritan authorities disdain, not music in worship per se, but rather musical excesses and "popery." See Scholes, *The Puritans and Music,* for documentation that challenges stereotypical views of Puritans as musical iconoclasts. On the problem of the term "Puritan," see Christopher Hill, *Society and Puritanism in Pre-Revolutionary England* (Hammondsworth: Penguin, 1964), ch. 1.

56. Austern, "Alluring the Auditorie," 354.

57. Prynne, *Histriomastix,* in Austern, "Alluring the Auditorie," 352

58. Ibid.

59. Wright, *The Passions of the Minde in Generall,* in ibid.

60. Austern, "Alluring the Auditorie."

61. Morley, *A Plaine and Easie Introduction to Practicall Musicke*, in Austern, "Alluring the Auditorie," 354.

62. Austern, "Alluring the Auditorie," 353.

63. Thus Rosalind in *As You Like It*, Act III, sc.2 [as Ganymede, to Orlando]: "Hee was to imagine me his Love, his Mistris: and I set him everie day to woe me At which time would I, being but a moonish youth, greeve, be effeminate, changeable, longing, and liking, proud, fantastical, apish, shallow, inconstant, full of teares, full of smiles; for everie passion something, and for no passion truly any thing, as boyes and women are for the most part, cattle of this colour" (Shakespeare, in Austern, "Alluring the Auditorie," 352).

64. Butler, *The Principles of Musick*, in Austern, "Alluring the Auditorie," 353.

65. *Histriomastix*, in Austern, "Alluring the Auditorie," 353.

66. Austern, "Alluring the Auditorie." According to Austern, even the advent of modern science continued to support belief in constructs of Woman and Music as dangerous creatures. Though music was reconstrued scientifically as "vivified air" by Francis Bacon, it remains a cleansing or contaminating force, this because "sensory effects were transmitted to the soul via the spirit—a subtle vapour that relayed those sensory impulses that entered the body" (351). Even though Bacon dissected music's body more empirically (cf. *Sylva sylvarum* in Weiss and Taruskin, *Music in the Western World*, 191-93), he still construed it as a gendered, engendering discourse. (Perhaps Bacon had more confidence in the composers' controlled, 'rational' manipulation thereof for purely dramatic effect): "It hath been anciently held, and observed, that the *Sense of Hearing,* and the *Kindes of Musicke,* have most Operation upon *Manners*; as to Incourage Men, and make them warlike, To make them Soft and Effeminate, To make them Grave, To make them Light, To make them Gentle and inclined to Pitey. &c" (Bacon, *Sylva sylvarum* [1629], in Austern, "Alluring the Auditorie," 351).

67. Thus Sorge: "Just as in the universe there has always been created a creature more splendid and perfect than the others of God, we observe exactly this also in musical harmony. Thus we find after the major triad another, the minor triad, which is indeed not as complete as the first, but also lovely and pleasant to hear. The first can be likened to the male, the second to the female sex. And just as it was not good that the man (Adam) was alone, thus it was not good that we had no other harmony than the major triad; for how far would we come in a progression from one chord to the other?" (Sorge, *Vorgemach der musicalischen Composition* [tr. A. Dixon Reilly], 179f., in McClary, *Feminine Endings,* 11).

68. John Dennis, *An Essay on the Opera after the Italian Manner,* in Smith, *Handel's Oratorios and Eighteenth-Century Thought,* 82.

69. Lavington, *The Influence of Church Music,* 11-15, in Smith, *Handel's Oratorios,* 46.

70. Smith, ibid., 74.

71. Ibid.

72. Miller, *Harlequin Horace* II, in ibid.

73. Aaron Hill, *The Tears of the Muses,* in ibid., 81.

74. Bedford, *The Great Abuse of Musick,* in ibid., 86.

75. Hill, *Works* 2/1754, in ibid., 79.

76. Wesley in Temperley, "Wesley, John," *New Grove Dictionary of Music and Musicians*, 303.

77. Bernard Germain Lacépède, "*La Poétique de la musique* (1785), vol. 1, bk. 2, excerpted in Lippman, *Musical Aesthetics: A Historical Reader*, vol. 1, 385f.

78. Kierkegaard, "The Immediate Erotic Stages or The Musical Erotic," 81.

79. "Man's concept is spirit and we must not allow ourselves to be put off by the fact that he is also able to walk on two legs. Language's concept is thought, and we must not let ourselves be put off by the view of certain sensitive people that its greatest significance is to produce inarticulate sounds" (Kierkegaard, ibid., 75f.).

80. Cf. Kierkegaard, "Immediate Erotic Stages," 71-84. "If this spirit of the sensual erotic in all its immediacy demands expression, the question is: what medium lends itself to that? What must be especially borne in mind here is that it demands expression and representation in its immediacy. In its mediate state and its reflection in something else it comes under language and becomes subject to ethical categories. In its immediacy it can only be expressed in music. . . . In the erotic sensual genius, music has its absolute object. This of course by no means implies that music cannot express other things, but this is nevertheless its proper object" (75f.).

Kierkegaard explains the genesis of these distinctions as follows: "Sensuality as a principle, then is posited with Christianity, and similarly the sensual erotic as a principle . . . as a power, as a realm characterized by spirit, that is to say characterized by being excluded by spirit, if I imagine it concentrated in a single individual, then I have the concept of the spirit of the sensual erotic . . . which Christianity first introduced to the world, if only in an indirect sense" (ibid.).

81. Ibid., 78f.

82. Ibid., 75.

83. See ibid., 63-65. Thus: "In saying that when language stops, music begins, and in saying, as people do, that everything is musical, we are not going onwards but back. That is why I have never had any sympathy—and here perhaps even the experts will agree with me—for that purified music which thinks it can do without words. For as a rule it thinks of itself as being above the word, in spite of being its inferior. . . . For music always expresses the immediate in its immediacy. . . . In language there is reflection and therefore language cannot express the immediate. Reflection kills the immediate and that is why it is impossible to express the musical in language; but this apparent poverty of language is precisely its wealth. For the immediate is the indeterminable and so language cannot apprehend it, but the fact that it is indeterminable is not its perfection but a defect" (80).

84. In the *Concept of Dread*, we learn that this "full might of sensuality" involves a complete absence of self-directing will; it is "a womanish debility in which freedom swoons" (ibid., 55). Don Giovanni's endless (yet futile) pursuits are meant to thwart the very dread that plagues both subject and object. Romance is but a denial of the existential meaninglessness endemic to aesthetic life. For Kierkegaard, the happiness, beauty, peace, harmony, and joy that men pursue in "feminine youthfulness" veils an "anxious . . . dread of nothing" (*The Sickness unto Death*, 158). Woman is this manhole. Terry Eagleton points out that in this later work Kierkegaard homologises sensuality, dread, and Woman more explicitly: "Dread is the 'inexplicable nothing' which shadows all sensuality, the faintest, purely negative trace of spirit lurking within it, and thus a suitable image of the innocent, treacherous female" (Eagleton, *The Ideology of the Aesthetic*, 179). See Eagleton's helpful discussion of this notion of dread as well as Kierkegaard's concept of the aesthetic (versus those of the ethical and religious) in chapter 7 of *The Ideology of the Aesthetic*, 173-95.

85. Kierkegaard, "Immediate Erotic Stages," 101. Kierkegaard continues: "This is something music is excellently fitted to accomplish, since it is far more abstract than language and therefore does not express the particular but the general in all its generality, and yet it expresses the general, not in reflective abstraction, but in the concreteness of immediacy."

86. "Don Giovanni . . . is from tip to toe a seducer. His love is not of the soul but sensual, and sensual love is not according to its own lights faithful but absolutely faithless; it loves not one but all, that is to say, it seduces all. For it exists only in the moment, but the moment, in terms of its concept, is the sum of moments, and so we have the seducer" (Kierkegaard, "Immediate Erotic Stages," 100).

And later: "This force in Don Giovanni, this omnipotence, this gaiety, only music can express, and I know no other description for it than 'exuberant good cheer.'"

"These considerations bring us back to the main topic of this inquiry, that Don Giovanni is absolutely musical. He desires sensually, seduces with the demonic power of sensuality, he seduces all. The spoken word is no part of him, for that would straightaway make him a reflective individual. He has no substance of this kind but hurries on in a perpetual vanishing, just like music, of which it is true that it is over as soon as it stops playing and only comes back into existence when it starts again" ("Immediate Erotic Stages," 107f.).

87. "Immediate Erotic Stages," 97.

88. "[With the birth of Christianity] the whole world became an abode for sensuality's worldly spirit. . . . The Middle Ages have as much to say of a mountain not found on any map; it is called Venusberg. There the sensual has its home, there it has its wild pleasures, for it is a kingdom, a state. In this kingdom language has no home, nor thought's sobriety, nor the laborious business of reflection. All one hears there is the elemental voice of passion, the play of the appetites, the wild din of intoxication; indulgence, only, in an eternal tumult. The first-born of this kingdom is Don Juan. That is not yet to say that it is the realm of sin, for we must grasp it at the moment when it appears in aesthetic indifference. Not until reflection enters does it present itself as the realm of sin, but then Don Juan is slain, the music comes to an end, one sees only the despairing defiance which impotently casts its negative vote but can find no constituency, not even in musical sounds" ("Immediate Erotic Stages," 97).

A *musically* conceived Don Giovanni is, therefore, Dread writ large, oozing the spirit of sensuality as no literary persona ever could. "[T]he ear in that dying string of the violin stroke has a presentiment of all the passion. . . . [A]s if in the deep darkness it were born in dread . . . but his dread is his energy. . . . Don Giovanni's life is not despair; it is the full might of sensuality" ("Immediate Erotic Stages," 130). With these words, the aesthete A admires Mozart's operatic overture. Its labia birth Don Giovanni—Dread's love-child—musically begotten and therefore full and perfect. Such gorgeous dread is the Don's lifeblood; as music, it keeps him alive.

89. See "The Aesthetic Validity of Marriage" and "Equilibrium between the Aesthetic and the Ethical Development of Personality," in ibid.

90. "Immediate Erotic Stages," 129.

91. Ibid., 62.

92. Cf. more positive reassessments of Kierkegaard by Berry, Bertung, Watkin, Perkins, and Howe, in *Feminist Interpretations of Søren Kierkegaard*, Leon and Walsh, eds.

93. Women's histrionics find their antecedents in the theatre: "Was Wagner a musician at all? At any rate, there was something else that he was more: namely, an incomparable *histrio*, the greatest mime, the most amazing genius of the theater ever among Germans, our *scenic artist par excellence*. He belongs elsewhere, not in the history of music: one should not confuse him with the genuine masters of that" (Nietzsche, *The Case of Wagner*, 172).

94. Nietzsche, *Joyful Wisdom*, trans. T. Common, in *The Complete Works*, 319f., cited in Oliver, "Woman as Truth in Nietzsche's Writing," 72f.

95. Nietzsche, *The Case of Wagner*, 191.

96. Ibid., 184.

97. Nietzsche, in Köhler, *Nietzsche and Wagner: A Lesson in Subjugation*, 163.

98. Nietzsche, *The Case of Wagner*, 170.

99. Ibid., 171.

100. Ibid., 166.

101. Ibid., 155.

102. Ibid., 183.

103. E.g., the medieval "Dutch Masters," Handel, Mozart, Beethoven, and Rossini (Nietzsche, *Nietzsche contra Wagner*, trans. W. Kaufmann, 668).

104. Ibid.

105. Nietzsche, *The Case of Wagner*, 173.

106. Nietzsche, *Nietzsche contra Wagner*.

107. Köhler's descriptor of their relationship. See chapter 3, "The Euphoric Acolyte," *Nietzsche and Wagner: A Lesson in Subjugation*, 36-52.

108. Nietzsche, *The Case of Wagner*, 164.

109. Ibid., 177f.

110. Oliver, "Woman as Truth in Nietzsche's Writing," 68.

111. Ibid., 70f.

112. Cf. ibid., 68-72.

113. Thus Nietzsche exhorts: "The world with which we are concerned is false; it is 'in flux' as something in a state of becoming, as a falsehood always changing but never getting nearer the truth; for there is no 'truth'" (Nietzsche, in ibid., 78).

114. That said, Oliver comments: "Art enables us to act . . . her illusions give life a foundation (although illusory). . . .The will to illusion, then, is a survival mechanism, an instinct which protects us from a deep look into the horror of nature (which . . . is the affirming woman – the will to power)" (Oliver, ibid., 75). Note then that Nietzsche even genders his sacrosanct will to power female.

115. Oliver also points out that the terrifying Dionysian life force itself—the will to power—is feminine and, according to Nietzsche, is mirrored in the fact that "there are women, who, wherever one examines them have no inside, but are mere masks." This does not make them shallow, but rather, like the Original Mother of Creation—the will to power—such women are unfathomably deep. "The Dionysian force—the will to power—is not a reactive force; rather it is the origin of all force. Yet it is a myth, an origin which does not exist" ("Woman as Truth," 75).

116. "Woman as Truth," 158ff.

117. Ibid., 182f.

118. Ibid., 158f.

119. Ibid.

120. Ibid.,157.

121. Ibid.

122. Ibid., 166.

123. Ibid., 158.

124. Nietzsche, *The Case of Wagner*, 161. Wagner thus takes his place in a regrettably long line of German artistic geniuses who have been corrupted by "the eternal feminine" in all its physical and metaphysical guises.

125. Susan Bernstein concurs here. See her engaging analysis of Nietzsche's use of the feminine operation, as well as visual and musical metaphors, in "Fear of Music? Nietzsche's Double Vision of the 'Musical Feminine.'"

126. This negative enumeration of the German masses is in fact Wagner's own. Or so Nietzsche intimates. It occurs in part of a fictional conversation that Nietzsche composes between Wagner and some of the latter's younger artist-sycophants. See Nietzsche, *The Case of Wagner*, 167-69.

127. Ibid., 167.

128. Squire, *Church Music*, 66.

129. Ibid., 18.

130. The tacitly gendered rhetoric of purity is also in evidence in the lines that follow the above: "Although from early synagogue times until long after the time of Christ there was a similarity between the music of the temple and of the synagogue; that of the synagogue was always restricted to pure singing, i.e., instrumentally unaccompanied. . . . Singing by the assembled people (the women perhaps did not sing) was carried on in congregational style. The rabbis and cantors led the exercises" (Squire, *Church Music*, 22). In my view, implied here is that liturgical song was at its purest, not only when instrumentally unaccompanied, but also when women's voices did not add their specific timbre to the song. Again, Squire ignores the gender politics endemic to notions of aesthetic purity.

Similarly unphased by the sexist undertones in another later musico-historical development, Squire (in his discussion of secular music's crossover into medieval Christian music, and certain authorities' reactions to this threat to music's purity) includes without comment the same passage from John of Salisbury cited in chapter 2 above: "Music defiles the service of religion. For the admiring simple souls of the congregation are of necessity depraved—by the riot of the wantoning voice, by its ostentation, and by its womanish affectations in the mincing of notes and sentences" (Salisbury, in Squire, *Church Music*, 111).

131. McClary, *Feminine Endings*, 10; her emphasis.

132. *Harvard Dictionary of Music*, Apel, ed., s.v. "Masculine, feminine cadence." Cf. also *New Harvard Dictionary of Music*, Randel, ed., s.v. "Masculine, feminine cadence."

133. Schoenberg, *Theory of Harmony*, 96, in McClary, *Feminine Endings*, 11.

134. Adorno continues: "[T]he eunuch-like sound of the jazz band both mocks and proclaims, 'and you will be rewarded, accepted into a fraternity which shares the mystery of impotence with you, a mystery revealed at the moment of the initiation rite'" (Adorno, "Perennial Fashion—Jazz," *Prisms*, 129).

135. Maynard Solomon, "Charles Ives: Some Questions of Veracity," *Journal of the American Musicological Society* 40 (Fall, 1987): 467.

136. Solomon in McClary, 17. Cf. McClary's discussion of the same in *Feminine Endings*, 17-18.

137. Pseudo-Basil, *Commentary on Isaiah* V.158 in MacKinnon, *Music in Early Christian Literature*, #143, 70.

138. Ibid.

139. Quasten, *Music and Worship*, 81-82. There is also ample evidence that women played, sang, and danced as equal participants in Egyptian, Greek, Ionian, Roman, and Jewish rituals and worship until these freedoms, like others, were reduced or abolished entirely. (Cf. Quasten, *Music and Worship*, 76-77; and Carol Meyers, The Drum-Dance-Song Ensemble."

140. *Didascalia of the Three Hundred Eighteen Fathers* [c. 375], in Quasten, *Music and Worship*, 81.

141. Ibid., 82f.

142. Jerome, Epistle CVII, *Ad Laetam* 4, in MacKinnon, *Music in Early Christian Literature*, #322, 142.

143. Jerome, Epistle CVII, 8, in MacKinnon, *Music in Early Christian Literature*, #324, 142.

144. Jerome, Epistle LIV, *Ad Furiam de uiduitate seruanda* 13, in MacKinnon, *Music in Early Christian Literature*, #320, 141.

145. Quasten includes an excerpt from Lucian of Samosata's *Dialogue of a Courtesan* here: "She played the cithara and danced more elegantly than was becoming to an upright woman, and she could do many other things which minister to voluptuousness" (Quasten, *Music and Worship*, 83).

146. Arnobius, *Adversus nationes*, 2.42 in Quasten, ibid.

147. Jerome, Epistle LIV, *Ad Furiam*, in MacKinnon, ibid., #320, 141. Thus Jerome elaborates: "Oh if you could see your sister and if it were possible to hear in person the eloquence of her holy lips, you would perceive the mighty spirit within her tiny body and hear the entire content of the Old and New Testaments bubbling up from her heart! Fasting is her sport and prayer her recreation. She takes up the tympanum in imitation of Miriam and after Pharaoh is crowned sings before the choir of virgins: 'Let us sing to the Lord, for he has triumphed gloriously; the horse and the rider he has thrown into the sea' (Exodus 15.1). These she instructs as harpists for Christ, these she teaches to be citharists for the Saviour. Thus she passes the day and night, awaiting the coming of the bridegroom with oil ready for the lamps. You, too, then—imitate your kinswoman" (MacKinnon, ibid., #320, 141).

148. Epistle CVII, *Ad Laetam de institutione filiae* 4, in MacKinnon, ibid., #322, 142.

149. Isidore of Pelusium, *Epist.*1.90 in Quasten, *Music and Worship*, 85.

150. See *Carmina* 1.3.2, in Quasten, ibid., 84.

151. Isidore of Pelusium, *Epist.*1.90, in Quasten, ibid., 81.

152. Quasten, ibid., 79.

153. "When the holy Ephraem saw how all were being torn away by the singing (of the heretics) and since he wanted to keep his own people away from dishonorable and worldly plays and concerts, he himself founded choirs of consecrated virgins, taught them the hymns, and responses whose wonderful contents celebrated the birth of Christ, his baptism, fasting, suffering, resurrection and ascension, as well as the martyrs and the dead" (anonymous author, *Bibliotheca Orientalis* I, in Quasten, ibid., 79).

(Also of hagiographical interest in this account is the author's subsequent characterisation of Ephraem as a redemptive father figure who imparted actual *laws* of song to these women, thereby preserving Christian harmony in the face of the "dishonourable and worldly" pagan music: "He had these virgins come to the church on the feasts of the Lord and on those of the martyrs, as they did on Sundays. He himself was in their midst as their father and the citharist of the Holy Spirit, and he taught them music and the laws of song" (ibid.).

154. Quasten, ibid., 92. The employment of choir boys as lectors, moreover, lent further ecclesial agency to these young singers.

155. Lucian of Samosata, *Imagines* 13, in Quasten, ibid., 87.

156. See Quasten, ibid., 87-92.

157. Austern, "Sing Again Syren," 425.

158. "Since I may facion this (ideal) woman after my minde, I will not onlye have her not practise these manlie exercises so sturdie and boisterous [as tennis, feats of arms, and hunting], but also even those that are meete for a woman, I will have her do them with heedfulnesses and with the soft mildenesses that we have said is comlie for her. And therefore . . . in singing or playing upon instruments [I would not have her use] those hard and often divisions that declare more counninge then sweetnesse. Likewise, the instruments of music which she useth (in mine opinion) ought to be fitt for this purpose. Imagine with your selfe what an unsightly matter it were to see a woman play upon a tabour or drum, or blowing a flute or trompet, or anye like instrumente: and this is because the boisterousnesse of them doeth cover and take away the sweete mildnesse which setteth so further everie

deed that a woman doeth" (Castiglione's Lord Julian Medici, from *The Courtier*, in Austern, "Sing Again Syren," 430).

159. Someone easily seduced by feminine beauty would be thoroughly ravished by a woman's music. Neoplatonic physiology offered a modern scientific explanation for this double whammy:

"Renaissance thought regarded the soul as a substantive entity, physically affected by the five senses. Corporeal perception reached the soul through the spirit, a subtle vapor that relayed those sensory impulses that entered the body. This spirit could wander out through the eyes and infect the blood of another at a glance, thus uniting the spiritual and the physical" (Austern, "Sing Again Syren," 425f.).

"But unlike the visual invitation to earthly love and spiritual rapture, music touched the very soul as it reached the body and intermediary spirits, drawing it through the ear to become one with universal harmony. This direct seduction of the soul by music resulted from a substantive similarity between the two, for both music and the soul were regarded as vivified air." Here Austern cites Robert Burton: "because the spirits about the heart, take in that trembling and dancing aire into the body, are moved together and stirred up with it, or else the mind as some supposed, harmonically composed, is roused up at the tunes of musicke" (Burton, *Anatomy of Melancholy*, in Austern, "Sing Again Syren," 426).

160. Thus Robert Burton in his *Anatomy of Melancholy* laments: "A thing nevertheless frequently used, and part of a Gentlewoman's bringing up, to sing, to daunce, and ply on the Lute, or some other instrument, before she can say her *Pater Noster*, or ten Commandements, 'tis the next way their parents think to get them husbands, they are compelled to learne, and by that meanes, *incestos amores de tenero maditantur unque*; Tis a great allurement as it is often used, and many are undone by it" (Austern, "Sing Again Syren," 431). As indicated above, for most people this strategy was risky, and did not assuage women musicians' seductive powers; women were strongly advised to sing and play for their own private consolation (see Austern, "Sing Again Syren," 434f.). According to Austern's research, these musical norms surface in and are reinforced by Elizabethan literature (435-47).

Like the Pietists discussed in chapter 1, for some Elizabethans, music's effects were not entirely self-determined; they depended on the (male) listeners' preoccupation as well—be it with the woman or with God, lust or love. Thus the generally held view that an individual's proclivities would determine music's effeminizing strength: "But whom I praie you, doth (music) make effeminate? Surely none but such as without it would bee. . . . [I]t is indeede as fire to flare, and as wine to drunkarde, if flare be easily inflamed, is the fault in the fire or if a drunkard be easily overcome with wine, is the fault in the wine?" (*The Praise of Musicke*, 58, in Austern, "Sing Again Syren," 436f.). Similarly, Thomas Wright comments: "Let a good and godly man heare musicke, and hee will lift up his heart to heaven: let a bad man heare the same, and hee will convert it to lust" (*The Passions of the Minde in Generall*, in ibid., 437). And Bacon ultimately concluded that "Musicke feedeth that disposition of the Spirits which it findeth" (*Sylva sylvarum*, in Austern, "Sing Again Syren," 427).

160. Austern, "Sing Again Syren," 431f.

161. Erasmus can also be included among these proponents. He cautioned, however, that the musical "folly," "frivolity," and "foulness" of his day could irrevocably contaminate Christian girls. In the following passage, note also his astute sense that music's own body could exude fleshly connotations: "But in our music, apart from obscenity in texts and subjects, how much is frivolity, how much is folly? There existed in former times a kind of performance in which, without words and only by pantomime, anything that was desired could be represented. In the same way in modern songs, even if the text is not sung, the foulness of the subject can be understood from the nature of the music. Then add to this the sound of frenetic pipes and noisy drums combining with a frenzy of movements. To such music young girls dance, to this they are accustomed, and yet we think there is no danger to their morals" (Erasmus, *Omnia opera* V717F, in Miller, "Erasmus on Music," 348).

162. Austern, "Sing Again Syren," 428. Thus Richard Mulcaster advocated: "reading well, writing faire, singing sweete, playing fine, beyond all cry and above all comparison, that pure excellencie in things ordinary may cause extra-ordinary liking; or else in skill of languages annexed to these foure, that more good giftes may work more wonder" (*Positions wherein those primitive circumstances be examined, which are necessary for the training up of children*, in Austern, "Sing Again Syren," 429).

163. Philip Stubbes believed that music's sexual liability entirely eclipsed its spiritual possibilities: "And if you would have your daughter whoorish, bawdie, and uncleane, and a filthie speaker, and such like, bring her up in musicke and dauncing, and my life for youres, you have wun the goale" (*Anatomie of Abuses*, in Austern, "Sing Again Syren," 432f.).

164. Thus Powell: "In stead of Song and Musicke, let [girls] learne Cookery and Laundrie. And in stead of reading *Sir Philip Sidney's Arcadia*, let them read the grounds of good huswifery. . . . Let

greater personages glory their skill in musicke, the posture of their bodies, their knowledge in languages, the greatnesse, and freedome of their spirites: and their arts in arreigning of mens affections at their flattering faces. This is not the way to breed a private Gentleman's Daughter" (*Tom of all Trades*, in Austern, "Sing Again Syren," 431).

165. Some scholars contend that even virgins who became lectresses and deaconesses outside the convent also may have served as cantors (Quasten, *Music and Worship*, 80-81).

166. J. Michele Edwards, "Women in Music to ca. 1450," in Pendle, *Women and Music*, 22. Singing liturgical music was the central communal activity in most convents. The education of novices focused on reading and singing, to encourage participation in collective worship. One woman in the convent served as cantrix, an opportunity for leadership which did not exist outside the convent. More than a conductor, the cantrix also chose repertoire, held rehearsals, supervised the copying of music and illumination work, managed the library, and supervised liturgy. She would have been among those most likely to compose texts and music for religious services.

167. See Monson, *Disembodied Voices: Music and Culture in an Early Modern Italian Convent*, 6f. and 36-40.

168. See especially Monson, ibid., and Kendrick, *Celestial Sirens*.

169. Monson, ibid., 37; emphasis mine. The ineradicable male ambivalence toward nuns' singing is succinctly expressed in another passage from the same report to the archbishop: a certain Don Leone strongly objected to the "frivolities" that had come to characterise convent life at Santa Cristina in Bologna—the keeping of pets (dogs and birds), the reading of dubious recreational materials, card and dice playing at Christmas, but most of all, the singing of frivolous songs, sometimes in the company of men: "They spend feast days in idle songs to the organ and in frivolous music. . . . (They have) conversations and friendships with (male-singers). . . . They spend too much time singing and playing (.) Some singers and organists have too much freedom, and sing and play vain things (.) Sometimes (male) singers sing with the nuns (.) They invite the magistrates for Holy Week and to Easter compline" (Don Leone, report to Archbishop Paleotti [1576], in Monson, ibid.). But because the nuns sometimes sang in mixed company in their parlours, beneath this more 'neutered' complaint of musical "frivolity" lies a deeper fear of the redoubled sensuality that women making music embody, not to mention fear that music will arouse female erotic desire. The author Monson also detects a fear of sexual misconduct that such social musical events in mixed company might hold: "Typically, behind the regular echoes of distraction and time-wasting, the paranoid fear of sexual contact also resonates" (ibid.).

170. Monson, ibid., 85.

171. Consider for example Thomas Coryat's renowned description of the courtesan's musical prowess: "Moreover shee will endevour to enchaunt thee partly with her melodious notes that shee warbels out upon her lute, which shee fingers with as laudable a stroake as many men that are excellent professors in the noble science of Musicke; and partly with that heart-tempting harmony of her voice. Also thou wilt finde the Venetian Cortezan (if she be a selected woman indeede) a good Rhetorician, and a most elegant discourser, so that if shee cannot move thee with all these foresaid delights, shee will assay thy constancy with her Rhetorical tongue" (*Coryat's Crudities*, 267, in Monson, ibid., 85).

172. Feminist musicologist Susan McClary has also analysed Monteverdi's political use of a courtesan's emasculating musical prowess in his opera *L'Incoronazione de Poppea* as a veiled critique of the actual erosion of patriarchal control in seventeenth-century Venice (see *Feminine Endings*, chapter 2).

173. Feminist ethnomusicologist Ellen Koskoff's term, discussed presently.

174. Koskoff, *Women and Music in Cross-Cultural Perspective*, 6.

175. Ibid.

176. Ibid.

177. McClary, *Feminine Endings*, 8.

178. Historian and literary critic Stephen Jay Greenblatt's term, also adopted by McClary. See Greenblatt, "The Circulation of Social Energy," *Shakespearean Negotiations*, 1-20.

"Inebriate Bewitchment"[1]

Harmony's Eternal Return

IN THE LAST TWO chapters, we have watched the seemingly neutral rhetoric of purity and dangers, or community as unison and symphony, escalate into portraits of music as redemptive virgin or distracting, lascivious whore, images which, moreover, justified the circumscription of acceptable musical practices for women. In the process, music becomes Woman, a gendered *and* engendering discourse. One almost prefers, however, the coy mistresses of Kierkegaard and Nietzsche to the eternal return of the ancients in twentieth-century musico-theological reflection. While all these theological offerings are undoubtedly meant to translate the wonders of human musicality into astute theological insights, the unfortunate by-product of such generous hermeneutics is its unintentionally sexist oversights. Music is occasionally linked to human sexuality by analogy—both providing means for transcendent union with God. For example, musico-theological visions of unity, number, and order surface continually in *Sacred Imagination: The Arts and Theological Education*—a 1994 thematic study issued by the journal *Theological Education*.[2] None of the contributors who discusses music and theology uses, or proposes the use of, insights in musicology as part of their pedagogical resources—a glaring omission given the interdisciplinarity of the topic. Nor do any of the scholars question the ideological implications of the notions of harmony, unity, and transcendence to which they appeal. None acknowledges music's socialising clout in the shaping of human identity. Music's relationship to sexuality receives four lines in one article by Max Stackhouse, and honourable mention in another by Edward Farley.[3]

Given all the above materials, it is rather surprising that contemporary theologians continue uncritically to avail themselves of canonical models and (patristic) authorities. Scholars remain unaware of the gendered connotations within their own musico-theological rhetoric. For example, in a (consciously inclusive) historical survey of Christian music, stylistic changes during the time of the Counter-Reformation are described in implicitly gendered terms:

> The effects of the Renaissance penetrated the Roman church's music only slowly. The Church was a benevolent employer of the most brilliant composers, allow-

ing them gradually to transform medieval styles to Renaissance ideals without restricting their creative freedom. When serious change was finally imposed on musicians—well into the 16th century—the result of the pruning (some say) was *a leaner and stronger* Christian music, to which the Roman Catholic Church still refers to as its musical "golden age."[4]

"Penetrating" musical innovations aside, this passage evokes a hierarchical contrast between a "hipless," hard-body aesthetic ideal, and its replacement of an inferior, zaftig antecedent. The reference is subtle, harmless perhaps, until read on the heels of the two previous chapters. The anatomical metaphors also illustrate that music continues to "have" a body that behaves a certain way.

I. Barthian Mozart:
"You wanted only to make pure music"

Karl Barth's oft-quoted musings on Mozart do much to sustain both the musico-theological value of harmony and order and the protection of music's ideological immunity. Admittedly, this is recreational writing for Barth, but his work commands such authority within Christian circles that it is taken seriously as theologically insightful, (even meriting a one-volume reprint with an effusive prologue by John Updike). The usual suspects—purity, transcendence, and music's infusion of right character—organise Barth's reading of Mozart's music. To Barth, Mozart enacts his own compositional dialectic, one which imbues temperance in its auditors:

> What I [Barth] thank you [Mozart] for is simply this: Whenever I listen to you, I am transported to the threshold of a world which in sunlight and storm, by day and by night, is a good and ordered world. Then, as a human being of the twentieth century, I always find myself blessed with courage (not arrogance), with tempo (not an exaggerated tempo), with purity (not a wearisome purity), with peace (not a slothful peace). With an ear open to your musical dialectic, one can be young and become old, can work and rest, be content and sad: in short, one can live.[5]

Barth above all reinstates moderation as music's greatest theological significance: "In Mozart there are not flat plains but no abysses either. He does not make things easy for himself. But neither does he let himself go; he is never guilty of excess."[6] When Mozart's music does become turbulent, it ultimately remains a credal affirmation of harmonic resolution and order beneath all existence: "What he translated into music was real life in all its discord. But in defiance of that, and on the sure foundation of God's good creation, and because of that, he moves always from left to right, never the reverse. This, no doubt, is what is meant by his triumphant 'charm.'"[7]

The *fons et origo* of Mozart's oeuvre, and its revelatory gift to us, is this affirmation of divine harmony and order which we cannot always perceive around us, but of which his music reassures us. Like a good Pythagorean composer, Mozart learns from creation and the cosmos, assimilates God's ways, exercises freedom while yet under 'his' laws, and frees us into life, into faith in God's victory. His transmission of God's ultimate order represents "a sounding out of God's glory,"[8] a "channelling, and reflecting" of "divine energy."[9] Barth and his junior commentator Updike thus paint a classically inspired, Christian portrait of Mozart. Also analogous to Boethius's 'baptism' of Pythagoras, Barth's Mozart rivals Christ in his supernatural powers. In his glorification of Mozart (and Updike's recapitulation thereof[10]) quasi-christic attributes are ascribed to the composer; this even though Barth asserts Mozart's "full humanity" and qualifies his accolades by emphasising that Mozart's music remains a "supplement" to divine grace.[11] Mozart becomes an omniscient, living parable of perfect harmony who writes a "begotten" music. He personifies universal Man—without sinful excess, and with freedom through submission, with kenotic creative purity, with childlike simplicity. In short, Barth's rhetoric portrays Mozart as the omniscient possessor and revealer of invisible truths: "Imposing limits, he tells us how everything is. Therein lies the beauty of his beneficent and moving music. I know of no other about whom one can say quite the same thing."[12] And in another address: "Knowing all, Mozart creates music from a mysterious center and so knows and observes limits to the right and the left, above and below."[13] Also, like the Word-made-flesh, Mozart "maintains moderation."[14] Free of excess, his wise ways warrant imitation:

> This implies that to an extraordinary degree his music is free of all exaggeration, of all sharp breaks and contradictions. The sun shines but does not blind, does not burn or consume, Heaven arches over the earth, but it does not weigh it down, it does not crush or devour it. Hence earth remains earth, with no need to maintain itself in a titanic revolt against heaven. Granted, darkness, chaos, death, and hell do appear, but not for a moment are they allowed to prevail.[15]

Mozart's music, moreover, because timeless and absolute, and composed from a "mysterious center," exudes the eternal Logos, presumably because Mozart has a direct line to God: "Could it be that the characteristic basic 'sound' of both the earlier and the later Mozart—not to be confused with the sound of any other—is in fact the primal sound of music absolutely? Could it be that he discovered and struck this 'tone' in its timelessly valid form?"[16]

Mozart, *secundum Barth*, is the incarnate icon of God as all in all. His music not only reflects cosmic order, revealing the divine, but also "participates" in (i.e., identifies with) all humanity.[17] Mozart, furthermore, is omniscient, at least in his "universal," self-transcendent understanding of the entire human condition. Tempted by discord yet harmonically resolved, Mozart calls us to a similar confession of our universal strengths and weaknesses.[18] Apparently (and here unlike Jesus *perhaps*), Mozart "never knew doubt," and always affirmed in his work that evil had its limits, that the divine Yes countered the No.[19] In effect then, Barth ascribes to Mozart two natures—perfect humanity and divinity. The pool-playing fun-lover also possesses an originary, decontextualised divinity, which other composers do not: "Question: How then did he know all things so clearly, as his music reveals? . . . I do not know the answer. He must have had organs which, as if to belie that extraordinary seclusion from the external world, made it in fact possible for him to apprehend universally what he was able to state universally."[20]

Writing his own Mozartean "legend" in the same breath that he condemns others,'[21] Barth's Mozart incarnates and expresses in his music our full humanity, yet without committing the sin of excess—the equivalent of musico-theological perdition: "It is precisely the absence of all demons, just this stopping short of extremes, just this wise confrontation and mixture of the elements which—once again—are the constituents of that freedom with which Mozart's music renders the true *vox humana* through the whole scale of its possibilities—unsubdued, but also undistorted and without convulsions."[22] One will note in the above a rhetoric of freedom through submission—the ultimate christic trait, which surfaces continually in Barth's musings.

But having jubilantly identified essence and existence, harmonized universals of immanence and transcendence, Barth can still assert: "There is no Mozartean metaphysics." Notwithstanding that homage to contingency, Mozart's music still incarnates perfect freedom: "In the realms of nature and spirit, he sought for and found only the opportunities, materials, and tasks for his music. With God, the world, himself, heaven and earth, life—and, above all, death—ever present before his eyes, in his hearing, and in his heart, he was a profoundly unproblematical and thus a free man: a freedom, so it seems, *given* to him—indeed *commanded* and therefore exemplary for him."[23] As we shall see in other twentieth-century theologies of music, this communication/mediation of transcendent freedom remains the primary locus of music's theological significance.

Barth asserts that Mozart's music is also pure in that it is untainted by subjectivity[24]—by which our theologian means showy virtuosity. This kenotic simplicity is also attributed to Mozart's freedom to compose in "sovereign submission."[25] Like the gospel, Mozart's music incarnates a new "covenant" in its marriage of freedom and the law: "From the beginning, he moved freely within the limits of the musical laws of his time, and then later ever more freely."[26] Mozart's yoke is ever easy, his burden light: "Mozart's music always sounds unburdened, effortless, and light. This is why it unburdens, releases, and liberates us."[27] And in another context, Barth invites readers to "consider how this man, while truly mastering his craft and always striving toward greater refinement, nevertheless manages never to *burden* his listeners—especially not with his creative labors! Rather, he allows them to participate afresh in his free, let us now say "childlike," play."[28] The limited range of Barthian metaphors evokes a Mozart who is at once the kenotic Christ and the infant Jesus. Barth's Mozart/Jesus idealises the personification of human play in perfectly balanced degrees of intensity and freedom. Mozart obediently becomes a child (as, of course, Jesus himself exhorted). But even here, innocence exudes omniscience, for Mozart composes with a *metaphys-*

ical grasp of alpha-and-omega logic: "Beautiful playing presupposes an intuitive, childlike awareness of the essence or center—as also the beginning and the end— of all things. It is from this center, from this beginning and end, that I hear Mozart create his music."[29]

Barth's authoritative perpetuation of musico-theological metaphysics is also evident in the ideological immunity that he grants Mozart. For Barth, to read Mozart's music through the lens of politics or religious humanism (as Kierkegaard and Goethe did) is anathema; Mozart's music is pure and free.[30] The purity of Mozart's oeuvre should not be sullied with political eisegesis. He miraculously transcends the politically socialising forces which the rest of humankind, immersed in history, cannot escape. In fact, Mozart has the power to free those who are slaves to ideology:

> And now, in our attempt to define this special quality, it may be appropriate to focus on the concept of *freedom* from still another direction. As performer and composer, Mozart always had something to say, and he said it. But we should not complicate and spoil the impact of his works by burdening them with those doctrines and ideologies which critics think they have discovered in them but which are in fact an imposition. There is in Mozart no "moral to the story," either mundane or sublime.[31]

Mozart never forces anything on the listener, taking or demanding us to take political positions: "Mozart does not wish to *say* anything: he just sings and sounds. Thus he does not force anything on the listener, does not demand that he make any decisions or take any positions; he simply leaves him free."[32] Barth is not so magnanimous, imposing as he does his mandatory listening posture on Mozart's audience: "But he never becomes truly tragic. He plays and never stops playing, and the listener who does not himself sway and soar, who does not play along with him, is not truly hearing him. But neither is one truly hearing him if, as happened in the nineteenth century, he is heard as a musician of mere facile gaiety."[33] While Mozart never preaches, "just sings and sounds," Barth certainly gives us a lengthy exposition of this pure sounding. And while Mozart's music may free us, Barth burdens him (and us) with his own utopian cravings for harmony, existential perfection, and superhuman freedom.

II. "Touches of Bliss," "Traces of Transcendence": Hans Küng's Mozart

In 1991, some thirty years after Barth, Hans Küng similarly tries to identify the musical and extramusical elements that compose Mozart's mystique and to reach the "deepest foundation" of Mozart's genius, uncovering roots that other theological and musicological articulations have missed.[34] Küng is less effusive, seeking to steer a middle course between two extremes in Mozart reception— "metaphysical exaggeration" and the reductionistic "cool cutting down" of Mozart by "radical American critics," foremost among whom he ranks Susan McClary.[35] However, the initial "sobriety of critical theology" that Küng injects into Mozart reception devolves into musico-theological cliché.[36] Witness the broader conclusions that Küng draws from his inquiry:

> Truly, more than any other music, Mozart's music—though it is not heavenly music but completely earthly music—seems to show in its sensual yet unsensual beauty, power, and clarity, how wafer-thin is the boundary between music, which is the most abstract of all arts, and religion, which has always had a special connection with music. For both, though they are different, direct us to what is ultimately unspeakable, to mystery. And though music can become a religion of art, the art of music is the most spiritual of all symbols for that "mystical sanctuary of our religion," the divine itself. In other words, for me Mozart's music has relevance for religion not only where religious and church themes or forms emerge, but precisely through the compositional technique of the non-vocal, purely instrumental music, through the way in which this music interprets the world, a way which transcends extra-musical conceptuality.[37]

Prior to this traditionalist reinstatement of music's mystical transcendence of the conceptual, Küng corrects myopic articulations of Mozart's genius; reading Mozart as a fellow Roman Catholic, Küng detects a "reality" far deeper than an all-consuming passion for music out of which Mozart composes. From his faith perspective, Küng hears Mozart's self-proclaimed abiding within "the mystical sanctuary of our religion."[38] Küng also hears Mozart fleshing out attempts "to achieve eternal bliss," tastes of which any catechetically informed Roman Catholic believed to be procurable.[39] The core roots of such musical essays thus lie in "a deeply grounded belief in God," and, moreover, in what Mozart himself describes as an "entire and steadfast submission."[40]

Originally critical of Barth's constraining dogmatic lenses, Küng's reading of Mozart trades in dogmatics for catechetics. This is doubly disappointing given that Küng initially insists upon, and begins by, reading music within its determinative socio-political context. He even recognises the decisive role that the listener's biases play in defining all music's meaning, yet his thematic emphases and preoccupations remain traditionalist and conclusively determine the direction his inquiry takes. More specifically, such thematics are further quests for unity, harmony, and order. For example, Küng defines Mozart's uniqueness as rooted in the higher unity that "the totality of his music" exudes, and in its "freedom of the spirit" (both of which stem from complete submission to God).[41] As before, such unity lies in the balanced integration of sacred and secular ideals, of personal and regional styles, of childlike innocence and prophetic iconoclasm, of a musical "humaneness" that refutes prior ascriptions of Mozart to "demonic" and "divine" categorical poles. Like Barth, Küng also hears Mozart affirming the existential triumph of Yes over No. Finally, Küng uncovers musical elements that generate a "mysterious" order, not just through its "superhuman sense of form," but more significantly, through its genesis in "good Catholic religious experience."[42] Having found this last missing piece of the puzzle that is Mozart's mystique, Küng can explain why previously, when Barth asked Mozart in a dream "what 'dogma' and 'dogmatics' were," Barth received no reply; quite simply, "the author of the monumental thirteen-volume *Church Dogmatics* had asked [Mozart] about the dogmas of the church instead of about good Catholic religious experience—of which Mozart had spoken in connection with the *Agnus Dei*."[43] Had Barth and others attended to Mozart's understanding of religious experience, they might have grasped the centrality of his Catholicism to his creative powers. For Mozart had revealed the following in a letter:

> [I]f someone has been introduced since earliest childhood, as I have been, into the mystical sanctuary of our religion; if there, when you did not yet know how to cope with your dark but urgent feelings, you waited for worship with an utterly fervent heart . . . and at the communion the music spoke in quiet joy from the hearts of those kneeling there, *Benedictus qui venit*, then it is all quite different [than Protestant insensitivity to the *Agnus Dei*]. . . . [O]nce you really take in again words which you have heard a thousand times, in order to set them to music, it all comes back. It stands before you, and moves your soul.[44]

Küng's *via media* further derails in the contradiction that, from the outset, he consciously situates himself between Barth's effusive, markedly Protestant definitions of Mozart's *je ne sais quoi*, and the psychoanalytic demystifications of the latter by Jewish agnostic Wolfgang Hildesheimer, and yet Küng does eventually side with Barth[45] (notwithstanding Küng's 'Catholic' amendment).[46]

Most ironic in my view is Küng's use of erotic metaphors to describe the increasingly disembodied "traces of transcendence" that Mozart's music provides. Thus in his more personal, closing "confessions," he states:

> [T]he most important thing may be whether, in studying or simply sampling it, we open ourselves completely to this music, let it take us over, enter completely into it. . . .
>
> If we do this, we can experience that Mozart's music in particular is the lofty art of transcending, understood—primarily in musicological terms—as the art of exposition, variation and transition. . . .
>
> If I try to surrender completely to Mozart's music, without outside disturbances . . . *I suddenly feel how far I have got away from being confronted with the body of sound: I hear only the form of the music, music and nothing else.* It is the music which completely surrounds me, permeates me and suddenly echoes from within. . . . I detect that I am directed completely inwards, with eyes and ears, body and spirit; the self is silent, and all external factors, all encounter, all the split between subject and object has for a moment been overcome. The music is no longer something over against me, but is what embraces me, penetrates me, delights me from within, completely fulfils me. The statement comes to mind: 'In it we live and move and have our being.'[47]

Throughout this final meditation, Küng translates his sensuous perceptions into hyper-rational testaments to the transcendence of limits through formal perfection. Within another litany of Mozart's balancing acts, Mozart's untexted adagio movements utter a "new language of the soul," a "new melody of humanity," akin to "spiritualised love" and "contemplation."[48] From such intensely sensual transport, Küng ultimately hopes that other people, whatever their creed or context, will recognize in Mozart's music "the sound of infinity":

> With keen ears . . . [they] may also perceive in the pure utterly internalized sound, for example of the adagio of the Clarinet Concerto, which embraces us without using words, something wholly other: the sound of the beautiful in its infinity, indeed the sound of an infinite which transcends us and for which "beauty" is no description. So here are cyphers, traces of transcendence. In this overwhelming liberating experience of music which brings such bliss, I can myself trace, feel and experience the presence of a deepest depth or a highest height. Pure presence, silent joy, happiness. To describe such experience and revelation of transcendence, religious language still needs the word God, the nature of which (according to Nicolas of Cusa) makes up that *coincidentia oppositorum*, the reconciliation of all opposites, which is also characteristic of Mozart's music.[49]

Here the irony redoubles as music's overpowering body becomes a "cypher," synonymous, moreover, with "traces of transcendence." Using metaphors of sexual relations, Küng still manages to inscribe himself within and perpetuates the musico-theological politics of transcendence chronicled thus far.

Moreover, while he acknowledges their status as "personal confession," his closing remarks rhetorically urge his audience to allow Mozart to restore to them the same powers of "reason" that he has received:

> Some one might ask whether these experiences might not have ended up making me a fanatic, a Mozart fanatic or, even worse, a religious fanatic. But none of this has to do with mystical transports, madness or ecstasy. . . . I am not suddenly losing all reason when I listen to Mozart's music. Rather, my reason is being restored. Indeed, now and then I am transported to that peace which transcends all critical and even theological reason. For that I can never be grateful enough to Mozart, and such peace is something I wish you all.[50]

III. Russell N. Squire:
Another Musical Ethic of Purity

We have already glimpsed in chapter 2 Russell N. Squire's perpetuation of the rhetoric of effeminacy in his denigration of post-1054 Eastern church music. His supposedly objective survey reflects an uncritical preoccupation with the chastity and virility of Christian music—outgrowths of yet another musico-theological ethic of purity akin to that of Barth. Furthermore, this ethos is developed by the author's near deification of his own musical favourites: Ockeghem and Palestrina, thus placing Squire within the same rhetorical "tradition" as Barth and Küng on Mozart, and (as we shall see) Pelikan on Bach. Here again, Squire promotes purity and musico-spiritual "nobility" as supreme religious values—as the guarantors of Christian musical decorum. Ockeghem's music embodies such values: "In his church music, he maintained remarkable polyphonic balance, making use of both full and divided choirs. He observed the ecclesiastical tonalities carefully, and followed his texts sensitively, in noble, dignified musical language evidencing the purest of musical ideals, all in keeping with the highest liturgical requirements."[51]

According to Squire, Palestrina's music promotes these same timeless, canonical values in the sixteenth century: "a man who wrote sincerely, devoutly, majestically, and in greatest purity . . . like the name of Moses in his age, or of David in his, Palestrina's name above all others, has stood for the best in sixteenth-century choral writing."[52] Squire ascribes even *chastity* to Palestrina's most celebrated composition: "Palestrina's *Mass of Pope Marcellus* while unsurpassed by any of his other works, was perhaps equaled many times. It does not represent a 'new music' or a new style, but rather in purity, chastity, and technical subtlety, it represents one of the mountain peaks in the age of choral music—an age which began at least as early as the fourteenth century."[53] Palestrina himself, however, was less convinced of his own unfailing devotion as a composer, compromising his virility by dabbling in lascivious compositional waters, as we saw in chapter 1. In Squire's closing remarks on Palestrina, he decontextualises the composer from his cultural milieu in order to grant Palestrina the ideological immunity that, as we have seen, always seems to allow great Christian composers to express (and achieve) spiritual transcendence in and through their music: "No doubt, Palestrina's music possessed an other worldliness, and a universality which kept it apart from the immediacies of local interpretive idioms."[54] (Squire's Palestrina is also "bipolar"—having ascribed to Palestrina an otherworldliness, he nevertheless rejects Romanticism's characterisation of Palestrina's music as "disembodied."[55])

Squire laments music's later loss of virginity after Palestrina—guardian of Christian musical chastity—dies. (Squire does concede, however, that, in the right hands, musical innovation can be spiritually edifying). One may note, for example, the rhetorical pillars of "character" and chastity in the following description of music in the seventeenth century:

> [A]s was inevitable, among the musically artistic clergymen who were not religiously sensitive, there arose (and still exists) an intermixing of church, religious, artistic, and secular factors that brought about, in too many instances, *the formation of a conglomerate which, because of its lack of character*, has hindered the fruition of the church's musical enterprise into authentic religious service. *The purity, the austerity, the virginity* that characterized the best of the older Roman or medieval music (which to be sure, is still performed), is no longer embraced as the ideal in the newer Roman music.[56]

Showing partisan colours yet again, Squire maintains that, in the nineteenth century, the liturgical rigour of the Roman church preserved a musical and spiritual order that Protestantism could not.[57] He contends that the latter's musical demise is symptomatic of, even as it contributes to, a more general "religious anarchy" (the enemy of all good music, as we have seen).[58]

IV. Another "Transcendentalist": Gerardus van der Leeuw

Encouragingly enough, Gerardus van der Leeuw does not reduce music's quintessential theological value to its numerical properties.[59] He deems dance the "original" art, and thereby asserts the centrality of human embodiment to all theologies of the arts.[60] Moreover (and in dramatic contrast to the early Christian authorities discussed in chapters 1 and 2), van der Leeuw revalorises the drum as the "original, basic instrument."[61] Indeed, his eventual metaphysical derailment is especially surprising given van der Leeuw's retrieval of a dancing Christ,[62] and his phenomenological observation that, both biblically and philosophically,[63] humans apprehend God as ordered, and ordering, *movement*.[64] This very material, dynamic starting point, coupled to his foregrounding of dance and human embodiment, might have engendered a more incarnational rendering of music's theological significance. However, his grounding of music's theological import in its emergence from rhythm, movement, and dance dissolves into metaphysics, this despite his original phenomenological critique of the latter.[65]

In a section entitled "Theological Aesthetics of Music," van der Leeuw establishes two points of contact between religion and music that allow the articulation of music's theological significance: "Where does their unity lie? . . . [F]irst, the 'other world,' the new creation; and second, the inclination to the absolute, which is called silence. Or are they perhaps identical?"[66] Here van der Leeuw, the phenomenologist, makes a fatal shift, casting his lot with disembodiment, and thus effecting the standard hierarchy of values endemic to masculinist thought. For van der Leeuw, as for some church fathers, "actual" music is inaudible; the truest music is unencumbered by materiality.[67] His illustrations reinforce this conventional metaphysical hierarchy.[68] For example, as a closing *apologia* for music *qua* silence, van der Leeuw (quoting Herman Rutters) invokes Bach and his *Art of Fugue*: "We recognize through this music that Bach belongs to another world, to which we cannot find entrance. Here is music in its pure, abstract essence. . . . Chaos is ordered to a cosmos. . . . [I]t belongs to that mysterious atmosphere where the physical becomes transformed into the metaphysical. It is a symbol."[69] Read in the context of the present book's last two chapters, it would seem that here again, music (like Woman) is "deception," and only if it is disembodied through some singing silence can music's integrity be restored. Thus, "[c]omplete music is silent. Sound, for it, is a resistance conquered."[70] Music-as-"problem" (echoes of Woman-as-problem) is solved when music subordinates itself to the wholly Other.[71] (Theology, incidentally, becomes the quintessential—because "eschatological"—music. Theology is itself "the praise of God.")[72]

And, of course, with masculinist élan, Mozart and Bach are swept into this metaphysical tide; the latter is ordained a priest—Lutheran consubstantiator of opposites. Thus, in a discussion of "ecstatic music," an aria from Bach's *St. Matthew Passion*[73] mediates a "heavenly immateriality."[74] It illustrates that "[m]usic, freeing itself from the world, rises up to heaven in silent or occasionally loud ecstasy."[75] Mozart is divinised, and like Barth, the former's eternally childlike nature is also decisive in van der Leeuw's appreciation of him; both Mozart and his *oeuvre* incarnate the musical harmonisation of beauty and holiness. He is certainly not a product of his times.[76] The musical translation of Mozart's puerile innocence effects "a gentle melancholy," which is "peace" and "harmony"—"a foretaste of the calm of paradise."[77] Van der Leeuw therefore concludes his "phenomenology" with a theological synthesis of the arts. This would seem at cross-purposes with his originally more modest "search for comprehensible associations" among them.[78] In this concluding systematisation, music is aligned with the Spirit of God (vs. Image or Movement of God). More specifically, music's connection to the Spirit of God obviously points to the Holy Spirit, and therefore, warrants Trinitarian theological elaborations of their interrelationship. Correlatively, music's evanescence heralds a divine "Demolishing" (vs. divine "Speaking" or "Forming") which corresponds to the phase of eschatology in the divine arc of creation, redemption, and eschatology.[79] Such theologising hardly denotes the author's original agenda of rudimentarily grasping "phenomena themselves in their simple existence," or the bracketing of "truth behind the appearance."[80] In short, despite van der Leeuw's initially holistic claims, and his attempt to dissolve sacred/secular dichotomies, and despite his revalorisation of dance, the seemingly ineradicable desire for disembodied transcendence gets the last word. Indeed, in the final section on music, his rhetoric becomes progressively metaphysical, almost anagogical.[81] We are here, it would seem, far from the dancing Christ.

V. Oskar Söhngen:
Doktor of "Unity, Number, and Order"

While less well-known to North American scholars, the most systematic twentieth-century theology of music has been written by the Protestant scholar Oskar Söhngen. Its basic contours were translated into English in the form of a widely cited article, written in 1982.[82] According to Söhngen, throughout Western history, music has always borne witness to the fact that "Unity, number, and order rule everywhere in material nature."[83] On the basis of this canonical presupposition, Söhngen designs three categories with which to frame music's religious significance. First of all, *music as science* imparts knowledge about the nature of *Deus artifex*.[84] As structured sound, music is inherently mathematical and subject to the same laws that govern the cosmos: "The realm of sound is not chaotic matter from which the art of sound brings forth order. Music is not only art of sound, but also kingdom of sound, not only historical spirit but also ideal Logos."[85] After a historical survey of this enduring thematic (Pythagoras, Augustine, Boethius, and others), Söhngen praises its "resurrection" in the twentieth century. Many disciplines—from chemistry to crystallography, from astronomy to atomic physics—testify to the timeless truth that "music is developed out of and upon the basis of the sounding order of creation."[86] From music's "ontic" unity, number, and order, Söhngen concludes that "God himself wanted to arrange his praise in this manner."[87]

Söhngen formulates the second realm of music's theological significance, *music as worship,* by way of Augustine, Aquinas, Luther, and Calvin. Söhngen deems music the superlative medium for satisfying humanity's desire "to enter into immediate relationship with God."[88] Music acquires this second, functional aspect, moreover, by way of its ontological *numerositas.*[89] Furthermore, human engagement of the latter as a means of worship makes musical composition "one of the highest creations of the human *spirit.*"[90] Also problematic in this portrait of music as worship is Söhngen's uncritical endorsement of preserving the primacy of text over music in Roman Catholic musical decrees, the *Motu proprio* of 1903 and the *Constitutio de sacra liturgia* of 1964.[91]

A similar logocentrism pervades Söhngen's third category as well: music is *creatura evangelistica*[92] because, following Luther, both music and gospel are divinely inspired *auricularia.* This shared heredity implies that music's *telos* is kerygmatic; music's highest purpose is "to seize and spread the gospel" since it can accompany the Word with overwhelmingly persuasive power.[93] As such, music possesses an intrinsically "ecumenical character."[94] A consequence of this kerygmatic *telos* is the creation of social harmony. Söhngen proffers one listener's remarks after hearing the motet "Jesus and Nicodemus" by Ernst Pepping (1901-81): "Never before have we had such a strong impression that the Gospel has moved right into the body as in this music."[95] But can the gospel penetrate the body without textual domination? Clearly the answer is no, as Söhngen's entire theory is eclipsed by the "missionary position" his theology of music assumes. (In addition to these constraining metaphysical lenses, further evidence of Söhngen's hermeneutical conservatism lies in his use of the Trinity to structure further musico-theological inquiry.[96])

VI. Doctrinal Fixations, Specious Contextualities: Jaroslav Pelikan's Bach

Jaroslav Pelikan's *Bach among the Theologians* reinforces the same traditional musico-theological values as those of Barth, Küng, Söhngen, and, of course, their Greek antecedents. The rhetoric of unity, transcendence, and music's revelatory power, as well as deliberations over sacred/secular evaluative criteria, constitute the main themes that Pelikan uses to identify the theological import of Bach's oeuvre. As a Protestant historian of Christian doctrine, Pelikan is predisposed to interpret Bach within a very traditional hermeneutic framework. The title states his basic objective of placing Bach "among the theologians."[97] Such traditionalism is exacerbated by Pelikan's failure to consult musicological sources other than canonical commentaries upon Bach.[98] Pelikan does make occasional, obvious criticisms of these works—on which he heavily relies nonetheless—questioning for example, Schweitzer's and Spitta's hyperbole while indulging in his own. Conservatism aside, the more impoverishing element in his method is its *textual*, that is, logocentric, axis:

> Having now come, in my work on the fifth and final volume of *The Christian Tradition*, to the period of Bach, I have, here in *Bach Among the Theologians*, employed the texts of his sacred music as a case study in the methodological problem of how to handle the liturgical and biblical setting of Christian thought. My underlying conviction is that both the Christian tradition *and the music of Bach* can be understood better through such scholarly investigation.[99]

Rather than considering "the circulation of social energies" in Bach's music (as, for example, Susan McClary has done),[100] Pelikan's way of contextualising Bach's music consists of a discussion of the latter's relationship to his contemporaries: August Hermann Francke, Erdmann Neumeister, Samuel Werenfels, and Georg Friedrich Handel.[101] In part 1 of his book, Pelikan further "contextualises" Bach's church music by identifying the four influential currents in his compositions: Reformation theology (mostly Luther), the Enlightenment, Confessional Orthodoxy, and Pietism. Before substantiating this schema by assigning chorale texts to each category,[102] Pelikan falteringly seeks to add further contextual nuance by sketching "the four seasons of J.S. Bach" (making with this coinage a reference to Vivaldi's substantial influence upon Bach's composition). Under this arbitrary rubric, Pelikan observes that "the four seasons of the church year . . . determined the rhythm of Bach's musical activity and set the program for his works as both composer and performer."[103]

In chapter 3 of his book, the principles of reason, order, and number take center stage as theologically significant elements in Bach's musical evangelism.[104] As an introduction to his summary and musicological discussion of "the mathematical and numerological quality" in some of Bach's works, Pelikan then situates Bach within the tradition discussed in chapter 1 above, all this by way of a summary of music's valence as mathematical microcosm of both God's macrocosm and God's own nature. Here though, Pelikan is careful to point out that rationalist philosophers of Bach's day were trying to avoid connecting mathematics to metaphysics.[105] So as not to mislead the reader, however, Pelikan concludes that, despite Bach's shared Enlightenment interest in mathematical structure, his life's work remains a musical confession of tried and tested faith.[106] Bach's continual use of Luther is not the only evidence of his deep assimilation of Reformation theology. Bach himself becomes—to use a cliché which Pelikan alludes to in his dedication—the fifth evangelist.[107] Within this chapter, Pelikan also recycles another Enlightenment theme: music as character-building pedagogue.[108] Additionally,

Pelikan asserts that Bach's adoption of Luther's chorales in his *Christmas Oratorio* exemplifies the composer's thoroughgoing transmission of Lutheran "christocentric existentialism."[109]

As Mozart is to Barth and Küng, Bach is to Pelikan: an icon of existential truth and Christian heroism, more specifically in his embodiment of that same creative obedience that brings freedom. In a flurry of transcendentalist rhetoric, Pelikan quotes Paul Hindemith to summarise Bach's theological significance, and our "most precious inheritance," namely the latter's possession and transmission of truth, his artistic excellence, and his exemplary freedom in artistic submission.[110] Here again, music dialogues with theology via the well-worn theme of humanity's struggle for transcendence.[111] Not surprisingly, this corollary to such obedient harmonisation of opposites is a "sublime unity."[112]

In chapter 4, Pelikan takes up the additional extramusical issue of debating whether Bach was a pietist or an orthodox confessionalist, or both.[113] Ultimately, Bach's music epitomizes a new form of universality—an "evangelical catholicity."[114] As further testament to Bach's catholicity, Pelikan believes that Bach's Passions according to St. Matthew and St. John represent musico-theological commentaries on the atonement that effectively promote the enduring value of this medieval doctrine for the modern era.[115] Once again, therefore, the dogmatic lenses dictate the theological value to be retrieved from Bach's oeuvre.[116] In light of Bach's musically rendered vision of Christian unity, Pelikan elevates evangelical catholicity as a unifying principle for his own theological purposes, *and* as the musico-theological measuring stick of great art.[117]

Pelikan uses his conclusion to rehash yet another standard musico-theological debate: whether to characterise Bach as an essentially sacred or secular composer.[118] Pelikan decides that he is both. He is also concerned lest the dispute become trivialised, seemingly blind to the fact that the debate itself *is* trivial—yielding little musico-theological insight into Bach's music.[119] By labouring Bach's superhuman status and celebrating his achievement of fusing sacred and secular, Pelikan himself trivialises Bach, or at least Bach's theological significance.[120] Pelikan pronounces Bach "a complex of opposites" (and then indulges in his own psycho-biography by describing Bach as resembling Luther in his combination of "a simplicity, almost a naiveté, at one level, with not only profundity but ambiguity at another").[121]

Pelikan's preoccupation with unity as evangelical catholicity (i.e., with Bach's eclipsing of denominational categories), with the composer's negotiation of freedom and finitude, with musical reflections on number and order (not to mention symbolic and formal translations of trinitarian truths),[122] and with the relationship between Bach's musical forms and their sacred functions keeps his musico-theological insights well within traditional discursive parameters. Furthermore, his basic drive to thematise Bach's "theology" into clearly defined theological currents—Luther/Reformation thought, Rationalism, Confessional Orthodoxy, and Pietism (as well as atonement theory)—constrains the musico-theological imagination. It is as if Bach harnesses these four movements to create a teutonic synthesis of tempered passion, faith, reason, and doctrine (the four seasons of J. S. Bach), all in order to offer the Western world another inspirational icon of harmonic transcendence. The banality of such hackneyed rhetoric stifles genuinely creative reflection upon the theological significance of Bach's oeuvre.

Thus, Pelikan's excessive attention to text and metaphysical or liturgical concepts precludes any focus on music's bodily repercussions and their theological import. While Pelikan does cite musicologists, whereas other theologians discussed above have not, his sources are traditionalist and therefore do nothing to destabilise the conservative musico-theological worldview that shapes his argument. Pelikan is blind to any sense of creative innovation because his analysis of Bach's music is really an exegesis of chorale texts with only an occasional nod to musical motifs, symbolism, and key changes. Freed from traditionalism (a word that Pelikan has publicly eschewed) and a logocentric hermeneutic, very different theological insights might emerge. Or, if one cannot escape the intimate union of music and text that inevitably defines Bach's "theology," one could at least discuss the corporeal, performative significance of this wedding as musicologist Suzanne Cusick does, and whose alternative insights I engage in chapter 4.[123] Another option would be to study Bach's compositionally iconoclastic and rebellious role in the history of Western music, a historical reality that Pelikan the historian ignores, but to which McClary the musicologist carefully attends.

VII. Jeremy Begbie: Musical Temporality and Improvisation as Doctrinal Exegetes

Jeremy Begbie's discussions of musical time and improvisation offer initially progressive theological approaches to music. In his elucidation of fresh "possibilities" of "interaction between music and theology," Begbie is rightly critical of the standard suspicions attributed to music throughout history—its materiality, its distractive power, its supposedly threatening "transience," and its "capacity to manipulate."[124] He too urges the need both for more reflection upon nontexted music and for more treatment of music as a set of embodied practices.[125] To these ends, he does derive overlooked theological insights from the natures of musical time and improvisation. But ultimately his theologising reduces music to a mere proof-text for biblical doctrine. Music thus remains an evangelistic revealer of Christian truths.[126]

Dissatisfied with some composers' attempts to suspend time in music (often either to simulate the eternal as does Olivier Messiaen, or to effect a misguided escapism from mundane temporality), Begbie wants to affirm rather than deny music's temporal physicality. He maintains that Augustine's Christology—and even those modern christologies which maintain "a pernicious dichotomy between time and eternity"—perpetuates a negative view of temporality.[127] Obversely, Begbie argues that music's quiddity affirms the goodness of time.

Rather than a symptom of our flawed mutability, for him time is part of God's well-ordered creation. Music helps to "redeem the time," so to speak. Its unfolding pattern of beats/notes palpably renders past, present, and future totally inter-dependent in a concrete, sensuous form.[128] Time in music exudes "a dynamic inter-relatedness," which is vital to music's existence and logic. Contra popular theological opinion, musical time therefore is no "absolute receptacle or inert background." According to Begbie, musical works "enfold" both their own past and ours (as we listen to them) in their ever-unfolding future, and thus musical events reveal time to be life-sustaining and essentially good.[129] By extension, music confirms the biblical doctrine that creation is good. Moreover, the nature of musical time also ratifies the doctrine of the Incarnation. In Christ, time is recon-figured,[130] and so too, music reconfigures time. Musical time "entails an interpen-etration of the temporal modes of past, present, and future."[131] Given the interdependence of the notes' unfolding—past into present into future, with none being "mutually exclusive"—music "'takes' our time and 'returns it' to us reshaped." In Christ's life, death, and resurrection, "[t]he worst of humanity's past is judged and buried in the grave; the glory of the past, especially Israel's past, is not lost but carried forward, renewed, and directed toward a future."[132] Music is analogically revelational.[133]

Because music's temporal nature imitates salvation history, the respective harmonic fulfilments of music and resurrection-faith paradoxically both "ease tension and intensify it."[134] Through its delicious tensions and resolutions, music intensifies Christian hope. Like the resolution effected in the incarnation, music heightens and strengthens our hope for the not-yet.[135] With a quotation from Zuckerkandl's *Sound and Symbol,* Begbie concludes that our awareness of music's sacramentally "healed temporality" "bears a striking correspondence to the dynamic at the heart of redemption, through which creation's temporal disrup-tion is in some manner amended. This correspondence opens up enormous pos-sibilities for the theologian who seeks to expound the temporal facets of salvation, and not least as they are concentrated in the *anamnesis* of the eucharist."[136] Begbie even enlists Barth's "notorious adulation" and "fulsome eulogy" of Mozart to defend his own reading of music as a sign that "limited duration can be beneficial, and moreover, can be known as divine generosity."[137] Such musical experiences also teach and model for us "the biblical art of patience," so eloquently described by Paul in Romans 8.[138]

Admittedly, this is a highly creative reading of musical time. But Begbie's attempt to expunge human ambivalence toward time is a modified form of the spiritual escapism through music that he rejects.[139] Perhaps music edifies by forc-ing us to embrace transience as well as our (ineradicable) ambivalence toward finitude rather than priming us to write theological equations for harmonically resolving them. Also problematic here, while Western tonal music serves Begbie's theological agenda very well, atonality—developed between and after two faith-shattering world wars—shuns harmonic resolutions.[140] He presumes that most

Western music operates "according to teleological principles" where tensions are eventually resolved. Such scholarly prerogatives may seem above criticism. Yet in my view, the persistence of such harmonically-driven musico-theological models into the twenty-first century flags an urgent need to inflect musico-theological discourse with the more dissonant tone and content of theologies constructed "after Auschwitz."[141] (Catherine Pickstock exhibits a similar 'ahistorical' penchant for happy endings, discussed below.)

As his second thematic focus, and against those who have maligned its chaos and "emotional" excess, Begbie rightly seeks to retrieve improvisation as theologically valuable. The church could learn much from improvisation, for the latter models "the constitution of personal particularity through reciprocal musical dialogue."[142] Furthermore, if we re-view musical improvisation as a "particularising process,"[143] and as the "exploration of occasion,"[144] music-as-social-process clearly affords musicians "an immediacy with personal exchange" and "uncommon opportunities for profitable 'dialogical interrelations.'"[145] This revising could inform ecclesiology. As a further liberating insight, in improvisation the player becomes both performer and composer, thereby "disrupting conventional barriers between 'composer,' 'performer,' and 'audience,' for an improviser is (normally) all three concurrently."[146] Moreover, as a great infuser of anticipation and hopefulness, improvisation can also inform the doctrine of the Holy Spirit for us: "Pentecost was a divine 'exploration of occasion' if ever there was one. . . . Life in the Spirit, therefore, involves a combination of faithfulness and particularizing what is received in the present in anticipation of the future. This is the dynamic of musical improvisation."[147]

Finally, Begbie rightly emphasises the acute embodiedness that improvisation foregrounds.[148] Music teaches us to avoid "over-intellectual accounts of what it is to be human, or accounts which suggest patterns of oppressive domination in relation to the nonhuman order."[149] Begbie's rereading of improvisation, with his awareness of constrictive theoretical frames and false dichotomies, resonates with this book's agenda, though we may draw different conclusions from these critical revisions. For, interestingly enough, in Begbie's rereading of jazz's theological significance, the erotic lifeblood of jazz improvisation is, at best, only implied and thus given surprisingly short shrift. Instead Begbie shifts his attention almost immediately to the divine; the improviser imitates/intimates the "integrity" of divine freedom and creativity. (Begbie also includes here yet another thematic variation upon the composer–improviser's freedom through submission.[150])

In sum, while the freshness of Begbie's insights are laudable, and while he initially seems to read music as a socialising force and to criticise theological clichés, his doctrinal apologetics leads him to construe tonality's narrative form as a seemingly preordained teleological principle and to use music for validating biblical doctrines (creation, the incarnation, and the Holy Spirit). Such proof-texting, so to speak, indicates a basic failure to take music seriously as a cultural document— a decontextualising modulation that theologies of music cannot afford to make.

Part of the problem may lie in his failure adequately to ground his analysis in musical practices of particular historical contexts, interpreting music as a cultural document— a shared set of codes and social conventions that have "*social* histories marked with national, economic, class, and gender—that is, political—interests."[151] Instead, Begbie's universal assertions about two musical properties perpetuate the popular value judgment that music "by nature" transcends its socio-cultural roots. (This internal cross-purpose to Begbie's original critique is graphically illustrated by his use of a poem that praises the "mutinies of living," "a love of deviance, our genesis in noise" to undergird an ironically "deracinated" conclusion that music simulates "the [ultimately good and harmonically resolvable] dynamics of the creation of the cosmos").[152]

Finally, Begbie's enlistment of musical "tension and release" can be read very differently if, instead of eschatology, one relocates this pattern in the equally valid context of human sexuality. Love-making may also be proleptic in its extramusical significance (and, as we have seen, is often construed as a proleptic form of transcendence—a cliché of which I'm sure Begbie would be critical). But music's connection to sex, and the latter's theological significance, need not always take us back to teleology and harmonic resolution, even if we connect it to the incarnation.

VIII. John Michael Spencer: Music "in the Deity's Time—the wholly unformed pure mood"[153]

A far more misleading venture that contrasts with Begbie's basically intelligent undertaking is that of John Michael Spencer. Spencer claims to have created a new discipline, "theomusicology," which—understatedly expressed—is in fact not musicological at all. With the exception of a few pages in which he uncritically discusses the work of Peter Kivy,[154] Spencer claims to be in dialogue with numerous and varied disciplines—none of which is musicology. This "dialogue," moreover, consists of brief historical descriptions of each movement or field, which Spencer usually connects to theomusicology by arguing that they share a common, emancipatory goal.[155] Theomusicology is "musicology as a theologically informed discipline . . . principally incorporating thought and method borrowed from anthropology, sociology, psychology, and philosophy. . . . [I]ts analysis stands on the presupposition that the religious symbols, and canon of the culture being studied are the theomusicologist's authoritative/normative sources."[156]

Also problematic, instead of considering music's actual bodily effects, Spencer plans to examine "the depths [never defined] of sacrality, secularity, and profanity in the music of civilization's many cultures." By doing so, theomusicologists will "increasingly discern how particular peoples perceive the universal mysteries that circumscribe their mortal existence."[157] In light of the present chapter and the last two, readers will question such mystifications, cognizant now of music's incontestable circulation of acutely contextual social energies—erotic and political—rather than some static repository of "universal mysteries," however defined. Spencer believes that plumbing these "depths" will reveal "how the ethics, theologies, and mythologies to which they [peoples] subscribe shape their worlds and *the* world."[158] While this objective seems more contextually informed, what he actually does is identify elements from these three meaning-systems exclusively in the *texts* that the music accompanies and in the political activism of its performers and composers (e.g., Paul Robeson and James Brown). Indeed, Spencer seems oblivious to the absence of commentary on actual music in his theomusicology. This *in nuce* is the problem with his approach. He never really gives even one articulation of music's theological significance but simply enumerates possible modes for its study, even though sociologies, anthropologies, psychologies, and philosophies of music (not to mention musicology itself) have themselves already connected music and religion.[159]

Spencer's sources and norms are of equally questionable value; his unlikely antecedent is Jean Jacques Rousseau. Again, Spencer is uncritical of Rousseau's musical logocentrism. Nor—oddly enough given the topic—does he concern himself with Rousseau's musical writings. Rousseau's actual philosophy of music is archly conservative.[160] More troublesome still, even though he eventually draws from Afrocentric "discourses,"[161] a resource which has been ignored in theologies of music (and which I shall use in chapter 6), his fundamental "mentor" is Augustine. And even here, Spencer consults not the *De musica* or the *Confessions*, whose metaphysical cant was criticised in chapter 1 above, but the *City of God*. Consulting the latter, Spencer cannot resist erecting a "trinary domain" of sacred, secular, and profane realms. Unfortunately, this appeal to such tired hermeneutic categories to comprehend artistic human creativity stymies this author's musico-theological reflection. Unless gifted with considerable exegetical skills, it becomes difficult for one to rely so heavily on a fourth-century worldview to theologise about music in the late twentieth (or twenty-first) century. Spencer has made Augustine the ultimate resource for his model because it allows him to embrace Augustine's interpretive "absolutes" rather than to recognise their historical contingency.

Leaping from antiquity to bourgeois Vienna, C. G. Jung next guides Spencer's reading of music's theological significance. Despite sharp and widespread critique of Jungian epistemology by critics of anti-Semitism and by feminist theorists, Spencer does not bother to qualify his "dialogue" with Jung but instead adopts wholesale Earl E. Thorpe's (equally uncritical) application thereof.[162] Dehistoricising music's theological significance, Spencer (via Thorpe) promotes instead the "archetypal" forms of music that transmogrify into musical "Mandalas"—"symbols of wholeness . . . intended to bring cosmos out of chaos [and restore] balance between the unconscious mind and the ego."[163]

This now familiar preoccupation with transcendent universals surfaces again in Spencer's promotion of dialogue between literary criticism and theomusicology, both of which supposedly "*comprehend ultimate reality* through the study of music."[164] In this dialogue, Spencer connects music and gender, extra-musically at best. Spencer assumes that music *only becomes gendered in its connection to literature.*[165] In his second "dialogue" with women's studies, Spencer simply urges the assimilation of Cain Hope Felder's threefold (gender-race-class) biblical hermeneutic.[166] Felder's research calls theomusicologists not to read music as a gendered discourse but to perform a "priestly," healing role ("theomusicotherapy").[167] Feminist musicology, a more contemporary resource, has established a more direct connection between music, sex, and gender, one that can renovate his musico-theological reflection. As with Begbie and all the other previous masculinist examples, the biggest aporia in Spencer's new discipline is its insufficient attention to music itself as a discourse or semiotic "body." Even when Spencer ascribes a redemptive sacrality to blues and jazz, his conclusion mystifies music's powerful effects—the latter "emanating" from the godhead and/or the collective human unconscious.[168] Spencer is more intent upon portraying the blues as (deceptively secular) rituals, worship, prophesy, and meditations on theodicy—in short, the eternal return of the same old ingredients in theologies of music. These digressions fail to locate the theological significance of music in the music itself.[169]

Oblivious to New Musicology, he chooses instead to consult Andrew Greeley and other sociologists of religion as well as to Camus's existentialism to understand the blues.[170] While his chapter on theodicy is useful in drawing together the theological undercurrents in diverse blues music and in thematising them articulately enough, in this chapter he resorts again to Jungian theories of the Self to force the blues into an overarching framework of wholeness and integrity.[171] Thus, most ironically, in the name of theological liberation from Eurocentric norms, Spencer still employs variants of Western notions of harmony and order; more specifically, psychic wholeness and integrity become Spencer's ultimate theological values, and music's theological significance lies in its instillment of the same:

> Blues singers' defiant denial of the "heaven" and "kingdom come" abstractions . . . was typically followed by a search to acquire or construct a heaven of their own. . . . To this end, Texas Alexander was wistful in "Yellow Girl Blues." In order to gather a cluster of brown-skinned women around his throne, he decided to get himself a "heaven kingdom" of his own. . . . Henry Thomas, in "Texas Worried Blues," . . . [i]n order to give all "good-time women" a home, . . . decided, like Alexander, that he was going to build himself a heaven of his own.[172]

Even in his later books, Spencer never really constructs a new theological model. When he does make some initial attempt to do so in *The Blues and Evil*, it is always with recourse to merely textual analysis of the music in question, and to canonical (musico-theological) debates, resources, and tropes. While his study of the blues is of value in its summary of both blues lore and of other authors' insights, Spencer's reliance on traditional theological interpretive categories/lenses (even if more Afrocentric than Christian)[173] limits the theological riches which blues music might have offered. In *The Blues and Evil*, Spencer criticises white scholars for reducing the blues to a mere "object of study," when in fact it is "a racial disposition."[174] Yet he himself is reductionistic in locating the significance of blues *music* in its textual messages and in the political iconicity of its performers.[175]

Spencer is also silent about the sexism, that is, the objectification of women, in blues songs and fails to nuance his critique of the commercialisation of black music.[176] Profits empowered black people, especially women, even as white music markets exploited their cultural heritage and creativity.[177] To reinstate the blues as a deeply spiritual, theological, "racial disposition" is not the concern of "theomusicology" as I would define it, nor as the (interdisciplinary) term itself implies. Of all musical genres, it seems odd that the critical nexus of music and sex in blues music is made an aside rather than the primary theological issue. Spencer's lack of interest in gender may explain this inattentiveness, even though the blues' sexy reputation and blues women's notoriety for the same would have made this the likely place to begin one's theological inquiry. Most ironically, given his desire to make blues a sacred medium, when Spencer does celebrate the erotic content of blues music in his conclusion, he still keeps religion and sex, politics and sex quite separate. For, according to Spencer, sex *replaces* religion as a preoccupation of the blues. It also replaces questions of theodicy and social justice. Where sex prevails, blues singers cease to be prophets and priests, becoming instead mere "performers."[178] Furthermore, "cosmology" (here Spencer really means religious worldview) dissolves when sexual thematics dominate the genre.[179]

In short, Spencer's own narrowly *theological* worldview has not allowed him to broaden his own hermeneutical horizons. Reading feminist and queer musicology would force him to make other musico-theological connections, reading blues music even against itself, to portray it less as an underdog that needs defending or vindication and more as a powerful iconoclast that shatters theological models. Spencer's preoccupation with theological apologetic—arguing that blues music is essentially theological, moral, and ethical—distracts him (*pace* Augustine) from the music itself and the circulation of (conflicting) social energies therein. His dichotomising begs more careful consideration of the inherent *ambivalence* of the blues. For example, where whites call it irreligious or profane, Spencer calls the blues profoundly theological (until urbanisation and capitalism drained its prophetic/priestly messages). Surely a "both/and" reading would be more accurate. Then blues could actually be a "synchronous duplicity" (Spencer's coinage) which does not separate sex, religion, and "cosmology" as Spencer unfortunately does; a separatism, moreover, that African holism (which he supposedly endorses) should contravene.[180] Spencer thus perpetuates the false dichotomies that he criticises, because he simply reverses the dualisms in his analysis without playing with the creative tensions, the insoluble contradictions of blues music, portraying them as *both* problem and opportunity for black self-expression.[181]

IX. Greeley, West, and Dyson— Spencer's Kindred Spirits

There are a handful of "theomusicological" connections made between music and sex in Spencer's introduction to his later compilation of various scholars' essays, *Sacred Music of the Secular City*, but the volume remains principally a theological apologetic for those who still read pop, rap, jazz, soul, and blues as purely secular. (Unfortunately, in the introduction, Spencer transmits a very inaccurate reading of Ellen Koskoff's objectives in *Women and Music in Cross-Cultural Perspective*.[182]) Extensive critique of each article in this anthology is not possible here. Fifteen of the twenty articles are text-based defences for the theological value of each genre—blues, pop, rap, and jazz.[183] With the exception of one article, music's bodily effects as a resource for theological reflection are ignored.[184] Contributions from prominent social critic Michael Eric Dyson as well as from theologians Andrew Greeley and Cornel West warrant critical response.

Andrew Greeley situates Madonna's "Like a Prayer" within the tradition of erotic mystical discourse. Both the video and music evoke "(if unintentionally) the sandalwood themes of the Song of Songs."[185] Greeley also acknowledges that "sexual passion may be revelatory" and applauds Madonna's transcendence of Catholic guilt—this by way of her Catholically rooted, "sacramental imagination"—such that she harnesses the latter and unleashes the sacred musical erotic in her video.[186] Unfortunately, however, Greeley focuses on the video not the music, and on the significance of Madonna's undulating body instead of the music's body. The music itself is not clearly designated as the locus of "revelation." (In any discussion of Madonna, moreover, one must at least mention the—for some feminists—problematic ideologies of female subjectivity and womanhood that Madonna glorifies and that render her a dubious icon of liberation, spiritual or otherwise.[187])

Using this same sacramentalist lens to assess Bruce Springsteen's theological value, Greeley reframes him as a liturgist and Meistersinger (again, owing to the singer's Roman Catholic upbringing). Springsteen engages his divinely ordained "dancing self,"[188] his God-given "frolicsome modality of being."[189] Because Springsteen taps into his "preconscious" self wherein "Spirit speaks to our spirit," he inspires "grace, hope, renewal."[190] Such is Greeley's evaluation of "Tunnel of Love." This emphasis on pop psychology and pop religion (i.e., the "preconscious") and on both these pop artists' subconscious retrieval of Catholic sacraments and symbols from their pasts deters us from apprehending the *music's* power as a socialising, engendering force. Though Greeley qualifies that he has "no desire to claim Springsteen as Catholic in the way we used to claim movie actors and sports heroes,"[191] his baptism of secular artists with Catholic sensibilities still seems a superficial articulation of their music's theological value.

Unlike Greeley's sacramentalist celebration of Madonna and Springsteen, Cornel West's "Sex and Suicide" reductionistically vilifies Prince's impact on today's youth. According to West, Prince's music only worsens black teens' downward spiral into sex, drugs, and suicide insofar as Prince contributes nothing to the reality of the "abundant life promised and provided by Jesus Christ."[192] Prince exploits, even heralds, a "dark, *anarchic* future" as prelude to the apocalypse.[193] With this sharp dismissal, West fails to admit the contradiction between Prince's vibrant, envigorating music and his (to West) nihilistic texts. West might reply that Prince's music "sugar-coats ideology." However, in a more "difficult" reading, I suggest that, rather than promoting escapism, Prince's music energises and grounds body and soul, enabling not only survival but also continued struggle against oppression. Genuinely *musical* analyses would constructively attend to such contradictions rather than dismiss or ignore their transgressive potential.[194]

In one of his two articles on rap music, Michael Eric Dyson astutely warns against knee-jerk Christian censorship of the ultraviolent, misogynist rap music of 2 Live Crew, elucidating the political hornet's nest that such racist and reductionistic censorship masks.[195] However, like his more pessimistic colleague Cornel West, Dyson does not consider the polysemous role of the music itself as accomplice *or* rebel to offensive texts. Does it sweeten a revulsive pill or tell a different story from that of the text? The music's multivalent potential is not adequately acknowledged. As for rap's religio-sexual import, Dyson equivocates in his second article; he is disturbed by rap's transmission of "the ornamental and orgiastic elements of sexual fulfilment," not to mention its perpetuation of "machismo,"[196] but such shocking "sexual excess" represents a reactionary extremism that could in fact teach Christians to correct the church's repression of the body and human sexuality.[197] Dyson further recognises rap's vital role in shaping human (here African American) identity.[198] However, he locates this socialising force exclusively in the texts rather than in the *music's* influence upon our bodily behaviours and postures. Acknowledgment that rap's textual nihilism might be duking it out with the music's kinetic recharging of our bodies would strengthen Dyson's countercultural assessment. So, for example, *pace* West and Dyson, women rap-lovers may ingest horrifying texts while the music leaves them physically empowered—revolted by many lyrics even as their bodies groove in oblivion. Are flesh and music thus conscientious objectors to the text, thereby undermining the latter's effects?

I do not wish unequivocally to devalue the theological analyses of these contributors but to call for an alternative to such ceaselessly text-driven readings—a truly interdisciplinary approach that effects imaginative shifts. Rather than expanding our musico-theological vocabularies, the songs discussed above are recontextualised within extant theological frameworks. This is not to reject music's constructive role as a life-giving liberating practice. However, sometimes it evokes other kinetic, rather than logocentric, "dangerous memories" (Metz).

X. "Subordinate But Not Inferior":
Catherine Pickstock's Musical Compromise

As part of the apologetics launched by the Christian radical orthodox movement to counter postmodern deconstructions of religious truths, Catherine Pickstock writes an "appeal" not only for "a restoration of the integrity of the Western (Platonic-Christian) vision of musical theory," but also for the resurrection of the Western (Platonic-Christian) worldview *in toto*—its cosmology, psychology, and political ideals.[199] She reinstates an Augustinian form of music's metaphysical meaning and elaborates its broader cosmic, existential, and ethical directives as a counterresponse to postmodern "nihilistic" worldviews and music philosophies: "I argue that this nihilism [evidenced in postmodern definitions of music], despite its exhaustive claims as to the universality of the flux, is an arbitrary phenomenology; and that the Augustinian tradition can once again become available as a theologico-musical key to ontology, psychology and to the political order. However, for this to become a coherent possibility, it is necessary that music be understood as a metaphysical category."[200]

Pickstock begins with a detailed exposition of Augustine's allegedly more relevant and appropriate musical metaphysics in the *De musica*. Augustine's Christian theological meaning-system enables him to understand music's spatial and temporal evanescence in positive terms; he holds "space and time in balance under transcendence."[201] Music constitutes and offers auditors "echoes of eternity."[202] For human benefit, it also "stabilises" flux, so to speak: "in music we hear the flux only as articulated, and articulations only in flux."[203] In contrast to such balanced integration, all Eastern religious, Enlightenment, and postmodern portraits of musical temporality and harmony are grounded in (and reinforce) erroneous *hierarchies* of space and time. Such hierarchies then feed flawed, nihilistic cosmologies, anthropologies, and ethics. For example, in antitranscendent, postmodern readings of music (cf. Lacoue-LaBarthe), "time and space become separate and are distorted as 'opposites' of one another. . . . It is therefore no accident that the very thing which postmodernism *most* denies is music, for its core belief is that flux and articulation are both necessary to each and yet mutually canceling."[204] Only Augustine's metaphysics of music offers a life-affirming, hopeful, and egalitarian model. Equally *avant la lettre*, Augustine's conception of "recursive judgement (*numeri judiciales*)" in the *De musica* reflects and evokes an open-ended "perspectivalism," worthy of adoption today for it does not result in a debilitating relativism. Thanks to his extensive musical speculations, Augustine "is able to recognize that judgement gives birth to contrasting customary norms which can themselves undergo change, and yet be integrated within an overall sense of rightly judged proportion. For one can have a sense of different customs fitting different times and places."[205] It is thus by decontextualising Augustine—focusing on the 'universal' theological and anthropological conclusions that can be drawn from his *musica speculativa*—that Pickstock can recast Augustine as a holistically minded, democratic thinker.

Music's democratizing, conciliatory powers, moreover, stem from the (to modern minds) unlikeliest of roots: its numerical *ontos*. Pickstock explains how all of Augustine's musico-numerical speculations are not cold, disembodied *mathesis*, but a timely testament to music's literal and symbolic translation of the thoroughgoing relationality that composes divinity and humanity, cosmos and *polis*.

> Any rhythmic proportion is given by Augustine the name of "number." Created reality itself consists, for his adapted Pythagorean view, of nothing but numbers. This is equivalent to saying that it consists in nothing but relations ordered in certain regular and analogical proportions. . . . [T]he entire cosmos itself is not a total 'thing' . . . it is rather an assemblage of all the relations that it encompasses. . . . One might say that the totality of reality is not one big note, but instead, as Augustine says, a poem or song (*carmen*), and so, in other words, the total series of numerical interactions.[206]

Furthermore, Augustine's profound musico-numerical investigations inform his doctrines of creation *ex nihilo* and the incarnation and render these more accurate, calibrated depictions of the natures of the cosmos and (human) being than any other subsequent meaning systems have offered. For example, music's seemingly destructive, fleeting evanescence and impermanence is a microcosm and proof-text for creation *ex nihilo*: "The alternation of sound and silence in music is seen by Augustine as a manifestation of the alternation of the coming into being and the passing into non-being which must characterise a universe created out of nothing." In music's alternation of sound and silence, we can hear "at once the abyss of finitude and a participation in the plenitude of the infinite."[207] This musical *analogia entis* explains other aspects of Christian creation, for example, its anthropological dilemmas, and their resolution by the incarnation. Pickstock (via Augustine) reframes all social and political strife as "marks of our created finitude"—dissonant signs that we are out-of-step, but that Immanuel realigns:

> The ontological dialectic of being and non-being in creation, reflected in music as the alternation of caesura and sounding note, is re-doubled by a salvific dialectic of discordance and concordance, which here constitutes the theme of sacrificial passion. Earlier we saw that for Augustine salvation means that everything is in its own proper time and place, that everything is separated by the appropriate intervals. Now we can add that in a post-fallen world, the proper time and place is always the place of the Cross, or rather the temporal passage through the Cross.[208]

Hence, for Pickstock, the ultimate musical consummation of the "cosmic poem" is nonmusical. It lies in Christ's restoration of "perfect harmonic relation" with the "divine Father."[209] The creation and existence of music, its arithmetical essence, so astutely interpreted by Augustine, intimates and anticipates eternity's well-pro-portioned spatio-temporality, the final cosmic cadence, as it were, to the proleptic harmonic resolutions that have been effected in Christ's passion and resurrection. Pickstock elaborates: "[O]nly God incarnate possesses the correct ordering of soul and body, and this can be mediated to us only by physical means. . . .That which is beyond the world, the ultimate measure, nonetheless *contains* the world. As Christ's perfectly ordered body is inserted into a world of sin, this order is mani-fest as the suffering of Christ's body. This suffering is for us the first mode of access to a perfected music and beauty."[210] This musically inflected doctrine of the pas-sion communicates ethico-political mandates. Within salvation history, the per-fect harmony and proportion of the Christ sets the tone not only for human musicality but also, more importantly, for humanity's spiritual, social, and ethical striving. Recuperated into Christ's perfect harmonic relationality, we are called to "sound our right note in the cosmic poem."[211] Creating social harmony lies in our own christically imitative practice of a radical interdependence: "My recognition of the rhythm of the other . . . is a necessary aspect of my own rhythm, in the same way that cultural expressions have validity only through the enterprise of har-monising one culture with another, one age with another, without obliterating their differences."[212] From Pickstock's perspective, therefore, Augustine's numeri-cal speculations reflect *in nuce* a sense of music's prophetic, analogic connection to the incarnation; music both heralds and reiterates the incarnational mandate that all people must find their proper "sounding" in space and time.

Whatever reintegrative powers Pickstock salvages from a fifth-century meta-physical notion of musical *numerositas* she simultaneously obliterates with her lopsided insistence that the harmony and order which humanity "instinctively" craves lies in global conversion and obedience to Christian tenets—creation *ex nihilo*, the Incarnation, and a triune God: "For against fashionable invocation of the non-Western, the pluralistic and the postmetaphysical, this essay has sought to show . . . exactly why only this Western musical succession foreshadows a possible future political 'equality' or harmony. . . . [T]he traditional view holds in balance time and space under transcendence."[213] Music it would seem is quintessentially Christian; it "compels us to come in":

> It is impossible rationally to resolve the *aporias* of time. Neither a pure flow nor pure present moments make any coherent sense. And yet in music we hear this impossible reconciliation. To believe the evidence of our ears is therefore to deny nihilism. Moreover, it is to believe in transcendence. More it is to believe in the healing of time, and therefore, sacramentally, to receive the incarnation of God in time, his Passion and resurrection. . . . We are spared a denial of hearing har-mony through our acknowledgement of the triune God. Furthermore, our hear-ing of the harmony despite and through undeniable worldly disharmonies can be taken as more than a mere mitigation of noise [Attali] only if we take this har-mony to be the echo of the re-beginning of human music in time by God him-self.[214]

It is ironic that Pickstock champions democracy yet enlists such dangerously supersessionist—today, colonialist—sources and norms to flesh out her musical utopia. Pickstock states that for Augustine and other pious disciples democracy will organically unfold since good music instills an "unconscious regulation of all bodily movements by the soul" so long as the soul (in charge of the body) "actively receives" musical experiences and recognises therein "the memory of divine transcendence."[215] By contrast, for Augustine: "[d]omination [vs. 'genuine persuasion'] of others through music can be achieved only through a distortion of musical harmonies in which psychic ends are manipulated towards false material goals of power for its own sake, knowledge for its own sake, and attainment of desire for its own sake, which is possessiveness. Hence Augustine . . . democratises the notion of musical *ethos*."[216] Aside from her failure to recognise that *all* music manipulates, one must ask *whose* measuring stick will differentiate coercion from persuasion, distortion from attunement. Unless she has tacitly reinstated the tetractys of the decad, Pickstock never explicitly defines the content of specifically musical distortions. Her transposition of this distinction between musical domination and persuasion to true and false material goals begs the question: If communal consensus depends on our tuneful ability to "adequate" God's "perfect measure," which of the "elect" will standardise or receive the tablets of true proportions, rhythms, and intervals?[217] Will veteran Christians "regulate" or fine tune the notes that newer converts sound in the cosmic poem, or will conversion itself instill perfect pitch and metre at Pickstock's Woodstock, each of us marching to our designated (no doubt "judiciously" intuited) drum?[218]

Another inconsistency in Pickstock's ode to "holistic" metaphysics occurs in her interconnection of music and the incarnation. Like an ancient allegorist (and several modern scholars discussed above), Pickstock evacuates music's "deepest" essence and meaning—relocating it elsewhere, namely, in the Eucharist. According to Pickstock, once Augustine has affirmed that Christ incarnates and atones a "perfected music and beauty,"[219] he establishes this corollary: "the highest music in the fallen world, the redemptive music, is initially corporeal [Christ's body] rather than psychic, although it is the *cure* of the soul. It is none other than the repeated sacrifice of Christ himself which is the music of the forever repeated Eucharist."[220] According to this musical ontology, the truest music one can "hear" and participate in is the incarnation: "As Christ's perfectly ordered body is inserted into a world of sin, this order is manifest as the suffering of Christ's body. This suffering is for us *the first mode of access* to a perfected music and beauty."[221] Thus while "good" music's symbolic resonances help sustain humanity by providing foretastes of eternal perfection, such manna is more readily available through faith in the incarnation and regular participation in the Eucharist. "Undistorted" musical creations become the lowly *imago* of harmony incarnate. Using terms and logic reminiscent of Barth's notorious A-is-to-B anthropology, Pickstock suggests that music, like Barth's woman, becomes "subordinate but not inferior."[222] Amplifying the irony of this campaign for Christian democracy against postmodern solipsism, Pickstock, in this final metaphysical flourish, effects her own "deconstructive" variation: she erases music, "deferring" *real* or *true* music to the Eucharist. How holistic is a model that claims to be musically grounded yet ultimately finds a better music outside music's body—a salvation offered once for all through the Logos-made-flesh?

Equally disturbing in Pickstock's musically dis-located Christology is the manner in which her resurrection of overarching, relational, harmonic resolutions denies the "eternal" problem of an irresolvable plurality of conflicting beauties, truths, and moral goods, and the utterly irreparable devastation they inflict in the name of democracy or theocracy. Against the backdrop of Pickstock's eternity, such horrors are mere appearances: "every apparent discord can, in the course of musical time, be granted its concordant place."[223] But such "apparent" agonies are precisely the makings of terminally dissonant human tragedies (Auschwitz and 9/11, to name just two), atrocities that Pickstock rejects as musico-theologically untenable and that her Augustinian model can supposedly "harmonise." *Peu importe* the global terror ravaging Christ's body today, (tonal) music's happy endings—"the evidence of our ears"—will spark, bolster, or restore faith in divine sovereignty. Methodologically, Pickstock's hymn to Christ's perfected music and beauty means that the gored horror of Christ's crucified flesh, the tragic betrayals and misprisions he suffers, and most importantly, the musico-theological insights that these discords might afford, are aestheticised away. Contrast this musical vision with religionist Kathleen Sands's insistence that all any religious meaning system can intone for the twenty-first century is "a limping jig of grace"—a soft-shoe of humble, makeshift strategies that might choreograph "our messy multiform continuance."[224]

There is a more rudimentary blind spot in Pickstock's Augustinian theology of music. She fails to mention the famous passage from the *Confessions* where Augustine's love affair with music is highly conflicted. Chronologically, the *Confessions* is a later work than his *De musica*. It is characterised, moreover, by Eugene TeSelle as "a kind of first *Retractatio*"[225] *and* a work which is profoundly shaped by Augustine's "newly acquired understanding of the bondage of the will."[226] Margaret Miles, by reading the *Confessions* in context, links music to other seductive, troublesome feminine figures, all of whom informed the wider (gendered) politics in his worldview. Even Pickstock's hermeneutic of generosity vis-à-vis Augustine cannot erase the fact that he adopts a philosophical legacy and writes at a time in which music-as-Circe flourished. (Pickstock might counter here that: No, the "agony" of Christ's "perfected music" resolves Augustine's self-acknowledged, auditory lapses.[227] Unfortunately, however, the music tempting him was sacred—Pickstock's supposedly pristine, innocent, non-manipulative "echoes of eternity.")

Finally, part of Pickstock's recuperative agenda is the exoneration of Augustine from the "crude dualisms" that he has been accused of instigating, but which,

according to Pickstock, he preempts through his belief in transcendence: "Augustine's synthesis of the spatial and the temporal, of articulation and flow, produc-
ing the best possible expression of the eternal music, is a distribution of the
spiritual and the real which disallows any crude dualism, for his transcendent context, as we have seen, releases the ultimacy of such contraries by encompassing and
redeeming them."[228] However, the cure is worse than the ailment. For, if we read
Augustine 'holistically' in context, there is arguably no "cruder" dualism than sexism, and, "subordinate but not inferior" classes or clauses aside, Pickstock's 'tran-
scendentalism' strikes the ears as more discordant than harmonious. (All of this
notwithstanding Pickstock's affirmation that the body has the 'noble' task of
reminding the soul of the truer, "plenitude of eternal beauty.")[229] Not surprisingly,
to revalorise Augustine's musical ethos, Pickstock must ignore the legacy of effeminate slurs that its proper maintenance has perpetuated. (Boethius—the more
explicit of the two fathers in his connection of music and effeminacy—is also
"sterilised" in Pickstock's model.[230]) While Augustine may have implied, dissolved,
or ingeniously erased dualistic façades between men and women in his holistic
cosmology, the politics of transcendence that he promotes cannot be ideologically
immunised through decontextualisation. Nor does Augustine's rejection of dom-
ination-as-tyranny preclude other, subtler forms of domination from shaping his
musico-theological schema. This is why feminist readings of androcentric silences
and of gender dichotomies in his texts are essential. Admittedly, with overly post-
Cartesian mindsets, we often misread Augustine, Plato, and Pythagoras and
bypass the holistic, integrative impulses in their ideas. However, correcting
myopic and "crassly dualistic" critiques of Augustine does not make him 'prob-
lem-free.' Sexism *is* crude dualism, one to which the fathers—even the visionary
Augustine—inevitably fell prey, despite the egalitarian seeds that radically orthodox rereadings unearth (or inseminate).

    In this survey of well- and lesser-known scholars' musico-theological reflec-
tions, I have shown that masculinist theologies of music have not recognised, let
alone criticised, the treatment of music as the gendered, en-gendering discourse
which their earlier, *and* clearly influential, antecedents developed. Even in the
twentieth century, and partly because of this hermeneutical blind spot, theologians have not considered the theological riches that an intimate examination of
music's relationship to sex might unearth; it is precisely in music's constant appeal
to our erogenous zones that materials for imaginative theological construction
can be culled. While I too shall adopt organising principles from the tradition in
what follows, I purposely leave behind conventional musico-theological debates
and disrupt the hegemonic conceptual content of those Christian principles that
I retain. It is to this project of reconstruction I now turn.

Notes

1. George Steiner's characterisation of the 'cult' of Heidegger in postmodern discourse. See Steiner, "Inebriate Bewitchment," review of *Heidegger, Philosophy, Nazism* by Julian Young, *Times Literary Supplement*, 4924 (15 Aug. 1997): 11.

2. See *Sacred Imagination: The Arts and Theological Education*, Waits, Yates, and Merrill, eds., special issue, *Theological Education* 31, no. 1 (1994).

3. See Stackhouse, "Ethical Vision and Musical Imagination," and Farley, "Music and Human Existence: A Response," in *Sacred Imagination*, 149-64 and 175-82, respectively.

4. Wilson-Dickson, *History of Christian Music*, 72.

5. Barth, *Wolfgang Amadeus Mozart*, 22.

6. Ibid., 34.

7. Ibid., 33f. I hear in the following passage shades of the metal ("iron zeal") that Plato wanted music to instill in his warrior–citizens, and which the exemplary Mozart and his music embody: "But neither is one truly hearing him if, as happened in the nineteenth century, he is heard as a musician of mere facile gaiety. *Behind his play there is an iron zeal.* How simply the man worked during his short lifetime: during his journeys or in the company of others or simply playing billiards, with melodies singing in his head, shaping, unfolding, and integrating and bringing them out complete in an unceasing flood, as though he were simply writing letters—that was his prodigious achievement" (47; emphasis mine).

8. Updike in Barth, *Wolfgang Amadeus Mozart*, 8.

9. Ibid., 10.

10. See ibid., 7-10.

11. Ibid., 22.

12. Ibid., 34.

13. Ibid., 53.

14. Ibid., 51-52.

15. Ibid., 53. Updike concurs, underlining Barth's point that Mozartean moderation terminates in a very positive "upsetting of the balance . . . in which joy overtakes sorrow without extinguishing it, in which the Yea rings louder than the ever-present Nay" (Updike in Barth, *Wolfgang Amadeus Mozart*, 11 reiterating 55).

16. Barth, *Wolfgang Amadeus Mozart*, 28f. This is Mozart's *fundamentum*, his "center." Barth elucidates this Mozartean quality with reference to Goethe, and the latter's own literary command or "sovereignty": "For the rest, Goethe referred to the 'incomparable genius' of Mozart (unfortunately, we do not know in what sense), he mentioned him in the same breath with Raphael and Shakespeare, and he deemed only Mozart capable of setting his *Faust* to music. I find it hard to compare them, because the Mozartean *center* is not ultimately the same as the Goethean *sovereignty* and because that imbalance between the two opposing aspects of life which is so decidedly characteristic of Mozart— that triumphant turn, i.e. Mozart's *freedom*—does not, if I am correct, have any counterpart in Goethe" (58).

17. Barth expounds: "Mozart is universal. One marvels again and again how everything comes to expression in him: heaven and earth, nature and man, comedy and tragedy, passion in all its forms and the most profound inner peace, the Virgin Mary and the demons, the church mass, the curious solemnity of the Freemasons and the dance hall, ignorant and sophisticated people, cowards and heroes (genuine or bogus), the faithful and the faithless, aristocrats and peasants, Papageno and Sarastro. And he seems to concern himself with each of these in turn not only partially but fully; rain and sunshine fall on all. . . . Can one ever listen enough to what happens in a Mozart orchestra, how the components are introduced, unexpected but always with perfect timing, in their own height or depth and tone color? It is as though in a small segment the whole universe bursts into song because *evidently the man Mozart has apprehended the cosmos and now, functioning only as a medium brings it into song!* Truly, we can call this incomparable (Barth, *Wolfgang Amadeus Mozart*, 34-35; emphasis mine).

18. "The true listener may regard himself as also called to this freedom—to see himself as the person he really is: as the cunning Basilio and the gentle Cherubino, as the hero Don Giovanni and the coward Leporello, as the tender Pamina and the raging Queen of the Night, as the all-forgiving countess and the terrifying, jealous Electra, as the wise Sarastro and the foolish Papageno. They lie hidden in all of us. He may see himself as still living but destined for the grave—as we all are" (Barth, *Wolfgang Amadeus Mozart*, 53-55).

19. Barth, *Wolfgang Amadeus Mozart*, 35.

20. Ibid., 36-37.

21. Barth insists: "There is no substance to the legend of a Mozart of pure grace, a legend so ardently proclaimed by the nineteenth century, which then, not unexpectedly, turned its back on him. But neither is there any substance to the 'demonic Mozart' which our century wishes to substitute" (Barth, *Wolfgang Amadeus Mozart*, 54).

22. Barth, *Wolfgang Amadeus Mozart*,

23. Ibid., 51. Updike gives an exegesis here, and endorses Barth's elevation of "freedom" as Mozart's musico-theological import. To Updike, Mozart is the "ideal man": "It is his consideration of Mozart's freedom that Barth becomes most theological, most instructive, and even most musicological: this ideal man, Mozart, carrying the full baggage of human woe and of temporal convention and restraint, possesses his freedom through a 'triumphant turn' out of 'Nay' into 'Yea.' This turn is construed as more admirable than Goethe's sovereign humanism or Schleiermacher's location of a neutral center whereupon balance can be achieved: '[Now quoting Barth] What occurs in Mozart is rather a glorious upsetting of the balance, a turning in which the light rises and the shadows fall, though without disappearing, in which joy overtakes sorrow without extinguishing it, in which the Yea rings louder than the ever-present Nay.'"

Updike continues: "'Though without disappearing'—thus the theologian acknowledges the inextinguishable problem of evil. He implies a cosmic paradigm in the way in which Mozart sweeps into his magnificent lightness everything problematical, painful, and dark. Mozart's music, for Barth, has the exact texture of God's world, of divine comedy. Hearing it, he is 'transported to the threshold of a world which, in sunlight and storm, by day and by night, is a good and ordered world.' The order is, in Mozart, deeply assimilated and not a kind of exoskeleton, a message, as in Bach" (Updike in Barth, *Wolfgang Amadeus Mozart*, 10-11).

24. One type of Mozartean "objectivity" consists of the following: "Mozart's music is not, in contrast to that of Bach, a message, and not, in contrast to that of Beethoven, a personal confession" (Barth, *Wolfgang Amadeus Mozart*, 37).

25. "Whether in *this* earlier or *that* later stage, he heard the same sounding cosmos with the same ears. And in every instance, he never wished merely to display his technical prowess, but only to place himself at the service of *Frau Musica*, to whom he had dedicated himself from childhood. It is this *sovereign submission* at all stages of his artistic career which may be taken as a distinct feature of what was unique and special in the man" (Barth, *Wolfgang Amadeus Mozart*, 51; second and third italics mine).

Nor does Mozart use music to "reveal himself" for "personal confession" as Beethoven did, or to "reveal doctrine" as Bach did (even though Barth makes Mozart the incarnation of cosmic harmony!) (Barth, *Wolfgang Amadeus Mozart*, 37). Rather, Mozart transparently becomes, as it were, the Way, Truth, and Life; or in Updike's paraphrase, Mozart "embodies the vital, 'living God'" (Updike in Barth, *Wolfgang Amadeus Mozart*, 12).

26. Barth, *Wolfgang Amadeus Mozart*, 46. Here is the rest of the passage: "But he did not revolt against these laws; he did not break them. He sought to be himself and yet achieved his greatness precisely in being himself while observing the conventions which he imposed upon himself. We must be aware of both these elements together. This is the mystery behind which we must seek his special genius if we are to appreciate the superiority with which he moved within his artistic and human surroundings. To this day he seems to us an eagle soaring above the concert hall."

27. Barth offers an example here: "This is so in his famous minor-key compositions; this is so when he composes *opera seria*—even in the sacred works culminating in the Requiem, even in the Freemason melodies, even when he becomes solemn, melancholy, and tragic. But he never becomes truly tragic. He plays and never stops playing, and the listener who does not himself sway and soar, who does not play along with him, is not truly hearing him" (Barth, *Wolfgang Amadeus Mozart*, 47).

28. See Barth, *Wolfgang Amadeus Mozart*, 28-30.

29. Ibid., 16f.

30. This prevails even when Mozart's music accompanies mediocre libretti—"creations of these third- or fifth-rate authors" (ibid., 52).

31. Ibid., 51. Barth continues with the following qualifications: "He certainly consulted closely with the librettists for his operas, but not at all to arrive at some agreed-upon profound meaning! . . . Thus Mozart's *Figaro* has nothing to do with the ideas of the French Revolution, nor *Don Giovanni* with the myth of the Eternal Rake (Kierkegaard notwithstanding!). Nor is there a Mozartean 'philosophy of *Cosi fan tutte*'; and we should not claim to hear much of a religious humanism or of other political mysteries when we listen to *The Magic Flute*. If we judge from his letters, the fact is simply—

whether we like it or not—that he was never directly or specifically affected by nature around him or by the history, literature, philosophy, and politics of his time. With regard to these he had no special conclusions and theories to present and proclaim" (Barth, *Wolfgang Amadeus Mozart*, 51f.).

32. Ibid., 37.

33. Ibid., 47.

34. Küng, *Traces of Transcendence*, 20.

35. Ibid., 12, 16, and 75 n. 34.

36. Ibid., 12.

37. Ibid., 33f.

38. Ibid., 25.

39. See Küng's speculation as to the influence of Roman Catholic catechisms on Mozart's composition in *Traces of Transcendence*, 21-24.

40. Ibid., 24; Mozart writes of this submission in a letter to his father from Paris, 9 July, 1778. See Mozart, *Letters of Mozart and his Family*, ed. and trans. Emily Anderson, 3rd ed. (revised by Sadie and Smart) (New York: Macmillan, 1989), 561.

41. Küng, *Traces of Transcendence*, 14.

42. Ibid., 10.

43. Ibid.

44. Mozart, letter to Johann Friedrich Doles, cantor of the Thomaskirche in Leipzig, 1789 collected in Rochlitz, *Verburter Anekdoten* (n. 18) 494f., in Küng, *Traces of Transcendence*, 25

45. On Küng's agreement with Barth, see ibid., 18-20.

46. On his Catholic amendment, see ibid., 10.

47. Ibid., 29ff.

48. Ibid., emphasis mine.

49. Ibid., 29-35

50. Ibid., 35.

51. Squire, *Church Music*, 86. Surprisingly, given his musical ethic of purity, Squire defends the infiltration of (presumably impure) secular tunes into Ockeghem's sacred vocabulary as testament to the latter's compositional finesse. If anything, Ockeghem's acts of baptism redeemed these "carnalities" from musical perdition—musical Pygmalions: "Mention was made above of the divergence between Ockeghem's secular music and sacred. Because of the opprobrium that is usually heaped upon such practice as indicative of the deterioration of the spiritual feeling of the day, it should again be noted that the secular melodies were mostly used in modified situations and forms. As [musicologist] Lang has pointed out, they would be recognizable in their secular reference only by the most erudite of musical scholars, and such recognition would lead some observers to feel that the melodies had been ennobled by their being judged worthy of a place in which to exalt the spiritual ideal" (ibid.).

52. Squire, *Church Music*, 97.

53. Ibid., 100.

54. Ibid., 102. Squire's musical ethic of purity is further evidenced in his characterisation of medieval Western music as being of a "nobler," that is to say, *non-worldly* style than that of the apostolic age: "In the medieval church there arose an exclusively vocal music which rejected support of instruments of music; it was characterized by a melodic quality that broke with the earlier metrical music of classical prosodic measure; it possessed a distinctive sacred style that in no way resembled secular music. The church avoided *the peril of introducing an alien drama* into the holy rites, exercising instead the nobler power of creating an atmosphere in which there was no worldly custom or worldly association" (ibid., 66; emphasis mine). (It is also worth noting that Palestrina's freedom from the "immediacies" of the local did not prevent him from becoming wealthy by a second marriage to the widow of a fur trader.)

55. Ibid., 108. "It should be remarked that while the romantic tradition had it that Palestrina's music possessed no earthly reference, was spirituality altogether disembodied as it were, the truth is that his works glow with passionate feeling, exultation, sorrow, jubilation, and all the other ranges of emotional color that human beings call upon for their best artistic revelation" (ibid., 103).

56. According to Squire, German sacred music suffered a similar fate in the seventeenth century—a bastardization produced by the excessive mixture of too many different stylistic influences. The end result according to Squire was the eclipse of sacred music's universality by provincialism, its "lofty ideals" by "decadence": "Unfortunately, this development in the music was often marked by an ostentatious concert style which betrayed a decadence into formalism and unseemly provincialism. This artificiality continued as a partial factor in the music of the German church through the seven-

teenth and eighteenth centuries. The *loss of the original spirit* of the German Reformation, evidenced in the great patriotic hymns of faith, was thus threatened when the choirs began to sing buoyant melodies accompanied thinly in the manner of the Italian music" (Squire, *Church Music*, 121). Praetorius, Schütz, and Bach heroically salvaged sacred music's other-worldly essence: "Perhaps it was the work of only a few, like Praetorius, Schütz, and others, who, preserving the most *lofty ideals* made it possible that out of ominous decadence there arose the cantatas and passions of Johann Sebastian Bach" (ibid., emphasis mine).

57. Ibid., 156f. Thus Squire: "A critical observation may be in order at this point. The absence of a liturgy in much of Protestantism (which Protestantism often has been proud to point out) has not always been a blessing. While the deteriorations that have set in from time to time in both Roman Catholicism and Protestantism will not allow for saying that the music of one is superior to that of the other, it is true that the basing of its music in history and tradition (only made possible in a well-regulated liturgy) has enabled the Roman Catholic church to revive the good quality of its musical offering after every siege of decline" (ibid.).

58. Particularly noteworthy in the following passage is Squire's definition of music's overarching telos as a vital catalyst for transcendence and human transformation: "The very nature of declines in Protestantism allows for kinds of religious consciousness that amount almost to religious anarchy. The feeling that music should be an expression of the people who use it is in keeping with the democratic spirit of Protestantism; but often this spirit is allowed to deteriorate into something less than one of *responsibility* [Squire's emphasis]. *Protestantism should train itself away from irresponsibility—and, of course, all should recognize that music is not mere self-expression; music is a transcending force for helping in the influence of the human spirit.* Tawdry, or inconsequential, or bad, music begets a like quality in the whole religious life and expression of the people who produce such music" (ibid., 157; emphasis mine). Note here, as before, that music's ultimate musico-theological significance is located in its effects upon the spirit over against the body (or the "flesh").

59. Van der Leeuw, *Sacred and Profane Beauty*, 253.

60. Ibid., 213.

61. Van der Leeuw explains: "Music is rhythm, melody, and harmony. Of these, rhythm is the most primitive. In primitive culture, melody plays a much less important role, and harmony is usually completely absent. Since rhythm is a constituent of music, but actually belongs to the dance, this means dance is more primitive than music, and that we have already said what is most important about music in our discussion of the dance and of verbal art. Everything that was true of the work song is also true of verbal art. Everything that was true of the work song is also true of music. Rhythm constrains the gods; it can only be strengthened by the effect of melody" (*Sacred and Profane Beauty*, 213).

62. Unfortunately, however, this trope from "The Hymn of Christ" in the apocryphal *Acts of John* is used to exemplify the ultimate form of "mystic contemplation . . . current in Gnostic circles" and the implications of Christ's physical dancing are gradually allegorised away. Thus in his section on "Dance as the Movement of God," van der Leeuw states: "Finally, we must consider briefly the third kind of ordered progress, that of wandering, or pacing. Here the dance has lost its immediate, concrete goal, and in addition, the exuberance of ecstasy is lacking. The dance becomes contemplative and reflects the highest form of movement, the movement of God. The movement of God's love in Christ is apprehended as a dance which Christ performs with his twelve disciples." Van der Leeuw then cites numerous examples of this 'Lord of the Dance': medieval songs, Bernardine mysticism, Gregory of Nazianzus, St. Basil, Dante, Vondel (see *Sacred and Profane Beauty*, 29-32). (And it bears mentioning that, despite the possibility of their ritual dancing, there is strong evidence in Gnostic sources to indicate a general contempt for the body harboured by many if not all Gnostic disciples.)

63. "The dance, as such, is nothing other than ordered movement. The man who invented the dance did not only discover himself, he discovered God. For he stepped into a new dimension of his existence. . . . The man who dances discovers that there is a power which enables him to develop a new essence, so to speak" (van der Leeuw, *Sacred and Profane Beauty*, with reference to Robert Marett, *Faith, Hope, and Charity in Primitive Religion* [Oxford, 1932], 73).

64. "[F]or the Bible, movement is everything; God is movement. . . . The dance is the discovery of movement external to man, but which first gives him his true, actual movement. In the dance shines the recognition of God, himself moving and thereby moving the world" (van der Leeuw, *Sacred and Profane Beauty*, 73f.).

65. Originally the author seemed ambivalent toward the project of musical metaphysics, carefully refuting the "trinity of Schopenhauer-Nietzsche-Wagner" (*Sacred and Profane Beauty*, 248, see 245-48) from whose idealism he nonetheless extracts something of value for his phenomenology:

"Music dramatically raises us above the accidental and lets us differentiate between essence and appearance" (248). Nevertheless, music is not to be "dissolved" into "a universal idea that pretends to be true reality. . . . [F]igures must be created, not only in painting and poetry, but also in music, even if their forms are of a completely different sort than those of the pictorial arts" (249). Despite such insistence upon music's inherent materiality, this series of assertions still leads van der Leeuw to interpret music as pointing beyond itself to a hidden essence, namely the Supernatural, the religious: "The reason that we ultimately discard the attractive theory of Schopenhauer is that we are not concerned with a metaphysics, but with a theology of music. . . . True reality lies for us, not in absence of images, but rather in the image itself, indeed in the image of God. . . . And above all, the path from art to theology, from God's creation to human creation, is to be found in the image of God as completely other reality—not then in the beautiful sound, but in the image where art *represents*, does music have its origin" (254).

66. *Sacred and Profane Beauty*, 259.

67. Ibid.

68. Van der Leeuw begins with Romain Rolland: "Our music is a deception. Our scales, our sound sequences, are an invention. They correspond to not a single sound of reality; compared to real sounds they mean an intellectual compromise, the application of a metrical system to eternal movement" (Rolland, *Jean Christophe: Journey's End* [New York, 1913], in van der Leeuw, *Sacred and Profane Beauty*, 259). Next, to strengthen his case for "truest" music's inaudibility, van der Leeuw transmogrifies the music of the spheres, reinstating this trope as an intimation of the "meta-music" that human being echoes. Here he quotes Camille Mauclair on "meta-music": "Beyond music there is a highest language. . . . [T]hat is the rhythm which proceeds from the universe and of which we are no more than a mere echo. . . . [T]he meta-musical state is silence, for rhythm makes no more sound than the movement through the ether" (Mauclair, *Essais sur l'émotion musicale*, vol. 2: *Religion de la musique* [Paris, 1909], in van der Leeuw, *Sacred and Profane Beauty*, 259f.).

69. Van der Leeuw enlists Herman Rutters here: "*The Art of Fugue* is perhaps the purest manifestation of absolute music, of abstraction. But the sound is already something concrete, and even more so the timbre. . . . But when we bring these timbres into connection with the *Art of Fugue*, do we not thereby drag it down from the height of its abstraction to the lower atmosphere of the concert?" (Rutters, "J. S. Bach's *Die Kunst der Fuge*," *Alg. Weekblad voor Christendom en Cultuur* 7 (1931), no. 25 in van der Leeuw, *Sacred and Profane Beauty*, 260).

70. Van der Leeuw, *Sacred and Profane Beauty*, 260.

71. "Temporarily, we are happy that music is not silent, that it resounds in all its timbres. But we must not forget that the precondition and background for its sounds is the great silence of God. Music comes to us as in a dream" (van der Leeuw, *Sacred and Profane Beauty*, 260).

72. "Holy music is always a hymn, *laudes* in the ancient sense, the praise of God sung before his face. And behold, for here we have arrived imperceptibly in the midst of theology. For the original and only true meaning of the word 'theology' is the same as hymnody, the praise of God. Theology is not a kind of philosophical justification of belief. This occurs there; but *it is essentially eschatological music*" (*Sacred and Profane Beauty*, 261; emphasis mine).

73. Namely, "*Aus Liebe will mein Heiland sterben.*"

74. Van der Leeuw, *Sacred and Profane Beauty*, 233.

75. Ibid., 253. Bach's achievement of "loud *pianissimi*" in the *B Minor Mass*'s "*Incarnatus est*" and "*Crucifixus*" . . . "express[es] what is inexpressible" (237). Bach's compositional use of silence suggests not "inactivity," but "the greatest receptivity and highest activity," not to mention a fulfilling christic kenosis (237f.). This is the case in "the choral recitative in the *Christmas Oratorio*, "*Er ist auf Erden kommen arm*,' where the soprano voice sings the drawn-out notes of the ancient chorale to the delicate accompaniment of the oboe, giving rise to an impression of loneliness, as though representing the kenosis, the self-emptying of Christ. Here we stand in the immediate presence of utter abandonment, which discloses itself in miraculous fashion as richest communion" (237).

76. Thus (quoting Jacques Maritain) van der Leeuw insists: "The most noble and most beautiful [example of harmony in music] is probably found in Mozart. To attain that harmony, one must either remain a child or become a child once more. . . . Here we find the guilelessness, the unselfconsciousness, which Maritain demanded of a holy work of art: 'Mozart's essence is not the man himself, but this gift within him, the charisma of sounds, the angel which dictates the music to him'" (Maritain, *Religion and Culture* [1931], in van der Leeuw, *Sacred and Profane Beauty*, 244).

77. Van der Leeuw, *Sacred and Profane Beauty*, 243.

78. Here are his original objectives: "We shall see ourselves confronted with the question of the

ultimate value of the holy, the beautiful, the good, and the true, independently and in relation to one another. But our analysis is not philosophical or dogmatic. It is phenomenological. . . . Where history asks, 'How did it happen?,' phenomenology asks, 'How do I understand it?'; where philosophy examines truth and reality, phenomenology contents itself with the data without examining them further with respect to their content of truth or reality. We do not intend to pursue causal relationships, but rather to search for comprehensible associations. Further, we do not intend to investigate the truth behind the appearance, but we shall try to understand the phenomena themselves in their simple existence" (*Sacred and Profane Beauty*, 5f.).

79. Van der Leeuw, *Sacred and Profane Beauty*, 328.

80. Ibid., 5.

81. In a closing section entitled "Eschatological Music," he claims: "The highest and best music is that which is more than music; not that which sounds with voice and instruments, but that which our voices and instruments remind us of. . . ."

"In this sense, music is the last thing, that which remains. In the heavenly city which the Revelation of John describes, there is no more image and no temple: 'The final thing is song.' The heavenly song cannot be heard on earth; it is that *canor* of which the mystics speak, the song which sounds first above, then within, the human being. Earthly music can only remind us distantly of this song. The most beautiful music is only an echo of the eternal *Gloria*" (van der Leeuw, *Sacred and Profane Beauty*, 261).

82. Cf. Patricia A. Kazarow, "Text and context in Hildegard of Bingen's *Ordo virtutum*"; Paul Westermeyer (in his category of music's theological ontology), "Reflections on Music and Theology," 185f.; André Kraege (in his discussion of music as *creatura evangelistica*),"Luther: Théologien de la musique," 457f.; Gunter Scholtz (in his discussion of the perennial tensions between music and text in sacred song), *Schleiermachers Musikphilosophie*, 25 n. 21.

83. Söhngen, "Music and Theology," 3.

84. Ibid.,14.

85. Ibid.,6.

86. Ibid.,7.

87. Ibid.,6.

88. Ibid.,10.

89. Here is Söhngen's logic: "Augustine sees in music an excellent means of elevating the soul to God and to its return into God. The sacred words when sung move the mind 'more devoutly and ardently in the flames of piety' (*Confessions*, 10.33). But at the same time Augustine, influenced by Neoplatonic ideas, can combine the *anagogē* to God with Pythagorean number theory. Thus, the caption to the fourteenth chapter of book VI of his *De musica* reads: 'The soul, through the principle of numbers and of order—which it loves in matter—is called to the love of God'" (Söhngen, "Music and Theology," 10).

90. Söhngen, "Music and Theology," 6; emphasis mine.

91. In the former, "the demand is placed on church music 'to add greater efficacy to the text in order that by means of it the faithful may be the more easily moved to devotion,'" and in the latter, "sacred music increases in holiness to the degree that it is intimately linked with liturgical action, winningly expresses prayerfulness . . . and enriches sacred rites with heightened solemnity" (Söhngen, "Music and Theology," 11).

92. For the sake of greater specificity, I have embellished Luther's (and by extension Söhngen's) denomination of music as *creatura* with the adjective *evangelistica*.

93. See also Söhngen, *Theologie der Musik*. The third part of this very comprehensive study is summarised in the article cited above. On the basis of Söhngen's tripartite model, I concluded that music is related to theology because its ontic features and worldly functions inform theology proper (music as science), theological anthropology (music as worship), and soteriology (music as *creatura evangelistica*). I also demonstrated that specific compositional techniques of Olivier Messiaen implicitly translate Oskar Söhngen's tripartite theory into actual musical practice. See my "The Nature of the Relationship of Music and Theology according to Oskar Söhngen and Olivier Messiaen" (master's thesis, McGill University, 1990).

94. Söhngen, "Music and Theology," 15.

95. Ibid.

96. "It would be intriguing to develop the three forms of a theology of music in trinitarian fashion, according to the following areas: 1) music in the realm of creation; 2) the Christ hymn and the *musica crucis*, cultic music is contrasted with religious music; 3) music as work and instrument of the

Holy Spirit, instrumental music and the phases of music as stations on the way to the eschaton. I have pursued this elsewhere" (Söhngen, "Music and Theology," 15; see also Söhngen, *Theologie der Musik*, 262-340).

97. Pelikan, *Bach among the Theologians*, 102-3.

98. These include Robert Lewis Marshall, Denis Arnold, Paul Hindemith, Albert Schweitzer, Friedrich Smend, Philipp Spitta, Christoph Wolff, *The Bach Reader* (ed. Hans T. David and Arthur Mendel), and, most notably, for Pelikan's theological agenda, Martin Petzoldt's anthology *Bach als Ausleger der Bibel*. For his critical survey of Bach scholarship, see Pelikan, *Bach among the Theologians*, chapter 10.

99. Pelikan, ibid., x.

100. See, McClary, "The Blasphemy of Talking Politics during Bach Year."

101. Thus, Pelikan spends four pages comparing Bach's *Passions* to Handel's *Messiah* only to conclude "[t]here is certainly enough also in the Messiah to offend the non-believing listener, not to say the listener for whom the Hebrew Bible is the primary Scripture rather than only the first part of Scripture; nevertheless it is far easier to treat it as a concert piece, whose theological content, while never irrelevant to the interpretation, need not get in the way of the performance. With Bach's Passions the situation is quite different. Both the objective basis of the piece, from the Gospels, and the subjective elements, in the arias and chorales, presuppose and seek to achieve an element of engagement in the audience that is appropriate to the church rather than to the concert hall" (Pelikan, ibid., 78).

102. Throughout the book, for that matter, Pelikan supplies copious details about the genesis of many of Bach's chorale settings and cantatas not to mention borrowings from them, overlap between them, and reworkings thereof. Apparently many of Bach's cantatas and chorale settings reflect his "celebration of the musical heritage of the Reformation" (Pelikan, ibid., 15).

103. Pelikan then gives examples of chorales from each liturgical season, pointing out that the longest season after Trinity Sunday was the most challenging for Bach's creative energies. Thus Pelikan argues that the church year is pivotal to comprehending the magnitude of Bach's musico-theological value. He makes the profound connection that "[w]hat has recently been said of the medieval *Corpus Christi* plays would apply no less to Bach's music: 'The liturgical year is the context in which the church commemorates, day by day, all history'" (Anne Thorn Higgins in Pelikan, 3). Cf. Anne Thorn Higgins, "Time and the English Corpus Christi Drama" (Ph.D. diss., Yale University, 1985) 22. Pelikan also emphasises that Bach would often compose chorales/preludes out of a "preoccupation with time and transiency as this had been sacralised by the four seasons of the Christian year" (Pelikan, ibid., 12).

104. Pelikan attributes these compositional forces to Bach's exposure to Enlightenment thought. He even portrays Bach and Voltaire as "near contemporaries": "Johann Sebastian Bach was a near contemporary of Voltaire, who, to many in his own time and in ours, seems to embody the spirit of the Enlightenment in its assault upon the Church. Voltaire was born, as Francois-Martie Arouet, in 1694, nine years after Bach, and died in 1778, twenty-eight years after Bach. What is more, not only did their lives intersect in time, their careers almost intersected in space as well. For from 1750, the year of Bach's death, to 1753, Voltaire resided at the court of Frederick the Great of Prussia" (Pelikan, ibid., 29).

105. Here Pelikan relies on Ernst Cassirer's *The Philosophy of the Enlightenment*: "Enlightenment 'philosophical thinking tries at the same time to separate itself from, and to hold fast to, mathematics; it seeks to free itself from the authority of mathematics, and yet in so doing not to contest or violate this authority but rather to justify it from a new angle'" (Cassirer, 15, in Pelikan, ibid., 32).

According to Pelikan, Bach shared Frederick the Great's interest in "mathematical analogies . . . as illustrations of the existence of inexorable laws of necessity throughout nature." This description of the significance of mathematical analogies for Frederick and Bach is transferred and cited from a *totally* different context, namely, Harry A. Wolfson's discussion of the different "attitude of mind" between Spinoza and Descartes (Wolfson, *The Philosophy of Spinoza: Unfolding the Latent Processes of His Reasoning*, 2 vols. [Cambridge, Harvard University Press, 1962] 1:53, in Pelikan, ibid., 31f.).

106. So for example, in contrast to Johann August Ernesti's positivist approach to Scripture, Bach's musical treatment thereof reflected a continued belief in Scripture's revelatory potential. Furthermore, accounts of Bach composing upon his death bed "And now I Step before thy Throne" lead Pelikan to conclude, that in Bach's artful blend of enlightenment and mysticism, music is offered to its *fons et origo*—the ever-inscrutable God of created order and reason: "For after having stood before the most enlightened throne of the *Aufklärung* at Potsdam three years before and having demonstrated to the king there both his brilliant rationality and his virtuosity, he now stood before another Throne

and another King, who dwelt indeed in rationality but even more in mystery. And in the words of one of Bach's young theological protegés, 'All that the advocates of materialism could bring forward must collapse before this one example'" (Pelikan, ibid., 41).

107. Pelikan, ibid., 26. This evangelism, remarks Pelikan, is not only "material" but also "formal" (27). Bach had to navigate "both the musical limitations and the musical opportunities coming out of Luther's reformation." This feat "represents his heritage to later generations" (28).

108. The issue of music and pedagogy arises because Pelikan devotes the rest of this chapter to Bach's debate with Ernesti (Pelikan, ibid., 31-34). Their impasse, according to Pelikan, is symptomatic of the frustrating spirit of Enlightenment "pragmatism and utilitarianism" under which devoted church musicians like Bach were forced to work (34). For Ernesti, music's primary purpose should be pedagogical.

Ernesti discouraged equal time traditionally given to music and theology in the Thomasschule "on the principle that it was the purpose of the curriculum to combine music and theology in promoting piety and building character" (37) Quoting J.F. Kohler's first-hand account of this 'duel,' Pelikan writes: "'Bach began to hate those students who devoted themselves completely to the *humaniora* and treated music as a secondary matter"; on the other hand, Ernesti for his part "became a foe of music. When he came upon a student practicing on an instrument, he would exclaim: 'What? You want to be a beer-fiddler, too?'" (Kohler, *Historia Scholarum Lipsiensium*, in Pelikan, ibid., 37).

109. Even when he uses complex structures in his *Jesu meine Freude,* for example, they do not eclipse the work's "theological cantus firmus," namely, "the centrality of Jesus Christ as the beginning and the end of faith" (Pelikan, ibid., 26). This is also most evident in Bach's oppositional juxtaposition of a majestic bass aria's song of praise, and a tender children's carol: "In that contrast between his settings of the "*Grosser Herr und starker König*" of the bass aria and of the "*Herzliebes Jesulein*" of the chorale, Bach was affirming the totally objective and yet utterly subjective character of the faith in the Word-made-flesh, and thus making his own Luther's christocentric existentialism" (26). Bach's continual use of Luther is not the only evidence of his deep assimilation of Reformation theology. Bach himself becomes—to use a cliché which Pelikan alludes to in his dedication—the fifth evangelist (ibid.). This evangelism, remarks Pelikan, is not only "material," but also "formal" (27). Bach had to navigate "both the musical limitations and the musical opportunities coming out of Luther's reformation." This feat "represents his heritage to later generations" (28).

110. "Recognition of human excellence in its highest form, knowledge of the path that leads to it, the necessary done with dutifulness and driven to that point of perfection where it outgrows all necessity—this knowledge is the most precious inheritance given us with Bach's music" (Hindemith in Pelikan, ibid., 28).

111. Two other passages reflect the goal of transcendence through submission as a primary musico-theological value and norm: "Artists have had to limit themselves because they were finite and because the matters they described were finite too. But Christian artists have felt able to claim that they were not dealing only with the finite and the temporal. Like Bach, they have stood before earthly kings; but Bach's last composition, '*Vor deinen Thron tret' ich hiermit* (And now I step before thy throne)' (BMV 668), has become a mythic symbol of how they have also stepped before the eternal throne itself. A Christian artist like Bach was therefore *a citizen of the Eternal City*, praising a God who was almighty and everlasting. *Thus it would seem that he of all artists could be liberated from this finiteness which so easily besets us and be free to soar, unfettered and unbounded, in the timeless and spaceless realms of the absolute*" (Pelikan, ibid., 122; emphasis mine).

Of even more concern, in the following section, Pelikan seems dangerously close to attributing to Christian art privileged access to the divine, and supercessional communication thereof (somewhat like Squire): "In a sense, it is true that Christian art has been an expression of boundless freedom, for it has been the worship of the eternal God, not of idols. Thus Christian artists have succeeded in creating beauties that seemed to be not of this mortal realm. The antiphons in Bach's setting of the '*Sanctus*' for the *Mass in B Minor* have seemed to many hearers not only to fill the earth and the heavens with the glory of God, as the words '*Pleni sunt coeli et terra gloria ejus*' declare *but to go beyond their periphery into the very presence of the Almighty.* Bach's artistry in the Mass has indeed bespoken a boundless freedom" (Pelikan, ibid., 122; emphasis mine).

Pelikan never explains how music enters "the presence of the Almighty." Like Barth before him discussing Mozart, Pelikan adds the qualification that this grand musical feat requires great humility, and the, I daresay manly, negotiation of freedom and form: "But it has done so by voluntarily binding itself to form. The God whom the *Mass in B Minor* adored was not some Timeless One who lived in endless self-contemplation as the unmoved Prime Mover, but the Holy One who was available within this bounded existence through the boundedness of the historical figure of Jesus Christ. Like all authentically Christian art, Bach's Mass concerned itself with the absolute and the Eternal as this had been revealed in Christ" (122). Here again, Pelikan chooses to emphasise, yea require, (Christian) art to meditate upon, and testify to timeless absolutes.

112. Pelikan further locates the theological richness of Bach's music in his achievement of a (for the listener) consolidating "thematic unity," this via Bach's interspersion of well-known chorales from the liturgical year in the Passions as commentary on the Passion narrative, a compositional choice which simultaneously educates the congregation, while testing their powers of reconnaissance in an enjoyable way: "the chorales of the Bach Passions become a leitmotiv that cuts horizontally across Bach's sacred music and gives it a special sort of thematic unity" (Pelikan, ibid., 79). Later he argues: "Far from being a 'liturgical monstrosity,' therefore, Bach's *Mass in B Minor* is a liturgical, theological, and aesthetic celebration of the Evangelical Catholicity that marked his entire lifework. More perhaps than any other of his sacred compositions, it brought together the disparate elements of his thought and work and united them in a sublime unity" (127). And lest we forget, only solid roots in tradition can afford such a priceless theological attribute: "In addition to bringing out contrasts and implicit connections in the text of the Mass, Bach also illuminated the text by bringing out its full scope and meaning as affirmed by the Catholic tradition. This function of the music comes into evidence in the *"Benedictus"* and the *"Agnus Dei,"* which Bach managed to relate to his whole conception of the Mass" (ibid.).

113. Trinitarian orthodoxy seems central to Bach's musical composition as evidenced in the B minor *Credo,* his setting of catechism hymn preludes in the *Klavierübung,* and his setting of Luther's Creed (*Wir glauben*). Bach is also orthodox in his musical endorsements of praying to both Christ and the Spirit in certain chorale texts (see Pelikan, ibid., 47-50). Other chorale texts used indicate an ortho- dox insistence upon *sola fide/sola scriptura.* Bach's interaction with Erdmann Neumeister sealed this alliance with confessional orthodoxy (see Pelikan, ibid., ch. 4). Nevertheless, one cannot ignore the "evangelical catholicity" which Bach's writing of both the *Magnificat* and the *Mass in B Minor* reflects (55). To make Bach's "true catholicity" even more evident, namely that Bach straddles both Protes- tant and Catholic camps, Pelikan quotes lines from Bach's chorale, and extensively from Joseph Sit- tler's reading of Bach: "Putting Bach into contrast with the present, which he calls 'a time whose Christian inheritance is so pale that it can play both Parsifal and the St. Matthew Passion on Good Fri- day and perceive no opposition in content,' Sittler ascribes to Bach 'not an amorphous spirituality without intelligible content or historic roots, but a very definite faith that was as vital and palpable for him as the stones of the Church of St. Thomas in Leipzig.' He therefore feels able to declare: 'I have yet to find in Bach's confessions, either by word or by the implications of his life or in the content of his music, any concern for religion save as that work meant to him the common faith of his people and church and time. The good city of the consummation toward which his soul pressed was not Parnas- sus but Jerusalem; the songs which drew from him the wondrously sweet and devout arias of the can- tatas were not the songs of Pan but the songs of Zion; the spirit whose might he invoked in his labors was not the Goethean spirit of the Cosmos but the *Heiliger Geist* of his stout faith; the river at whose waters he 'sings the song of Zion in a strange land' is not the mythological Lethe but historical Baby- lon'" (60).

Nor does his orthodoxy preclude the influence of Pietism upon his music. "All the attempts by Orthodox Lutheran confessionalists, in his time or in ours, to lay claim to Bach as a member of their theological party will shatter on the texts of the cantatas and the Passions, many (though by no means all) of which are permeated by the spirit of Pietism. Above all, the recitatives and arias for individual voices (which he seems to have been willing to use), ring all the changes and sound all the themes of eighteenth-century Pietism: all the intense subjectivity, the moral earnestness, and the rococo metaphors of Pietist homiletics, devotion, and verse" (57).

114. See Pelikan, ibid., chapter 9, "Aesthetics and Evangelical Catholicity in the *B Minor* Mass," 116-27.

115. "That Anselmic doctrine of redemption as satisfaction rendered through the blood of Christ is a crimson thread that runs through Bach's [*St. Matthew*] Passion" (Pelikan, ibid., 95). Pelikan elab- orates: "Read as a dogmatic treatise, the *St. Matthew Passion* is a defense, against the theories of Reimarus, of the orthodox interpretation of the death of Christ as a voluntary act of satisfaction ren- dered by Jesus Christ to the justice of God. Whatever some of the avant-garde theologians of Bach's time may have begun to suppose about 'the intention of Jesus and of his disciples,' Bach seems to have been quite content, in *The Passion of our Lord according to Saint Matthew,* to work within the schema first systematized by Anselm. . . . Bach's *Saint Matthew Passion* rescued 'satisfaction' from itself by

restoring it to a context in which it could give voice to central and fundamental affirmations of the Christian gospel" (100f.). Despite the interpretive shift which eighteenth-century Enlightenment Rationalism introduced (reflected in Reimarus's work), Bach preserved Anselm's doctrine of atonement *but* (and here is the important nuance for Pelikan) in "devotional" terms akin to Anselm's *Meditation on Human Redemption* rather than in the "rational-apologetic" terms of *Cur deus homo* (100).

Conversely, (ever the exemplum of compositional moderation) in the *St. John Passion*, Bach 'sings' of *Christus victor*. While Bach's *St. Matthew Passion* constitutes "the most powerful musical vindication ever composed of that medieval [atonement] theory, . . . Bach's *St. John Passion* is the vindication, no less powerful, and moving, of another theory, the theory of 'Christus Victor', for which Bach had to reach over Protestant Orthodoxy to Luther, and over the Middle Ages to the Greek church fathers of the early Christian centuries" (106). Chapter 8 explores this second christological theory.

Pelikan finds evidence of the atonement as thematic in Bach's other works too: "It has become customary for theologians to contrast the idea of atonement as satisfaction à la Anselm and the idea of atonement as victory à la Luther and the Greek fathers, usually at the expense of the former. By solemnizing the former in his *Saint Matthew Passion* and celebrating the latter in his *Saint John Passion*, Bach demonstrated once again his refusal to choose from among alternatives that had equally legitimate authority in his tradition. Indeed, he even brought the two images of atonement together in, of all places, his *Christmas Oratorio* (BMV 248). For as has been mentioned earlier, he closes the sixth cantata of that work with the musical theme that runs through the *Saint Matthew Passion*, the Lenten chorale, '*O Haupt voll Blut und Wunden*,' but in the key of D major and with trumpets. But the words under which he puts this *Saint Matthew Passion* chorale are '*Christus Victor*' words, more appropriate to the *Saint John Passion* than to the *Saint Matthew Passion*—and (so, at any rate, it would seem to modern sensibility) more appropriate to the *Saint John Passion* than to the *Christmas Oratorio*" (115).

116. Pelikan reads, for example, Bach's *Et in unum dominum* from Bach's *Mass in B Minor* through traditional symbolic/dogmatic lenses: "The canonic duet of soprano and alto in Bach's Mass, '*Et in unum Dominum*,' has indeed been interpreted as *a musical representation of the orthodox dogma of the Council of Nicea* that the Father and the Son were distinct and yet equal. That makes it all the more striking that Bach should follow it with one of his best 'step-motifs' in the '*Et incarnatus est*,' with the descent of the infinite into the finiteness of the flesh. *Nor was this combination of the boundless freedom of the Eternal with the boundedness of the Incarnate confined to the Mass in B Minor. It runs, for example, throughout the Christmas Oratorio*" (ibid., 122; emphasis mine).

Pelikan also emphasises the Mass's essentially doxological tone and function, concluding that for Bach "the highest activity of the human spirit was the praise of God, but that such praise involved the total activity of the spirit" (ibid.). From this conclusion, he formulates a corollary which is strikingly similar to Barth's fascination with the freedom which comes from submission and obedience: "As the praise of the eternal God, therefore, Christian art was an expression of boundless freedom; but as the praise of the God who had limited himself in the incarnation, it bound itself to form. The conception of art as freedom and release from the bonds of finiteness was an ancient one, found in certain Greek views of the artist as one set apart from the ordinary limitations of human life" (121).

117. Pelikan's discussion of Bach's *B Minor Mass* in chapter 9 further transmits the tradition of locating its theological significance in its "synthesis" of Protestantism and Catholicism. In fact, part of the *B Minor's* value becomes no less than the very maintenance of "the continuity of the church itself" (ibid., 120).

118. Here are the terms with which he introduces and frames the standard debate: " In each of the preceding nine chapters, the place of Johann Sebastian Bach in the musical and theological context of the first half of the eighteenth century has emerged from a comparison and contrast between him and one of his contemporaries—Antonio Vivaldi, August Hermann Francke, George Frederic Handel, Hermann Samuel Reimarus, Samuel Wesenfeld, Franz Josef Haydn. But for this final contrast and comparison of Bach with his own time, the most striking contemporary contrast is with none of these, but with himself. For the issue that any interpretation of Bach's music or of Bach's personality must confront is what Leo Schrade has called 'the conflict between the sacred and the secular' in him and in his work. . . . Was he a 'staunch Lutheran' of parsonage legend. . . . Or would it be more accurate to demythologize this legend and to see in him a secular modern man who did what he had to do . . . but for whom the music was the thing and the text was incidental? Which trilogy explains which: the *Brandenburg Concertos*, *The Art of the Fugue*, and the *Well-Tempered Clavier*—or the *Saint Matthew Passion*, the *Saint John Passion*, and the *B Minor Mass*?"

"As such questions make all too obvious, it is easy to caricature both sides in the dispute and, in the process, to trivialize the dispute, indeed, to trivialize Bach himself. Yet a dispute there is" (Pelikan, ibid., 130-31).

119. Pelikan raises a possible objection to his own discussion of Bach: like other scholars, he has misconstrued Bach as essentially religious despite the latter's vast secular output (ibid., 133). In response to this charge, Pelikan rejects descriptions of Bach as either "staunchly Lutheran" or "radically secular" by raising the intentionality fallacy from which such categorisations arise (133-32). Here, Pot calls Kettle black, given that Pelikan has been reading Bach's mind and his intentions throughout his book (cf. esp. his reading of the *B Minor Mass*).

120. "The Bach of the Peasant cantata, the partitas, and the concertos was not 'too secular.' These were rather, the expression of a unitary (if to modern eyes sometimes inconsistent or even self-contradictory) world view, in which all beauty, including 'secular' beauty, was sacred because was one, both Creator and Redeemer" (Pelikan, ibid., 139).

121. Pelikan, ibid., 140. He quotes Denis Arnold whose ultimate conclusion Pelikan thinks an important way to understand Bach: "Bach may have been a mystic, an ecstatic—but that view may shed more light on [Albert] Schweitzer's mentality than his subject's. He may have been a convinced Lutheran who sought his salvation in writing music and persuading others to virtue. He may be considered the last of the medieval craftsmen in music, the product of a Germany which missed the Renaisssance" (Arnold in Pelikan, ibid., 140). All such "essentialist" speculation about Bach's spirit aside, we would do best to remember, prompts Pelikan, that Bach was quite simply "a thoroughly professional musician, doing his job day in, day out" (ibid.). This commitment, and the last theological word (seemingly for Pelikan the most important) which spawned it, lies in the simple fact that: "Bach began his compositions by writing '*Jesu Juva*' and closed them by writing '*Soli Deo Gloria*.' Throughout all his composing," states Pelikan, Bach's "craftsmanship," and the guiding force of his credo: '*Soli Deo Gloria*' ensured the authenticity, sincerity, and holiness of his entire oeuvre" (ibid.). In my view, this hortatory *adieu* hardly represents the theological meat that careful attention to Bach's music might offer.

122. Cf. Pelikan, ibid., 46-49 and 123-25.

123. Cf. Suzanne Cusick, "On A Lesbian Relationship with Music."

124. Cf. Begbie, "Theology and the Arts: Music," 686-89. Begbie explores these themes of improvisation and time with impressive range and clarity in his later work, *Theology, Music and Time* (Cambridge: Cambridge University Press, 2000).

125. Begbie, "Theology and the Arts: Music," 686.

126. Another terminological oddity: Begbie (via Jacques Attali) wants to theologise *through* music rather than about it, believing that "through it new features of theological truth are apprehended and familiar features apprehended in fresh ways" (Begbie, ibid., 687). (To Begbie, Attali makes music "a way of perceiving the world" rather than a mere "object of study"; cf. Attali, *Noise*, 4.) The distinction seems semantic, since to talk *about* music's theological significance is to identify its contribution to theological discovery, and therefore to theologise *through* it.

127. Begbie, ibid., 688f.

128. Here Begbie cites Zuckerkandl, *Sound and Symbol*.

129. Begbie, ibid., 692.

130. Begbie explains: "In Christ's life, death and resurrection, creation's past, present, and future are re-integrated, made to co-inhere. In the risen and ascended Christ, there is a kind of newness which neither negates time nor grows old" (ibid., 692).

131. Begbie, ibid., 692.

132. Ibid.

133. "The past of a musical occurrence does not retreat into an ever-receding 'beyond,' but is carried by its constant future orientation, borne along by its waves of tension and resolution. Musical events do not fall backwards into vacuity: They are new in the sense of being *always new*. . . . As musical occurrences anticipate their future they carry their past; as their future is *un*folded, their past—and ours—is *en*folded. This is the dynamic into which we are invited and caught up by music" (Begbie, ibid., 692).

134. Ibid.

135. Music's temporal structure operates chiefly through a hierarchy of metrical waves of tension and resolution. . . . However strong the sense of resolution may be at any particular level, *there will always be a higher level (or levels) in relation to which every resolution process generates a heightening of tension, giving rise to a stronger reaching out for further resolution.* The correspondences between

this and the character of Jewish and Christian hope are remarkable and hardly need to be pointed out (Begbie, ibid., 692; emphasis mine).

136. Begbie, ibid., 692f.

137. Ibid., 690. Here is Begbie's reading of Barth: "Mozart appears in the midst of a discussion of the 'shadowside (*Schattenseite*)' or negative aspect of the universe. . . . Mozart's music appears as articulating the praise of creation in all its aspects: It sings the praise of the cosmos in its 'total goodness,' *including its shadowside.* Mozart's music contains its 'No' but this is the 'No' of the shadowside, not evil. . . . In Mozart's music, therefore, creation praises God in its very finitude and thus shows what authentic praise truly is. This is what gives Mozart's music its 'freedom,' its light and effortless quality. It is the freedom of creation, liberated to praise God, in and through its God-given temporal limitations."

138. Here Begbie rightly emphasises music as process, and for him, music refines and sustains our ability to wait: "[M]usic invites us to discover a kind of patience which enlarges and deepens us in the very waiting. . . . In effect, music says to us: 'There are things you will learn only by passing through this process, by being caught up in this series of relations and transformations'" (Begbie, "Theology and the Arts: Music," 691, quoting Rowan Williams, *Open to Judgement: Sermons and Addresses*, 247).

139. Here is Begbie's apologetic: Music "is the art-form most prone to the supposed destructive effects of time. *And yet*, music can also be ordered, glorious, and enhancing, the very opposite of futile. Music can 'sound forth' the theological truth that limited duration can be beneficial" (Begbie, ibid., 690).

"Our interaction with time need not be characterized by struggle, competition, intrusion, or invasion, nor by retreat, evasion, or escape. Music, in this context, has inestimable potential in demonstrating that these two broad routes do not exhaust the possibilities: Music can provide a concrete means of establishing a more contented 'living peaceably with time' than our contemporary existence seems to offer" (Begbie, ibid., 691).

140. Admittedly, atonality has its own highly mathematical, excessively intellectualist, and, therefore, masculinist proclivities, but I still maintain that Begbie's presupposition of a purely tonal framework of tension and resolution weakens the relevance of his theology of music for a postmodern context.

141. For examples of such theologies, see, for example, Darrell J. Fasching, *Narrative Theology after Auschwitz: From Alienation to Ethics* (Minneapolis: Fortress Press, 1992); Clark M. Williamson, *A Guest in the House of Israel: Post-Holocaust Church Theology* (Louisville: Westminster John Knox, 1993), and Sands, *Escape from Paradise.*

142. Begbie, ibid., 694. This is a phrase that Begbie borrows from a poem by Peter Riley "as [c]ited in [Roger] Dean, *Creative Improvisation* (Milton Keynes, 1989), p. xvi" (Begbie, ibid., 698 n. 39).

143. Begbie, ibid., 695.

144. Riley, in Begbie, ibid., 694f.

145. Begbie, ibid., quoting E. Prévost, 694.

146. Begbie, ibid., 693.

147. Here is the doctrinal/musical exposition in full: "Pentecost was a divine 'exploration of occasion' if ever there was one. Furthermore, this particularizing activity is a function of the Spirit's eschatological ministry to anticipate here and now in ever fresh ways the Father's final, eschatological desire (2 Corinthians 1:22; Ephesians 1:14; Romans 8:23): The particularizing engenders hope. Life in the Spirit, therefore, involves a combination of faithfulness and particularizing what is received in the present in anticipation of the future. This is the dynamic of musical improvisation" (Begbie, ibid., 695).

148. "Insofar as improvisation is a thought process, it is not so much imposing a grid of pure thought on acoustic phenomena, it is rather . . . thinking *in* physical sound—notes, melodies, harmonies, meters. You indwell these physical realities, and establish them as you rearrange them. . . . Related to this, embodiedness is especially crucial to improvisation, for the embeddedness of music in the physical world is mediated through our own physicality" (cf. Begbie, ibid., 695f.).

149. Begbie, ibid., 696.

150. "The fact that the improviser's freedom is discovered in what we have called a 'courteous interaction' might well provide models of divine freedom and creativity which do greater justice than some to the materiality of God's presence to the world in Jesus Christ, in and through whom creation's integrity is neither over-ridden nor ignored but established and renewed" (Begbie, ibid., 696).

151. Cf. McClary, "Introduction," in *Feminine Endings.*

152. Begbie, ibid., 696.

153. Spencer, *Theological Musicology,* 6.

154. Ibid., 109-11.

155. Here is Spencer's opening summary of his interdisciplinary method: "What I intend to illustrate in Part Two (chapters 4 through 10) is that theomusicology can, and at its best does, involve dialogue with different disciplines—folklore, literary criticism, sociolinguistics, biblical exegesis and so forth—as well as a gamut of historical epochs and movements—slavery, abolitionism, the Reconstruction, the Great Migration, the Social Gospel, American Communism, the Civil Rights Movement, American Pragmatism, popular culture, postmodernism, and so forth. In this dialogue I seek to determine what each of these areas of interest and discipline can say to theomusicology and what theomusicology can say to them as each lifted voice vollies for authority in an effort to impact the world. To find out, I place theomusicology directly in the midst of thirty-five textual discourses centered around these other disciplines and historical epochs and movements" (Spencer, *Theological Musicology,* xii).

156. Here is his definition of this new approach in full: "*Theomusicology*—musicology as a theologically informed discipline—is a musicological method for theologizing about the sacred, the secular, and the profane, principally incorporating thought and method borrowed from anthropology, sociology, psychology, and philosophy.

"What distinguishes the method of theomusicology from pure social science investigation is that its analysis stands on the presupposition that the religious symbols, myths, and canon of the culture being studied are the theomusicologist's authoritative/normative sources. For instance, while the Western music therapist would interpret the healing of the biblical patriarch Saul under the assuagement of David's lyre as a psychophysiological phenomenon, the theomusicologist would *first* take into account the religious belief of the culture for whom they even had meaning" (Spencer, *Theological Musicology,* 3).

157. Spencer, *Theological Musicology,* xi.

158. Ibid.

159. For example, the following project has already been addressed *ad nauseum*—the religious content of seemingly irreligious music—and hardly requires the creation of a new discipline: "Referring to a blues song or a rap as a *hymn* (which is, after all, the root of the word "hymnody") seems quite contradictory to the very nature of blues and rap as musics of radical oppugnancy toward the hypocrisy and slavocracy of institutionalized religion and the ruling culture. This is why the thought and method of a new discipline—theomusicology—are needed: Theomusicology is able to recognize aspects of sacrality in the sphere and the music of the secular" (Spencer, *Theological Musicology,* 12).

160. Note again in the following passage how musicology is glaringly absent from his "scientific," interdisciplinary framework: "Jean Jacques Rousseau's method of considering the sacred canon of nature (or natural law) in conjunction with the social sciences is the general concept on which this method is based. Rousseau, of course, considered human response to music to be the consequence of physiological and moral (rather than theological) stimuli. . . . The theomusicological method is therefore one that allows for scientific analysis, but primarily within the limits of what is normative in the ethics, religion, or mythology of the community of believers being studied" (Spencer, *Theological Musicology,* 3ff.).

161. See Spencer, *Theological Musicology,* 114-15 as well as another honorable mention of African holism on p. 148. See also p. xxvi in the introduction to Spencer's *The Blues and Evil.*

162. Earl E. Thorpe, "Slave Religion, Spirituals, and C.G. Jung," and "African Americans and the Sacred: Spirituals, Slave Religion and Symbolism," unpublished conference papers; cf. Spencer, *Theological Musicology,* 163 n. 3 and n. 4.

163. Spencer, *Theological Musicology,* 9.

164. Ibid., 93.

165. Consider the following superficial point of contact Spencer makes between music, race, and gender politics via literature. Quoting Helen Taylor, "'I would suggest that the southern Local Color Movements in which a number of prolific and critically acclaimed women writers were prominent, must also be seen as a political enterprise codifying and to some extent moulding the values of its time, especially in relation to issues of gender, race, and region in the postbellum South'" (Taylor, *Gender, Race, and Region in the Writings of Grace King, Ruth McEnery Stuart, and Kate Chopin* [Baton Rouge: Louisiana State University Press, 1989], in *Theological Musicology,* 93). Spencer then supposedly makes this vague connection explicit: in his own study of gender and race in Southern black literature, Spencer concludes (note his simplistic terminological conflation of "gender" and "feminism"): Helen

Taylor's study of Grace King, Ruth McEnery Stuart, and Kate Chopin gives "special attention to the interrelationship between gender (feminism), race (racism), and region (regionalism). Theomusicology shares her intention and is interested in her findings. The fictional regionalism these women wove with words created a mythic world of white nostalgia that impinged upon black reality, creating the trappings out of which early blues emerged" (Spencer, *Theological Musicology*).

Spencer continues: "Stuart for instance, repeatedly characterized black men as not only economically powerless but dependent, frequently ill or dying, and thus as feminized and on a par with weak white women (102). This, according to Spencer, corroborates Taylor's thesis that "[t]he construction of a postbellum national culture . . . required a mythos of blacks who—though emancipated—were controlled, tamed, and feminized" (101). Along with these rather indirect connections between gender and racism that Spencer finds relevant to theomusicology, the "symbiotic relationship" that black women's fiction shares "with musical minstrelsy—both of which impinged upon black (religious) reality" will somehow (tangentially) contribute to theomusicologists' "quest to comprehend ultimate reality through the study of music" (93).

166. "Citing biblical evidence, Felder declares that the Household of God has the familial obligation of obliterating the patriarchal tradition that excludes women from church leadership positions. This is especially true of the black church, he says, for black women face the odds of racist white feminism, and male chauvinism" (Spencer, *Theological Musicology*, 137). See Cain Hope Felder, *Troubling Biblical Waters: Race, Class, and Family* (Maryknoll, NY: Orbis Books, 1988).

167. "Theomusicology can never simply be scholarship for its own sake. As a partner in the task of theological critique, the theomusicologist always must maintain the indispensable element of priestliness, which I have termed 'theomusicotherapy' in chapter 3" (Spencer, *Theological Musicology*, 60-61).

168. Here is the connection between music and sex that Spencer makes: "Akin to the effect of archetypal jazz on Sartre's Roquentin, the effect of archetypal blues on Ellison's Trueblood is one of redemption rather than devastation. This is especially provocative considering that jazz and blues (particularly during the time of Sartre and Ellison wrote these novels) had been accused of every possible kind of ribaldry, from inflaming eros to diverting spiritual progress. It may seem paradoxical that Tolstoy's Pazdnyshev, an educated Russian aristocrat, comments similarly about Beethoven's 'Kreutzer Sonata'—that it is demonic because it is, in Knapp's words, 'a metaphor for lovemaking, with its ultimate culmination in the orgasm' (71). However, archetypal music, the music of the collective unconscious, is no respecter of conscious musical forms and public opinion. . . . Hence, claiming that archetypal music has numinosity and is sacred, and in intimating that it emanates from God, Knapp's book has penetrating implications (Knapp, *Music Archetype, and the Writer* [University Park: Pennsylvania State University Press, 1988] 4, 57)" (Spencer, *Theological Musicology*, 108).

169. Spencer neglects the music precisely because he becomes caught up again in traditional debates—is blues music sacred or secular, is blues the devil's music or a commentary upon God and evil? To read the blues in a "new way," Spencer applies old tropes—Adam as tragic hero, the Prodigal Son, the Trickster, blues as devil's music (Spencer, *The Blues and Evil*, 16). (Spencer even uses a very complicated, multilayered story about incest to discuss accepting life and God's mysterious ways—accepting life's unpredictability as one response to the "why" of theodicy.)

170. Spencer uses Camus to reframe blues musicians, not as atheists who deny "heavenly abstractions (cf., e.g., Paul Oliver), but as "rebels" who, as Camus noted, "defy" more than they "deny" (Spencer, *The Blues and Evil*, 85, esp., 84-89).

171. Here he uses pastoral (Jungian) psychotherapist John Sanford to read the blues; see Spencer, *The Blues and Evil*, chapter 3, esp. 71-74. As one brief example, "Because the church refused to accept the shadow side of God, which was the permissive side of God's personality, 'blues people' had to fashion a 'new god'—the blues god,' whose personality was the positive element of the bifurcated African trickster-god (73f.)

172. Spencer, *The Blues and Evil*, 86.

173. Spencer sets out to prove that, contrary to white (and some black) scholars' theses, the blues music and musicians were deeply theological, ethically engaged, prophetic, and priestly. This would be more evident, Spencer proposes, if we read the blues from the context of its roots, namely, from the African worldview with its more duplicitous trickster-god: "a personage that is both superhuman and subhuman, male and female, sacred and profane, benevolent and malevolent, and who walks with a limp because one foot moves in the realm of the mundane and the other in the realm of the divine. This trickster figure is not only symbolic of what blues is when personified, but prototypical of a par-

adigm of personality and morality in African-American cultural history" (Spencer, *The Blues and Evil*, xxvi).

174. Spencer, *The Blues and Evil*, xxv.

175. Moreover, this logocentrism also results in what I regard as another equally problematic form of reductionism: Spencer claims that essentially the blues explore, ponder, and bear witness to "the truth" of human being (Spencer, *The Blues and Evil*, 37 and 59).

176. Uncritical of sex in the reception and analysis of blues, Spencer is also superficial in his comments about class which now strongly divides African Americans. He believes that as a black man—albeit an upper middle-class professional/academic, he will read the blues more authentically than white people. (He does discuss the emergence of the middle class and its effects on blues' thematics, but this is another topic.) Moreover, he claims he can provide "thicker" descriptions of their meaning (Spencer, *The Blues and Evil*, xxivf.), and yet he then reduces the blues to being an overarching, generic "symbol of black cultural and ontological reality" (xxvi), unilaterally defining their collective essence as a quest for truth and honesty rather than palliative or escape, ignoring their symbolic polyvalence according to the sex/race/class of its auditors.

177. Moreover, in a chapter on portraits of sin and justification in the blues (another traditional, theological lens), Spencer discusses women in the blues in very peculiar terms. In a section called "The Blues God," Spencer totally ignores male objectification of women in men's blues songs, reframing them as examples of a humanly instituted, realised eschatology. As one example, "Blues singers' defiant denial of the 'heaven' and 'kingdom come' abstractions . . . was typically followed by a search to acquire or construct a heaven of their own—a heaven where the spirit of the 'blues god' could reign. To this end, Texas Alexander was wistful in 'Yellow Girl Blues.' In order to gather a cluster of brown-skinned women around his throne, he decided to get himself a 'heaven kingdom' of his own" (Spencer, *The Blues and Evil*, 86).

And then, Spencer erroneously lumps Bessie Smith's lament alongside the above male fantasies: "Bessie Smith sang the same thing from a female perspective in her 'Workhouse Blues,' except that she produced more constructive sounds from behind the mask. She wished she had a heaven of her own so she could give all the 'poor girls' a long happy home" (ibid.).

Earlier in his discussion of justification in the blues (Spencer, *The Blues and Evil*, 57-63), Spencer offers a very bizarre portrait of women via an equally bizarre reading of Nietzsche's infamous statement: "'Supposing truth is a woman—what then?' This query opening Friedrich Nietzsche's *Beyond Good and Evil* (1886) raised a question that has confused scholars about the place of woman in the morality of blues and as regards the blues singer's consciousness of sin. If truth were a woman then man would be 'justified' in loving her so, despite the opposing mandates (or misconceptions) of Christianity. But woman was no 'truth,' she was the one about whom the truth was told in the blues, and this seemed to give female 'blues people' some degree of affirmation. That women felt affirmed in blues sung by men is the most reasonable way to explain why they were generally so supportive of the blues" (57). Arguably, women supported the blues because it provided them an empowering forum of self-expression and subsistence, regardless of what men were singing about them.

178. Spencer, *The Blues and Evil*, 126.

179. "In urban blues, since a single theme had to be chosen over the many, it was almost always the theme of sexual prowess and unrequited love that won out" (Spencer, *The Blues and Evil*, 127).

Such weighty, religious concerns as the 'problem of evil' were no longer preponderantly pondered. . . . Although the reality of the 'strong sense' of evil still existed doctrinally for black urban blues singers, urban blues, in relation to its precursor, registered an increasing subjugation of traditional southern cosmology beneath the predominant themes of sex and love (Spencer, *The Blues and Evil*, 137).

180. In his discussion of blues musicians' "retention" of elements of African voodoo-hoodoo, Spencer identifies the "blues singer's holistic worldview"— "an African-centered synchronous duplicity that is the 'truth of our being,'" as crucial to preserving some black musical heritage in the face of African puritanism (Spencer, *The Blues and Evil*, 14).

181. Another example of premature harmonic resolutions: After firmly demarcating the unfairly opposite camps of church vs. blues musicians, and profiling blues musicians who (like the African trickster-god) kept one foot in each camp, Spencer remains surprisingly uncritical of the coercion of blues musicians into renouncing the blues life for gospel music when they faced ostracism from church communities. Spencer decides to resolve this problem by reading this as their fulfilment of a prodigal-son, socio-cultural role—this trope being to Spencer an important musico-theological interpretive

tool (cf. Spencer, *The Blues and Evil*, 63). Rather than suggesting that blues music undermines the legitimacy of such theological species, or lamenting the performers' unfortunate capitulation to such ultimately untenable moral dichotomies, Spencer prefers the closure of theological narrative, so to speak.

182. Spencer accuses feminist ethnomusicologists, as social scientists, of failing to engage in the kind of "critical hermeneutics" which would promote women's liberation. Koskoff and the other contributors unthinkingly leave other specialists to tackle the "'broader' social, legal, and *ethical* dimensions" of the fieldwork presented in Koskoff's volumes (Spencer, "Introduction," *Sacred Music of the Secular City*, 6). According to Spencer, only three of the fifteen articles show hints of critical hermeneutics. Spencer thinks that women-ethnomusicologists do not want to be perceived as compromising their objective research with a feminist agenda. The authors in *Women and Music* exhibit a "hesitancy to make the transition from historical exegesis to critical hermeneutics, where the scholar would make the research speak explicitly to what seems to be (based on the articles in Koskoff's book) a universal female longing for liberation from male domination" (7). These scholars are masking a "(potentially) feminist subtext." I would argue, however, that there is nothing "subtextual" about Koskoff's hermeneutically critical conclusion: "The theme of devaluation concerning women and their musical activities resounds throughout the papers collected here. . . . [W]e must . . . begin to address the valuative role music plays in defining and reflecting established social and sexual orders and in acting as an agent in maintaining or changing such orders" (Koskoff, "An Introduction to Women, Music, and Culture," in *Women and Music in Cross-Cultural Perspective*, 15).

Spencer argues that theomusicology fully achieves the proper shift "from historical exegesis to critical hermeneutics," and directs readers "toward social praxis" (Spencer, "Introduction," *Sacred Music of the Secular City*, 9). By contrast, Spencer contends that Koskoff and her colleagues mute their protest because they themselves remain oppressed by masculinist anthropological methods. I would contest that Spencer and his contributors' theomusicology has hardly transcended oppressive masculinist themes or even more stifling musical logocentrism. He thus accuses Koskoff and the other contributors to her anthology of a failure of nerve—not daring "to step out of disciplinary bounds." (8). All of these articles, however, represent a broadening of extant methodologies, a challenging of previous approaches to, and studies of, women and music.

Furthermore, Spencer still promotes the false dichotomy between religion and (social) science. He says he is not deeming theology queen of the sciences, but consider the grandiosity, the scholarly hubris, of the following mandate: "Perhaps the ethnomusicologist who accused me of trying to recrown theology [queen of the sciences] thought I was suggesting that theomusicology claims privileged access to truth. If it appeared I was suggesting a certain sacred status for our discipline, it is probably because the ethos of this systematic musicology, birthed from the potentially prophetic loins of theology, is characterized by human quest for divine wisdom about self, community, humanity, and the God therein. This wisdom is crucial in the context of human encounter with the very soul of other individuals, communities, nature, and the cosmos and a better world. . . . [Theomusicology attempts] "to read the 'soul history' of cultures. Who can deny that this is a high calling?" (13).

I do not want to be accused of the same complex—demanding that contemporary theologies of music turn their attention solely to the relationship between music and sex as the primary source for theological reflection. Begbie's interests take him in other directions, as do Pelikan's, as did Barth's. But at the methodological level, my proposal of an alternative "root-metaphor" (McFague), namely, music as metaphor for sexual relations, is a strategic perspectival shift, one which generates an acute hermeneutic of suspicion. Through it, the metaphysics and silences of other approaches are thrown into sharp relief.

183. The articles can be loosely grouped under two thematic foci, both of which are logocentrically derived: music as emancipatory force, and correlatively, the musical artist (or even the genre itself) as prophet and/or preacher. Both are exemplified in Spencer's introduction to rap. Against particularly white vilifications of rap music, Spencer defends rap "as a music of spirituality with potential "utopian aspirations." . . . [R]ap has a theological aspect that is epitomized in the idea of soteriological knowledge or rap gnosticism." He defends this position by quoting band names and the messages in their lyrics: "Poor Righteous Teachers, the Intellectual Hoodlum . . . songs such as 'Knowledge is King' by Kool Moe Dee and 'Holy Intellect' by PRT (which the rap says are 'holy as the mind')" (Spencer, *Sacred Music of the Secular City*, 266). Rappers are "sidewalk prophets" (267). Admittedly, the words in rap music define the genre, but is it theology purely by virtue of those rappers who express "utopian aspirations"? Once again, Spencer wants to make "this aspect of transcendence" (ibid.) the focus of our theological attention, as well as the usual topics of the false dichotomy between sacred and

secular, and the (by now hackneyed) reconceptualisation of art as prophecy. "Theomusicology" must also broaden its analytical scope to illustrate how rap's "kinetic orality and affective physicality" shape subjectivity as much as, if not more than, the texts.

184. The late Larry Neal, for example, offers an insightful essay on the origins and ethos of the blues, one meant to defend their "fleshy" themes (Neal, "The Ethos of the Blues, 45ff), and their double-edged portraits of "the realities of the male-female relationship." But to do so, he appeals to their lyrics (ibid.). Moreover, he argues that the "didactic and moralistic impulse underlying the blues is often obscured by the fact that many blues songs seem to be inordinately concerned with the sex act" (ibid.). In fact however, "[t]he essential motive behind the best blues song is the acquisition of insight, wisdom" (37). And later: "The blues are primarily the expression of a post-slavery view of the world. They are linked to the freeing of the individual spirit" (41). He even argues "Like any artist, the blues singer has the task of bringing order out of chaos" (43). As I shall demonstrate in part 2, the sexually-charged musical idioms supporting both musical types challenge such clear distinctions, and analyses that ignore this mislead the reader. This becomes even more obvious when blues idioms support Gospel texts. Excessively text-based critiques, as always, miss the chance for more multilayered musico-theological reflection.

185. Greeley, "Like a Catholic: Madonna's Challenge to Her Church," 245.

186. Ibid., 247.

187. Cf. esp. bell hooks, "Madonna: Plantation Mistress or Soul Sister," *Black Looks: Race and Representation* (Cambridge, MA: South End Press 1992), 157-64, and "Power to the Pussy," in *Outlaw Culture: Resisting Representations* (New York: Routledge, 1994) 9-23.

188. Greeley, "The Catholic Imagination of Bruce Springsteen," 235.

189. Ibid., 233.

190. Ibid. 235.

191. Ibid., 241.

192. West, "Sex and Suicide," 252.

193. Prince preaches sex as an "opiate," and sexual liberation as a "form[s] of negative transcendence" (West, "Sex and Suicide," 252). Prince does not respond constructively to, but rather (note West's concern for social and musical order): "Although the Christian quest for transcendent meaning in life and history is rejected in Prince's lyrics, the idea of divine intervention in the form of eschatological catastrophic presence is preserved. In the interim, life is a party, a sustained effort to stay alive by feeling "alive," keeping the adrenaline flowing for the purpose of frequent climax. This viewpoint, reflected and condensed by Prince in his music and his performance style, promotes and encourages an orgiastic way of life in which sex is an opiate of the people. The major alternatives are drugs and suicide—both strongly rejected by Prince" (ibid.; emphasis mine).

"[W]e are impelled into a pulsating world of surfaces, seeking to secure some vitality and vigor for our desperate selves" (251).

194. In another pessimistic article, West offers a survey of Afro-American pop music which identifies the watershed events in this development: Michael Jackson's innovations, the rise of bebop and rap. West is troubled by the hopelessness and the purely "cathartic release" which rap music tends to provide ("On Afro-American Music: From Bebop to Rap," 293). He identifies rap as the "last form of transcendence available to young black ghetto dwellers, yet it, tellingly, is often employed to subvert, undermine, and parody transcendence itself" (294). As in his analysis of Prince, West ignores the music's contradictory message; he writes of its "accenting syncopated polyrhythms, kinetic orality, and sensual energy in a refined form of raw expressiveness" but dismisses these elements' reviving effects (ibid., 292). For West, the texts cancel out the music's influence ("its virtuosity lies not in technical facility but rather street-talk quickness and linguistic versatility," ibid.), and he predicts that, unless rappers preach "moral visions" and "give existential hope to the underclass and poor working class in Afro-America," the future of genuinely Afro-American music is bleak (294).

195. "The critique of 2 Live Crew must not, however, feign socio-political innocence, cultural purity, or moral neutrality. Similar cases for censorship and obscenity could be made against comedian Andrew Dice Clay's white racist routines and misogynist monologues, or rock group Guns N' Roses' homophobic harangues and racist lyrics (Dyson, "Rights and Responsibilities: 2 Live Crew and Rap's Moral Vision," 277). And later: "Only political naiveté or insularity would conclude that the right to free expression has been equitably applied throughout its torturous tenure; as the old saw goes, the right to a free press belongs to those who own the press. . . . While 2 Live Crew's right to express its artistic worldview should be protected, even by the most fervent feminist, that artistic worldview, which has profoundly disturbing social and cultural meanings, must be strongly and vociferously crit-

icized. . . . But the implicit and racist swipe at young black male culture in the whole affair must not be overlooked when calls for legal response go forward. Informed criticism yes, reactionary censorship no" (ibid., 280).

196. Dyson, "Rap Culture, the Church, and American Society," 271.

197. Dyson thus advocates: "Dialogue about rap, culture, and sexuality also forces the church to be more open and direct about its ambiguous theology of embodiment, to rethink its rigid conceptions of sexual identity, and to reexamine its contradictory and hypocritical codes of sexual behavior" (Dyson, "Rap Culture," 272).

198. Rap offers auditors and performers "an ontological stance," "a way of being in the world" ("Rap Culture," 269). Rap music also has redemptive force in its "art of historical retrieval": "rap artists help illumine fugues and movements that have given insight and inspiration in hard times" (272). It is an extension of black oral culture (ibid., 270).

199. Pickstock, "Music: Soul, City and Cosmos after Augustine," 268.

200. Ibid., 244.

201. Ibid., 269

202. Ibid., 261.

203. Ibid., 269.

204. Ibid. See Philippe Lacoue-LaBarthe, *Musica Ficta: Figures of Wagner* (Stanford: Stanford University Press, 1994). For Pickstock's critique of the same, see especially Pickstock, "Music," 252-55.

205. Pickstock, "Music," 258.

206. Ibid., 247.

207. Ibid.

208. Ibid., 265f.

209. Ibid., 249.

210. Ibid., 264.

211. Ibid., 258.

212. Ibid., 266.

213. Ibid., 268.

214. Ibid., 268f.

215. Ibid., 255f.

216. Ibid., 263.

217. Ibid., 249.

218. On the moral/ethical import of *numerii iudiciales*, see Pickstock, "Music," 255-58.

219. Ibid., 264.

220. Ibid., 264f.

221. Pickstock elaborates: "[B]y participation in Christ's sufferings, this discordance [of body-soul relations] can be transfigured into a rightly ordered music. This redemptive process most of all fulfils Augustine's contention that nothing falls outside the harmony of the cosmic poem. . . . [E]very apparent discord can, in the course of musical time, be granted its concordant place" ("Music," 264f.).

222. Barth, *Church Dogmatics*, vol. 3, sec. 4; ed. G. W. Bromiley and T. F. Torrance, "The Doctrine of Creation" (Edinburgh: T.&T. Clark, 1961).

223. Ibid., 265.

224. Sands, *Escape from Paradise*, 136.

225. TeSelle, *Augustine the Theologian*, 189.

226. Ibid., 190f.

227. Pickstock, "Music," 264.

228. Ibid., 268.

229. Ibid., 264. Thus Pickstock situates the body as follows: "[A]lthough the beauty of the body is subordinate, nevertheless it has its own proper beauty which is qualitatively distinct, not merely a quantitatively lesser degree of psychic beauty. . . . The body has a beauty of its own which it can communicate to the soul, and provides an irreplaceable assistance to the soul in reminding it of the plenitude of eternal beauty."

Elsewhere, Pickstock applauds the body's "lowly perfection": "There is a generosity in Augustine's invocation of the plenitude of Being . . . he recognises that a lower and limited harmony can still possess a certain inimitable, although lowly, perfection, like that of the body" (Pickstock, "Music," 267).

230. Cf. ibid., 244f.

Part Two: Reconstruction
A Feminist Theology of Music

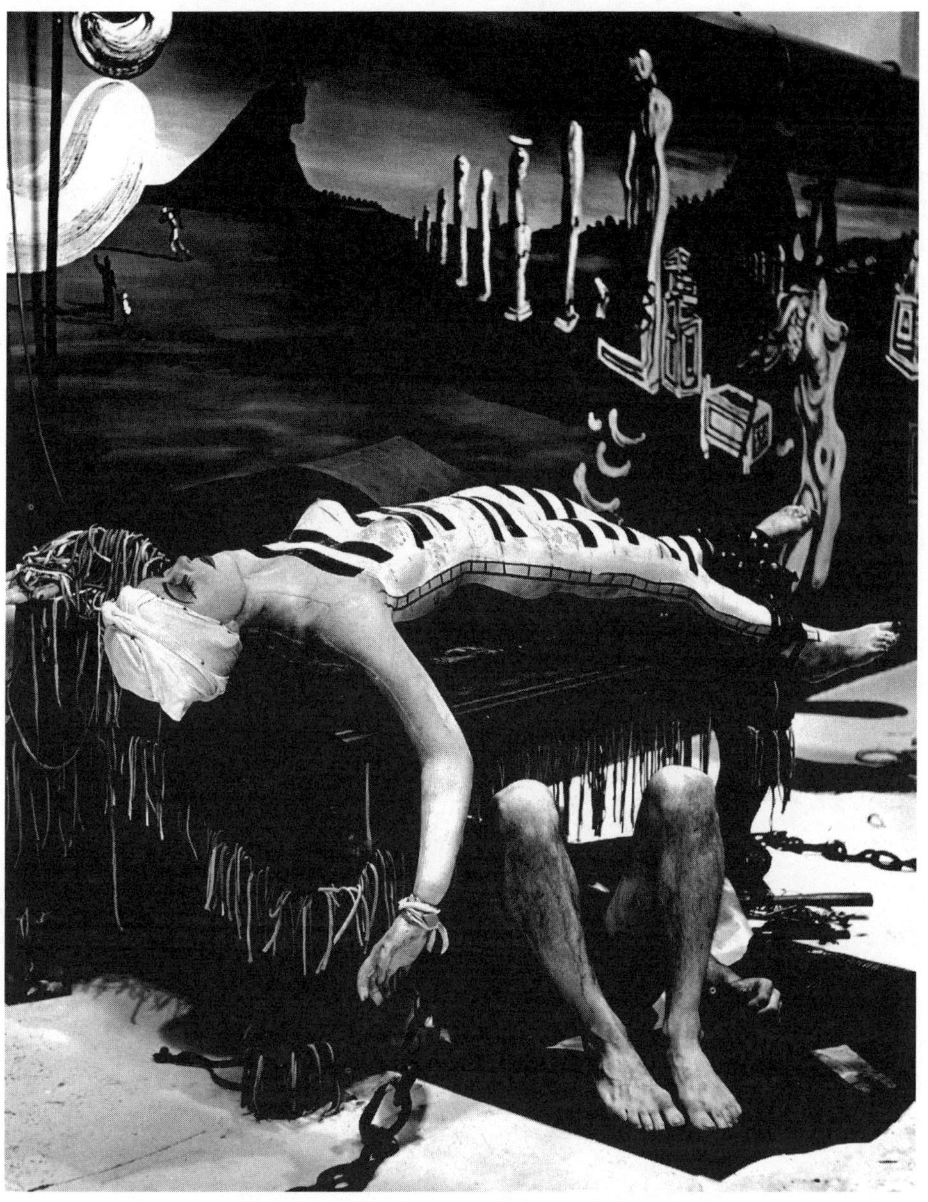

Salvador Dali, *Dream of Venus*, photo Eric Schaal, courtesy Princeton Architectural Press

Who will write us the new laws of harmony?
We have no further use for well-tempered clavichords
We ourselves are too much dissonance.

Walter Borchert

<table><tr><td>CHAPTER
FOUR</td><td># Critical
Counterpoint</td></tr></table>

Critical Counterpoint

Arpeggiating a Feminist Theology of Music[1]

PART ONE HAS ILLUSTRATED the need for an alternative approach to music's theological significance, one that incorporates rather than ignores the intimate
connection between music and human sexuality that feminist musicologists have
already begun to explore in their own field. Moving now from critique to reconstruction, if music is *positively* reframed as the metaphor for sexual relations that
it has always been, what specifically *theological* interpretive keys might revalorise
the connection between music and sexuality, and furnish conceptual pillars for a
feminist theology of music? To make this model genuinely interdisciplinary and
provocatively intertextual, I shall dialogue with a variety of feminist and music
theorists whose insights have already spawned important re-visionings within
history, literature, biblical studies, theology, and music. Such collaborations mul-
tiply creative new directions that previously narrow musico-theological discourse
has foregone while at the same time illustrating how departures from canonical
sources and symbols hardly impoverishes but rather enriches musico-theological
reflection. If nothing else, the previous chapters have shown that music is by
nature intertextual.

First, one must develop the theological implications of music's sexual
metaphoricity. Our epistemological dig site therefore shifts to the borders and forbidden territory of extant musico-theological discourse. Second, in this strange
land, women musicians—heretofore neglected in theologies of music—will sing
the new song. Following Elisabeth Schüssler Fiorenza, a feminist theology of
music will make these women's "values, insights and visions integral to the
[musico-]theological discourse of the Church."[2] To both ends then, I plumb the
works of two historical and two contemporary female musician–composers, challenging thereby the hegemony of music's symbolic function as revelator of divine
and transcendent harmony and relocating music's theological significance in its
erotic sway. Although my historical examples come from the Middle Ages and the
sixteenth century, eras in which women uncritically assimilate masculinist transcendental ideals, *in their musical practices*, these women engage music's disruptive power and promote (knowingly or not) a more embodied theology of music

119

or at least proffer seeds for its contemporary germination. I begin with Hildegard of Bingen (1098-1179), whose musical "activism" flags a third revisionist shift.

I. Placing the Cornerstone:
Hildegard of Bingen

It is not incidental that, even in his vastly comprehensive *Theologie der Musik*, Söhngen makes no reference to Hildegard's music or thought. And because the other theologians discussed in chapter 3 ignore the gender politics of human musicality, they too overlook the constructive potential she offers us. Consideration of Hildegard's musico-theological apologetics, tactically devised in the face of drastic clerical opposition, proffers a third methodological corrective to the excessively metaphysical/speculative conceptualisations of music's relation to theology discussed above: Hildegard's reflection on both individual and collective musical experience reminds us that *a feminist theology of music must mine concrete musical experience for its insights*; precisely those intense, bodily musical experiences that addled church fathers, Reformers, Puritans, and modern commentators, even Adorno. In accordance with a dynamic of mutual causality, praxis must determine the content of theoretical statements about music's theological meaning. Here Hildegard is exemplary. Unlike her male predecessors and contemporaries, her understanding of the relationship between music and theology does not develop from a formal philosophical or theological education, but instead from: (1) her inspired visions; (2) her richly imagistic assimilation of Wisdom literature; (3) her experiences of communal musical worship; and (4) her gynecological studies. These nonmetaphysical resources, furthermore, shape each other. For example, this priority of experience over metaphysics is particularly evident in Hildegard's musico-theological characterisations of Adam, Satan, Mary, and Jesus. These exegetical portraits do not emerge from her enchantment with music's *numerositas* but from her attentiveness to the voice of the "living light," that source of all Hildegard's visions and of many of her theological insights. As an additional, "unorthodox" resource, her articulations of the nature of the relationship between music and theology emerge from her very unsystematic sapiential Mariology— hardly the locus of masculinist musico-theological reflection.[3] In short, Hildegard is an invaluable source and revisionist norm, because it is on the basis of her acutely embodied mystical experiences, her composing, and her communal relationships, that music becomes metaphorically significant regarding divine– human relations. Again, more important still than her four nonmetaphysical sources, Hildegard's theology of music emerges from hours of singing, from intuitions born of resonating vocal chords, a fluid column of air, and the beat of a human heart.

While it may be questionable to read her compositions as "erotic mappings" (though one scholar has done so as we shall see), for those who seek to theologise about music in a new way, Hildegard's sensitivity to the body's vital role in music-making and her creative embroidery of an ancient christological trope will furnish a new thematic for this feminist theology of music, one that initiates the "redemption" of the flesh in musico-theological discourse. And although her music is not an intentional "fabrication of sexuality" (McClary), it certainly constitutes a graphic historical example of music's function as a metaphor for socially prescribed gender relations.[4] This particular male–female clash (the interdict and ban on all liturgical singing which the prelates of Mainz imposed on Hildegard's community at Rupertsberg in 1178) forces her to reflect with urgency on the meaning of music for individual and collective devotion and to develop an unequivocal *apologia* for its necessity.[5] While centuries earlier the church fathers hammered out musical policy in reaction to the threat of pagan and gnostic influences upon their congregations— adopting measures which very often silenced women's singing in church—Hildegard's musico-theological rationale reconstrues any such preventive (or punitive) silencing, male or female, as demonic. As we shall see in her conceptions of Adam and Satan, when the music stops, the devil moves in. Though Hildegard would most certainly have scorned "fleshly" musical media, her position does contest any sexist double standards in musical worship. This is because, for Hildegard, in the eyes of God human beings are basically musical beings. (And her insistence upon humanity's innate musicality led to very different theological implications than those of Boethius, discussed in chapter 1 above.) This battle also illustrates how, particularly when studying women musicians and composers, it is often not only concrete musical experiences but also the latter's double-duty as *political weaponry* that prompts new musico-theological insights, whether theirs or ours. Music's politically galvanizing force consolidates women's power. Musical bans merely mute the undeniably energising force that singing the ferial and festal liturgy affords these women.[6] Uppity nuns' musical disobedience and its supposed threat to their soulful purity must be squelched by "castrating" their musical virility (though, in fact, such artistic potency eroded clerical might more than sororial virtue).

A New Tonic

Aside from her exemplary emphasis upon praxis (and her status as a woman composer), there is another good reason for making Hildegard the inspiration for a new framework. Although she is not a feminist or even a proto-feminist within the Christian tradition, she does develop (albeit unsystematically) her own "theology of the feminine." Barbara Newman identifies her as the first Christian thinker "to deal seriously and positively with the feminine," especially the 'feminine' aspects of the divine.[7] For Hildegard, the feminine is the immanent divine principle, the mediating power "in God which binds itself most intimately with the human race and through it with the cosmos."[8] Many feminists would reject this essentialist, masculine/feminine dichotomy, so typical of Neoplatonic, sapiential theology such as Hildegard's.[9] One cannot, moreover, erase the fact that Hildegard uncritically assimilated Boethius's theology of music. Nevertheless, both Hildegard's conflation of earthly and heavenly feminine biblical figures—*Sapientia, Caritas*, Eve, Mary, and *Ecclesia*—and her consequent ascription of a redemptive role to the female body lead her to delineate a more intimate relationship between music and theology, one which is not developed by masculinist depictions of music as the ideal salvific, evangelical medium, or as the mirror of divine mathematical principles. Hildegard's theological readings of these female figures, most notably her depiction of a musical symbiosis between Mary and Jesus, imply that music is 'quintessentially' theological because it is essentially *incarnational*.[10] Stated otherwise, the basic presupposition for a theology of music is not (*pace* Söhngen et al.) that music is inherently theological, but rather, that human beings are inherently musical. Boethius recognised humanity's essential musicality but metaphysically disembodied this principle in the name of God. By contrast, Hildegard's thoroughly musical conception of the *imago dei* trans-fuses Word with flesh.

This incarnational approach to music's relation to theology (as opposed to a mathematico-philosophical one) constitutes the most important way in which a feminist theology of music would differ from its antecedents. The masculinist devalorisation and/or subordination of actual music-making as a set of (dangerously evocative) embodied practices clashes with the centrality of the incarnation in Christian theological models. Admittedly, through overuse in theological discourse, the term "incarnational" has been emptied of its radicality, becoming perhaps as much a cliché as the trinitarian conceits used by Barth, Söhngen, Pelikan, and Spencer, discussed above. However, feminist scholars are reviving the incarnation's discursively flesh-toned dissonance. Closer attention to four other musical images in Hildegard's theology will initiate a reconceptualisation of incarnation as the new cornerstone for a feminist theology of music. In the process, another crucial ingredient besides this new incarnational mode will emerge.

"Fluted Vault of Desire":[11]
The Body as Musical Instrument

In the masculinist theologies of music surveyed above, the theological, liturgical, and sociological import attributed to music rarely if ever emphasises the most obvious fact that the human body is a musical instrument—a resonant chamber, capable of song, uniquely disposed to fashion and play musical instruments (this despite the ancients' own sense of the inherent musicality of speech, a conviction which led them to wed music and words indissolubly). Our very existence is sustained and regulated by the rhythmic pulsations of heartbeat and breath. Human speech itself "in-corporates" elements of pitch, timbre, and rhythm. The potential for theologising about the body as musical instrument is usually allegorised away in Christian interpretations of scripture. The likeness of humans to musical instruments is spiritualised.[12] By contrast, this sheer fact of creaturely embodiment profoundly shapes Hildegard's theology, cosmology, and anthropology.[13] And unlike John Donne, who thinks that only in our death would we "be made thy musique,"[14] Hildegard thinks of herself in this life as one of God's musical instruments, more specifically as God's trumpet, or as one of his trumpet notes; as such, she is ordained to interpret and herald the content and meaning of her divinely inspired visions to other Christians. Thus in a letter to her friend Elisabeth von Schönau, she writes:

> Those who long to perfect the works of God . . . should leave heavenly things to him who is heavenly; for they are exiles, ignorant of the celestial, only singing the hiddenness of God, in the same way as a trumpet only brings forth sounds but does not cause them: another must blow into it, for the sound to emerge. So too I, lying low in pusillanimity of fear, at times resound a little, like a small trumpet-note from the living brightness.[15]

Admittedly, this portrayal of prophets as trumpets is a common trope in early allegorical readings of the Psalms. However, if read in conjunction with her medical treatises, Hildegard blurs conventional distinctions between the literal and metaphorical in ways that conventional allegory does not.[16] Thus as a physician trying to explain why the elements affect women more than men and why humors "are more plentiful" in women, God's prophetic little trumpet note describes the female body as "open like a wooden frame in which strings have been fastened for strumming."[17] This conception of herself as a musical instrument, and more importantly, the positive retrieval of the female body thereby, constitutes *in nuce* the incarnational change of key a feminist theology of music must elaborate. Hildegard's characterisations of Adam, Satan, Mary, and Jesus further establish this shift from the numerico-metaphysical to the incarnational *and* illustrate the theological riches of women's musical theory and practices.

Adam and Satan:
The "Untuning"[18] of Celestial Music Incarnate

In addition to her gynecological insight into music's theological import, Hildegard's perception of the human body as musical instrument may have influenced her interpretation of the Fall. Harmony, symphony, and song are aural "lenses" through which Hildegard reads the significant events and figures in salvation history.[19] Thus, before the Fall, Hildegard characterises Adam, the prototype of all human beings, as heavenly music incarnate: "in Adam's voice before he fell there was the sound of every harmony and the sweetness of the whole art of music. And if Adam had remained in the condition in which he was formed, human frailty could never endure the power and the resonance of that voice. . . . [H]e who, still innocent before his fault, had no little kinship with the sound of the angels' praises."[20] This sacramentalist use of harmony, wholeness, and integrity seems traditional, but Hildegard develops unique theological implications from this musical metaphor. In opposition to this prelapsarian Adam, Hildegard depicts Satan as utterly incapable of song. She blames Satan, *not Eve*, for destroying the original divine–human harmony; Satan "drew man out of the celestial harmony and the delights of paradise."[21] These musico-theological portraits become pivotal in mounting a counterargument against the clergy of Mainz when they threaten to silence convent music. For the clergy's threats squarely place them in Satan's camp; thus she elaborates:

> But when his deceiver, the devil, heard that man had begun to sing through divine inspiration, and that he would be transformed through this to remembering the sweetness of the songs in the heavenly land—seeing the machination of his cunning going awry, he became so terrified that . . . he has not ceased to trouble or destroy the affirmation and beauty and sweetness of divine praise and of the hymns of the spirit.[22]

Hildegard the composer, furthermore, musically elaborates this theological trope in her *Ordo virtutum*. In it, therefore, Hildegard's interdisciplinary oeuvre becomes musico-theological praxis incarnate. For in the *Ordo*, the character of the devil is never allowed to sing. Is it coincidental, moreover, that in the performance of the *Ordo*, practical exigencies of convent life dovetail with theological dictates, such that Satan, the only male part in the play, would be sung by a priest or monk since either would probably be the only male voice in the convent?[23] It is as if the *Ordo* underlines her conviction—voiced in her appeals to the prelates, and in her music—that only Satan silences bodily song.

Chora-l[24] *Antiphon: Jesus in Mary*

Before proceeding to the third and fourth incarnational *leitmotifs* in Hildegard's theology, it is important to emphasise again that her incarnational penchant does not negate Hildegard's subscription to the more traditional metaphysical understanding of music's relation to theology. Following Boethius and Augustine (via the teachings of Bernard of Clairvaux), Hildegard recognises music's reflection of divine unity, number, and order. For example, she gives the perfect fourth and fifth special symbolic significance in her compositions.[25] In accordance with philosophical and theological tradition, she also believes that human music blends symphonically with that of the cosmos and the heavenly choirs. Nevertheless, Hildegard's images of her own body as a trumpet, of prelapsarian Adam as heavenly music incarnate, and of Satan as its antithesis, illustrate that her fundamentally musical worldview gives equal attention to the fact that *Deus artifex*[26] places our souls in musical bodies. As we shall see in the two following examples, her musical characterisations of Mary and Jesus constitute both the culmination and redemption of such musical embodiment.

Additionally, this eternal/pre-existent symbiosis provides an alternative understanding of music's soteriological significance to those discussed in chapter 3. For Barth, Pelikan, and Söhngen (who take their cues from Luther) this significance resides in music's ability to seize and spread the gospel. Music is thus quintessentially *creatura evangelistica*. Hildegard, however, perceives a much deeper intimacy between the gospel and music. *Music and harmony constitute Christ's very nature.* Intentionally or not, with this insight Hildegard retrieves the ancient image of Jesus as the Song of God—a trope which apologists such as Clement of Alexandria used in the second century:[27]

> Behold the might of the new song! It has made men out of stones, men out of beasts. Those, moreover, that were as dead not being partakers of the true life, have come to life again, simply by becoming listeners to this song. It also composed the universe into melodious order, and tuned the discord of the elements of harmonious arrangement so that the whole world might become harmony....
>
> A beautiful breathing instrument of music the Lord made man, after His own image. And He Himself also surely, who is the supramundane Wisdom, the celestial Word, is the all-harmonious, melodious, holy instrument of God. What then, does this instrument—the Word of God, the Lord, the new Song—desire? To open the eyes of the blind and unstop the ears of the deaf, and to lead the lame or the erring to righteousness.[28]

In that context, the Christ came to be known as "the new Orpheus."[29] But the corporeal implications of this musical trope were allegorised away.[30] By contrast, and even more significant for a feminist theology of music, Hildegard chooses to couch this image of Jesus as the New Song within the context of her intense devotion to Mary—an earthly woman whom Hildegard is perfectly willing to conflate with the divine figure of *Caritas*.[31] Hildegard emphasises that it was only from the (musical) "instrument" of a woman's body that God's incarnate song could resound.[32] Thus, in her famous hymn to the virgin, "*Ave generosa,*" she writes:

> For your womb held joy/ *when all the harmony of heaven resounded from you/* for, virgin, you bore the Son of God/ when in God your chastity blazed.
>
> Your flesh held joy/ like the grass when the dew falls/and floods it with living green/ So it was in you also / O mother of all joy.[33]

As with her musical characterisation of Satan in the *Ordo virtutum*, Hildegard's theology shapes her musical practices, this time in the setting of Marian texts. In them, she accentuates Mary's crucial musico-theological value. For example, the above verse of "*Ave generosa*" underscores the importance that Hildegard attributes to Mary's embodiment of the redemptive Song of God: in this verse, the hymn's melody reaches its highest point (a high c') on the word *symphonia* (harmony),[34] and it returns to this highest note again during the verse's final line: "when your chastity grew radiant in God." The high c' is an entire octave plus a sixth away from the lowest note in the hymn. With this melodic gesture, Hildegard is no rebel—for it undergirds a celebration of the womb's harmony and chastity.

Nevertheless, its soaring range is still highly unorthodox for medieval liturgical chant.[35] More important still, in this dramatic leap and elsewhere Hildegard continually makes Mary the "concert master" par excellence of God's creaturely symphony, precisely because cosmic harmony is taking fleshly form within the confines of her womb.[36] This sustained revalorisation of the female body is even more graphically expressed in Hildegard's "Symphony of Virgins," where Mary sings:

> O Son beloved,
> whom I bore in my womb
> by the might of the circling wheel of the holy
> God who created me
> and formed my whole frame
> *and set in my womb*
> *all manner of music*
> in all blossoms of melody:
> now a throng of virgins
> follows me and you.
> Deign to save them. O Son most lovely![37]

These examples also illustrate that, for Hildegard, Christ becomes not only the Word-made-flesh, *he is God's music-made-flesh*.[38] Consequently, if one extends this theological root-metaphor, all creaturely singing finds its beginning and end in the Song of God, and hence human music-making bears witness to God's immanence, to the Christ who dwells within us. In short, music's salvific and evangelistic power does not consist in its power to seize and spread the gospel, however important this function may be; rather, it lies in the concrete fact that Jesus, the incarnate song of God, celebrates and redeems human embodiment. Unlike previous spiritual allegorisations of this musico-christic trope, Hildegard fleshes out a more genuinely incarnational musical "Christology," so to speak. Jesus is the most divinely inspired, perfectly tuned, and perfectly played musical instrument, whose music restores harmony to divine–human relations. In Christ's body, the player, the instrument, and its music become one. But, contrary to the harmonic ideology that I criticised in part 1, *such unity is effected through disintegration*; namely, the collapse of bodily boundaries or "integrity" in Mary's womb. Moreover, this harmonisation is not metaphysically, but corporeally "conceived" by way of a *chora*-l antiphon, placental coalescence. As shall be seen presently, this location of music's salvific activity within the body of Christ finds its natural counterpart in the human body itself. The salvific, harmonising power of the Song of God resounds in the human singing that it inspires, sustains, and ultimately composes, suggesting perhaps a new musical trope: *I am the Lute, You are the Strings*.[39]

Fine Tuning: Music as Salvific Integrator of Soul and Body

In his *De institutione musica*, Boethius discusses the Pythagorean belief that musical harmony unites the entire structure of soul and body. As distinct from *musica mundana* (the music of the spheres which the movement of celestial bodies generates and which orders the elements and seasons) and *musica instrumentalis* (human music-making), Boethius calls the internal force that binds the irrational and rational parts of the soul together *musica humana*.[40] Following Boethius, Hildegard believes that music unites body and soul, and that the soul is symphonic in nature; that is, "the whole structure of soul and body is united in musical harmony."[41] It is important to my study, however, that Hildegard blurs the boundaries between *musica humana* and *instrumentalis*. For, as mentioned above, she argues that by silencing song in her convent, the prelates not only severed human fellowship with the "angelic praise in heaven,"[42] but, graver still, they also disrupted the inner harmony of body and soul.[43] Although she accepts the traditional, spiritual understanding of music as transcending its literal effects, she cannot agree that music's spiritual essence mysteriously perdures in the absence of actual music.

To defend her position, Hildegard compares this unifying, interior effect of music to God's harmonisation of the divine and human natures in Christ. Liturgical song unites soul to body and rational praise to spiritual melody in the same way that God harmonises human nature with the divine in Christ.[44] In liturgical singing, writes Hildegard in her *Scivias*, "the words symbolize the body, and the jubilant music indicates the spirit; and the celestial harmony shows the Divinity, and the words the Humanity of the Song of God."[45] This image of music as an indispensable integrator of soul and body prompts another shift in the relationship between music and theology: as spokesman for the tradition, Söhngen locates the salvific activity of music in its evangelistic potential and in its use as a medium of worship; by contrast, Hildegard focuses on its salvific, integrative effect within the human body, and, *pari passu*, within the ecclesial/monastic community.

Unfortunately, the above analogy may reveal an element of dualism that would contradict the centrality of the body to Hildegard's theology of music. For, according to this analogy—body/soul : words/music, etc.—Hildegard associates *words* with the body and music with the *spirit* in a seemingly logocentric, metaphysical equation. She also categorises praise as rational and melody as *spiritual*. Barbara Newman has rightly emphasised that Hildegard's holistic cosmology does not erase her dualistic anthropology.[46] That is, although Hildegard celebrates the cosmic significance of Woman and elevates the feminine aspect of God and humanity to a position of equal importance with the masculine, as a child of her times and a consecrated virgin, she nevertheless regards women as essentially inferior to men and maintains an aesthetic and moral disdain for postlapsarian sexual intercourse. Although such dualisms in Hildegard's thought must be acknowledged, I would emphasise that the locus of their reconciliation or recollection is still the human body. Furthermore, music (particularly singing) actually unsettles theoretical dichotomies such as body/soul or body/spirit and underlines the problematicity of such constructs.[47] Even Hildegard seems to recognise that any theoretical distinctions between the rational and spiritual (or among body, soul, and spirit) dissolve in the act of singing. Music may be spiritual for Hildegard, yet she is acutely aware that without the resonant chamber of the body, sustained creaturely union with the divine would be impossible.[48] Admittedly, Hildegard characterises the *soul* as symphonic in nature[49] and the body as simply the garment of the soul,[50] yet Peter Dronke provides a crucial nuance here: "*symphonia* is something that is of necessity both material and immaterial. . . . Earthly music emerges from the earthly—yet is not earthbound. It 'leaps up to God'—not by overcoming its physical components, but in the act of affirming them."[51] Additionally, Dronke contends that for Hildegard "any symphony of voices and instruments on earth, which is directed heavenwards, is a means of reintegration, of bringing the lost human-heavenly condition alive again."[52] Melody is not, for Hildegard (as it was for Augustine), a problematic, potentially sirenic distraction of "sweet skilled voices." (It should also be remembered that this ancient dichotomy between body and soul was not regarded as purely negative or antithetical. Temptation, sin, and disharmony were the result of the body/soul's struggle against fleshly concupiscence.)

Theology in a New Key: Fugal Possibilities

This reading of Hildegard's musico-theological significance is a departure from Patricia Kazarow's 1993 appreciation of Hildegard's oeuvre. In Kazarow's view, Hildegard's music becomes yet another harbinger of number and order.[53] (Kazarow uses Söhngen as well.) Hildegard's understanding of the body as musical instrument, her characterisations of Adam, Satan, Mary, and Jesus in musical terms, and her emphasis on music's deep-seated integrative power within the human body, all suggest an important directive for revising musico-theological frameworks that formerly focused on music-as-science; as the "highest creation of the human *spirit*"; or as something that is aurally received to move the spirit and convert the soul.[54] It is indeed surprising that traditional theologies of music ignore the valuable insights that might be gained from a sense of singing as first and foremost a physiologically complex activity. Hildegard's attention to, and awareness of, the centrality of human corporeality in music-making reminds one that music has bodily effects as much as soulful ones, and that the latter depend on the former. Again, Newman insists that the tension between Hildegard's holistic cosmology and her dualistic anthropology cannot be resolved.[55] However, in my view, Hildegard's understanding of music as both corporeal and spiritual and as a sign of God's radical immanence prefigure the feminist theological attempt to dismantle the rigid, hierarchical polarities that order our world. In Hildegard's theology, music represents the "dancing still point"[56] in which any conscious distinctions between transcendence and immanence, or divine inspiration and creaturely fulfilment, dissolve. In this way human singing and music-making—even its erotic and iconoclastic genres—actuate the embodiment of divine aesthetic pleasure and purpose. As Dronke points out, Hildegard knew that "music represents a way in which human beings can still incarnate beauty in an earthly mode."[57]

Erotic Undertones in Hildegard's Theology of Music

Having reinstated the crucial importance of the body in musico-theological reflection, we may now consider in more detail the relationship of music to sexuality, though Hildegard may represent a less graphic incarnation of their confluence. Here however, Bruce Wood Holsinger disagrees. Holsinger attempts to eroticise a body-centered reading of Hildegard's music, perceiving as he does a sexual thematic in her chant: "In the context of medieval Christianity, a religion whose orthodox proponents constantly insisted on the miracle of Christ Himself as its kernel of legitimacy, Hildegard's music was for herself and the women in her abbey an escape into a form of spirituality that centered around the female body and female homosocial and homoerotic desire."[58] Holsinger thus challenges what he terms "asexual" readings of Hildegard's work (those of Newman and Dronke, for example) with his own homoerotic rereadings of the same.[59] (Kazarow's reading of Hildegard's music, as we have seen, is also "asexual," using Oskar Söhngen to read Hildegard's musical metaphysics and to focus on the musico-numerical symbolism in her chant.) Holsinger is unsatisfied with such orthodox approaches.[60] In his view, "there is a fundamental affinity between female spiritual devotion and female sexuality" underlying Hildegard's composition and the choral singing of her community.[61] A heterosexist perspective has blinded us to "the centrality of homoerotic desire to women's religious experience and expression."[62] On the basis of his analyses of two marian hymns, he argues that:

> a group of nuns, led by Hildegard, living in intimate proximity, raising their voices together in song, allow[ed] music itself—the actual music produced by and resonating between the bodies of the nuns as well as the music that emerges from the bodies of the Virgin and the feminized Church on Earth—to create and enliven the social, devotional, and erotic bonds both between one another and between themselves and God. Music, always a somatic phenomenon for Hildegard, allows women to voice their fleshly and spiritual desires for the female body in a way that transgresses—textually and musically —the careful devotional boundaries established by the medieval Church.[63]

Holsinger's reading of Hildegard, his identification of a homoerotic theme in her music and texts, is arguably anachronistic. Historian Caroline Walker Bynum, among others, has rightly warned against the use of contemporary "clinical" categories and concepts to interpret medieval psychology and behaviour, the notion of "homoerotic" being one of them. Holsinger himself acknowledges this problem but sees it as sanctioned by a hermeneutic of generosity.[64] Holsinger is trying to open up—though perhaps too widely, as some scholars have understandably argued—imaginative musicological space which previous over-spiritualised readings of Hildegard's music and theology foreclose. While his identification of a homoerotic subtext in Hildegard's musical compositions is eisegetical, his creative interpretation may bolster the argument that, at the very least, the tradition contains seeds for a contemporary theology of music that enunciates music as an embodied practice and as an engagement of human sexuality.[65]

II. Kindred Body: Suzanne Cusick's Lesbian Musicology

Hildegard's prescient treatment of music as a set of embodied practices has a contemporary analogue within feminist musicology. Had masculinist theologians discussing music's theological significance been more genuinely interdisciplinary, they might have assimilated the reinstatement of the body in musical analysis which feminist, queer, and other "new" musicologists have been promoting since 1989. Their recuperative strategies enrich my own and further support the aptness of placing the incarnation center-stage in contemporary musical reflection. More specifically, there are mutually validating affinities between the incarnational approach to music outlined above and Suzanne Cusick's feminist musicological rereading of music as a performative, bodily event. Cusick's iconoclastic scholarship engages precisely the kind of creative metaphor-making that theologians who seek to define music's meaning can no longer afford to ignore. Moreover, her embodied approach to music leads Cusick to reconceptualise a formerly scorned musical gynemorphism, thereby opening even more imaginative space for musico-theological reflection.

Trained in traditional musicology, Cusick questions her discipline's own logocentrism, its "apparent preoccupation with the textlike nature of music, that is, with the grammar and syntax of pitches and durations."[66] She subsequently enlists feminist theory to effect an analytical shift from the textual to the corporeal in musicological analysis. In her own way, Cusick reverses the ancient theory-practice hierarchy and value judgments; concrete experience has taught her that she gains more understanding of a musical work when she analyses it as a performer rather than as a musicologist.[67] Musical performance has been long neglected in musicological analysis. Cusick objects to this disembodied musical theorising and phrases her objections in uncannily theological terms that echo my own critique of extant theologies of music: "we have changed an art that exists only when, so to speak, the Word is made flesh, into an art which is only the Word. Metaphorically, we have denied the very thing that makes music, the thing which gives it such enormous symbolic and sensual power."[68] Cusick recognizes that this disembodiment of embodied creativity has "theological, moral, and class implications."[69]

She provocatively reads a sexist subtext in this prioritisation of text over bodies, one which makes her recuperative strategies acts of "musical liberation," so to speak; composition and performance themselves have been tacitly, "complementarily" gendered.[70] If composition is "mind," and performance is "body," then the association of body with *woman* implies that bodies performing music are, metaphorically, *female*. This gendered equation would in turn explain why performing bodies are less valuable objects of study for musicologists than the "male-identified" musical score.[71] (This also offers one explanation of Adorno's knee-jerk perception of jazz's freer, less textually dominated style as emasculating.) By treating music first and foremost as a performative, bodily event, Cusick literally retrieves the subtext, revalorising the musical body, the music-made-flesh, smothered beneath textual analysis. But she does not stop here. She also reconceptualises her lived relationship to musical bodies. Once Cusick's focus shifts without shame or ambivalence to the performing musical body, her sharper attunement to music's bodily resonances—its erotic flood of "desire and delight" (Miles)—sparks a new "subjective" correlative in her theorising: Cusick spurns the masculinist music-as-text to explore music's body, her "new found land."[72]

No longer a textual object, Cusick embraces music's erotic powers as sexual subject, sonic lover. In her article "On a Lesbian Relationship with Music: A Serious Effort not to Think Straight," Cusick arrives at this more positive construal of music-as-lover by studying the vital interdependence, even the conflation, of her sexuality and musicality.[73] This confluence, and the erotic metaphor it spawns, further heals the mind–body split that has infected music. This conflation hinges on Cusick's mutual redefinitions of human sexuality and musicality, using the former to understand the latter. Most simply defined, and minus its usual phallocentric trappings, sexuality denotes "a way of expressing and/or enacting relationships of intimacy through physical pleasure shared, accepted or given."[74] This predication is equally applicable to music-making. For through music, human beings undeniably share, give, and accept very physical pleasure. Physical pleasure circulates through musical activity such that, for Cusick and for musicians/music-lovers, music becomes "the most intense and important way one's identity is expressed or enacted," and just as important to self-definition as one's sexual identity. Music is thus an extension, or even precondition, of Cusick's sexuality. Consequently, she uses the visceral image of "bleed-through" to describe the intimate "proximity" of human musicality and sexuality: "If music isn't sexuality, for most of us, it is psychically next door."[75] Clearly the above conflation is only possible if, like Cusick, one rejects excessively genitalised definitions of sexual intimacy and redefines human sexuality as something much more diffuse.[76] She is able to re-vision sexuality and musicality as such because, as a lesbian and therefore exempt from the sexual power dynamics of the phallic economy, her sexual identity allows her "not to think straight." To Cusick's lesbian musings, it is nevertheless important to emphasise that music still penetrates the body, but perhaps in a seemingly non-phallocentric mode and irrespective of sexual orientation.

Paideia Revisited

Cusick promotes the musical porosity that church authorities dam(n)ed and makes it pivotal to her own brand of *paideia*. As a professor, in her "erotic pedagogy,"[77] she encourages her students to open wide and receive music-as-lover and to approach "her" more lovingly.[78] Such musical education subverts today's (masculinist) musicological objectives of teaching students both analytical *and* performative "mastery" (as well as the historical use of music to mould virile, self-controlled "heroes"). Conventional analytical tools, for Cusick, constitute reductionist, albeit "discursively valued strategies" (e.g., Schenkerian analysis, formal melodic/harmonic schemata).[79] To resist dissecting music's body with such controlling devices, Cusick attends to "less valued, 'sensual' features like texture and timbre."[80] Further extending her erotic metaphor, Cusick believes that this subversive listening posture teaches students a new strange "position" within the power/pleasure/intimacy triad which musicality and sexuality share.[81]

This very positive metamorphosis offers us another creative reading of music as a metaphor for sexual relations. Furthermore, Cusick's musico-erotic union evokes an additional, latent (yet very orthodox) dimension within this budding musical Christology: in mystical discourse, Christ—now as God's Music-(not Word) made-flesh—is often described as an erotic lover. Meditating upon her own performance and listening practices, Cusick both personifies and catalyses her own style of erotic, mystical union, yet this communion is acutely embodied. It is indebted, moreover, as much to *maternal* experience as to amatory. That is to say, Cusick strives to teach both "the primal joys of fixation and mother-substitute love" as well as the wondrous "immersion" in music that paradoxically affords freedom from "solipsism." The effects revivify: "As a listening posture, this refreshes and renews me . . . and enables me to return to the world that is the 'not I' with the same intense attention, both sensual and cognitive. Like good sex, it is an experience that re-teaches me how to relate to the world, how to have the nerve to open myself to it."[82] Intimations of such brave supersonic openings resound in Hildegard's Mary.

Also like Hildegard, Cusick's performance practice informs her (admittedly much more iconoclastic) grasp of music's vital, sacred power. This is most evident in her description of the undeniable erotics of organ-playing (included in her deliberations over "Who's on Top?"). In the following passage, one notes not only the unequivocally positive rhetoric with which she renders her embodied analysis of a Bach canonic variation, but also the dramatic contrast of her appreciation of Bach's theological significance vis-à-vis Pelikan's:

> I love using my body to release the power of the uncanonic melody's climax. . . .
> I love using my body to enable the existence in the air of a model of independent
> intimacy, I love feeling like I'm on top, controlling with skilled hands the articu-
> lation of snippets of the chorale in the uncanonic melody, and I especially love
> the climax because it is at that moment that the music gets away from me, at that

> moment that she is on top in the sense that because of my hands' work *she* has all
> the power. And I am reduced to rapture by that power's release. . . . [A]m I play-
> ing *Von Himmel hoch*, or is she playing me?[83]

Here Cusick shamelessly "confesses" her dalliance with musical sin: "This is dangerously close to public sex—in a Lutheran church."[84] *Pace* Pelikan, from Cusick
we also learn the *bodily* basis of music's theological meaning in her reading of
another work—*Aus tiefer Not*. While playing this fugue, the body cries out "in
deepest need" for a polyvalent grace, this because the performer must struggle to
keep the piece going when a *double* pedal line is introduced; five independent lines
of music must now be played with only two hands and two feet.[85]

Like Hildegard's perception of the female body as musical instrument,
Cusick's music-as-lover tests the limits of our distinction between the literal and
metaphorical. As a performer, Cusick transmits embodied love, allowing God's
music to take flesh through hers. Seemingly "on top" at the console, like Mary she
submits, becomes the music, and thereby magnifies the Lord. In this sacred *conjunctio*, subject–object distinctions "harmoniously" disintegrate. Like mystics
longing to become Christ, Cusick welcomes the erasure of her own atomistic identity, effecting in musical performance a loss of self in the Other so common to
mystical discourse. Yet, Cusick recognises and insists that such "spiritual" union,
such "transcendence," is achieved through the most sensual, polymorphously sexual, means.

This is the irony that masculinist models and musical taboos repressed: it is
only through the intensity of music's bodily effects that its spiritual value and
power are unleashed. Centuries after Hildegard, Cusick elatedly describes "all
manner of music and blossom of melody" humming through her frame; her being
plucked and strummed like a lute, delighted and terrified, as Mary was, that at
least in some erotic, corporeal way (if not in her womb), God's music-made-flesh
ravishes her own. Unlike male theologians, Cusick finds God reflected, not in the
contemplation of music's unity, number, and order, but in "her" disruptive iconoclasm:

> I suspect for all of us the originating joy of it comes from assuming more varied
> positions than we think we're allowed in regular life, positions that enable us to
> say "yes" or "no," to immerse, to initiate, to have simultaneous but independent
> climaxes, to escape a system (maybe, it was always the phallic economy) of bewil-
> deringly fixed categories, to wallow in the circulation of pleasures that are beyond
> danger and culturally defined desires. Restoring that joy to ourselves—in our
> musics, our musicalities, our musicologies— may require of us all the foreign-
> ness of thinking that comes of not "thinking straight."[86]

And so, in these boldest closing reflections, music and sex cease to be "next-door
neighbours of the soul" and effectively move in together.[87] Jezebel meets *Incarnatus est*. Here either–or demands for clarity confuse. Divine intercourse comes pre-

cisely in surrendering to music as an unwieldy, sometimes overwhelming Other. Unlike Plato and the fathers, Cusick sanctifies music's destabilising, disintegrating erotica as *Immanuel . . . Emmanuelle?*

And while one dare not universalise or essentialise Cusick's articulation of her experience of music-as-lover, insisting rather that the conceptual content of the lover-trope be contextually determined, the body and human sexuality (however constructed) must be reinstated in musico-theological interpretive frameworks.

Given Hildegard's emphasis upon Christ as God's music-made-flesh and upon humanity's intrinsic musicality, a feminist theology of music will be incarnational rather than mathematico-metaphysical. Thus, numerical relations interconnecting music, body, soul, cosmos, and God are replaced with incarnate flesh and blood, with the interconnective tissue of God's fleshly song nascently resounding in Mary's womb. With this concrete shift (and in light of the critique in part 1), *human sexuality* rather than *numerositas* and harmony has become the interpretive key to understanding music's theological significance. Drawing parallels between Hildegard and Cusick's sources and norms, and considering the theological implications of Cusick's redefinition of music as lover, music, sex, and mystical discourse further converge so that by reading music as metaphor for sexual relations, God's music-made-flesh becomes our lover. As such we (re-)consecrate music's gloriously seductive powers. Opening to "her" embrace, we kinetically redefine music's originary telos as passionate lover, magnifying Song. In the following chapter, other nuns making music supply further metaphorical resonances and christic grist for feminist musico-theological reflection.

Notes

1. An earlier version of the first half of this chapter was published in article form: "Immanence as Music Incarnate: Prelude to a Feminist Theology of Music," *The Annual Review of Women in World Religions,* vol. 5 (New York: SUNY Press, 1999): 90-116. My thanks to SUNY Press for permission to reproduce it here.

2. Schüssler Fiorenza, *Bread Not Stone*, xx.

3. This sapiential Mariology is exemplified in the writings of St. Bernard, Godfrey of Admont, and St. Peter Damian. It assumes the preexistence of Mother and Son together, hidden in the mind of God from eternity. Both Mary and Jesus reveal the secret for which the world was made (Newman, *Sister of Wisdom*, 161).

4. This represents a further historical validation of Ellen Koskoff's observation that music functions cross-culturally as a "metaphor for sexual relations." Cf. Koskoff, *Women and Music*, "Introduction."

5. Even if, *or precisely because,* Hildegard and her charges were not blatantly expressing sexual desire through their music, the fight between Hildegard, her nuns, and the male authorities illustrates Koskoff's transhistorical observation that music functions as metaphor for sexual relations (cf. chap. 2 above). That is to say, the nuns' socio-cultural role as virgins forced the erasure of female sexuality in their music-making; their freedom of musical expression was strictly circumscribed by the cultural roles they were assigned—their symbolisation of asexual purity. As consecrated virgins, Hildegard and her nuns were expected to exude musical "chastity" in their music-making. Any 'lascivious' tones they bodied forth would violate their prescribed cultural function as harbingers of musical purity. The latter role was/is in keeping with music's socio-political role as a metaphor for sexual relations (Koskoff).

6. Hildegard and her charges were subject to the Cistercian (musical) reforms being enforced at that time. According to medieval musicologist and historian Richard Hoppin, the Cistercians wanted their music to be just as "pure" as the rest of their daily living: "no chant should have a range of more than ten notes" (Hoppin, *Medieval Music*, 72). The *ambitus* of Hildegard's chants often exceeded this prescription (see here Holsinger, "The Flesh of the Voice," 105-8).

7. Newman, *Sister of Wisdom*, xvii and 35ff. According to Newman, Hildegard showed much more "interest in the feminine" than any of her "male predecessors and contemporaries." At the end of *Sister of Wisdom*, she writes: "It seems obvious that Hildegard's interest in the feminine per se exceeded that of her male predecessors and contemporaries; that she felt a strong affinity for the traits she perceived as essentially feminine (such as virginity, fruitfulness, natural and artistic beauty, and loving-kindness); and that she had a visionary and poetic gift which makes her images of the feminine, inter alia, particularly memorable. But to go further, to argue that her symbolic thinking took the shape that it did because she was a woman, would be to go too far" (257).

8. Newman, *Sister of Wisdom*, 250.

9. Newman extensively documents the Neoplatonic influences that shaped Hildegard's theology. See *Sister of Wisdom*, chaps. 2 and 6.

10. Margot Fassler emphasizes the centrality of the incarnation to Hildegard's understanding of music in convent life but does not develop its theological implications. See "Composer and Dramatist," in *Voices of the Living Light*, ed. Newman, 149.

Despite Hildegard's Neoplatonic theology, I also believe that her elevation of the feminine to equal importance in the redemptive process, and her blurring of the hierarchical distinctions between earthly and heavenly, divine and human, anticipate feminist principles. I shall elaborate this affinity in section 2 of this chapter.

11. Adrienne Rich, from "Transcendental Etude," *The Dream of a Common Language: Poems 1974-77* (New York: W.W. Norton & Co., 1978) 72.

12. For example, Chrysostom on Ps. 41: "Here there is no need of the cithara, nor taut strings, nor the plectrum and technique, nor any sort of instrument; but if you wish, make of yourself a cithara, by mortifying the limbs of the flesh and creating full harmony between body and soul. For when the flesh does not lust against the spirit, but yields to its commands, and perseveres along the path that is noble and admirable, you thus produce a spiritual melody" (*In psalmum xli*, 2; #169 in MacKinnon, *Music in Early Christian Literature*, 81). Or Athanasius: "[T]he senses in the body are tuned like a lyre; when an understanding mind guides them, then the soul distinguishes and knows what it is doing" (*Oratio contra gentes* 31, in Skeris, *Chroma theou*, 93). And Eusebius allegorises Ps. 97:4-6: "For the kithara is called the harmony of the body with the soul. And this law is clearly seen to be fulfilled in the churches, since we strike up the divine melody with the pneumatic kithara. Indeed, we make our own mouths into rational kitharas, and we use the teeth instead of strings, the lips instead of bronze. And when the tongue is set moving more quickly than the plectrum, then it accomplishes the fully harmonious sound of the struck notes, for the mind moves the tongue (just as) the right kind of musician, acting with full knowledge, brings about similar movements" (Eusebius, *Commentary on Psalms* [authorship in this section of the *Commentary* disputed], in Skeris, *Chroma theou*, 113).

13. Cf. Newman, *Sister of Wisdom*, esp. 55-64.

14. Cf. John Donne, "Hymne to God my God, in my Sicknesse," in John Hayward, ed., *Donne: The Penguin Poetry Library* (London: Penguin Books, 1950), 177.

15. Hildegard, *PL* 197, 217f., in Dronke, *Women Writers of the Middle Ages*, 149.

16. With Hildegard, it is impossible to compartmentalise her compositional, artistic, prophetic, and medical pursuits.

17. Hildegard, *Causae et curae*, in Holsinger, "The Flesh of the Voice," 98.

18. "Untuning," of course, is an allusion to John Hollander's classic work *The Untuning of the Sky: Ideas of Music in English Poetry: 1500-1700*.

19. Dronke, *Women Writers of the Middle Ages*, 197.

20. Hildegard, Ep. 47, *PL* 197, in Dronke, *Women Writers of the Middle Ages*, 198. In this letter, Hildegard goes on to portray David and the prophets in musico-theological terms: the prophet David discerns that the human soul is symphonic and therefore exhorts people in Psalm 150 "to proclaim the Lord on the lute and play for him on the ten-stringed psaltery." Similarly, the prophets compose psalms and craft musical instruments so that listeners might "recall that divine sweetness and praise by which, with the angels, Adam was made jubilant in God before he fell" (ibid.).

21. Dronke, *Women Writers of the Middle Ages*, 198. Hildegard's equation of Satan with non-musicality leads her boldly to conclude that the prelates' interdiction of singing is of demonic inspira-

tion: "So you and all prelates must use the greatest vigilance before stopping, by a decree, the mouth of any assembly of people singing to God. . . . You must always beware lest in your judgement you are ensnared by Satan, who drew man out of the celestial harmony and the delights of paradise" (Hildegard, *PL* 197, 218, in Dronke, 198).

22. Ibid.

23. See here Audrey Ekdahl Davidson, "Music and Performance: Hildegard of Bingen's *Ordo virtutum*," 1-29, and also Fassler, "Composer and Dramatist," 168-75.

24. This wordplay engages Kristeva's redefinition of the *chora*: "a womb or nurse in which elements are without identity and without reason. The chora is a place of a chaos which is and which becomes, preliminary to the constitution of the first measurable body . . . [T]he chora plays with the body of the mother—of woman—, but in the signifying process" ("Le Sujet en Proces," *Polylogue* [Paris: Seuil, 1977] 57, trans. and cited in Oliver, *Reading Kristeva*, 46). In functional terms, as Elizabeth Grosz explains, the *chora* provides "the energetic force" without which an infant cannot gradually enter the linguistic, communicative realm of the Symbolic. More essentially, the *chora* constitutes "the undifferentiated bodily space the mother and child share . . . the unnameable, unspeakable corporeality of the inextricably tangled mother/child dyad" (Grosz, "Chora," *A Feminist Dictionary of Psychoanalysis*). Kristeva tends to characterise music and poetry as hybrid products of both semiotic and symbolic utterances (see, *Desire in Language*, 133).

As for the metaphorical resonances of "placenta," literally this organ is the vital mediator between mother and child, providing nourishment and oxygen to the fetus from the mother's body, and returning fetal wastes into the mother's circulatory system for discharge (see *The Columbia Encyclopedia*, 6th ed. [New York: Columbia University Press, 2002]).

25. For actual examples of her symbolic use of the perfect fourth and fifth, see Kazarow, "Text and Context," 145-47.

26. Söhngen connects music to *Deus artifex* using music's mathematical properties rather than music's enlistment of human embodiment (Söhngen, "Music and Theology," 3). Cf. my discussion of Söhngen in chapter 3 above.

27. Newman, "Introduction," *Symphony of the Harmony of Celestial Revelations*, 21.

28. Clement of Alexandria, "Exhortation to the Heathen," *The Ante-Nicene Fathers*, vol. 2, 172.

29. This conflation was further developed in the high Middle Ages. As one example, Jacobus de Cessolis interprets: "What is the melody of Orpheus's voice but the sermons that Christ delivered and His marvelous teachings? What is the harp He played but the mysteries of the Passion He received on the cross, which was the true harp, whose strings were the sinews, bones, and flesh of Our Redeemer, stretched out like the strings on a guitar on the tree of the cross?" (*Dechado de la vida humana* in Surtz, *The Guitar of God*, 73). Cf. also John Block Friedman's *Orpheus in the Middle Ages* (Cambridge, MA: Harvard University Press, 1970). This imagery also evokes George Herbert's poem "Easter"; see n. 39 below.

30. For example, Eusebius: "He called and healed generously, with that human instrument which he bore, like a musical man showing his skill on the lyre and healing . . ." (*Demonstratio evangelica* 4.13.4, in Skeris, *Chroma theou*, 108) Or in his Tricennial Oration 14.5: "Thus, I say, did our common saviour prove himself the benefactor and preserver of all, displaying his wisdom through the instrumentality of his human nature even as a musician uses the lyre to evince his skill. The Grecian myth tells us that Orpheus had power to charm ferocious beasts. . . . But he who is the author of perfect harmony, the all-Wise Word of God, desiring to apply every remedy to the manifold diseases of the souls of men, employed that human nature . . . as an instrument by the melodious strains of which he soothed, not indeed the brute creation, but savages endued with reason" (Eusebius, in Skeris, *Chroma theou*, 118).

31. Newman, *Sister of Wisdom*, 156ff.

32. Ibid., 179ff.

33. Hildegard, "Hymn to the Virgin," in prose translation by Newman, *Symphony of the Harmony of Celestial Revelations*, 123-25; italics mine.

34. It should be noted here that the words *symphonia* and *(h)armonia* are "overlapping terms" (Newman, *Sister of Wisdom*, 11). During the Middle Ages they could be used to mean either melody, harmony, or music in general, either vocal or instrumental. Musical theorists such as Cassiodorus and Isidore of Seville used the word *symphonia* to refer to consonant intervals such as the fourth, fifth, and octave. Later the word became the name of several different musical instruments—a form of timbrel, a hand-drum, and the hurdy-gurdy (ibid.).

35. Holsinger, "The Flesh of the Voice," 106. For a more detailed analysis, and provocative extramusical interpretation of this hymn, see Holsinger, "The Flesh of the Voice," 100-10.

36. Mary was depicted in musical terms by other theologians as well. In the Office for the Nativity, she becomes "the new Miriam, the sister of Moses, leading the redeemed people of God out of exile with timbrels and dancing" (see Exod. 15:20, discussed in Newman, *Sister of Wisdom*, 180). Also, in one of his sermons, Ambrosius Autpertus contrasts Eve and Mary: "Eve sorrowed, but Mary exulted; Eve carries weeping in her womb, but Mary carried joy. . . . Mary may now play on her instruments, the Mother strike the cymbals with swift fingers. The joyful choruses may sound out and songs alternate with sweet harmonies" (Pseudo-Augustine, *Sermo*, 194.1-2; *PL* 39:210, in Newman, *Sister of Wisdom*, 180).

37. Newman, *Sister of Wisdom*, 181; italics mine.

38. Newman, *Sister of Wisdom*, 180.

39. One is reminded here of George Herbert's poem "Easter":

The crosse taught all wood to resound his name,
Who bore the same.
His stretched sinews taught all strings what key
Is best to celebrate this most high day.

George Herbert, "Easter," in *Herbert: The Laurel Poetry Series*, selected with an introduction and notes by Dudley Fitts (New York, Dell, 1962), 58.

In fact, this new christological trope is paralleled by other popular musical images which were associated with Christ's passion and circulated during the Middle Ages. However, usually the human creature, not Christ, is the lute whose strings Christ plays and tunes. Sor Juana Ines de la Cruz offers one (yet again overlooked) poetic resonance: "I seem to see all the limbs and veins and joints of my body transformed into the strings and keys or pegs of a guitar and Our Lord playing on them with His most holy hands, playing on them as upon an instrument or guitar and making a very sweet and gentle harmonious sound" (Sor Juana, *Vita*, in Surtz, *The Guitar of God*, 68). Note however the allegorical translation of this image's polyvalence.

Another male poet, Jorge de Montemayor, actually does construe Christ as an oddly composite guitar and guitarist in one of his poems (1554): "Christ was the instrument that played at the Last Supper. The twelve strings He played were the twelve Apostles, but one of them (Judas) was out of tune" (Surtz, *The Guitar of God*, 84 n. 39).

40. Newman, "Introduction," *Symphony of the Harmony of Celestial Revelations*, 19.

41. Ibid.

42. Hildegard, in Newman, *Symphony of the Harmony of Celestial Revelations*, 25.

43. Newman, ibid., 27.

44. Ibid.

45. Hildegard of Bingen, *Scivias*, 3.13.12, 631.

46. Newman, *Saint Hildegard of Bingen: Symphonia*, xviii.

47. My thanks to Eric Beresford for help in articulating this "ambivalence," and music's exacerbation thereof, more precisely.

48. Newman comments: "To silence music in the Church is to create an artificial rift between earth and heaven, to put asunder that which God has joined together" (Newman, *Symphony of the Harmony of Celestial Revelations*, 25).

49. Ibid.

50. Newman, *Sister of Wisdom*, 94.

51. Dronke, *Women Writers of the Middle Ages*, 199; italics mine.

52. Ibid., 198. Holsinger (whose provocative defence of a homoerotic element within Hildegard's music and thought hinges on her promotion of the body's centrality to human devotion) interprets the real referents in this analogy from the *Scivias* to be the *liturgy* and the *earthly body* of Christ: "music vivifies the liturgy just as the 'celestial harmony' vivifies Christ's earthly body" (Holsinger, "The Flesh of the Voice," 97f.). This analogy stems from Hildegard's recognition that music is "vital to bodily existence" (98).

53. Kazarow reads Hildegard's *Ordo virtutum* at the four medieval levels of interpretation that were applied to biblical texts at that time (see "Text and Context," 142-51). At the symbolic level (#3), using the standard numerico-mathematical lens, Kazarow carefully analyses the various musical gestures with which Hildegard underlines the person and centrality of Jesus Christ in her theology: "With Pythagoras in mind, then, on this third level, the musical figure of the rising fifth expanding to the octave followed in most cases by a descending whole tone, can be viewed as a symbol of the Incarnation. . . . The intervals formed in this figure . . . are perfect. These are then followed by imperfect intervals. . . . In each instance, the underlying text relates directly to the Incarnation, the Word of God, the

'perfect' and 'imperfect' (in musical terms), that is, the divine and human manifested in Jesus Christ" ("Text and Context," 145f.).

And, reaffirming once again Hildegard's exemplary musical communication of traditional theological values—order and community—Kazarow later concludes that Hildegard's "mystical marriage of music and theology . . . communicates to her listeners as much today as in her own era, a 'sense of wholeness and completeness which is ideally the entelechy of creative effort'" (151, and citing Barbara Jeskalian, "Hildegard of Bingen: Her Times and Music," *Anima* 10, no.1 [Fall 1983]: 13).

54. Söhngen; cf. chapter 3 above; emphasis mine.

55. Newman, *Sister of Wisdom*, 251. For an excellent, nuanced discussion of Hildegard's radical yet dualistic anthropology, see Newman, *Sister of Wisdom*, chaps. 4 and 7.

56. T.S. Eliot, "Burnt Norton," Four Quartets, in *Collected Poems 1909-1962* (London: Faber and Faber, 1963) 191.

57. Dronke, *Women Writers of the Middle Ages*, 197.

58. Holsinger, "The Flesh of the Voice," 122f.

59. Ibid., 119

60. "[D]iscussing Hildegard's music formalistically or mathematically, however, would be to ignore how the abbess actually described and experienced music" (Holsinger, "The Flesh of the Voice," 100). Holsinger therefore concludes: "Framing expressions of desire within an exclusively feminine context, Hildegard's music exceeds and transcends the norms of twelfth-century plainchant and refuses to fit into neat, mathematical models constructed by medieval music theorists and contemporary musicologists. Hildegard gave flesh to the voice and voice to the flesh not for aesthetic gratification, but for the affirmation of femininity and the sonorous expression of body, sexuality and devotional desire" (122f.).

61. Ibid., 118.

62. Ibid., 119. According to Holsinger, in her theology of music and her musical practices, Hildegard actualised and sanctioned the "ideal religious matrix of music and body." This is not surprising, claims Holsinger, given that medieval musicality (especially that of nuns) included a profound awareness of "music's ability to stimulate and enliven the human body." Citing Pseudo-Origen of Alexandria, Augustine, Boethius, and Hrotsvit, among others, Holsinger goes so far as to propose that "to many medieval Christians, the most fundamental attribute of music was its inextricability from bodily experience. . . . Indeed from the early Middle Ages, Christian writers made explicit connections in exegetical and devotional works between music and the body" ("The Flesh of the Voice," 94f.). The first two chapters of my project, however, might challenge any unequivocally positive conclusions that one might derive from this assertion.

63. Ibid., 108.

64. Ibid., 119.

65. In his own way, and to further a different scholarly project, Holsinger also advocates that we look to Christian women's musical practices as instances of both theological innovation and women's socio-political empowerment: "although Hildegard described herself as a 'poor little female,' complained of living in an 'effeminate age,' never advocated female ordination, and was never accused of heresy, her music is nonetheless a many-layered site of struggle with the patriarchal traditions of Christianity and the church" ("The Flesh of the Voice," 133).

66. Cusick, "Feminist Theory, Music Theory," 13.

67. "My musicological *habitus* inclines me to think about music's fixed, textlike qualities, an inclination that is perpetually at odds with the way my performing self inclines me to think about and respond to music" (Cusick, "Feminist Theory, Music Theory," 9-10).

68. Ibid., 15.

69. Ibid., 16. For example: "Identification of both composer and music as mind may be our discipline's version of what Donna Haraway calls the 'god trick,' the epistemological illusion of all-encompassing, and thus objective, knowledge" (ibid.). Cusick, therefore, proposes her own feminist strategy of recuperation. Feminist musicologists will shift their attention to music as "the practices of performing bodies" that enact, not only metaphors of gender, but also "the constitution of gender itself" (17). Thus Cusick outlines a feminist "embodied music theory" (20) to counterbalance extant "composer-identified [music] theory" so that we might "resolve or transcend the mind/body problem" and "explain how musical practices engender us" (22).

70. If one accepts that our gender identity is "the cumulative result" of socially encoded "gendered" acts which we perform over and over (cf. Judith Butler), musical performances are also "socially recognizable" acts (Cusick, "Feminist Theory, Music Theory," 14). Cusick links music and

gender identity via this shared prerequisite of performance. Like gender identity, musical performance represents a "socially recognizable" act, and in music, argues Cusick, "gender is performed " (ibid.).

The impetus for Cusick's reflection is her puzzling over the work of a female composer—the Trio in D minor, op.11 by Fanny Hensel Mendelssohn. Cusick struggles to read the work with a feminist hermeneutic which would resist sheer textual dissection. Instead, by physically playing the work, Cusick discovers its metaphorical content (ibid., 10); only a pianist, because taxed by performing this composition, can grasp the subtle engendering the composition exudes. The piano's role seems "cast and gendered feminine in relation to the theme-declaring strings whose role I heard as gendered masculine" (16). The Trio does not fit the usual trio textures to which our ears have grown accustomed. "Strings and piano might as well live in separate worlds, worlds separated with a rigidity that is unparalleled in the trio literature as I know it. . . . [T]he piano in its ceaselessly supporting role has both the most difficult part and the most crucial part in articulating the tonal plan of the movement's sonata form" (ibid.). Though Cusick's analysis of the piece remains a work in progress, her consideration of this instrumental "struggle" and its potentially gendered overtones only surfaced from her very unorthodox musicological focus upon musical bodies, rather than themes and tonal plans, an analytical stance that affords her clues to moments in the music where "difference has been inscribed, described, or reconciled" (13). Thus, she concludes, "When I write an essay on Hensel's Trio, I will want to argue that Hensel's script for the metaphorical social actions that resolve imbalances in her sonata-form movement is only readable if one acknowledges the inextricable presence of the body in music—a presence both musicology's and music theory's focus on the intentions and the texts of composers scrupulously denies" (15f.).

71. Theorists have prioritised the exposition of "practices of the mind (the composer's choices)." In other words, "We locate musical meaning in the audible communication of one creating mind to a cocreator, one whose highly attentive listening is in effect a shared tenancy of the composer's subject position" (Cusick, "Feminist Theory, Music Theory," 16).

72. An allusion to John Donne's "Elegie 19": "Licence my roaving hands, and let them go,/ Before, behind, between, above, below./ O my America! My new-found-land. . . ."

73. Cusick, "On a Lesbian Relationship with Music," 73. Cusick elaborates: "For some of us, it might be that the most intense and important way we express or enact identity through the circulation of physical pleasure is in musical activity, and that our 'sexual identity' might be 'musician' more than it is 'lesbian,' 'gay,' or 'straight'" (70).

74. Cusick, "On a Lesbian Relationship with Music," 71. Cusick cites Foucault here. Similarly Foucauldian, in her musico-sexual equation, Cusick inserts the inescapable variable of power: "All relationships are agreements about the distribution of power, agreements negotiated in varying degrees of intimacy. The *most* intimate are negotiated in large part through the circulation of pleasure" (ibid.). Sexual identity becomes "the enacted structure of the power/pleasure/intimacy triad" (ibid.). In our society, this enacted structure, in combination with the gender identity of Cusick's chosen partner, makes her a "lesbian." Lesbians are not beholden to the conventional resources for sexual pleasure and erotic experience (72ff.).

75. Ibid., 71.

76. Ibid., 73.

77. I see affinities between Cusick's approach and bell hook's notion of an erotic pedagogy. Cf. hooks, "Eros, Eroticism, and the Pedagogical Process." In this essay, hooks advocates: "Professors rarely speak of the place of eros or the erotic in our classrooms. Trained in the philosophical context of Western metaphysical dualism, many of us . . . enter the classroom to teach as though only the mind is present, and not the body (191). . . . One of the central tenets of feminist critical pedagogy has been the insistence on not engaging the mind/body split" (193).

78. Cf. the subsection entitled "Who's on Top?," in Cusick, "On a Lesbian Relationship with Music," 74-78.

79. Ibid., 77.

80. Ibid.

81. Ibid., 74.

82. Ibid., 75.

83. Ibid., 78.

84. Ibid.

85. Cf. Cusick, "Feminist Theory, Music Theory," 18-20.

86. Ibid., 80.

87. Ibid., 78ff.

Twisted Sisters' Theological Grist

Music as Redemptive Transgression

IN CHAPTER FOUR, I cursorily introduced the notion of imitating Christ as one way of understanding the "genetic" connection between the New Song and human musicality: "The salvific, harmonising power of the Song of God resounds in the human singing that it inspires, sustains, and ultimately composes, suggesting perhaps a new musical trope: '*I am the Lute, You are the Strings.*'" To add more conceptual substance to this symbiosis we turn to the nuns of Santa Cristina in *seicento* Bologna. Reinterpreting the compositional and musical practices of these overlooked Italian celebrities substantiates another episode in music's historical engendering and, more importantly, further inflects the incarnational content of our new model. Reflection upon the nuns' musical disobedience—the discord between their imposed social iconicity and their defiant assertion of artistic freedom—evokes unexpected metaphorical resonances and elicits conceptual substance for elaborating the symbiotic thesis of lute and strings. Again, such renovations become possible only when music is theologically reconceived as a set of embodied practices that circulates myriad social energies, shaping human subjectivity in the process. As above, to remain more interdisciplinary than my masculinist antecedents, along the way I shall consult the work of other feminist theorists in a variety of fields. But first, a "Koskovian" parable:

In her tragicomic summary of the "History of Music," Renée Cox includes a sardonic synopsis of Wagner's opera *Tannhäuser*. In it, Tannhäuser is torn between two women: the sexually insatiable Venus (not to mention her entourage at the *Venusberg*—sirens, naiads, nymphs, and cupids), who will do anything to keep Tannhäuser her love slave, and the chaste virgin Elizabeth, who prays so hard for Tannhäuser's deliverance that she dies and becomes an angel. Venus, writes Cox, is a "musical nymphomaniac"; her music (and that of her disciples) is laced with chromaticism, dissonance, harmonic tension, and rhythmic syncopation.[1] She is a tonally unstable, restless whore. By contrast, Elizabeth's music is "clean, square, diatonic," composed of "pure, clear triads" in "perfect four bar phrases"; she is a virgin who longs to become "pure spirit" and who prays, in one aria, for otherworldly transcendence.[2] Even Tannhäuser's climactic invocation of Elizabeth's name will effect harmonic resolution and Venus's undoing. (She is "swallowed up by the earth."³) The hero triumphs, and an angel–virgin dies to defeat a wicked whore. As listeners, comments Cox, we actually want Venus to die, to relieve the tension that her "disturbing and seductive" musical presence instils.⁴

I. *Liaisons Dangéreuses:* Bolognese Nuns and Venetian Courtesans

In his fierce polemic against seventeenth-century modern music—that *seconda prattica* epitomised in Monteverdi's audacious madrigals—Archbishop Giovanni Maria Artusi calls both style and composer a "painted whore." He contrasts old and new musical techniques within a tacitly gendered grid of oppositions⁵ whose rhetoric I shall summarise (in italics) as follows: according to Artusi, the *preference of modern composers for dissonance, seventh chords, mixed modes, and a style of word-painting which flouts classical poetic principles of rhythm and armonia, effectuates an unnatural, monstrous birth.* Modern music stages a *bitter, ugly, stinking, masquerade* by deceiving the listener's senses with *frivolous ornamentation* and changing *appearances.* Like the seductress *Armida,* it infects men like a *sickness,* contaminating them with *melancholy,* and working its charms through the singer's "wild, eye-rolling, body-distorting gestures."⁶ᵗ The *stile moderno* arouses and destabilises body and soul with the *restless movement of its parts*—its chief (and unorthodox) harmonic means. These *pagan dregs* Artusi contrasts with the *rich, sweet, Christian wine* of traditional music: *begotten,* not *made,* of *one genus* and *mode* throughout, through which one *changeless essence* remains. This *stile antico* is grounded in the *truth* of *unchangeable harmonic categories.* Consonance rules; text is the happy "daughter "of *ritmo* and *harmonia;* form controls *materia.* Like a *sick* woman, modern music is excessively *wet, cold,* and *ugly,* while the *prima prattica* is *dry, hot, healthy, beautiful.* It is a *fragrant,* pure libation akin to the singing of the *nuns at Jerusalem* in Tasso's *Jerusalem Delivered.*⁷ Cusick concludes:

> The implied feminisation of modern music's listeners is more than confirmed when Artusi first cites Tasso's description of nuns in Jerusalem singing chastely, through the authoritative voice of Vario; they sing chastely, ignoring the jeers of the Saracens as if they were chattering birds, and then contrasts the chastity of the nuns' music with the condition of modern music: "How," he [Artusi] asks, "has he [Monteverdi] preserved it chaste if, corrupting it, he has made it become like a painted whore?"⁸

With this gendered diatribe, Artusi hits Monteverdi and his disciples below the belt. Real men don't do monody. They are not, nor do they create, monstrous Armidas. Their music should be worthy of nuns' angelic voices.

What would happen, however, if Artusi's beatific nuns began speaking in the tongues of painted whores? Despite their strict enclosure, this scandal in fact occurred, namely, in the convent of Santa Cristina della Fondazza in Bologna, the same city where Artusi developed his musical theory and presided as canon regular of San Salvatore. In his recent archival study of this convent, Craig Monson observes that nun-composer Sister Lucrezia Orsina Vizzana (1590-1662) uses strikingly modern musical idioms. Monson's analysis of Vizzana's compositions shows that a woman composer, locked inside a convent, somehow managed to incorporate such illicit "monstrosities" into some of the city's most innovative sacred music.[9] Despite constant censure from arch-conservative clerical (and occasionally civil) authorities, this virgin's whoring music thrilled most clerics and lay people, "luring" them into true spiritual ecstasy and eliciting descriptions of the nuns as angelic choirs. Vizzana's and her fellow sisters' crafty maintenance of their full-bodied musical expressivity epitomises the new musical ethos being proposed throughout this book. Monson's and Robert Kendrick's[10] respective archival accounts of nuns' musical activities in Bologna and Milan contradict the common assumption that Counter-Reformation musical norms were universally enforced. Moreover, they reveal that a gendered agenda lies hidden beneath church authorities' attempts to purge musical "profanities and barbarisms"—supposedly in the name of textual clarity[11]—since musical reform was stricter in convents than in monasteries.[12] Even nonmusical convent reforms were musically censorious: church authorities used freshly reinforced cloister walls not only to protect the nuns from contamination by the outside world but also to "disembody" or neuter women's singing for its gynephobic auditors.

Ironically, while these walls might have "contained" men's fears, they actually consolidated women's social power.[13] Archival evidence reveals a gaping hole between the church's theoretical reforms and the nuns' musical practices.[14] Given the tridentine ban on visits from external music teachers, how could eighteen of Vizzana's twenty motets (pub. 1623) have been written in the *stile moderno*? Records show that a request for instruction in this style was denied to other nuns in 1606. However, in 1605, by exploiting a rich banker's influence over the Roman curia (Count Romeo Pepoli), the nuns at Santa Cristina managed to gain permission for external musicians to perform in their external churches on feast days and funerals. Thus, Vizzana could absorb the innovative idioms seeping through the convent grates.[15] Furthermore, the nuns' parents were still allowed contact with their daughters in the convent parlours and could smuggle them gifts of modern musical scores. In fact, one Sister Alfonsina Ganassi's father, Alfonso, was a composer, wind player, and music teacher, who no doubt transmitted his innovative compositional techniques to the nuns along with samples of his work. (After 1623, the abbess of Santa Cristina stopped screening mail, thus opening another conduit for musical contraband.[16])

After the authoritarian Archbishop Paleotti died in 1610, the nuns secretly enjoyed eight years of music teaching from Ottavio Vernizzi, whom their abbess surreptitiously appointed *maestro de musica* of the convent.[17] Vernizzi worked closely with the innovative modern composers Ercole Porta and Adriano Banchieri. As members of the new *Accademia dei Floridii* in Bologna (est. 1614), these men even dedicated motet collections to Milanese nuns, presumably for performance.[18] They also had contact with Monteverdi and unrestricted access to his music.[19] Vernizzi's cosmopolitan tutelage afforded Vizzana and the other nuns of Santa Cristina long, intoxicating draughts of the polluted *seconda prattica*. In addition to this clandestine resumption of musical instruction (and no doubt to Artusi's horror), nuns would sing Aquilino Coppini's resettings of Monteverdi's scandalous madrigals to sacred texts.[20]

Clay-Footed Angels and Worldly Investments

Monson's and Kendrick's research also challenges Artusi's images of convents as "earthly Jerusalems"—peaceful oases where innocent creatures make music in perfect harmony.[21] Vicious, competitive feuds often erupted between nuns before they intoned ethereal strains, strife which some church authorities used to warrant a return to musical austerity. These heavenly creatures were not the submissive souls whom Artusi idolised. While the nuns certainly hoped to achieve spiritual transcendence through their music, they also recognised and enjoyed their status as central agents in the Milanese and Bolognese "symbolic econom[ies] of prestige."[22] Nun musicians were the "most precious symbol of patrician pride and piety, a piety that did not necessarily coincide with episcopal guidelines."[23] For these women, music became, therefore, a political weapon, a source of power, and a means of what is now termed "identity," one which assured these invisible women a formative role in the city's cultural (and therefore political) life—its "symbolic world."[24] Kendrick characterises the nuns as "social actors" whose incarnate union of virginity and musical virtuosity secured divine favour for the Milanese citizenry.[25] As spiritual intercessors and musical virtuosi, the nuns were international celebrities; their attraction of foreign "attention and patronage" justified the "city's claims to be a second Rome."[26] Individual nuns became famous,[27] their mystique and allure no doubt heightened by their physical invisibility. In order to maintain musical activity on their terms (and their families'), nuns shrewdly enlisted help from family members against clerics or played clerical allies off against the local archbishop. Kendrick and Monson observe that, despite thick convent walls and partly thanks to their existence, nuns' highly publicised musical virtuosity allowed them to project their voices very powerfully back into the urban communities. Any ecclesiastical reforms or punishments that threatened the city's musical prosperity were opposed by the patrician families whose money vitally sustained convent life. There were numerous clashes among the different aesthetic tastes of patron families, and these subsequently precipitated internal strife among nuns.

While the end product of this prestige economy might seem the food of angels to the outside listener, the wars waged to maintain this coveted cultural commodity belie supernatural accolades and reveal the mixed motives, earthly and spiritual, that fuelled both the nuns' creativity and the financial machine that sustained it. In short, tangled webs of intrigue bred these heavenly choirs. As active participants in this economy, these nuns acquired a musico-rhetorical power equal to that of their lascivious contemporaries—the infamous Venetian courtesans. In fact, Archbishop Litta would decry convents as "seraglios of singers" rather than terrestrial paradises, and nuns as "ill-concealed opera-singers."[28] However, while both nun and courtesan sang the same ravishing musical language, the nuns' virginity[29] and vocation sanitised their otherwise blasphemous tones. (When, however, has personal sexual "integrity" ever undermined the "sublimity" of Mozart's, Brahms's, Liszt's, or Wagner's masterpieces?) Text, context, and performer/auditor either sublimated eros to salvific ends or fatally unleashed it to seduce and effeminise.

Nevertheless, *both teleologies implicate the same gynephobic subtext.* Perhaps the "smoke-and-mirror" claustral walls allowed the spiritually ravished male imagination to distinguish between nuns' music and that of their secular antitheses. While walls ensured the fantasy of disembodied voices, could the "dangerously" similar physical erotics of singing for both nun and courtesan further dissolve popular distinctions between angelic and sirenic music? As mentioned in chapter 2, Monteverdi himself (more secure in his own masculinity perhaps) allowed a Venetian courtesan to emasculate three powerful men in his opera *L'Incoronazione di Poppea.*[30] According to Susan McClary, this work offered a veiled political commentary on the crumbling of patriarchal control at the end of the seventeenth century. In *real life*, however, Milanese and Bolognese nuns—like their Venetian "sisters"—also resisted patriarchal attempts to squelch their autonomy and social power, arguably emasculating clerical potentates *à la Poppea.*[31] In the process, and for my creative purposes, the nuns' politicking and their sensuous musical language melted the boundaries between sacred and secular, virgin and courtesan, that cloister walls and Artusi's slanderous denunciations sought to enforce.

Musicologist Anthony Newcomb has culled archival evidence from sixteenth-century Naples that further suggests the blurring of these boundaries, this time in the popular imagination; at the theatre, one male audience member described Cleopatra's singing as *spiritually* ravishing: "The sweetness and novelty of the singing transported everyone to Paradise. . . . The queen Cleopatra was Phomia, whose singing cannot be compared to terrestrial matters but to the heavenly harmonies."[32] And one final postscript definitively belies the nun–angel as "pure" fantasy: it seems that glimpses of actual nuns through convent grates (which had illegally been left open by the nuns) horrified some men; in 1612, visitor Jakob Sobieski was disgusted by "the age and physical repulsiveness of [one] Donna Grazia."[33] Apparently ugly nuns make bad angels.

Thus, once again, (post-tridentine) musico-theological prescriptions and transcendentalist rhetoric veiled male insecurities about identity and male ambivalence toward women and the body. In all these stolen and authorised liberties, it should be noted, the convent walls became, paradoxically, a source of modern women's creative freedom. More important to this project, however, is the fact that through a female composer, a choir of nuns, and the sanitising force of sacred texts and godly *affetto*,[34] this illicit musical language circulated through the bodies of all who assembled in the convent's internal and external churches, arousing and expressing the congregation's collective desire for God. Vizzana's dissonances, bold leaps, and unusual harmonic resolutions set to a psalm text (or even a portion of the erotically charged Song of Songs)[35] manipulated and channelled Christian desire in new, and apparently for some, very dangerous ways. Most participants, however, felt themselves in the presence of angels, receiving heavenly manna.[36] The nuns' passionate, uncompromising song and musical vision remind one that music is "quintessentially" fluid, mocking with its liquid body and aural effects the morally charged, aesthetic, and corporeal boundaries that individuals try to maintain. The clerics' tactics and the nuns' disobedience demonstrate that music's theological significance lies not in its incarnation of harmony and order—divine, cosmic, or human—but precisely in the *"promiscuity" and disintegration* which it breeds; in its disorderly conduct of "power, pleasure, and intimacy" between willing (or not so willing) bodies. If Christians are strings melded to Christ, the lute, such that the Song of God resounds in the human singing that it inspires, sustains, and ultimately composes, the nuns teach us that music-as-*imitatio* is acutely fleshly and inevitably transgressive. Previously a dangerously volatile, musico-theological problem, women making music now provide new metaphors for theological reflection about music as an imitation of Christ, illuminating their genetic connection. I choose therefore to redefine music theologically as redemptively transgressive, fleshly *imitatio*.

II. Fleshly Intertextuality:
Singing Nuns Meet Lochrie's Kempe

Other feminist theorists and historians, reading tradition against itself, have reconstrued the flesh as a spiritual boon rather than burden. In the remainder of this chapter, I would like to fortify and elaborate this redefinition of music as fleshly *imitatio* by establishing points of contact with the work of other revisionist scholars. As we continue this exodus from the conceptual confines of music as unity, number, and order, these interdisciplinary affinities will confirm music's rightful and appropriately disruptive place within the tradition of imitating Christ. To this end, Karma Lochrie's analysis of women's mystical discourse as imitative and praiseworthy "translations of the flesh" offers an informative conceptual model.

Lochrie enlists the Kristevan notion of abjection as a lens through which to revalorise women's social function as principles of fleshly contagion in general and, in particular, to reframe Margery Kempe's writing as an authoritative translation of her fleshly intercourse with Christ. Abject objects and states of abjection are really "safeguards," cultural "primers."[37] Constituting the subject's antithesis, whatever is designated abject in fact negatively mirrors the subject and, therefore, allows meaning construction—economies of sameness so to speak—even as abject objects mark the site of meaning's "collapse."[38] "It is thus not lack of cleanliness or health that causes abjection," writes Kristeva, "but what disturbs identity, system, order."[39] Via such "safeguards," Lochrie gradually revalorises women's association with fleshly transgression. Within the Christian tradition (particularly by way of Augustine and Bernard of Clairvaux), women become identified with the abjectly threatening flesh, that is, with any demonic, unspiritual forces and impulses.[40] Following St. Paul, the flesh is a source of sin, and the body is merely a "lackey" to its rebel sway.[41] As abjection, the flesh "does not respect borders, positions, rules." It connotes the "in-between, the ambiguous, the composite."[42] Within the triangulation of body, soul, and flesh, Woman inhabits the border between body and soul to become a "fissure" which the flesh exploits to lure men into sin. Woman invites abjection for she personifies the "principle of influx" which continually weakens delineations between body and soul.[43] For medieval women, the only foolproof remedy against such fleshly in-fluence is to seal their bodies and to remove them from the world. Thus nuns and anchoresses, (i.e., model/ideal Christian women) embrace chastity, silence, and claustration.[44] This becomes the redemptive, *prescribed* form of female *imitatio Christi*.[45]

And yet, here Lochrie introduces the double logic of the flesh. *Pace* Paul, Augustine, and Bernard, the flesh remains the "hinge of salvation,"[46] and therefore women-as-flesh are its spiritual vanguards (though clearly church authorities did not celebrate women as such). Women-as-flesh personify the originary Christian paradox: *the Word was made flesh*.[47] Moreover, the model for many forms of *imitatio* is the "crucified body of Christ itself."[48] In addition to these two sanctioned fleshly precedents, the risen Christ invites Thomas to penetrate his wounds, further rendering abjection the route to faith and to communion with God.[49] Thus, in Christ's exemplary incarnation, death, and resurrection, the Word-made-flesh actually grounds faith and knowledge of God in bodily wounds, "ruptures," and dis-integration.[50] Consequently, to imitate Christ's passion through forms of abject submission, Catherine of Siena will go so far as to drink pus from an invalid's wound; Angela of Foligno drinks lepers' bath water; Catherine of Genoa eats lice; and Julian prays for mortal illness.[51] Thus, if one accepts that the Word-made-*flesh* privileges bodily communication and reception of the gospel, and this very often via forms of abjection, then women's *imitatio* challenges the pejorative ideology of Woman as flesh.[52] (It should be noted that examples of male immersion in such abject imitative media do exist. Also, religionists Bernard McGinn and Amy Hollywood have challenged any universal generalisation of such female bodily forms of christic imitation.[53])

Lochrie's interpretive keys of abjection and Woman-as-flesh also help to explain the polarised purity and danger of both music as Woman and women making music. As forbidden fleshly fruit, music(-as-Woman) is "always straying, heterogeneous, dangerous . . . verging always on sin through its excess of desire."[54] Further, this elucidates its historical, censored engendering in polarised gynemorphisms. Lochrie's model also articulates in more specific, theological terms why women making music were such dangerous creatures, the object of male ambivalence. Given the transhistorical conflation of music and Woman illustrated above and Lochrie's revisionist, double logic of the flesh, fresh insights abound if we reconstrue music as abject *imitatio*; for, like Woman, music exudes "influx," that principle which continually erases body–soul boundaries. And women making music destabilise cultural codes and taboos, not by writing the body as Kempe did but by singing it, thus breaching remedial seals and confusing the body/soul distinctions that virgins were supposed to embody and uphold.[55] Music as fleshly Woman is a heterogeneous "composite" which does not respect "borders, positions, rules."[56] In terms of gendered identity, women, music, and flesh threaten masculine self-definition with effeminisation.[57]

Like the abject acts of Angela of Foligno and both Catherines of Siena and Genoa, nuns smuggled "polluting" musical practices into their convent for literal incorporation into their musical *imitatio*.[58] In their "whorish" music and their defiance of ecclesiastical decrees, nuns con-fused "perversion and perfection" and effected "contagion between the two."[59] An embodied practice, during any musical event, music's penetration of and circulation among assembled bodies, as well as music's own promiscuity all guarantee that auditors, performers—even the spiritual sonorities themselves—teeter upon the threshold of socially encoded abjection; worship thus becomes a requisite "straying into unstable territories, where the limits of the self are not clearly defined."[60] In short, Lochrie's precedent encourages us to reread *musical* taboos (like those concerning food or sexuality) as valiant attempts to protect the body and subjective identity from all forms of abjection.[61] Music radically challenges the reality of these constructed boundaries, whether the body is male and therefore "spiritually" grounded, or female and eternally mired in fleshliness. Music exposes the fragility, the evanescence, of notions of bodily integrity, the impossibility of their sustained, concrete realisation.

This instability, however, is salvific, and, when actively engaged, an act of imitative obedience. For we recall that, to those assembled, these delinquent singing nuns did not despoil music's alleged incarnation of divine unity, number, and order. To sing, in a sense, is "to open the sealed body,"[62] and yet the wings of nuns' song, however 'disobedient,' bring salvation, communion with God. Singing nuns are perceived as idyllic, angelic advocates and mediators for entire cities. Their literally "heaving powers of the flesh"—their voices, lungs, diaphragms, and shoulder blades—musically "topple" worshippers and themselves "into the love of God."[63] Augustine feared music's sensual, distractive powers, and Artusi its "contaminating" elements, but, according to the double logic of the flesh, music is a divinely ordained "token of defilement," "a means of perfection." Further, if theologically reframed within the practice of imitating Christ, music-making would seem a more positive manifestation of women's *imitatio* than the traditional tears, stigmata, nosebleeds, and smells which Lochrie enumerates.[64] Read from this new musico-theological perspective, perhaps it is not the nuns (or monks, though less censored) who were disobedient, but the church authorities who would sterilise their music and thereby depotentiate the fullness of Christ's fleshly presence. (Hildegard implies the same.)

Quoting Angela of Foligno, Lochrie reconstrues language itself as blasphemous inhabitant and invader of the flesh: "*And then the Word passed through me, touched all of me, and embraced me.*"[65] Perhaps, Angela's erotic description of verbal communion with Christ strengthens the case for erotically reframing *musical* communion with Christ as a penetrating musical lover. Like a liquid, melting Venus, music also passes through us, washes over us, strokes, penetrates, and envelops our bodies, immersing us in its sonic vibrations. Like Angela, the nuns of Santa Cristina and other women making music voice the same redemptive "blasphemy"—chastely, obediently, imitating Christ with each note. Here, however, instead of trembling limbs, crying, or fainting,[66] desire circulates through soaring high notes, daring *appoggiaturas*, and the sustained tension of harmonic suspensions and deceptive cadences. The "flesh of the voice," that liminal point where "music and body coincide most radically" (Holsinger), engages the abject in ways that seem blasphemous and sirenic but are thoroughly redemptive.[67]

Singing the Body

Grounded in Kristeva's feminist revalorisation of abjection, Lochrie's terminology for understanding Kempe's texts and, by extension, women's *imitatio* provides theological discourse with a more apt—because inclusive and creatively tensile—vocabulary for articulating not just music's fleshly double logic but also its theological significance. Neither Lochrie nor Bynum include nuns' musical activity as a daily, "transgressive," imitative practice. Here a theology of music can fill aporia in the *imitatio* tradition. Phenomenologically, the most rudimentary imitative practices of this affective spirituality consisted of human acts of "imagination and memory" which were translated into fleshly modes. Whether imagined or ascetically performed, disciples actualised "translations" of "Christ's bodily presence."[68] Could not music be described as yet another, more palpable rather than imaginary translation of Christ's bodily presence? While traditional practices made images seminal to achieving union with Christ, music's nonverbal gestures, harmonic patterns, and rhythms (while dangerously polysemic for some authorities) offered even more direct "recollection," perhaps even recapitulation, of divinity within the human body. Indeed, music could be a wordless translation of Christ's bodily presence.

Lochrie also construes the mystics' bodies as "mnemonics of suffering" that took shape from the mystics' meditation on images and the subsequent translation of the body into a suffering, somatic "sign of remembrance." Given the centrality of music in convent life, singing bodies were mnemonics of the first order. And while Lochrie identifies reading, pilgrimage, and meditation as the main ingredients in medieval christic imitation that then culminated in late fifteenth-century forms of bodily *imitatio*, music seems an even more vibrant and prior engagement of the body, contemporaneous as it was with the original imitative acts of reading, meditation, imagination, and recollection. Further, it enfleshed a bodily remembrance that was not predominantly privative in content like other ascetic practices—self-flagellation, fasting, and so on. For singing is also communal and interpersonal bodily remembrance, enacted collectively by the body of Christ rather than alone in one's cell. Late medieval women may have imitated Christ's humanity and bodiliness more graphically than in other epochs, and in terms of wounds, sacrifice, and intense corporeal suffering, but they also imitated him bodily every time they opened their mouths to sing or lifted a bow to their viols. These were, I daresay, synergistic recordings of the Song of God.

Music is also overlooked in discussions of imitative practices' exploitation of the body's porosity, mutability, effluvia, and heterogeneity. Like other historical imitative practices, in singing, music exploits the body's *porosity*. In performer and auditor, there is a corporeal reception and internalisation of the body of Christ as Song of God. Such holy communion permits the "internalisation of another's reality"—traditionally both a goal and sign of *imitatio*.[69] In listening, we allow God's Song to flood our being from without; in performing, it infuses us, and then from this initial in-corporation, we re-diffuse this christic presence. As noted in chapter 4, "all human music-making finds its beginning and end in the Song of God and thus bears witness to God's immanence, to the Christ who dwells within us." Quite obviously, this porosity, and the musical internalisation of Christ's body which it affords, effects the *bodily change* that imitators of Christ desired.[70] Similar to those imitative practices that required voluntary or involuntary manipulation of the body to "become Christ," musical performance demands corporeal manipulations of staggering complexity. Even as listeners, our bodies are (involuntarily) manipulated by the sounds made and received. Music *moves* performers and auditors, emotionally and physically.

Rightly or wrongly, both Bynum and Lochrie make much of medieval women mystics' miraculous (often involuntary) bodily effluvia. (Men also experienced similar spiritual side effects.) This recent scholarly preoccupation is nonetheless instructive, because it reminds us that music is *bodily effluvium;* it leaves one body to "anoint" another. The theological significance of music's liquidity has been overlooked. Moreover, recognising and foregrounding this sonic trait helps to explain music's dangerous promiscuity as well as its gynemorphic potency. To shift emphasis from music's "innate" harmony to both its messy fluidity and *our* innate porosity allows the relocation of music's theological significance in its disintegrative, destabilising sway.

Finally the unruly heterogeneity characterizing other imitative practices acquires new metaphorical resonances in musical *imitatio*. Perhaps the most resounding message in the fleshly Song of God is the quintessential *heterogeneity* of existence; Being as a forcefield, mimetically transmitted in music as unresolvable flux. In its volatile body music communicates a tangle of spiritual and physical desires that ultimately evaporate; such transience is musically signified with a 'final'—itself paradoxically impermanent—chord. The ineradicable heterogene-ity of the human condition is further evidenced in the conceptual collapse between imitating *and* becoming the Song of God when we make music. This musical dissolution of the self, as well as music's own spatio-temporal evanes-cence, affirms the metaphorical fleshliness of our existence, i.e., its ineluctable transience, the inevitable "straying into unstable territories" of human subjectiv-ity which, as imitators of Christ, we are called to explore and affirm. Masculinist theologies of music avoid such dystopian readings of music's theological value. Begbie and Pickstock we recall, foreground music's often troubling, spatio-tem-poral impermanence, but then try to harmonically resolve it. In chapter 6 I will proffer a concrete example of this discordant alternative.

Provoking another theological collapse, music indicates that our "unbearable lightness" bears embracing. Perhaps music is equally, and for all Christians, *imita-tio Mariae. My body doth magnify God's Song, attuned not to some originary har-mony, but to the primal fluidity, the endless unfolding and ultimate dissolution of the self.* Here I dissolve another old conceptual dichotomy already discussed (*in utero*) in chapter 4. In other words, while not an imitative prerequisite per se, it is impor-tant to note in this section on music's heterogeneity that music makes its own weighty contribution to the erasure of boundaries between christic and marian forms of imitation. Upon conception, we remember, Mary burst into song. More telling still, scripture does *not* have Mary singing, but music's powers irrevocably shaped our reception of her words—*Magnificat* and music having become insep-arable in tradition and our collective imagination. Christians making music imi-tate Mary by embracing the living Song of God. This is another important recuperation, given the absence of the significant treatments of Mary's *Magnificat* in musico-theological discourse. A feminist theology of music will construct a framework that builds its concepts from the overarching images of Jesus as God's music-made-flesh, and of Mary as the woman whose body allows this music to take flesh. In fact, maternal imagery can be a rich, neglected resource for musico-theological reflection. Kristeva's correlative notions of abjection and the semiotic, we remember, are indebted to her analysis of mother–child relational dynamics.

Elaborated otherwise, human song is simultaneously kenotic and plero-matic—an imitative, christo-marian circulation of God's music-made-flesh. Hildegard perceived this in her marian hymns. This elision has also been discussed elsewhere by Bynum, Ellen Ziegler, and E. Anne Matter.[71] In her depiction of the intense reception of Christ during the Eucharist, Bynum records that both men and women imagined themselves pregnant with Christ.[72] These reception metaphors can be applied to musical experience as well. Just as mother–child boundaries blur in the womb and as Christ is absorbed in the Eucharist, in music-making we receive or become "pregnant" with the Song of God. Thus, music's power to challenge conceptual boundaries between spirit and flesh, sacred and profane, clean and unclean also erodes traditional distinctions between the imita-tion of Christ or Mary.[73]

Ascetic renunciations, ministry to those in need, and simulations of Christ's passion are not the only expressive modalities of Christian desire and longing for the Beloved, nor the only signs/tokens of communion with Christ. For, like the ingestion of wafer and wine; like Mary conceiving the Song of God; or Mary lamenting and cradling the dead Christ in her lap—like any other embodied configuration of christic reception—in playing/listening to music we receive the corporeality of Christ, *and this outside "controlled" liturgical or monastic containers.*[74] In music's invasively promiscual embrace, *conjunctio is imitatio.* That is to say, if Jesus is the Song of God, human music-making, and/or our immersion in music, collapses the distinction between imitating and becoming Christ.

Tannhäuser's plight needs reconception. Painted virgin–whores capably intercede in a passionate play of musical *chair.*[75] Lucrezia Vizzana and her fellow sisters point to a reframing of music-as-love. In musical *imitatio,* lover and beloved become one resonant flesh.

III. Critical Interlude:
Music as *Imitatio Crucis*

As Christian technique of the self, affect and desire are physically materialised in music and signified through the body, through a sonic language of the flesh, translating rapturous and/or suffering love. Is it possible to extend the effluvial metaphor and reframe musical *imitatio* as an oozing wound, one of the mnemonics of suffering that Bynum and Lochrie discuss at length. In the next chapter, I shall explore this possibility, but it seems unlikely that most music can be characterised as an *imitatio crucis.* Lochrie and Bynum frame most imitative practices (especially women's) as participation in Christ's passion and suffering. This hermeneutic emphasis may be somewhat misleading to readers unmindful of these scholars' necessarily restricted historical focus; a wide range of imitative practices outside the gorier framework of *imitatio crucis* has always existed.[76] Extravagant forms of the latter were (like musical excesses) discouraged. (Bynum, and Lochrie do mention this imitative censorship and its use as a source of male control over female agency, as do historians Jo Ann McNamara, E. Ann Matter, and Ellen Ziegler.[77]) More broadly construed, the imitation of Christ's suffering was intended to link one to Christ's saving work.[78] Even if it is not *ipso facto* an imitation of Christ's passion, music seems to share this broader objective.

One might, however, describe music metaphorically as a "sweet wound" to borrow the (erotically charged) metaphor that Julian of Norwich uses to describe her intercourse with Christ. Her complex reaction to this encounter aptly describes the pleasure-pain of many types of musical experiences that all of us have undoubtedly had: "living and vivid and hideous and fearful and sweet and lovely."[79] With similar ambivalence, music penetrates our ears and flesh in both violent and tender ways. Its harmonic tensions—resolved or not—inflict a presumably desired wounding within its auditors. On the basis of Julian's metaphor, one can also reconceptualise music— particularly given its overlooked fluidity and our "troublesome" porosity—as simultaneous outpouring and infusion of life-blood.

Without actually *being* suffering, music has always offered an outlet for its expression. Music, moreover, may gesturally simulate suffering. For example, in Bach's chorale prelude for organ "*Erbarme dich*," the steady pounding chords conjure images of nails being pounded into Christ's hands. Indeed, flagellation and cries of anguish can be simulated with musical idioms. Such mimesis may even induce suffering-as-compassion perhaps, or it may draw people together during times of agony, offering a desired catharsis. Of course, it must also be said that the *act* of making such evocative music is not necessarily an imitation of the suffering Christ either. And yet, for some performers, singing the "*Crucifixus*" from Bach's *B Minor Mass*, or the *Seven Last Words from the Cross* (especially James MacMillan's, b. 1959) can be considered aesthetic yet physically painful incarnations of the crucifixion. Pangs of Gethsemane might reside in Suzanne Cusick 's aching need, and plea for "grace" when she plays Bach's "*Aus tiefer Not*" at the organ, this due to the double pedal line which leaves her body teetering, her powers of coordination ever on the brink of the collapse. Nevertheless, despite these intimate connections between music's metaphorical resonances with suffering, it would be difficult to argue that music, like a multitude of other imitative practices, stems from a desire to experience the blood and gore of Christ's passion. In certain extreme musical cases, however, it can become one hermeneutical option for articulating music's theological significance, as we shall see in chapter 6. Moreover, to counterbalance masculinist models' excessively harmonic frameworks, one might urge more attention to dissonance in theologies of music, allowing thereby a wide spectrum of musico-theological resources with which to accommodate the historically specific tragedies and horrors of our own postnuclear context.

That said, perhaps, for a "postnuclear" theological model, this suffering motif need not be the sole definer of christic *imitatio* and, by extension, of music-as-*imitatio*.[80] Preoccupation with the imitation of Christ's suffering, as Margaret Miles suggests, may represent the bias of one particular cultural code, a dated means of identity formation which should be less of a priority today.[81] Even Lochrie tempers her concentration upon Christ's passion in Kempe's and other women mystics' discourse by mentioning that rapture was as much the effect of imitative practices as suffering; the more crucial element, so to speak, was emulation of Christ's *humanity*.[82] In light of Miles's critique and Lochrie's qualification, it might therefore be more appropriate to frame music's ultimate imitative uses and effects in terms of rapture and desire rather than those of suffering. For while it may be difficult to construe music as the *imitatio crucis* that past imitative practices were used to recreate, music does at least offer a channel for not only the joy of being filled with Christ but also for the very emptiness that individuals are often attempting to fill by musical immersion. Thus a case can be made with music for broadening our conception of the tradition of the imitation of Christ. The very act of renovation reminds one that *imitatio* is itself an imaginative construction, a (constraining) "cultural code."[83] By intentionally shifting the emphasis from suffering to a more polymorphous and polysemic desire, *christomimesis* accommodates not just Christians' myriad engagements of music as a form of discipleship but also a wider variety of socio-political contexts and needs. For some, such adjustments court a dangerous relativism. Yet this seeming "disadvantage" affords precisely the necessary conditions for perceiving the centrality of music within this christic tradition, enriching thereby its continued relevance and potency.

These various elements from medieval *imitatio* have been enlisted for feminist theological purposes yet with the full understanding of Bynum's and other historians' objections to crass decontextualisations of the same. Bynum contends that "the practices and symbols of any culture are so embedded in that culture as to be inseparable from it." If, as Bynum argues, discussing medieval mystics' inedia with a nineteenth-century "notion of anorexia nervosa" is anachronistic, then she must also conclude that "mediaeval symbols, behaviors, and doctrines have no direct lessons for the 1980s."[84] I take seriously Bynum's warning against finding "direct lessons" for the late twentieth century in medieval symbols and images and her insistence that "[w]e cannot adopt such symbols as an answer to the impoverishment of twentieth-century images."[85] Nevertheless, I do think the tradition of imitating Christ can be reconstructed for modern times. Arguably, various modes of imitating Christ have transhistorically defined Christian identity. Even Bynum concedes that our fascination with the panoply of medieval "images and values" can stir us to find "richer ones for our own time," and therefore the former may at least "point the direction in which we should search."[86] What is more important to retain from her research is the basic purpose such symbols served: while they did not programme human activity, they enabled women to express and give meaning to certain "basic realities that all societies face: the realities of suffering and the realities of service and generativity."[87] Music is another system of cultural codes and symbols that has participated in the expression and ascription of meaning to basic realities. It offers an alternative means of addressing reality. Indeed, as we saw in chapters 1 and 2, while chaos loomed—so much of the world "unmastered" from antiquity to the Middle Ages—music itself bodied forth sonic symbols of harmony, hope, and transcendence (however fleeting) for people to feed on.

Faith in (and perhaps even the desire for) traditionally perfect harmony gradually disintegrated, at least among composers and philosophers. Nevertheless, music can still be recuperatively framed as God's (albeit fleshly and dissonant) Song. In the midst of our own "basic realities"—the suffering and chaos of global, accelerated change—music's own spatio-temporal transience reminds us that we are flesh-turning-dust and that harmonic order may cost too much. Music's easy manipulation of our desire, its ability to destabilise and disintegrate, all preach the precariousness of human identity and mock hubristic dreams of bodily transcendence. Music reminds us that peace and stasis are as fleeting as the final chord, as perfect or imperfect as the cadence which dies the moment it is born. In the next chapter, I shall further elaborate this intimate relationship between music, abjection, and (suffering) love, in a less aesthetically desirable version of music-as-wound, a metaphorical resonance already implied in the elective affinities established between music and the mystical imagery of Angela of Foligno and Julian of Norwich. This additional example may encourage future theologies of music to attend equally to discord and harmony, as befits our "nuclear world."[88]

Notes

1. Cox, "A History of Music," 403.

2. Ibid.

3. Ibid., 404.

4. Ibid. Of course, some listeners who enjoy the musical pleasure-pain that Venus induces, who identify with her aspirations, and lament their caricature, do not want her to die. My thanks to Mitchell Morris for underlining this very necessary qualification.

5. The conventional, gendered oppositions within which Artusi's rhetoric can be situated have been catalogued in table 1 of Cusick's "Gendering Modern Music: Thoughts on the Monteverdi-Artusi Controversy." Cusick provides two tables of gendered oppositions—the first, those characteristic of late Renaissance thought (table 1, 4), and the second—those used by Artusi (table 2, 8), which clearly overlap with those in table 1, and which "would have evoked in his readers a nearly irresistible association of modern music with the feminine" (cf. 4-9).

6. Ibid., 6.

7. Here is the passage Artusi uses from Tasso (tr. Nash). In it, Vario says: "But the people of Jesus do not for that fall silent from their soft chaste melody, nor turn toward those shouts or take more heed of them than they would of a flock of chattering birds; nor do they fear that because they loose some arrows they will succeed in disturbing their holy peace from so far away. Hence they are easily able to carry to their end the sacred hymns begun" (Canto 11, stanza 13; Nash, 235, in Cusick, "Gendering Modern Music," 13 n. 25).

8. Artusi in Cusick, "Gendering Modern Music," 13.

9. Monson, *Disembodied Voices*, 69.

10. See Monson, ibid., and Kendrick, *Celestial Sirens: Nuns and Their Music in Early Modern Milan*.

11. These are the epithets of Pope Gregory XIII cited above in chapter 2, from his Letter to Palestrina and Zoilo, October 25, 1577, in Strunk, *Source Readings*, 1st ed., 358.

12. Cf. Monson, ibid., chapter 2.

13. Cf. Monson, ibid., 7-11. Monson borrows the terms "women's sphere" and "women's (work) culture" from revisionist historians of the late 1980s to characterise convent life (8). He argues: "I have found the concepts of 'women's sphere' and 'women's (work) culture' . . . useful for understanding the convents of the post-Tridentine Catholic world" (9). . . . "The physical space of the post-Tridentine convent was an archetypical 'women's sphere' in both its positive and negative aspects. At least to some degree, these cloistered spaces, clearly conceived to promote separation and subordination, could be shaped to the advantage of those enclosed within them. Nuns found numerous ways to render these female spaces somewhat less private; that is, to open windows in convent walls without demolishing them. Music was, I suggest, a powerful tool for partial deprivatization of architectural spaces—one deliberately employed by nuns to forge affective and, in the broad sense, political links with networks in the outside, public sphere" (11).

14. Cf. Monson, ibid., chapter 3, and Kendrick, *Celestial Sirens*, chapter 4.

15. Monson, ibid., 60.

16. Ibid., 61.

17. Vernizzi was *maestro de musica* from 1615-23 (Monson, ibid., 58).

18. A 1608 collection of Coppini's *contrafacta* was even dedicated to a nun—Suor Bianca Ludovica Taverna in Santa Marta Convent, Milan (Monson, ibid., 65).

19. Monteverdi himself had "ongoing personal contacts" with his son Francesco, a law student and amateur musician in Bologna (Monson, ibid., 65).

20. Kendrick records the same antipathy for *contrafacta* in Milan; Archbishop Litta (Federigo Borromeo's reactionary successor) was similarly horrified by the use of "*canzoni profani accomodate sotto parole sacre*," and tried to ban such profanities from use. For Kendrick these two archbishops' "contradictory attitude towards contrafacta parallels the divided view of nuns' music itself" (Kendrick, *Celestial Sirens*, 423).

21. Cardinal Federigo Borromeo, an exceptionally ardent supporter of nuns' music in Milan, regarded nuns as the ultimate incarnations of "natural goodness in creation," "the most select portion of Christ's flock" (Kendrick, ibid., 75). He described convents as "*hortus delicarum*, the garden of delight" (161). Under Borromeo's sympathetic rule, "the nexus of polyphony and transcendence became increasingly central for both the prelate and his monastic charges" (156). (The impression of such otherworldliness was created in part by the walls between internal and external chapels.) All of Kendrick's sources attest to "a universal mental category of the monastery as earthly Jerusalem and its singers as terrestrial angels" as well as to a unanimous wonder at the incorporeal nature of nuns' music: "observers musical and unmusical over the two centuries from Morigia to Burney employed the same semantic field—'ravishing,' 'heavenly,' 'angelic' to describe sisters' music: not fanciful descriptions but rather a realised set of expectations embedded deeply in one city's culture" (162). One Angelo Bernardi even described nuns' polyphony as "a sonic representation of the divinely instituted essence of music itself" (162). *Note here again the masculinist desire for disembodied transcendence.*

22. Kendrick's term, *Celestial Sirens*, 416. During the Counter-Reformation and after it, "urban prestige was inextricably bound to spiritual fervour," an alliance which fuelled both patrician support and contestation of specific reforms (Monson, ibid., 6).

23. Kendrick, *Celestial Sirens*, 415.

24. Ibid.

25. Ibid., 432.

26. Ibid., 416.

27. Namely, Emilia Grassi and Lucrezia Vizzana in Bologna, and Claudia Sessa, Chiara Margarita Cozzolani, and Angela Maria Clerici in Milan.

28. Kendrick, ibid., 166. Kendrick comments: "Indeed, the tension between anonymity and renown for individual singers was implicit in all the external testimony. If prelates and curia were concerned to make monastic musicians as anonymous as possible (whether by discipline or by persuasion), still the musical dedications and the travellers' reports underline the fact that famous singers were well known by name in the city" (165).

29. Kendrick emphasises the direct connection between virginity and music in the popular imagination: both were "parallel habitats of the Holy Spirit" (ibid., 11). This powerful confluence was further intensified through "reference to the classic Mediterranean concepts: patrician *onore* represented by their status" (ibid.). Following medieval tradition, sacred virgins were urban intercessors through whose agency the patriciate could gain "access to supernatural realms" (ibid.). Their singing possessed profound "thaumaturgic efficacy" (14).

30. In *L'Incoronazione di Poppea*, Poppea manipulates and emasculates three men—her husband, Ottone, the Emperor Nerone, and Seneca the philosopher. Susan McClary characterises each male character's music as idiomatically effeminate: Ottone's musical utterances "droop flaccidly to its Tonic"; Seneca's speech degenerates into "silly madrigalisms"; Nerone passively replies to Poppea' s flourishes—her macho musical language resembles the powerful rhetoric of Orfeo in Monteverdi's earlier opera *Orfeo* (McClary, *Feminine Endings*, 49).

31. Here is McClary's thesis in full: "I am suggesting that as the potency of humanist discourse evaporated so did crucial assumptions concerning the potency of patriarchy, male domination, and masculine sexuality. The nadir of this decline is dramatized in *L'Incoronazione di Poppea*, as Poppea usurps and perverts to her own ends the tools of patriarchal persuasion, making pathetic victims of these last refugees of humanism" (ibid., 49).

McClary warns however, that while Monteverdi seems to applaud women's increased social power, perhaps he is simply expressing male anxiety over the treacherous "inner workings of the female mind" (50). She reminds us that, in the seventeenth century, many men thought "*castrati* enacted women better than women themselves." The seventeenth century was, moreover, witch-hunting season (ibid.), and Monteverdi's opera might thus be far from iconoclastic: "In this paranoid world in which women were often selected as scapegoats for the crumbling social order, such 'powerful' constructions could also serve to justify patriarchal backlash" (49).

Despite such negative repercussions, McClary opts for the more 'difficult,' optimistic reading; she interprets Monteverdi's "shift in gender representation" as implicated in "the more general crisis in all forms of authority—political, economic, religious, and philosophical—during the first half of the seventeenth century." As an act of resistance, Monteverdi's opera could be a veiled critique of the institutional status quo: "critiques are safer, after all, when displaced onto marginalised Others" (51).

32. Newcomb, "Courtesans, Muses, or Musicians?," 112 n. 30. Newcomb speculates that the singer was either a professional actress (a disreputable *métier* as we have seen) or, surprisingly enough, an aristocratic lady, a woman from the opposite end of the social spectrum; in Newcomb's words, "another musically cultivated *donna di palazzo*" (ibid.).

33. Kendrick, *Celestial Sirens*, 165.

34. This is a quality which Federigo Borromeo emphasised in his advice to nun musicians in Milan, and which Kendrick describes in his book: following "earlier Florentine aesthetics," Borromeo prescribed "three requisites for good music: good voice, technically competent composition, but most importantly, the *affetto*." *Affetto* manifested itself in simple singing style (though Borromeo was much more lenient here than his predecessors) and in the congregation's palpable increase in devotion as they listened to the nuns' singing (ibid., 158).

35. Monson analyses Vizzana's music in chapters 3 to 6 of *Disembodied Voices*.

36. Citing Caroline Bynum's work, Kendrick records one Protestant composer's continued visits to the convent to receive "spiritual nourishment" from the nuns' music. For Kendrick, this testimony "suggests a final symbolic valence, one that would continue to the end of the *ancien régime*: female monastic musicians who provided spiritual nourishment to the city" in the same way that nuns had been considered as "the preferred ritual custodians of the Body of Christ from the later Middle Ages onward, evident not least in the Elevation, Corpus Christi, and Double Intercession motets of Chiara Margarita Cozzolani" (Kendrick, ibid., 420).

37. Kristeva, *Powers of Horror*, 2.

38. Ibid. Kristeva continues: "The corpse, seen without God and outside of science, is the utmost of abjection. It is death infecting life. Abject. It is something rejected from which one does not part, from which one does not protect oneself as from an object. . . . [I]t beckons to us and ends up engulfing us" (4).

39. Ibid.

40. Lochrie, *Margery Kempe and Translations of the Flesh*, 3.

41. Ibid., 19. Lochrie explains: "Abjection is the result of the Fall whence the boundaries of the body and soul were violated. Because the flesh is heterogeneous—neither body nor soul, but carnal and spiritual at the same time—abjection poses a continual threat to the Christian subject" (39).

42. Kristeva, ibid., 4.

43. Lochrie, *Margery Kempe*, 21.

44. Ibid., 4. Women's bodies were ascribed a "natural grotesqueness" and a "dangerous accessibility" for fleshly powers.

45. Lochrie notes that, paradoxically, this female imitation of Christ's suffering humanity does not reflect or celebrate "women's own suffering humanity." Instead, manuals of affective spirituality construe Christ's suffering humanity as "a remonstrance to woman's frail flesh" (*Margery Kempe*, 27). As such, "the female religious's imitation of Christ was not scripted to allow her to transcend or to celebrate the 'frail flesh' without a certain masochism" (ibid., 19).

46. This connection is made by Tertullian via a pun on the Latin words for 'flesh' (*caro*) and 'hinge' (*cardo*): "*Adeo caro salutis est cardo, de qua cum anima deo alligator ipsa est quae efficit ut anima eligi posit a deo*" (cf. *De resurrectione caro* 8).

47. Lochrie, ibid., 42. Here is Lochrie's subversive rereading of Woman as flesh: "The perviousness of the flesh places the cultural value of the integrity of body and soul continually at risk. Woman defiles by crossing these boundaries and, hence, the larger cultural demarcations which depend upon them. . . . Such abjection exploits by overturning the medieval effort to exclude abjection and with it, the feminine, from religious experience. . . . If the female mystic chooses to occupy those borders, to confound them by transgressing them, she exploits the medieval association of flesh and feminine" (ibid., 38-39).

48. Ibid., 41.

49. Ibid., 42. Lochrie elaborates: "The fissured body of Christ calls for an act of defilement to con-

firm belief for the doubter as well as the believer. The invitation to immersion in Christ's side is common in the visions of female mystics" (ibid.).

50. Ibid., 41f.

51. Ibid.

52. Lochrie's exposition of the double logic of the flesh allows her to argue that women mystics, like Kempe, who 'write' their bodies subvert the social order which their place as flesh was meant to enforce. Kempe's literary translation of her fleshly mystical experience threatens 'divinely ordained' hierarchies. As woman mystic, Kempe reaps power "from the taboo which defines her and which she breaks with her speech" (*Margery Kempe,* 39). Lochrie quotes André Vauchez's study of late medieval mystics. Vauchez "recognizes that feminine mysticism in the late Middle Ages was 'profoundly subversive' because of the extent to which it drew attention to the rupture between divine love and intellectual understanding" (3). This explains why women emphasised "the physical aspects of mystical experience," believing that it afforded them 'privileged communication' with God, and an access to religious mystery otherwise denied them" (ibid.). Lochrie also cites Caroline Bynum's assertion that women mystics greatly profited from the "new access to divine love" which "bodiliness" afforded (ibid.).

53. Cf. McGinn, *The Flowering of Mysticism,* 15f. and 327 n. 70, and his review of *Holy Feast and Holy Fast,* in *History of Religions* 28 (1988): 90-92. See also Hollywood, *The Soul as Virgin Wife,* 27-29, and "Suffering Transformed," 87-113.

54. Lochrie, *Margery Kempe,* 44.

55. Ibid., 26f.

56. Kristeva, *Powers of Horror,* 4.

57. Lochrie, *Margery Kempe,* 39.

58. Ibid., 43.

59. Ibid.

60. Ibid., 38.

61. Ibid., 39. Lochrie explains the dialectic as follows: "Abjection is bound to the sacred in the form of taboo. That is, the taboo serves to exclude something—say, a food substance or sexuality—in order to secure the borders of the subject. At the same time, then, the sacred calls into being transgression, since it is transgression of the taboo, rule or law which gives rise to abjection" (ibid.).

62. Cf. ibid., 23-27.

63. Ibid., 39.

64. Ibid., 40.

65. Ibid., 45.

66. See ibid., 40.

67. Holsinger, "The Flesh of the Voice," 122.

68. Ibid., 28. That is, devotees reconstructed Christ's passion or pilgrimages to the Holy Land in their minds so that they might experience love, humility, longsuffering, and contempt for earthly things, all of which, represented imitations of Christ (ibid.). Lochrie explains the process in more detail: "From the signposts of memory are produced the stigmata of the body, but the suffering is never located in either place since the transference of knowledge is never complete. It is endlessly repeated, circulated, and succeeded by intervals of want and repletion.

"*Imitatio Christi* in the Middle Ages, then, is not simply a doctrine of suffering or mortification of the flesh. It is a semiotics of suffering, a complex system of signposts and tokens that do not always observe the boundaries of the physical, imaginary, and symbolic" (ibid., 36).

69. Matter, "Interior Maps of an Eternal External," 73. See also Bynum, *Holy Feast and Holy Fast,* 255-59.

70. See Bynum, *Holy Feast and Holy Fast,* 208-12, and Lochrie, *Margery Kempe,* 34-37.

71. According to Ziegler, Virgin-Child and Pietà statues reminded Beguine women "that the highest reward for the chaste and holy woman would be to embrace the presence of the living Christ" (Ziegler, "Reality as Imitation," 123). In her article, Ziegler considers the impact of Pietà and Virgin-Child statues on Beguine piety. While Pietà sculptures promoted compassion, and the tending of the sick and dying, they also encouraged the right reception of the body of Christ: "There is a 'reception' metaphor in the *Pietà,* which Beguines probably understood as a supplementary directive to the rules. In the latter, they were instructed to receive the Eucharist, and the image of the Pietà likely reminded them to do so. There is another possibility, here, that the Beguines were physically stimulated by the virgin's example of touching the body of Christ" (125). This corresponds, Ziegler argues, to her colleague Jo Ann McNamara's characterisation of the reception "dynamic" of the Eucharist, *yet* in medi-

tation upon marian statues reception is "dissociated from the formal liturgy and open[s] a path to God directly without intermediarie[s]" (ibid.). See also McNamara, "The Rhetoric of Orthodoxy" in the same volume.

72. Bynum, *Holy Feast and Holy Fast*, 268f.

73. As another historical example of the fluid boundaries between christic and marian *imitatio*, in her study of the life of Maria Domitilla, E. Ann Matter is struck by Maria's "identification of her 'virgin womb' with Mary's." More significantly, "in at least one vision Maria Domitilla is taken to the Virgin's breast and offered precious drops of the milk that nourished the infant Jesus" (Matter, "Interior Maps of an Eternal External," 68ff.). Here therefore, Maria imitates Christ, yet espouses a maternal role toward him as well. Matter wants to reconstrue this "meeting of Christ in a maternal role" by such women as Maria Domitilla Galluzzi, Veronica Giuliani, Agnes of Montepulciano, Catherine of Siena, and Margery Kempe as a "subset of the more pervasive *imitatio Christi*" (69).

74. It was precisely this direct access to God (without ecclesial mediation) achieved through women's mystical practices, offerings, and devotions ("purgatorial piety" for example) that threatened clerical authority (McNamara, "The Rhetoric of Orthodoxy" 21).

75. The word *chair* is intentionally singular and italicised. The wordplay is on the French "*chair,*" which means "flesh."

76. Helpful discussions of this broader "spectrum" can be found throughout Miles, *Fullness of Life*, and *Practicing Christianity*, chapter 2, as well as in essays by the authors cited above (cf. *Maps of Flesh and Light*).

77. For example, according to Ellen Ziegler, Beguine women followed Christ in more tempered modalities, simply "by dress, action, and prayer" (Ziegler, "Reality as Imitation," 114). Ziegler focuses on the practices of care-giving and nurturance which the sculptures of Virgin and Child and Pietà in beguinages modelled. These images promoted more "accessible" spiritual modalities during the fourteenth century: "Beguine rules codified female sanctity so that all women could adapt themselves to it. The art works in their churches further reinforced, prescribed, and modelled for these women compassion and other right, virtuous actions (ibid.).

However, Ziegler contends that the promotion of more modest forms of female *imitatio* was politically motivated—due to a clerical desire to "tighten control over what had become women's excessive and extravagant spiritual behaviour" ("Reality as Imitation," 112f.). In my view, *musical* practices can accommodate virtuosity, excess, and even the expression of suffering, pathos, or ascetic austerity if composer, performer, and audience desire this devotional vocabulary. Such musical extravagance, however, was not previously encouraged, as we have seen.

78. "By participating in the events surrounding Jesus's suffering and learning to feel and experience as Christ had felt and experienced, one explicitly linked oneself with the salvific work of Christ" (Ellen Ross, "She Wept and Cried Right Loud," 47).

79. Julian of Norwich, *Showings,* trans. Colledge and Walsh, 188, in Lochrie, *Margery Kempe*, 41.

80. See here Miles, *Practicing Christianity*, 37ff.

81. See ibid.

82. "Not all these corporeal imitations inspire suffering. . . . As much rapture as mortification attends these miraculous alterations of the body. In either case, the bodily component of mystical experience manifests a physiological and often literal conformity to Christ's humanity. For many female and some male mystics, the corporeal aspect of mystical meditation was neither metaphorical nor symbolic" (Lochrie, *Margery Kempe,* 14).

83. Both concepts—the body and imitation—are problematic because they are always culturally defined constructs whose diverse meanings often overlap or contradict each other (Lochrie, *Margery Kempe,* 15ff.). E. Ann Matter has, in fact, elucidated the negative constraints which the evolution of this "cultural code" of *imitatio* eventually placed upon women's subjectivity—their means of "self-expression" and "self-modelling": "It seems that women's experience of *imitatio Christi*, which began in the late Middle Ages as a radical, form-breaking type of self-expression, became by the sixteenth century a more conformist and less expressive manner of self-interpretation. This form of female piety came to be carefully regulated by the patriarchy of post-tridentine Catholicism" (Matter, "Interior Maps of an Eternal External," 72). Thus, like accounts of post-tridentine musical restrictions, such historical analysis reminds us that musical and spiritual practices are often circumscribed within polemical contexts where control of one group (often "dangerous" women) necessitates immutable legislation by another. As exemplum of this squelched potential, Matter discusses the life of Maria Domitilla Galluzzi d'Acqui, the main focus of her essay. One can never really gain access to this nun's "interior map": "For a modern evaluation of Maria Domitilla's interior map, it is therefore necessary

to take into account the problem of voice. That is, we need to consider the extent to which her most personal and interior expressions of self were spoken through, if not muted by, the external realities through which they were allowed expression" (73). In Matter's view, Suor Maria regarded her own body "as the executioner of an exteriority. If we look at her autobiography with the question 'who was she?,' we find her own narrative telling us that she was, as far as possible, someone else: Christ" (ibid.).

84. Bynum, *Holy Feast and Holy Fast*, 299.

85. Ibid.

86. Ibid., 302.

87. Ibid., 276.

88. Miles, *Practicing Christianity*, 3. Living as we do in a "nuclear world," Miles wants to complicate our adoption of traditional devotional practices by shifting their previous emphasis upon individual salvation to one of collective social responsibility: "Human beings have always lived in peril, vulnerable at any and every moment to accident, disease, and, ultimately and inevitably, death. But the possibility that humans could exterminate the human race and destroy life on the planet has existed only in approximately the last forty years. . . .

"The contemporary practice of Christianity cannot have as its goal individual happiness or even, in the traditional term, individual salvation. Rather, in the nuclear world, an 'examined life' is a moral responsibility. A life before God in our time requires a degree of social responsibility far greater than that recognized by most historical Christian writers" (ibid.).

"Foul Ooze"[1]

SIX

New Icons of Abjection

A S THE NUNS FOUGHT to preserve their musical integrity in Bologna, miles away on another continent much greater violence was inflicted on other allegedly "deviant" musical bodies. Plantation masters in both the American South and in other European colonies feared the chthonic, socially disruptive powers that their slaves' music exuded. A feminist valorisation of such fleshly transgression in musico-theological discourse has, therefore, a much older antecedent, namely, the "heterogeneous sound ideal" that shapes almost all African music.[2] Untapped roots for a more holistic theology of music lie in the musical practices and sacred aesthetics of this neglected precedent. Its ingredients merit a brief excursus, as does the symptomatic rhetoric with which white rulers derided this African musico-theological alternative. The mission to preserve music's (now white) chastity from new "pagan" assaults sparked invective against musical "miscegenation." In defiance, a nascent Afro-American gospel style asserted its redemptive hybridity.

I. Buried Treasure: Music's African Body

Unlike the normative European taste for tonal and textural harmonies discussed in part 1 above, many African tribes intentionally combine "timbres that contrast rather than blend" to create a "tonal mosaic."[3] This constitutes the African sacred musical ideal. It actually endorses song that is accompanied by musical instruments—drums, rattles, and bells, even dancing and hand-clapping—for *both* sacred and profane music. This unmistakably African "fusion" thus incorporates the very elements that the European quest for musical purity condemned.[4]

These practices are theologically sanctioned insofar as there is no sharp demarcation made in African religion systems between "sacred and profane realms of life or between the material and the spiritual."[5] According to music historian Samuel Floyd:

> there was in traditional Africa, no word for "religion" because the Africans' religion permeated, and was the basis for all aspects of life, including education, politics, harvesting, hunting, homemaking, and community welfare. Since religion permeated the everyday life of African peoples, the great number of religious

beliefs that existed were not systematized into dogmas, but appeared as ideas and practices that governed everyday life in the various communities.[6]

Thanks in part to the absence of hellenistic metaphysics (or Christian qualitative gaps), African anthropology and cosmology minimise the distance between God and humanity. While God remains "a creator and provider" ruling from on high, nevertheless, earth and heaven are "either close together or joined by a rope or bridge."[7] On the basis of this cosmology, and *contra* European norms, the combined effect of drum, dance, and song, because of their multisensory engagement of a believer's whole being, restores an intimacy between heaven and earth, rather than fleshing out their estrangement. This holistic, three-dimensional form of worship provides the most appropriate enactment and symbolisation of "intercourse between the material and spiritual worlds,"[8] thereby fulfilling the Africans' ultimate religious objective of union with the divine.

One qualification must be made here, however. Despite the holism grounding this alternative theology of music, African believers still worship a divine patriarch: "Like the Christian God, the African god is known as a High God, a Supreme God, a father, king, lord, master, judge or ruler, depending on the society doing the naming (or, in some matriarchal societies, Mother, although the image of God as Father is not limited to patriarchal societies)."[9] This, of course, complicates yet does not, in my view, completely abort the retrieval of a useable past within African religious musical traditions. For, instead of the cerebral contemplation of musical unity, number, and order prioritised in European theologies of music, music's rhythmic and timbral heterogeneity, as well as its intense engagement of the body, grounds African piety and renders the latter a welcome alternative resource for this revisionist project. Moreover, this model is instructive insofar as *dance* rather than text anchors a threefold medium for effecting spiritual communion.[10] This transvaluation of dance (and drum) over song also lends support to a praxis-based, staunchly non-logocentric approach to music's theological significance.[11]

Equally anathema to European mores is the genesis of drum-dance-song worship out of erotically driven polyrhythms that find expression in bodily movement. Ethnomusicologist Alan Lomax explains: "[T]he trunk and the pelvis of the dancer, and the hands and sticks of the drummers steadily maintain two separate and conflicting meters. This twisting pelvic style (and its reflection in hot rhythm) infuses African work and play with a steady feed of pleasurable erotic stimuli."[12] This sacred channel suggests an aesthetic version of what paleontologist Stephen Jay Gould calls "punctuated equilibrium"[13]—a balance forged between body movement and drumbeats—the two compositional pillars of most African music. As a pedagogical tool (and again in sharp contrast to Greek and Christian *paideia* discussed in part 1), in African cultures music and dance were and are intentionally used to "educate boys and girls for their adult sexual roles in a polygynous world."[14] Thus the polyrhythms, their erotic roots, and African musical *paideia* recognise and celebrate rather than suppress the vital "bleed-through" (Cusick) between music, sexuality, and "spiritual" communion.[15] White slave-owners could not appreciate such integrative feats, however. To them, African dance was more threat than "primitive" amusement, a "demonic," raucous amalgam. Once again, church leaders and slave owners resorted to vituperative, sexualised derogations to amputate its sway.

Barbarian Invasions and Musical Savagery

As testament to the perdurance of the early Christian musical ideals documented in part 1, an uncanny resemblance exists between ancient rhetoric against music of the flesh and that of Southern whites who decry the musical excess of slaves. The slaves' dancing, their use of instruments and drums, as well as their funeral rites, were all regarded by their masters as lascivious and wanton, exuding a "heathenish" extravagance. Archival sources indicate that when African slaves attempted to maintain their own devotional style, "the ceremonies and music of the ring [ritual] were looked on by most whites as 'idolatrous dancing and revels' and they were mightily criticized and suppressed in nearly all parts of the United States (New Orleans was perhaps the major exception)."[16] In another report, a plantation master deemed even slaves' Christianised worship "horrible howling," akin to satanic possession.[17] Frederika Bremer (on visiting Cuba in 1851) contrasts blacks' sensual inebriation, that is their "savage" "screeching" and "lawless" dancing, with the "spiritual intoxication" that converts (and proper Christian music) can remedy. (Artusi's contrast of pagan dregs and Christian wine comes to mind here; cf. chapter 5.[18]) Bremer therefore decides that blacks must assimilate European musical practices to be redeemed, likening Cuban blacks to "sour crab" apples, and converted mainland "negroes" to "noble, bright Astrachans."[19]

French monk Jean Baptiste Labat called African dancing "*déshonnêtes,*" "*indé-centes,*" "*lascives.*"[20] In the early 1700s, Anglican missionary Francis Le Jau tried desperately to end African dancing in South Carolina; it so defiled blacks that they were not allowed to take communion.[21] Along with dance, of course, playing musical instruments was particularly offensive. Before 1700, "drums, trumpets, and loud instruments" were prohibited as dangerously incendiary.[22] All of these accoutrements produced a "horrid noise" and "barbarous melody."[23]

Before their Christian "sterilisation," black funeral rites were the most egregious example of musico-theological barbarism, possibly because they embodied the most jarring confusion of music and emotional display. Like early Greek women's moirology, black lamentation was "heathenish." In such outpourings, the disciplinary restraint of the words was crushed by emotional excess. Whites regarded the slaves' full-bodied dirges at funerals as "barbarous," "strange and weird." One description of funereal call-and-response songs likens the latter's style to that of "sailors heaving at the windlass."[24] Part of this disgust was due to white perplexity over blacks' mixed emotions over death. In eighteenth-century Jamaica, missionary Charles Leslie condemns the coexistence of conflicting emotions in slaves' musical lamentation, pitying their belief that death could be a blessing: "all the while they are covering it with Earth, the Attendants scream out in a terrible manner, which is not the Effect of Grief but of Joy; they beat on their wooden Drums, and the Women with their Rattles make a hideous Noise."[25] Such apparent cheerfulness was anathema to the majority of white Christians.[26] (One white woman, however, is more appreciative of black lamentation, finding in the Other's grief/music a source of "thrilling" pleasure.[27])

The *"Master's [Musical] Tools"*[28]

General disdain for the black musical ethos stemmed from the whites' need to control their slaves and to confiscate any cultural heritage that might inspire slaves to mount collective rebellions. Whites constantly feared the political power of these musical practices; for, even after conversion, African music's distinct style and energising force galvanised and recollected slaves' indigenous identity and politico-religious hopes. African musical spontaneity and improvisation could turn docile hymns into battle cries.[29] However, like the nuns who would not allow their musical enthusiasm to be silenced, slaves—now in a far more dehumanising historical context—defied their masters' interdicts. As it circulated "competing ideologies," music-making became an important source of agency and political resistance.[30] For example, in the following passage, the christianised slaves' abject musical *practices* took assimilated white hymns hostage and literally mobilised them to rekindle black morale and solidarity "after hours":

> "Would your marster allow you to hold prayer-meetings on his place?"
> "No, my child; if old marster heard us singing and praying he would come out and make us stop. . . . Marster used to say God was tired of us all hollering to him at night.". . . None of us listened to him about singing and praying. . . . Sometimes when we met . . . we would put a big wash-tub full of water in the middle of the floor to catch the sound of our voices when we sung. *When we all sung we would march around and shake each other's hands, and we would sing easy and low, so marster could not hear us.* . . . Aunt Jane used to sing, 'Jesus? the name that charms our fears' . . . [and] 'Guide me, O thou great Jehovah.'"[31]

Converting slaves to Christianity thus proved a mixed blessing. Material profit for white businessmen was, after all, the primary impetus for converting slaves; the latter was supposed to improve, not diminish, productivity.[32] Yet using conversion to consolidate the ranks proved ineffective. Given music's already innate promiscuity, and its rebellious volatility, the musical freedoms that Africans took with Christian hymns might disrupt rather than domesticate. Consequently, because of this serious, unforeseen threat to social order, many whites repressed any form of black Christian music and preaching after the Nat Turner rebellion in 1831.[33] However, as in the early church, censorship of African style and/or content varied according to local authorities *and* from one denomination to another. Episcopalians were very strict,[34] while Baptists and Methodists allowed more spontaneous self-expression at their camp meetings.[35]

Perhaps the cruelest irony characterising African slave-conversions was the eventual rejection by converts of their original aesthetico-religious ideals. Many Christian slaves would reproach as demonic any traces of Africa's "timbral mosaic" in Christian song, espousing the derogatory views of their masters and missionary leaders.[36] To maintain this musical 'divorce,' white leaders strongly rewarded black prowess in psalm-singing—clergymen, for example, such as Presbyterian Samuel Davies and the Rev. Mr. Todd of Hanover.[37] Similarly, missionary Charles Colcock Jones (in rhetoric we have seen before) advises: "One great advantage in teaching them good psalms and hymns is that they are thereby induced to lay aside the extravagant and nonsensical chants, and catches and hallelujah songs of their own composing; and when they sing, which is very often while about their business or of an evening in their houses, they will have something profitable to sing."[38]

Exceptions to the Rule: Slave Music as Exotic "Other"

Despite these denigrations, scholars report some white appreciation for African music, albeit as musical exotica. While the unwieldy Other—black bodies making music—were uncivilised, sexually charged objects to be managed, if kept at a comfortable distance, they seem to become endearingly exotic delights.[39] Thus, Zephaniah Kingsley seems sincere in his lament of one white Christian missionary's purging of black customs:

> About twenty-five years ago [1804], I settled a plantation on St. Johns River, in Florida, with about fifty new African negroes, many of whom I brought from the coast [of Africa] myself. . . . I never interfered with their connubial concerns, and domestic affairs, but let them regulate these after their own manner. . . . I encouraged as much as possible dancing, merriment and dress, for which Saturday afternoon and night, and Sunday morning were dedicated. . . . A man, calling himself a minister, got among them. It was now sinful to dance, work their corn or catch fish, on a Sunday. . . all pastime or pleasure in this iniquitous world was sinful. . . . I cannot help regretting that honest well meaning men, with so much ability to do good . . . should so misapply their talents as to subvert all natural and rational happiness, and endeavor to render our species miserable.[40]

Admittedly, this portrait of white derogatory rhetoric and of the Master's insistence upon unity and order is anecdotal. Primary sources, as African-American historians know, are fragmented and often informal documents.[41] Nevertheless, there is sufficient evidence to demonstrate the gradual dilution of an African musical worldview into an Afro-European hybrid, the latter supposedly civilising the former. Fortunately for Western 'civilisation,' however, the African heterogeneous sound ideal defied complete extinction. Despite even the most repressive white opposition, valuable traces of it prevailed, albeit in the form of a musical compromise, as historian Dena J. Epstein remarks: "The fiddle may have been silenced and the dancers forbidden to cross their legs, but the droning [white] hymnody was transformed."[42]

This historical excursus demonstrates the preexistence of another, very different theology of music, one that has been eclipsed by the hegemony of masculinist models, most of which would now seem not only sexist but racist. The precolonial African sacred musical aesthetic offers a far more holistic theology of music than the masculinist models in chapter 3. In light of this excursus, it seems even more bewildering that African American scholar Jon Michael Spencer would make minimal use of this African sound ideal in his original outline of a "theomusicology" (1991). He pays homage to this holistic worldview only in his fourth book, *The Blues and Evil*, a theomusicological rereading of the blues. For his earlier methodological prolegomenon, however, he consults Augustine, Camus, Rousseau, and Carl Jung for his sources and norms. (In fairness to Spencer, he does discuss the political roots of black Christian music in two books that are historical surveys of black music, but in neither book does he connect these roots to a broad-gauge theomusicology.[43])

This recuperation of an aesthetic that honours the ineradicable bonds between music and sexuality, an alternative whose creative blood was banished to the abject margins of the Christian tradition, serves to contextualise our two final theological resources for a feminist theology of music. Both of them are from the twentieth century, and both embrace a heterogenous sound ideal. In them, music's gendered and raced bodies converge. For in the master's imagination, if music is a dangerous woman and white women making music are doubly wanton, then one can readily conceive the threat to social order and individual "purity" that black women's musicality would represent. In that masculinist imagination, such musicality was fueled by bigoted portraits of black women as either nymphomaniac Jezebels or as neutered, docile Mammies.[44] Women who enfleshed African, specifically musical, promiscuity were a severe liability to the status quo. One senses this fear of black women's musical powers (and the latter's successful disarmament) in the following account of a virtuoso black woman-violinist whose documented conversion seems remarkably reminiscent of Christian hagiography about repentant Magdalens:

> Not all fiddlers were men. Clarinda, in later life "a pious coloured woman of South Carolina," was born in 1730. She was brought up "in a state of ignorance unworthy of a Christian country," as evidenced by the fact that "she learned to play on the violin, and, usually, on the first day of the week, sallied forth with her instrument, in order to draw persons of both sexes together, who, not having the fear of god before their eyes, delighted like herself, in sinful and pernicious amusement." . . . Once while dancing she "was seized with fits, and convulsively

fell to the ground. From that moment, she lost her love of dancing, and no more engaged in this vain amusement." She became a preacher, the leader of a flock and led a blameless life until she died at the age of 102.[45]

(Epstein adds: "This story of a reformed fiddler is remarkable chiefly because it concerns a woman. Such tales of conversion are a standard feature of religious literature in nineteenth-century America."[46])

Constrained after baptism behind the rigid bars of spirituals, black women's musicality might be marginally redeemed. But what were the consequences if postbellum Christian black women devoted themselves to singing the blues, or—worse still—became virtuoso blues instrumentalists? Blues music was arguably the early twentieth century's "painted whore." I allude here to blues singer/guitarist Sister Rosetta Tharpe (1915-73). If, as established in chapters 4 and 5, imitating Christ involves defilement through abjection, then Tharpe's music, her fleshly misconduct, are in fact stigmatic perfection.

II. Sister Rosetta Tharpe: Prodigal Daughter, Gospel *Skandalon*

Tharpe was raised a gospel singer, but, like her contemporary Thomas A. Dorsey (Georgia Tom; 1899-1993), she was "seduced" from the straight and narrow into the nether world of blues music (a fall from grace immortalised in her rendition of "I Want a Tall Skinny Papa"). Originally she was allowed to pursue this double life within sacred and profane venues, without condemnation from church authorities. Presumably this was because the blues idioms which she used undergirded gospel texts—a hybrid practice that the black heterogeneous sound ideal tolerated. Tharpe often sang blues settings of sacred songs in theatres and clubs (e.g., "This Train," "Didn't it Rain Children").[47] Only purists who unilaterally espoused white sacred aesthetic ideals condemned this fusion. For many black people (especially later black scholars), the blues' celebration of the erotic served the cultural function of affirming life in the midst of death-dealing oppression, and thereby conveying resurrection hope.[48]

Like Christ, not only did Tharpe commerce with outcasts and sinners, her failure to stop doing so also resulted in her condemnation by religious authorities. Originally they tolerated her "double life," but when Tharpe released a blues record with another wayward sister, Marie Knight, the Baptist and Holiness Churches finally condemned her and refused to take her or Knight back into the fold. This excommunication occurred even though Tharpe was unswervingly committed to her faith. She managed to survive by touring in Europe and the United States and giving large concerts for white consumers of her now-fashionable blues/gospel hybrid. The cost, however, was a fuller exercise of her original musical "promiscuity,"[49] and, interestingly enough, the church's condemnation of Thomas Dorsey's schizoid musicality did not preclude his eventual exoneration.

He was given full pardon once he left his secular "mistress" for good (1929). But Tharpe never became a bona fide repentant Magdalen. Her exile is thus yet another example of music's function as a metaphor for gender relations. As with the nuns discussed in chapters 4 and 5, for whom music became a source of social potency in the face of clerical opposition, Tharpe's music also threatened to emasculate. Equally subject to censor was her virtuosity on the guitar—stereotypically a male pursuit. She would not relinquish this socially-coded, masculine activity. Nor, incidentally, did her predecessors of the 1920s; Memphis Minnie McCoy, as Big Bill Broonzy reported, "played the guitar like a man." (Blues scholar Paul Oliver adds: "These women were admired for the masculinity of their musical attack; traditional femininity was replaced by a bragging sexuality."[50]) Tharpe's audience appeal was also man-size. At the height of her career (and this on the "gospel circuit"), she performed before crowds of 17,000 and 27,000 people.[51] Tharpe was not alone here. Many other Christian black women made their mark as blues divas: Clara Smith, Sippie Wallace, Victoria Spivey, Ma Rainey, Mamie and Bessie Smith. Yet these hard-core blues women, ironically enough, were perhaps adjudged less "promiscuous" insofar as they did not feel the pull of two competing fields; they cast their lot in the world and suffered the disrepute and social stigma which, we have already seen, has dogged actors and minstrels—male and female—throughout history.

Thus, like Jesus, Tharpe destabilised the authority of cultural taboos, singing a gospel hybrid to sinners hungry for musical comfort. If one accepts, furthermore, Jacquelyn Grant's christological thesis that today the Christ is a black woman, that is, the "least" among humanity (since black women incarnate the nexus of all three forms of oppression—sex, race, and class),[52] then Tharpe imitates Christ by becoming him even more emblematically than the musical *imitationes* discussed in chapters 4 and 5. Abject music exudating from a black woman's body effects a sonic race-class-sex triumvirate that testifies to God's inviolate, erotically charged immanence within society's outcasts. Virtuoso instrumentalist, singing the "devil's music," mixing pagan dregs with heavenly manna (Artusi), this black *Christa* with a huge following epitomises the transgression of all previous musical taboos, incarnating a christic *skandalon* that unfortunately fell on many deaf (Christian) ears.

I do not want to idealise Tharpe. Her lifestyle was often as extravagant as her guitar riffs (even solo gospel performers, however, lived in opulence); Tharpe's life was an admixture of devotion and celebrity. Thus, another fracture of neat and tidy categories already evident in Tharpe's christic *imitatio* is the inevitable wedding of gospel and commerce. Christian notions of decorum and asceticism have always been suspicious of worldly extravagance. And yet, extravagance as much as abstinence marked the behaviour, works, and sayings of Jesus. Blues music, especially sung by a prodigal daughter, becomes the locus of both exploitation and proclamation; a confusing site of pollution and emancipation that mocks naive devotional demands for purity and integrity.

Abject Bread and Wine: Tharpe's Eucharistic Offering

The gender politics framing both Tharpe's oeuvre and blues' symbolic function as "promiscuous" threat to Christian purists' musical standards are not the
primary imitative dimensions of Sister Tharpe's music that I wish to accentuate,
however. As we shall see in the following analysis, Tharpe's musical prodigality
and excess make her "Black Women's Musical Jesus" par excellence. Tharpe's
praxis bears witness to the often tenuous line between holiness and sin. Her rendition of "Two Little Fishes and Five Loaves of Bread" incarnates the New Song's
confusing liminality in a sonically redemptive paradox that sacred-music legalists
could not grasp. Recorded live at the Apollo Theater, in this song Tharpe harnesses
music's promiscuity to salvific, christomimetic ends. The music's highly chromatic, erotic idioms intercourse with a sacred parable. First of all, the piece begins
with a sexually connotative vamp motif. In response to this erotically coded
incipit, our bodies "coil in Pavlovian anticipation"[53] even as we feed on a sacred
story. Given the text's rather banal form (four-line verses with refrain) and content (complete with moralising codetta),[54] it is the music's erotic energy that sustains our interest. Moreover, its most aurally stimulating measures are located in
the nontextual guitar solo that precedes the final hortatory verse and codetta.

The medium, then, seemingly contradicts the parabolic message. But the
medium is the message—the music, the parable. For, more than textual bread and
fish, the extramusical message lies in this sonic body of Christ's invitation; it bids
auditors to take and eat, that is, *to move and to physically/aurally taste*, the ever-
expanding ripple-effects of musical "desire and delight" (Miles). Here again,
music's jarring promiscuity redeems both a tired text and weary auditors.
Tharpe's New Song, therefore, is a reviving transfusion that renovates what would
otherwise be a merely textual ingestion of eucharistic symbols ("loaves and
fishes") within a well-worn tale. This rather bland "spiritual" fare is subordinate
to or, more importantly, translated into an aural and tactile feast which Tharpe—
imitating Christ—imparts to us through her own musical body. Moreover, rare
archival film footage of Tharpe's other performances allows us to watch her gyrate
and sway as the music feeds her own body,[55] and to witness how she visually
infused even more erotic lifeblood into Gospel texts, and also (by literal extension)
to her audience. Like Jesus before her, Tharpe's musical promiscuity incarnated an
iconoclastic gospel freedom which Barth on Mozart or Pelikan on Bach never
imagined.[56]

Additionally, Tharpe's guitar accompaniment—a taboo instrument, let loose
here to sing its own song before the final verse and pulsing with sexually connotative flat-seventh chords and syncopated rhythms—can also be reconstrued as
another musical incarnation of christic communion. Once again, in Tharpe's textless *imitatio*, "the Word passes through [her]," as it did for Angela of Foligno. Yet
another woman's musical discipleship renders the socially coded abject (here
blues music) "an instrument of power and a site of "privileged communication";[57]
Tharpe hosts, in effect, a eucharistic banquet in a nightclub. Thus, in blues music

more generally, and in Tharpe's musical exegesis of a feeding narrative more specifically, human sexuality is musically refracted as a sonic touch, as an anamnesis of the full-blooded erotic humanity which many white people feared. In this feminist theology of music, virtuoso blues, sung by someone of a historically "tainted" gender, race, and class, becomes the consummate icon of redemptive abjection.

One might conclude, therefore, that Tharpe's music proffers two broader, "promiscual" musico-theological corrections. The first revisionary insight is that it is precisely blues' (and jazz's) innate predisposition for musical "excess"—that is, its improvisational volatility—which makes it a preferred medium for the gospel. (Begbie, one may recall, does not identify the theological significance of improvisations in these terms.) Tharpe is most charismatic when she wails and lets loose, when her full-bodied enthusiasm, her supremely guttural offerings "topple abjection into the sublime."[58] God is received through an intensely curvaceous musical body, one which penetrates the assembled body of Christ. (Note here the musical metaphor's promiscuous, because ambivalent, transsexuality: music-as-Woman, performed by a woman, penetrates.) The same sublime excesses could also be attributed (at least to some degree) to Mahalia Jackson[59] and other gospel queens. Jackson herself still sings melodies that are full of (mysteriously baptised) blues idioms and its stylistic ornaments, a contradiction that mocks the application of conventional stylistic dichotomies, given that gospel and blues draw from the same African and slave musical roots. However, Jackson did not acknowledge this paradox. Rather she scorned blues music. Consequently, I would argue that, unlike Jackson, Tharpe's musically voluptuous body is "naked without shame."

Jackson and Tharpe seemingly incarnate and repolarise another musical, virgin–whore split, one that the nuns of Santa Cristina previously dissolved. But again, this divide does not hold; Tharpe was simply more "categorical," so to speak, more explicit than Jackson, in her suffusion of musical *imitatio* with human sexuality. Setting parables to the traditionally suspect genre of chromatic love songs, singing these in theatres and juke joints, Tharpe catalysed the free association (in her and her audience's body/minds) between music and "unclean" things. Both her music and life show her christically treading a precarious line, a music-making woman-as-flesh occupying a border position, or rather, marking the impossibility of such borderline distinctions. Thus she and her music are a living parable that effectively challenges legalism and dogmatism, whether musical or theological. Tharpe enfleshes a certain "excess of desire"[60] which demands outlet in taboo musical language. While she threatens "Christian decency" simply in her instrumental virtuosity, in my view, her virtuosic and improvisational prodigality expresses the effulgence of a godly desire.

The second revisionary insight Tharpe's oeuvre provides is that blues music can indeed be a christomimetic wounding. James Cone describes the blues as "an artistic response to the chaos of life. . . . The blues express a black perspective on the incongruity of life and the attempt to achieve meaning in a situation fraught with contradictions. The blues experience always is an encounter with life, its trials and tribulations, its bruises and abuses—but not without benefit of the melody and rhythm of song."[61] Blues music revives black body–souls with christic power *but without the luxury of ideological unity, harmony, and order.*[62] Rather than unity, harmony, and order, blues and jazz musicians glorify the creative tension which previous aesthetic prescriptions spurned. Quoting W. E. B. Dubois, Cone emphasises "the tension in the spirituals between hope and despair, joy and sorrow, death and life," and "the ability of black slaves to embrace such polarities in their music."[63] And unlike the harmonised "truths" in Spencer's theomusicology, blues musicians do not resolve these tensions but flesh them out in their intentional courting of disintegration via improvisation. This more balanced musico-theological appreciation of chaos and order, suffering and hope, harmony and dissonance (both musical and existential) makes the blues an emblematic form of *imitatio crucis.* Flowing from both "an openness to the intensity of life's pains" (Cone)[64] and a people's wounding by the violent brutality of other human beings, the blues' body itself simultaneously wounds and soothes.

Given these roots, Tharpe's sonic *imitatio,* enfleshed in the body of a vilified woman, becomes a paradoxical conflation of music as a healing wound, as symptom and cure, and thus another example of music's redemptive promiscuity. Reconstrued as such, Tharpe's "Loaves and Fishes" becomes both crucible and elixir, oozing wound yet bittersweet container of black identity with the crucified one.

III. Re-Vamping the Cross:
Diamanda Galas's *Imitatio Crucis*

If Rosetta's blues are a sweet wound, exudating the pleasure–pain of Christ's redemptive presence during dark times, Diamanda Galas's music is a lethal gash. Her "electroacoustic voice-work" is my fourth and final challenge to the location of music's theological significance in its harmonic purity and formal order. Her musical offering bolsters the theological revisions made thus far and allows further revisions of music's ethical, anthropological, and soteriological significance. Just as womanist theologian Jacquelyn Grant informed the preceding reading of Tharpe's music, I will engage a feminist philosopher, religionist, and biblical scholar in this final "interfacial" conversation.

Like Tharpe and the nuns of Santa Cristina (and even Hildegard to some extent), it is Galas's very disobedience which makes her a sound exemplum for a feminist theology of music. Within the gynemorphic framework sketched in part 1, Galas seems a castrating Fury—plunging her aural hostages into musical abjection. As a form of musical protest, her Plague Mass (performed in 1990 at the Cathedral of St. John the Divine) is a searing critique of Christian attitudes toward AIDS. Its début performance precipitated the enduring scorn of right-wing church authorities, and of her own church-musician father. The former have condemned Galas's music as "satanic."[65] The latter maintains that singers are "a bunch of whores."[66] Mocking such slurs, in her crucified musical flesh, Galas expresses both the agony of AIDS victims' suffering, and, at the same time, a righteous anger which shames auditors into repentance and activism. To this end, by spewing a toxic, often incoherent, stream of musical consciousness, Galas shatters all standardised definitions of music and the expectations that such constants have encoded in us. In Kristevan terms, Galas launches a Semiotic "guerrilla raid"[67] upon the musical Symbolic. In doing so, she deconstructs not only normative musical "bodies," but all notions of unified subjectivity. It is not too much to say that Diamanda Galas represents the nonpareil of promiscuously abject, musical *imitatio.* One concrete example from her CD/Video "Judgment Day" offers a broad sample of her musically iconoclastic palette.

In her "bastardised" rendition of "Were You a Witness?," Galas weds gospel favourites " Were You a Witness?" and "Were You There When They Crucified My Lord?" to hortatory rhetoric ("And on that holy day/bloody day"), thereby warping Good Friday piety into contempt for Christian voyeurism and complacency toward AIDS.[68] From the outset, such basic textual and then musical promiscuity muddle the listeners' kinetic and affective response. Throughout the piece, the galling complexity of listeners' reactions tells a corporeal, literally enervating tale of frustrated desire.

1. The Vamp Motif: Introducing and undergirding this textual mélange, the opening chaos of low, harmonically ambiguous bass chords creates even more somatically registered malaise. When the piano finally settles into a vamp motif, this recognisable erotic code offers some aural stability, although it is punctuated with the rich, octave-spanning chords one normally associates with Romantic piano concerti. The key is minor, but, given the black-leather visuals flashed earlier, this might simply connote a darker sexual thematic. Easing into this full-bodied vamp, our conventionally programmed musical sensibilities anticipate[69] musico-erotic pleasure. Instead, Galas as Grim Reaper/Dominatrix assaults us with a foul mixture of accusatory, grief-stricken questions. Each "Were you there?" is a double entendre: were you there as voyeurs indifferently watching AIDS victims die, or as lovers and friends, outraged and crushed by loss? The sexy bass vamp, especially its off-beat chordal commentary, becomes a knuckle-rapping, face-slapping interrogation.

2. The Melody: Further distorting music's normative body, Galas purposely disfigures her melodic lines. Initially, within the context of gospel or blues improvisation, they behave "reasonably" enough, but the text is then wrenched from even these freer rhetorical styles. Its verses are hissed, moaned, inflected with ululation, screams, and panting. Feigning musical personality disorder, Galas variously inhabits the voices and affectations of, I suggest, Paul Robeson, Jessye

Norman, Eartha Kitt, and the aesthetically "uglier" Janis Joplin. She also pushes the standardized use of vocal vibrato past its stylistically correct (and normatively pleasurable) limits. Symptomatic of imbalance, and an imminent musical break-down, Galas further perverts melody and meter via her "oral fixations" on "Some-times" and "Were You There" (complete with abrupt changes in volume), thereby heightening the tension in the listener's body with great effect. The listener teeters on the brink of musical abjection, until, finally, the inevitable musical eruption occurs, after which music's body emits a final, anguished scream.

3. Motivic Allusions: And still, in her rage and grief, Galas vamps. As the bass chords rock her back and forth, as she chants one word over and over in a breathy *pianissimo*, as she wraps her gaping mouth around the mike, Galas rhetorically inflects this dirge with cognitively dissonant, orgasmic overtones. Often in Galas's music, there is this promiscuous overlay of musical conventions which connote sex, love, madness, and death. This is precisely why her music is most disturbing. In all her works, Galas persistently weds music—via texts and allusive funereal motifs—to death and disintegration. As mentioned in chapter 5, we want to for-get that music dies; its body de-composes instantaneously—contravening perma-nence, presence, or stability.

4. Visuals, Musical Personae, and Galas's Ritual Body: Equally promiscuous is the confluence of abject musical personae in Galas's vocal styles; all are female fig-ures of excess, historically shunned by religious authorities as effeminising and /or contaminating. Her heterogeneous musical vocabulary evokes: (1) blues musi-cians—blues women were the 20s and 30s "painted whores" (Artusi)—con-demned by white, and many black, church authorities; (2) the pagan "womanish grieving" anathema to early Christian funeral rites; (3) the musical virtuosity and flamboyant makeup of opera diva Maria Callas.[70] Furthermore, stripped to the waist and drenched in stage blood (meant to represent the infected blood of AIDS patients), as Galas vamps and keens at the foot of a cross in the cathedral (or on stage), her ritual body visually conflates the Christ(a), the Magdalen, *Mater dolorosa*, and the diseased, hallucinating body–minds of AIDS patients (not to mention of course, the mad woman in the attic). The introductory tease of visu-als is promiscually abject as well—a jarring collage of rough-trade leather, a human fetus (aborted or *in utero*?), a mangled frog, a crucifix, a skeleton, a final dizzy spin of stained glass.

Galas's Musical Mnemonic of Suffering

Just as the nuns smuggled in musical contraband to commune with God, Galas incorporates the above marginal elements to accommodate her own more tormented "excess of desire."[71] While I have tried to retrieve and incorporate frag-ments lost from the tradition into a new model, Galas effects her own radical reworking of music's more prodigal elements. That is, her raw materials lie in the neglected margins (gospel and blues), and danger zones (Greek moirology) of traditional Christian compositional resources. But it is precisely such "pagan" pathos and the more inclusive palette of African-Christian music that provide Galas with the necessary materials for doing justice to the horrors of AIDS, meeting expressive needs which sacred Eurocentric Pablum cannot. (Traditionally, grieving the dead in Greek and black churches is much less reserved than that of white funerals.) Moreover, unlike the euphonious musical incarnations of *imitatio* which Hildegard and the nuns of Santa Cristina embodied, in Galas both music and the music-making body actually lose all aesthetic allure to become painful mnemonics of christic and marian suffering—repulsive, first-order forms of abjection. Galas "practices defilement to achieve [a very excruciating] grace."[72]

Revalorising Dissonance: Music as Suffering Love

We seem far from the joys of musical sex introduced in chapter 4 via the musical praxis of Suzanne Cusick. But perhaps Galas's music is a tragic "erotic mapping." If music is Cusick's lover, in Galas's work, music is the beloved crucified by AIDS and human indifference, at whose feet Galas wails and rages even as she simulates this crucifixion on her own body. In her music-made-flesh, music's body is stretched to the limits of its expressive potency, a lover infected, torn, ripped apart, deformed by pressure to obey "straight"-laced harmonic ideals. Refusing such self-betrayal, music's body breaks. In her performances, Galas's own reviled, revolting body also simulates the bodies of AIDS patients. People turn away from both. With her song's cubist disarray, Galas paradoxically overturns both Christian and musico-performative tableaux of civility. Thus Galas's music can be reframed, not as blasphemy, but as a much more graphic, oozing (rather than "sweet") wound of an *imitatio crucis*, abject effluvium. In her ritualistic body[73] and her brutalised musical flesh, as well as in her textual promiscuity, Galas fleshes out a "polyglot discourse" for imitating Christ, one which upends previous prescriptions for Christian identity formation.[74] As such, Galas can serve as one artistic response to Schüssler Fiorenza's plea for topical, emancipatory christologies.[75] Her polysemic cry from the cross represents "a set of rhetorical practices which unsettles [the] doctrinal formulae and traditional metaphorical systems" that ground extant christologies.

IV. *Ritornello:* Revamping Music's "Innate" Ethicality

"There are no prodigies in this realm," writes Adrienne Rich, *"only a half-blind, stubborn cleaving to the timbre, the tones of what we are."*[76] Galas's musical mnemonic of promiscuity brings us full circle as she manifests the thoroughgoing, "circular historicity of music and the body."[77] Her own body and her music's chronic shape-shifting, its foreign tongues, and abject "otherness" convey the precarious semiotic/symbolic balance struck in all musical bodies, *and* in

human subjectivity itself. Vamping her dangerous (kinetic) memories, aurally and visually, Galas exposes the fragility, the evanescence of notions of bodily integrity, and the impossibility of their sustained, concrete realisation.[78] This new musical ethos represents a radical departure from other masculinist models in which "virtuous" musical bodies erase inner discord by modelling and literally in-spiring either corporeal transcendence or some sort of hermetically sealed integrity. Constantly decomposing and recomposing itself, music shows itself to be a technique of the self, where the self and Christian identity are postcolonial, postnuclear, postmodern configurations—ever subject to change. Correlatively, Galas's relentlessly abject *imitatio* reminds us that "what is excluded can never be fully obliterated, but hovers at the borders of our existence, threatening the apparently settled unity of the subject with disruption and possible dissolution."[79] Of particular interest to theologians constructing ethical models, Galas's mnemonic of music's innate promiscuity teaches us to embrace the alterity *within ourselves* and in society.[80] We may shun this musical mnemonic of our own promiscual abjection, but such repression is futile.[81]

To add further nuance to engagements of music's body in ethical models, as we saw in chapter 3, traditionally when theologians promote music as a vehicle of political liberation, they really locate its power in the *textual* messages which music accompanies, or in the artist's social activism, rather than in the music's suasions. By contrast, Galas's use of texts is critically deconstructive—purposely nonsensical, one strand of a broader, semiotic assault. *Yet in the absence of the logocentric, music's fragmented body remains potent*, moving us—and this quite literally—out of complacency; receiving its blows, we cringe and squirm. Consequently, refuting any illusion of transcendent idealism, Galas's promiscual body of musico-cultural citations still affords an imaginative space for political resistance. While masculinist appreciations of music's potential as a liberating conduit for political texts are valid, as we have seen, they have ignored music's actual body too long, and this myopia itself harbours a gendered agenda. We must not only make a concerted effort to recuperate and revalorise the emancipatory power of music's disintegrating body, but also problematise any monochromatic[82] portraits of music as the galvanising, political "glue" among consolidated subjects.[83]

This tragic erotic mapping has further ethical implications: Galas's musical body supports Kathleen Sands's proposal that, instead of harmonically resolved "beginnings and ends," theologians and ethicists must more humbly conceptualise "our messy multiform continuance." In the face of "the daily proliferation of difference" and the no longer suppressible clash of competing definitions of the 'Good,' our task is simply to help the world "go on."[84] In Galas's similar refusal of "the closure of absolutes," her musical ethos constitutes what Sands calls "a tragic heuristic"—"a theatre for shared inquiry about conflict,"[85] as well as a real "*practice* of compassion."[86] That is, Galas's music represents the agonising, agonistic "work of holding open boundaries of thought and care that are wider than the bounds of what we can choose and affirm." Her musical body portrays a sonic redefinition of compassion as "opposition that is not benumbed to the enemy, negation that dares to understand."[87] Daring to give voice to tragedy, Galas teaches feminist theologians to promote music as a set of embodied practices which re-theorises corporeal subjectivity in ways that contradict the masculinist use of music as either subordinate undergarment to liberal notions of the subject and its agency or as utopian proleptic, a.k.a. soothing escape pod. Indeed, Galas's mnemonic of promiscuity reminds us of the impossibility of maintaining one, unified, universal body, or Ur-self even as her music models and inspires some imaginative yet profoundly embodied element of transcendence from our seemingly atomistic individualities and physical limitations. Her dramatised pastiche of abject bodies and their musical analogues model immersion in a shared project of kenotic selfhood which still affords at least some form of (promiscual) transcendence that all embodied creatures inevitably desire. "Any theory of human embodiment must take seriously the urge toward transcendence endemic to bodies."[88]

The above hermeneutical shifts counter the initial theological impression that Galas's "heterogeneous sound ideal" reflects the abject failure of language and art to contain grief or affirm meaning and beauty in the face of tragedy. Galas bodies forth the harshest of realities and the analogically disruptive musical powers which Plato and the church fathers "transcended" through cerebral/contemplative immersion in pure harmonies. A postmodern theology of music which takes tragedy seriously, that is, which acknowledges today's epidemic injustices and the irreconcilable pluralities of truths and goods, cannot afford to perpetuate such platonic naïveté. Like Tharpe in her musical milieu, Galas's musical abjection helps restore a balance to the expressive range of musico-theological meaning-making. Dissonance—previously deemed "demonic" and/or "feminine"—becomes a self-critical, musico-theological voice which questions the cogency of those absolutes which music previously signified—harmony, unity, and order. In her music and the worldview that inspires it, Galas relentlessly exposes the suffering, disintegration, and decentering forces which humans cannot escape.

But, in the anguished discord, both honesty- and integrity-as-disintegration are birthed. With acutest intensity, Galas will not let us forget that no pure, free-agent authenticity lies outside of the historical texts and tones which compose us. And yet, ironically enough, Galas's musico-rhetorical dementia also reflects the agency which even decentered subjectivity can achieve.[89] Galas's revamped, cruciform frame fills today's discursive/theological need for new models of human subjectivity; to quote Judith Butler, "radical rearticulations" of bodies "worth protecting . . . saving . . . grieving."[90] In effect, Galas puts not only Sands's and Schüssler Fiorenza's theories into musical practice, but also Judith Butler's model of subjectivity. Read according to the latter, Galas's abject musicality heralds the possibility for change inherent in the "slippages" that inevitably transpire because norms require constant reiteration to be materialised and naturalised. Such reiterations are never exact, and consequently, their attendant "gaps and fissures" destabilise normative constructions of body, sex, and gender, thereby inviting their own subversion.[91] Like sex and gender identities, Galas's musical body is never "thought" (more accurately played and sung) "outside the systems of citationality that give rise to it."[92] Inscribed on her fingers in the opening visuals, Galas insists, "We are all HIV positive." This conflation, combined with Galas's musical abjection, politically activates through the powerful medium of sound "those 'unlivable' and 'uninhabitable' zones of social life" whose inhabitants are the designated nonentities used by so-called normal people to "circumscribe" their own identity.[93] Moreover, to counter hegemonic "forces of exclusion and abjection," through her own musico-ritual body, Galas's "citational politics" makes the AIDS body normative and virile.[94] Refuting any illusion of either transcendent idealism or transcendent materiality,[95] Galas's promiscual body of musico-cultural citations still affords an imaginative space for political resistance.

Furthermore, Galas's archly fluid body of citations, and more generally, all music's "cultural instantiations" contradict any assertion of a "bodily remainder" that would transcend the reiterative production of selfhood. Correlatively (and supporting Butler's citational model of subjectivity), as invisible sound waves penetrating our own porous frames, music's materiality mocks our attempts to reify into "matter" an infinite "*process* of materialisation that stabilizes over time."[96] With consummate self-irony, music incarnates the constant evaporation of "boundary, fixity and surface."[97]

Thus, Galas's *imitatio*, her flagrant musical *délire*, is a dark, harrowing conversion—not perversion—of the gospel, a gospel which cannot be contained, terrifying in both its unanticipated freedom and the force with which it explodes previous incarnations—ever new.[98] This postmodern woman–mystic immerses herself in abjection in order adequately to imitate Christ's cruciform plea for justice, compassion, and mercy. Like Angela of Foligno, Galas knows that the gaping, pustuled wounds of suffering love can cleanse and feed. And thus, her raging discord heralds a more contemporaneous musico-theological attitude—aural crucifixions and tritone resurrections.

Notes

1. Aeschylus's description of the Furies in *Eumenides*: "[T]hey snore with breath that drives one back./From their eyes drips the foul ooze" (2.52-54).

2. Olly Wilson's descriptor for an African religious aesthetic; cf. "The Heterogeneous Sound Ideal in African-American Music," in *New Perspectives on Music: Essays in Honor of Eileen Southern*, ed. Josephine Wright, with Samuel A. Floyd, Jr. (Michigan: Harmonie Park Press, 1992), adopted by Floyd, in *The Power of Black Music*.

3. Wilson, in Floyd, *The Power of Black Music*, 28.

4. Ibid.

5. Ibid., 15.

6. Ibid.

7. Ibid., with a quotation from John S. Mbiti, *African Religions and Philosophy* (New York: Praeger, 1969) 52.

8. Floyd, *The Power of Black Music*, 23.

9. Ibid., 15.

10. Cf. ibid., 14-34.

11. Van der Leeuw's prioritisation of dance, therefore, suggests a consultation of non-Western sources and norms; cf. chap. 3 above. And yet, Lippman points out that originally, even the hellenic notion of music was comprised of three components: poetry, dance, and song. The commemoration of heroes and important "historic events" always engaged "a representational art of rhythm: music-poetry-dance. Hellenic theories of musical ethics are generally concerned with music in this fuller form" (Lippman, *Musical Thought in Ancient Greece*, 52). Christian adaptations of Pythagorean and Platonic musical ethoses did not retain this tripartite notion of sacred music.

12. Lomax, "Africanisms in New World Music," in *The Haitian Potential*, ed. Rubin and Schaedel (New York: Teachers College Press, 50), in Floyd, *The Power of Black Music*, 27.

13. I am using very loosely this scientific coinage of Stephen Jay Gould and Niles Eldredge. It is rudimentarily defined as follows in the *Oxford Dictionary of Earth Sciences*: "Evolution characterised by geologically long periods of stability during which little speciation occurs, punctuated by short periods of rapid change—species undergoing most of their morphological changes shortly after breaking from their parent species."

14. Lomax, "Africanisms in New World Music," 49, in Floyd, *The Power of Black Music*, 27.

15. Floyd, quoting Frances Bebey, concludes that the primary objective of African music is the translation of everyday experiences (though this often engages the supernatural) into "living sound" (*The Power of Black Music*, 14).

16. Ibid., 38, quoting Morgan Godwyn, *The Negro's and Indian's advocate, suing for their admission into the church* (London, n.p., 1680), 33.

17. Thus the slave in question recounts: "[F]or several nights after the [camp] meetings, the slaves had prayer-meetings in their houses, and sang and shouted greatly to the disturbance of the master. One evening the noise had been greater than ever, and, in the midst of it, the master sent for the leading black man. . . . *'Dick,' said the planter, 'what is the meaning of this hideous noise? If you were whipped by devils, you could not make a more horrible howling. Now, Dick, I can bear a great deal, but more of this I cannot stand. Now I say, Dick, stop it. . . .' 'Yes, massa; but the blessed gospel is from God, and if he command us to pray, and you command us not to pray, what shall we do, massa?'* (*National Anti-Slavery Standard* 25 (Oct. 15, 1864), in Epstein, *Sinful Tunes and Spirituals*, 232; emphasis mine).

18. Thus Bremer: "There is a vast, vast difference between the screeching improvisation of the negroes in Cuba, and the inspired and inspiring preaching of the Savior . . . which I have heard extemporized in South Carolina, Georgia, Maryland, and Louisiana. *And the low and sensual is that lawless life, and intoxication of the senses in those wild negro-dances, and those noisy festivities to the beat of the drum, compared with that life, and that spiritual intoxication in song and prayer*, and religious joy, which is seen and heard at the religious festivals of the negro people here" (Bremer, *The Homes of the New World*, II, in Epstein, *Sinful Tunes and Spirituals*, 90; emphasis mine). Bremer even thought whites could revise and teach more civilised versions of their original African songs to black children. According to Epstein, "[s]he described an idyllic vision of young white women teaching black children the songs and dances 'as they are practiced in their native land; those songs, for instance, with the chorus, which seems to be the heart of all songs among the natives of Africa'" (Bremer, in Epstein, *Sinful Tunes and Spirituals*, 90).

19. "Since I have seen in Cuba the negroes in their savage, original state—seen their dances, heard their songs, and am able to compare them with what they are at the best in the United States, there remains no longer a doubt in my mind as to the beneficial influence of Anglo-American culture on the negro. . . . The sour crab is not more unlike our noble, bright, Astrachan apple, than is the song of the wild African to the song of the Christian negro in the United States, whether it be hymns that he sings or gay negro [minstrel] songs that he has himself composed" (Bremer in Epstein, *Sinful Tunes and Spirituals*, 89).

20. Labat, *Nouveaux Voyages aux isles de l'Amerique* (Hague, 1726), in Epstein, *Sinful Tunes and Spirituals*, 30.

21. "I[t] has been Customary among them (our Slaves) to have their ffeasts [*sic*], dances, and merry Meetings upon the Lord's day, that practice is pretty well over in this Parish, but not absolutely: I tell them that[to] present themselves to be admitted to Baptism, they must promise they'll spend no more the Lord's day in idleness, and if they do I'll cut them off from the Communion" (Le Jau [1709], in Epstein, *Sinful Tunes and Spirituals*, 38).

Epstein includes a later account (1779) of slaves' Sunday dancing which may or may not refer to pre-convert activities. "Sundays and holidays are indeed allowed the negroes in Carolina. . . . Holidays there are days of idleness, riot, wantonness and excess; in which the slaves assemble together in alarming crowds, for the purposes of dancing, feasting and merriment" (Epstein, *Sinful Tunes and Spirituals*, 41). Eight months later he wrote "to the secretary of the society for the Propagation of the Gospel in foreign Parts (S.P.G.): 'The Lord's day is no more profaned by their dancings at least about me'" (38).

22. Ibid., 30.

23. John Oldmixon, *The British Empire in America*, in Epstein, *Sinful Tunes and Spirituals*, 31. "They have two Musical Instruments, like Kettle-Drums, for each Company of Dancers, with which they make a very barbarous melody" (ibid.).

Also, in the *Importance of Jamaica*, it states: "On *Sundays* . . . towards the Evening . . . some hundreds of them [the slaves] will meet together, according to the Customs of their own Country (many of which they retain) with Strum-Strums and Calibashes, which they beat and make a horrid Noise with (tho' some of the *Creol* Negroes are esteem'd for keeping just Time, and playing very well on the Violin)" (ibid.).

Little wonder, given its references to musical instruments, that we no longer sing the third verse of this version of "Swing Low Sweet Chariot" (pub. 1903):

Banjos pickin', Jews harps zoonin'
all de hebbenly ban'a-chunin',
Swing low, sweet charriyut.
Sing en shout bofe night en day,
Stop just long ernuff to pray,
Swing low, sweet charryiut."

(Anne Hobson, *In Old Alabama*, in Epstein, *Sinful Tunes and Spirituals*, 219).

24. Frederick Law Olmsted, *A Journey in the Seaboard Slave States*, I, 26-29, in Epstein, ibid., 235f.: "The hearse halted at a desolate place, where a dozen colored people were already engaged heaping the earth over the grave of a child, and singing a wild kind of chant. [After the sermon] an old negro . . . raised a hymn, which soon became a confused chant—the leader singing a few words alone, and the company then either repeating them after him or make [*sic*] a response to them, in the manner of sailors heaving at the windlass. I could understand but very few of the words. The music was wild and barbarous, but not without a plaintive melody. A new leader took the place of the old man, when his breath gave out (he had sung very hard, with much bending of the body and gesticulations). and continued until the grave was filled, and a mound raised over it" (ibid., 235-36).

25. Here is the quote in full: "They have no idea of Heaven, further than the Pleasures of returning to their native Country, whither they believe every Negro goes after Death: This Thought is so agreeable, that it cheers the poor Creatures. . . . They look on Death as a Blessing. . . . When one is carried out to his Grave, he is attended with a vast Multitude. . . . They sing all the way. . . all the while they are covering it with Earth, the Attendants scream out in a terrible manner, which is not the Effect of Grief but of Joy; they beat on their wooden Drums, and the Women with their Rattles make a hideous Noise. . . . [T]hey return to Town, or the Plantation, singing after their manner, and so the Ceremony ends" (Charles Leslie, *A New History of Jamaica*, in Epstein, ibid., 235).

26. Ibid., 234.

27. "Presently the whole congregation uplifted their voices in a hymn, the first high wailing notes of which—sung all in unison, in the midst of these unwonted surroundings—sent a thrill through all my nerves" (Fanny Kemble *Journal of a Residence*, St. Simon's Island near Georgia, winter 1838-39, in Epstein, ibid., 235).

28. Adaptation of an essay title in Audre Lorde's *Sister Outsider: Essays and Speeches*; 'The Master's Tools Will Never Dismantle the Master's House" (Trumansburg, NY: Crossing Press, 1984) 110-13.

29. For example, "they formerly on their Festivals were allowed the use of Trumpets after their Fashion, and Drums made out of a piece of a hollow Tree, covered on one end with any green Skin, and stretched with Thouls or Pins. But making use of these in their Wars at home in Africa, it was thought too much inciting them to Rebellion, and so they were prohibited by the Customs of the Island" (Sir Hans Sloane, *Voyage to the Islands* I in Epstein, ibid., 29).

30. McClary's term.

31. Lydia Maria Child, "Charity Bowery," in *The Liberty Bell*, in Epstein, ibid., 230; emphasis mine.

32. Former slave Alice Sewell (b. Nov. 13, 1851) reported, "Dey didn't allow us to sing on our

plantation, 'cause if we did we just sing ourselves happy and get to shouting and dat would settle de work" (Epstein, ibid., 231).

33. "[T]he whites reported it round among themselves that, if a note was heard, we should have some dreadful punishment; and after that, the low whites would fall upon any slaves they heard praying, or singing a hymn, and often killed them before their masters or mistresses could get to them" (Epstein, ibid., 229).

34. In the Episcopalian church, blacks worshipped in "segregated sections" of white churches: "No extemporary address, exhortation, or prayer was permitted." Epstein comments: "The strict control over the service exercised by the Episcopal Church would have prevented (or at least kept to a minimum) any blending of African religious practice with the formal order of worship, or any expression of ethnic cultural preferences except in ways too subtle to be detected. The development of any distinctive black religious song would thus have been tightly circumscribed" (Epstein, ibid., 196).

35. Epstein has noted that "widespread opposition" to black freedom of worship existed within these churches: "Even among the less formal Baptists and Methodists, there was widespread opposition to permitting blacks to worship as they chose. The more genteel objected to practices that were traditional at camp meetings, claiming that noisy, enthusiastic meetings were not a proper expression of religious feeling and disturbed the peace" (ibid., 196).

36. Epstein notes: "The acceptance by some blacks of the conventional evangelical attitude toward dancing and other amusements was demonstrated in a speech delivered by a black man, Abraham Johnstone, before he was hanged for his crimes in 1797. It could have been (and perhaps was) written by a white missionary: 'Above all my dear friends avoid frolicking, and all amusements that lead to expense and idleness'" (ibid., 111).

37. Davies writes in one of his letters: "I cannot but observe, that the *Negroes*, above all the Human Species that I ever knew, have an Ear for Musick, and a kind of ecstatic Delight in *Psalmody*; and there are no books they learn so soon, or take so much Pleasure in" (Samuel Davies, *Letters*, in Epstein, *A Journey in the Seaboard Slave States*, 104). One Revd. Mr. Todd reports: "The sacred hours of the Sabbath, that used to be spent in frolicking, dancing, and other profane courses, are now employed in attending upon public ordinances, in learning to read at home, or in praying together, and singing the praises of God the Lamb" (Todd, in Davies, *Letters*, in Epstein, ibid., 1977, 104f.).

38. Jones, *Religious Instruction,* in Epstein, ibid., 222.

39. Epstein explains this ambivalence thus: "In their writings [southern whites] one finds two apparently contradictory views of this music: close at hand it was often dismissed as mere noise or uncivilized barbarism, but at a distance it became beautiful, melancholy, and nostalgic" (225). She quotes two such attitudes held by Mary Boykin Chestnut (Camden, SC, 1861). Note Chestnut's concern over the singers' emotional excess, and its obscuring of the text:

"[There was] a very large black congregation. . . . Jim Nelson, the driver . . . a full-blooded African, was asked to lead in prayer. He became wildly excited, on his knees, facing us with his eyes shut. He clapped his hands at the end of every sentence, and his voice rose to the pitch of a shrill shriek, yet was strangely clear and musical, occasionally, in a plaintive minor key that went to your heart. Sometimes it rang out like a trumpet. I wept bitterly. It was all sound, however, and emotional pathos. . . . The words had no meaning at all. It was the devotional passion of voice and manner which was so magnetic. The Negroes sobbed and shouted and swayed backward and forward, women with aprons to their eyes, most of them clapping their hands and responding in shrill tones: 'Yes, God!' 'Jesus!' 'Savior!' 'Bless de Lord, amen,' etc. It was a little too exciting for me. I would very much have liked to shout, too. Jim Nelson when he rose from his knees trembled and shook as one in a palsy, and from his eyes you could see the ecstasy had not left him yet. He could not stand at all, and sank back on his bench. . . .

"Suddenly, as I sat wondering what next, they broke out into one of those soul-stirring Negro camp-meeting hymns. To me this is the saddest of all earthly music, weird and depressing beyond my powers to describe."

Epstein then adds: "Yet on March 13 of the following year she wrote: 'The best way to take the Negroes to your heart is to get as far away from them as possible'" (Chestnut, *A Diary from Dixie*, in Epstein, ibid., 225-26).

40. Kingsley, *Treatise on the Patriarchal or Co-operative System of Society,* in Epstein, ibid., 194. Another more appreciative white poet described slave rituals thus:

On festal days; or when their work is done;
Permit thy slaves to lead the choral dance,
To the wild banshaw's* melancholy sound.

> Responsive to the sound, head, feet, and frame
> Move awkwardly harmonious; hand in hand
> Now lock'd, the gay troop circularly wheels,
> And frisks and capers with intemperate joy,
> While those distinguish'd for their heels and air,
> Bound in the centre. . . .

(Grainger, "The Sugar Cane; A Poem" January, 1763, Basseterre [St. Kitt's], in Epstein, *A Journey in the Seaboard Slave States,* 32). Epstein includes the poet's footnote: "**Banshaw.* This is a sort of rude guitar, invented by the Negroes. It produces a wild pleasing melancholy sound."

41. Most early historical information comes by way of the West Indies (cf. Epstein, *A Journey in the Seaboard Slave States,* chapter 1). Here is a brief, explanatory excerpt:

"If the search for contemporary descriptions of black music is confined to mainland North America, an anomalous situation is revealed: the blacks arrived in the colonies in 1619, but almost nothing about their music has been found before the end of the seventeenth century, when they were already playing the fiddle. Very fragmentary accounts of music and dancing have been found from the mainland during the seventeenth century—not enough, by themselves, to present a convincing case that African music and dancing continued among the Africans after their arrival in the thirteen colonies. This lack of contemporary description becomes comprehensible when one realizes that the black population of the mainland colonies grew very slowly throughout the seventeenth century, and that it was widely dispersed among a much larger white population" (21f.).

"The cultural heritage brought from Africa, common to the slaves both on the mainland and in the islands, met with less overt opposition in the islands and so was able to maintain itself freely and for a longer time. The conditions in the islands which were conducive to the preservation of African cultural patterns included absentee landowning, with an accompanying lack of interest in the leisure activities of the slaves; frequent influxes of new arrivals from Africa; and a very high proportion of blacks to whites, ranging from 5:1 to as high as 23:1. The blacks on the mainland, relatively fewer in number and dispersed among a much larger white population, did not all come directly from Africa; slaves already "seasoned" in the West Indies were considered more desirable, since they could already understand some English or French and had become accustomed to plantation labor."

"However, the descriptions of African music from the islands were quite consistent with the more fragmentary accounts surviving from the mainland" (23f.).

42. Epstein continues: "[B]y the time contemporary reporters described it, black sacred music shared many points of stylistic similarity with secular black music: rhythmic complexity, gapped scales, overlapping of leader and chorus, bodily movement, extended repetition of short melodic phrases—all now recognized as characteristic of African musics" (*A Journey in the Seaboard Slave States,* 217).

43. Cf. *Protest and Praise: Sacred Music of Black Religion* (Minneapolis: Augsburg Fortress Press, 1990), and *Black Hymnody: A Hymnological History of the African American Church* (Knoxville, TN: University of Tennessee Press, 1992).

44. On the Jezebel/Mammy stereotypes, see Deborah Gray White, *Ar'n't I a Woman?: Female Slaves in the Plantation South.*

45. Epstein's synthesis of Abigail Mott, *Biographical Sketches and Interesting Anecdotes of Persons of Color,* in *A Journey in the Seaboard Slave States,* 114f.

46. Ibid., 115.

47. Cf. *Early Rhythm and Blues* (Mojo Records, 307, 1996).

48. Though without construing blues as a form of *imitatio,* black theologians have identified other christologically significant elements in the blues. James Cone in particular develops a theology of the blues in his book *The Spirituals and the Blues.* Cone's treatment of the intertwined themes of suffering and sex in blues music strengthens my own proposal that Tharpe as scorned and rejected blues singer became Christ. Cone argues: "[White] people cannot appreciate the feel and touch of life nor express the beauty of giving themselves to each other community, in love, and in sex until they know and experience the brokenness of existence as disclosed in human oppression. People who have not been oppressed physically cannot know the power inherent in bodily expressions of love. That is why white Western culture makes a sharp distinction between the spirit and the body, the divine and the human, the sacred and the secular" (*The Spirituals and the Blues,* 128). Thus Cone also collapses the distinction between spirituals, gospel, and the blues (ibid., 48). Blues music breaks the oppressive musical bonds of white aesthetic ideals.

49. Cf. Broughton, *Black Gospel: An Illustrated History of the Gospel Sound,* 83ff.

50. Oliver, "Blues," in *New Grove Dictionary of Music and Musicians,* 815.

51. Broughton, *Black Gospel,* 84.

52. Here is Grant's basic argument: "For Christian Black women in the past, Jesus was their central frame of reference. They identified with Jesus because they believed that Jesus identified with them. As Jesus was persecuted and made to suffer undeservedly, so were they. His suffering culminated in the crucifixion. Their crucifixion included rape, and babies being sold" (Grant, *White Women's Christ, Black Women's Jesus,* 212).

"But is this just another situation that takes us deeper into the abyss of theological relativity? I would argue that it is not, because it is in the context of Black women's experience where the particular connects up with the universal. By this I mean that in each of the three dynamics of oppression, Black women share in the reality of a broader community. They share race suffering with Black men; with White women and other Third World women, they are victims of sexism; and with poor Blacks and Whites, and other Third World peoples, especially women, they are disproportionately poor. To speak of Black women's tri-dimensional reality, therefore, is not to speak of Black women exclusively, for there is an implied universality which connects them with others" (216f.).

53. McClary's coinage, "Music, Pythagoreans, and the Body," 84.

54. Here are the lyrics:
A crowd of people/ went out in the desert
To listen to what the good Lord said.
All day long they heard/the good Lord's word
And they got hungry and had to be fed
On only two little fishes and five loaves of bread.

The Lord's disciples/began to get worried
And each of them had to scratch his head.
But what could they do cause each one knew
There was a big crowd that had to be fed
With only two little fishes . . .

The Good Lord stood up/ and told his disciples
To bring him the loaves of bread instead.
Bring the fishes by and let him try
A little idea he had in his head
About those two little fishes . . .

Guitar solo with piano and bass "commentary"

He broke the bread up/ and also the fishes
And then his disciples went ahead.
But the more passed round, the more they found
With lots left over when all had been fed
On only two little fishes . . .

Here what I said: If we all helped one another then the world would be fed
On only two little fishes and five—loaves of bread.

55. A brief clip of Tharpe performing can be seen in a documentary entitled "The Story of Gospel Music: Through Many Dangers," directed by Andrew Dunn and James Marsh, BBC, 1996. Aired on PBS television, *Great Performances.*

56. Cone argues: "Because we know that we have survived, that we have not been destroyed, and that we are more than the stripes on our backs, we can sing as a way of celebrating our being. Indeed, for black people, existence is a form of celebration. It is joy, love, and sex. . . . People cannot love physically and spiritually (the two cannot be separated!) until they have been up against the edge of life, experiencing the hurt and pain of existence" (*The Spirituals and the Blues,* 128).

57. Lochrie *Margery Kempe,* citing Vauchez, 3ff.

58. Ibid., 41.

59. Broughton describes Jackson's "risqué" performance style as follows: "For many churches they [her gospel ballads] raised the temperature higher than was proper and decent, for not only was Mahalia an excessive shouter, she was also a flirtatious entertainer known for her 'snake-hips' and for lifting her robe an inch or two when she got happy. . . .

"She roared and shouted like a Pentecostal preacher, she moaned and growled like the old southern mothers, she hollered the gospel blues like a sanctified Bessie Smith and she cried into the Watts' hymns like she was back in a slave cabin" (*Black Gospel,* 54).

60. Lochrie, *Margery Kempe,* 40.

61. Cone, *The Spirituals and the Blues,* 115-16.

62. "He [Dubois]called them sorrow songs, because they were 'the music of an unhappy people, of the children of disappointment; they tell of death and suffering and unvoiced longing toward a truer world, of mist wanderings and hidden ways.' . . . '[T]here breathes a hope [in them]—a faith in the ultimate justice of things'" (*The Spirituals and the Blues,* 12). Similarly, in Cone's discussion of the *spirituals*—the blues' progenitor and Tharpe's inspirational wellspring—he applauds black realism (as opposed to white transcendentalist ideology). (See ibid., ch. 5.)

63. *The Spirituals and the Blues,* 13.

64. Ibid.

65. Pope and Leonardi, *The Diva's Mouth: Body, Voice, Prima Donna Politics,* 237.

66. Pope and Leonardi, *The Diva's Mouth,* 269 n. 7. For a good introduction to Galas's performance art, see ibid., 228-42.

67. Terry Eagleton characterizes Kierkegaard as launching a "guerrilla raid" on all things metaphysical (Eagleton, *The Ideology of the Aesthetic,* 173).

68. Here is an abbreviated form of the basic text, minus Galas's lengthy interjections and digressions:

Were you a witness? (x2)
And on that holy day
And on that bloody day
Were you a witness
But to all cowards and voyeurs:
There are no more tickets to the funeral (x2)

Were you there when they crucified my Lord?
Were you there when they nailed him to the cross?
Sometimes it causes me to tremble, tremble, tremble
Were you there when they crucified my Lord?

Were you there when they dragged him to the grave? (x2)
Sometimes it causes me to wonder, wonder, wonder
Were you there when they dragged him to the grave?

Were you there when they laid him in the tomb? (x2)
Sometimes it causes me to wonder, wonder, wonder
Were you there when they laid him in the tomb?

69. McClary coins this Pavlovian metaphor in her discussion of "In the Midnight Hour," in "Music, the Pythagoreans, and the Body," 84.

70. Callas has been a great source of inspiration for Galas. She wears the former's signature large sunglasses and dramatic eye makeup, and in one interview proclaimed: "no diva performs without her *full* eye makeup" (Leonardi and Pope, *The Diva's Mouth,* 230f.).

71. Richard Gehr also discusses Galas's radical hybridisation of gospel music and Greek moirology: "Exploiting the parallels between Greek ritual lamentation and the connection of black women to the church in the American South, she transforms gospel clichés (Swing Low Sweet Chariot, Let My People Go) into *calls to arms*" ("Mourning in America," 118; emphasis mine).

72. Lochrie, *Margery Kempe,* 41.

73. Galas ritualises her body by simulating the crucifixion with it, and, in her *Plague Mass,* by uttering the words of institution from the liturgy: "This is my Body, My Blood."

74. Schüssler Fiorenza, *Jesus: Miriam's Child, Sophia's Prophet,* 28.

75. Ibid., 62f.

76. Adrienne Rich, "Transcendental Etude," *The Dream of a Common Language: Poems 1974-44* (New York: W.W. Norton, 1978) 72-77.

77. McClary, "Music, the Pythagoreans, and the Body," 84.

78. Theologian Jeremy Begbie, we recall, would prefer to harmonically resolve music's spatiotemporal evanescence. I think this is to miss the point entirely. Cf. chapter 3 above.

79. Grosz, *Sexual Subversions,* 71.

80. See Kristeva, *Strangers to Ourselves,* and also Kelly Oliver, *Reading Kristeva: Unraveling the Double-Bind.* Thus Oliver: "Kristeva's claim that alterity is within the subject undermines any notion of a unified subject" (13). Or stated otherwise: Galas's music underlines one of Kristeva's crucial insights from her study of abjection: "Like avant-garde poets, pregnant Madonnas, analysands undergoing analysis, we are all foreigners, 'extraterrestrials,' subjects-in-process. . . . We must learn to live within the flexible, always precarious borders of our subjectivity in order to learn to live within the flexible, always precarious borders of human society" (ibid.).

81. "It is *impossible* to exclude these psychically and socially threatening elements with any finality. The subject's recognition of this impossibility provokes the sensation Kristeva describes as abjection" (Grosz, *Sexual Subversions,* 71f.).

82. I use this adjective on the basis of Kathleen Sands's last chapter title: "A World of Color: The Promise of a Tragic Heuristic," 137-69 in her *Escape from Paradise.*

83. McClary likens music to "glue" in another context: "By around 1600, Italian music had produced not only the means for delineating affect and specific subjective images, but also the glue that held everything together: a set of procedures later known as tonality. From the moment tonality was 'naturalized' in eighteenth-century France as the product of mathematics and physical acoustics, it has been accepted as having nothing to do with social construction or passionate expression. It is simply 'the way music goes'" (McClary, "Music, the Pythagoreans, and the Body," 95f.).

84. Sands, *Escape from Paradise,* 168f.

85. Ibid., 174.

86. Ibid., 168.

87. Ibid. Earlier Sands explains: "Now the moral task can only be that of making the world go on. . . . To honor the plurality of truth is a practice of intellectual compassion; to honor the plurality of values is a practice of moral compassion. Were it a faith, compassion might seem to save us from the guilt of negating and destroying, but as a practice within a tragic world, it does not. But in the negating and the destroying, compassion holds open a space of memory and of longing—not an infinite space, but larger than the local world and its presiding deities" (16).

88. Hollywood, "Transcending Bodies," 13. This critical review provides an excellent synopsis of the main themes and problems in feminist theories of the body (cf. 13-18). Hollywood succinctly observes: "Human beings are their bodies, and yet bodies themselves continually push toward transcendence of bodily limitations, whether through the construction of artifacts, language, or other acts of the imagination [Leder 1990, Scarry 1985]; thus, as Paula Cooey suggests, discussion of embodiment is intrinsic to any account of human religiosity" (13). Later Hollywood remarks that the very "desire to transcend the limitations of embodiment" is "grounded in the body itself." Consequently, "politically motivated artists" often "use the transcending language of religion in their work" (cf. here Paula Cooey, *Religious Imagination and the Body*). Such assimilations may occur because "religious language and practice are most crucially about the human desire for transcendence of the limitations of the body" (18).

89. Cf. also Susan McClary's appreciation of Galas's iconoclastic portrait of female madness within the context of its more conventional renderings in Western music (*Feminine Endings,* 110-11).

90. Butler, *Bodies That Matter,* 16.

91. Ibid., 11.

92. Ibid., 16.

93. Ibid., 3.

94. Ibid.

95. According to Hollywood, these are the two problematic presuppositions of much feminist body-talk (Hollywood, "Transcending Bodies," 14).

96. Butler, *Bodies That Matter,* 9; emphasis mine.

97. Ibid.

98. Again I suggest that the musical force of her work, and its theological significance, lies in its power to destabilise both canonical texts and musical genres, using them against themselves; their meaning disintegrates, at the same time as it is synthesised into a powerful new message. Richard Gehr similarly describes Galas's work as both a sifting *and* recasting of historical texts and traditions: "By quoting the Bible, by making it her own and forcing it to serve her political and artistic needs, Galas audaciously appropriates the most connotatively charged text of Western culture. You can almost sense the verses she chooses stumbling beneath the weight of their historical and symbolic freight. . . .

Yet the verses stumble in other ways as well, moving in and out of the listener's sympathies. At times we hear the punitive God of the Old Testament, the strict father; at times the suffering Son, or suffering humanity. And the words seem at times an eloquent expression of realities we know, at times alien concepts wrestling to contain a contemporary culture that they were not designed to describe—and yet we still see them applied today, to suffocating effect" (ibid., 117f.).

 # "Sing for Our Time Too"[1]

Future Theologies of Attunement

DISENCHANTED WITH PRIOR intimations of nature's pretty harmonies, novelist Annie Dillard lauds its "abounding radicality, extremism, [and] anarchy." She deems creation "one lunatic fringe."[2] Feminist scientist Evelyn Fox Keller echoes this new perspective in more theoretical terms. She laments scientists' propensity for prematurely imposing "laws" upon nature. Masculinist scientific models are over-confident in their conviction that humanity's imaginative powers can create principles that are "fully adequate" for comprehending the natural world. The ultimacy of nature's multiplicity, its "prodigality and largesse," are too often minimised as exceptions to the rule.[3]

In effect, this book recuperates a similarly prodigal epistemology. In part 1, I diagnosed tacit strains of sexism and ideological escapism sustaining previously "harmless" theological accounts of music as science, music as revealer of divine harmonic laws. These incongruities weakened enlistments of music as trump-card proof of divinity's beneficence. In fact, numerous oppressive hierarchies produced tradition's musical parousias and their attendant musico-ethical distinctions between good and bad, sacred and profane. These required exclusionary gestures that belie music's divinely ordained, democratic *ésprit*. More specifically, a "symptomatic reading"[4] of historical and contemporary musico-theological discourse exposed the rhetoric of effeminacy and virility, and the polarised gynemorphisms in which masculinist musical taboos were expressed. In light of this critique (and with the help of feminist musicologists), music's unacknowledged role as a metaphor for sexual relations became apparent in these models.

The master's house dismantled, I constructed a feminist theology of music in part 2 with new tools, namely, images and metaphors culled from the vital intercourse between music and human sexuality, and from insights gained by the study of women's musical practices. From Hildegard, Jesus was redefined as God's music-made-flesh, and human music-making then became an imitation of Christ. From Lucrezia Vizzana and her fellow sisters, such musical *imitatio* was characterised even more specifically as redemptively abject—the nuns' fleshly musical transgressions dissolving the compartmentalisation of body vs. soul, sensuality vs. spirituality, christic vs. marian mimesis. Sister Rosetta Tharpe's promiscual blues further incarnated this new "heterogeneous sound ideal" while simultaneously reminding us of the latter's expurgation from the Christian tradition. And finally, the self-defined "intravenal voice work" of Diamanda Galas demonstrated in contemporary musical idioms the viability of a musically potent yet acutely decentered *imitatio crucis.*

This recuperative synthesis of lost tradition (Jesus as the Song of God) and revisionist history has laid a new musico-theological foundation: Music's theological significance now resides, not in its incarnation of harmony and order, but in its promiscuity and disintegration, that is, in its disorderly conveyance of power, pleasure, and intimacy among willing bodies. Correlatively, with this christomimetic reframing of women's varying degrees of musical iconoclasm, I have attempted to fulfill Elisabeth Schüssler Fiorenza's call for a "'women'-defined feminist theoretical space" within which to advance "christological meaning-making."[5]

Feminist demands for inclusive language in hymns melt but the tip of the *Venusberg.* When we fully embrace music as sirenic *imago* of sexual relations, with all the vibrant, dissonant, heterogeneous repercussions that such musico-sexual "bleed-through" breeds, we retrieve the revelatory bedrock which earlier theologians refused to mine in the name of a purer, disembodied God. Its initiation long overdue, the musico-theological possibilities of future dialogue between feminist theologies of music and other feminist theories are endless. Only a few can be alluded to in this brief final note, but even they point the way to the riches that lie beyond the present masculinist hermeneutical horizons.

For example, having blurred the boundaries between christic and marian *imitatio,* traditional understandings of salvation might be musico-theologically redefined in terms of invocation, modelled after Mary's *Magnificat.* This is salvation conceived as the giving of voice to God's radical, *yea discomfiting,* immanence. Such a voice is heralded in John Tavener's setting of "Thunder Entered Her," a poem on the Annunciation by Ephraem the Syrian ("the lyre of the Holy Spirit"). As another dialogical possibility, feminist theologians could elaborate upon Cynthia Willett's relocation of the "origin of ethics in music and dance," roots that Willett spots in the "affect attunement" of nonverbal, mother–child antiphony.[6] Finally, feminist theologies of music can consecrate a richer range of sonic and conceptual means for the construction of religious bodies—ritual, suffering, mystic, or christic. In these diverse modes of theological reflection, as both a toned interlocutor and a new thematic focus, human musicality provides an imaginative sound-bank (rather than think-tank) of authentically carnal/incarnate knowledge.

Cadenza

"Music is Love in search of a Word," feeding for now, without satiety, on sonic flesh and bone.... *"His stretched sinews taught all strings."* ...[7]

It is indeed disconcerting (though perhaps not altogether surprising, given the numerically based root-metaphor of *harmonia*) that the concept of love never figures prominently in masculinist musico-theological equations. Part 2 above suggests that a polysemically suffering or erotic love simultaneously feeds and answers musico-theological inquiry. If Jesus is both the Song of God and love incarnate, then music enfleshes divine love. Thus, for Hildegard, Satan—love's antithesis—cannot sing. Without love, we recall, St. Paul becomes a noisy gong, a clanging cymbal (1 Cor. 13:1).

Here, yet again, centuries after the great apostle, forgotten nuns sensually chromaticise love's necessity: Suor Juana de la Cruz has a joyous vision in which the Song of God embraces her so passionately that he plucks and strums her "limbs," "joints," and "veins," yet each tone sears her flesh with pain.[8] And, from Santo Domingo, Suor María,[9] another bride of Christ, yearns to be stroked by the musician whose bleeding hands and feet croon a gentle song, sweetest melody.

Notes

1. Homer, *The Odyssey*, 1.12: "Sing to me of the man, Muse, the man of twists and turns/ driven time and again off course . . . Launch out on his story, Muse, daughter of Zeus./ Start from where you will—Sing for our time too."

2. Dillard, *Pilgrim at Tinker Creek*, 144.

3. Keller, *Reflections on Gender and Science*, 164f.

4. Schüssler Fiorenza's coinage, *Jesus: Miriam's Child, Sophia's Prophet*, 124.

5. Ibid., 3 and 121 respectively.

6. Willett, *Maternal Ethics*, 45 and 89 respectively.

7. The first metaphor is from Sidney Lanier, "Symphony," in *Selected Poems of Sidney Lanier*, 58. The second christic image is from George Herbert, "Easter": "His stretched sinews taught all strings to celebrate this most high day."

8. Suor Juana de la Cruz, *Vida*, fol.6or, cited and translated in Surtz, *The Guitar of God*, 68: "Then the Lord embraced me and placed His feet on my feet and His knees on my knees—He purified them completely—and His palms on mine and His head and body against mine. And when He did this, what I felt was so intense that it seemed that there was a multitude of very sharp, burning nails piercing me. And there sounded a din all around as when they perform a Passion play, striking blows with a hammer. It [my body] was filled with His presence and with the taste and sweetness of His love. . . . I seem to see all the limbs and veins and joints of my body transformed into the strings and keys or pegs of a guitar and Our Lord playing on them with His most holy hands, playing on them as upon an instrument or guitar and making a very sweet and gentle harmonious sound" (ibid.).

9. "O sweet and good Jesus! . . . What sin untuned, your blood tuned. . . . O good Jesus, when I heard that music playing [probably a harpsichord or clavichord], my heart was hardened and my soul saddened, as I saw that I was not in tune so that you might play sweetly upon me. The instrument of my soul was not in concord so that you might touch it with the gentle hand of your love, of your will, for I had not come unto you so that the strings of its virtues might be cleansed with your most holy blood" (Suor María de Santa Domingo, *Libro de la oration de Sor María de Santo Domingo*, sig.C 6r cited and translated in Surtz, *The Guitar of God*, 72).

Works Cited

Adorno, Theodor W. *Prisms*. Trans. Shierry Weber Nicholsen and Samuel Weber. Reprint. Cambridge: MIT Press, 1983.

Alexiou, Margaret. *The Ritual Lament in Greek Tradition*. London: Cambridge University Press, 1974.

Aristotle. *Nichomachean Ethics*. Trans. Jack Thomson. London: Penguin, 1953.

Augustine, St. *The Confessions*. Trans. Henry Chadwick. Oxford: Oxford University Press, 1991.

Austern, Linda Phyllis. "'Alluring the Auditorie to Effeminacie': Music and the Idea of the Feminine in Early Modern England." *Music and Letters* 74/3 (1993): 343-54.

———. "Sing Again Syren: The Female Musician and Sexual Enchantment in Elizabethan Life and Literature." *Renaissance Quarterly* 42/3 (1989): 420-48.

Barth, Karl. *Wolfgang Amadeus Mozart*. Trans. Clarence K. Pott. Grand Rapids: Eerdmans, 1986.

Begbie, Jeremy. "Theology and the Arts: Music." In *The Modern Theologian: An Introduction to Christian Theology in the Twentieth Century*. 2nd ed. Ed. David F. Ford, 686-99. Oxford: Blackwell, 1997.

———. *Theology, Music, and Time*. Cambridge: Cambridge University Press, 2000.

Bernard of Clairvaux, St. *Sermons on the Songs of Songs*, vol. 3. Trans. Kilian Walsh. Kalamazoo, MI: Cistercian Publications, 1980.

Bernstein, Susan. "Fear of Music? Nietzsche's Double Vision of the 'Musical-Feminine.'" In *Nietzsche and the Feminine*. Ed. Peter J. Burgard, 104-32. Charlottesville, VA: University of Virginia Press, 1994.

Blackwell, Albert. "Schleiermacher on Musical Experience and Religious Experience: 'What Hath Vienna to do with Jerusalem?'" In *Friedrich Schleiermacher and the Founding of the University of Berlin*. Ed. Herbert Richardson. Lewiston, NY: Edwin Mellen Press, 1991.

Boethius. *Fundamentals of Music*. Trans. Claude V. Palisca. New Haven: Yale University Press, 1989.

Borchert, Wolfgang. "Das ist unser Manifest." In *Gesamtwerk*. Ed. Werner Rebhuhn, 369-76. Hamburg: Rowohlt/Verlag Hamburgische Bucherei, 1949.

Broughton, Vivian. *Black Gospel: An Illustrated History of the Gospel Sound.* Dorset: Blandford Press, 1985.

Brown, Peter. "Art and Society in Late Antiquity." In *The Age of Spirituality, Metropolitan Museum Symposium.* Ed. K. Weitzmann, 17-27. Princeton: Princeton University Press, 1980.

———. *The Body and Society: Men, Women, and Renunciation in Early Christianity.* New York: Columbia University Press, 1988.

Butler, Judith. *Bodies That Matter: On the Discursive Limits of "Sex."* New York: Routledge, 1993.

Bynum, Caroline Walker. "Introduction" to *Gender and Religion: On the Complexity of Symbols.* Boston: Beacon Press, 1986.

———. *Holy Feast and Holy Fast: The Religious Significance of Food to Mediaeval Women.* Berkeley: University of California Press, 1987.

Carson, Anne. *Eros the Bittersweet: An Essay.* Princeton: Princeton University Press, 1986.

Clement of Alexandria. "Exhortation to the Heathen." In *The Ante-Nicene Fathers,* vol. 2. *Fathers of the Second Century.* American ed. New York: Charles Scribner's Sons, 1908.

Clément, Catherine. *Opera, or the Undoing of Women.* Trans. Betsy Wing. Minneapolis: University of Minnesota Press, 1988.

Cone, James. *The Spirituals and the Blues. An Interpretation.* New York: Seabury Press, 1972.

Cox, Renée. "A History of Music." *Journal of Aesthetics and Art Criticism* 48/4 (1990): 395-409.

Curd, Patricia, ed. *A Presocratics Reader.* Indianapolis: Hackett, 1996.

Cusick, Suzanne G. "Feminist Theory, Music Theory, and the Mind/Body Problem." *Perspectives of New Music* 32/1 (1994): 8-27.

———. "Gendering Modern Music: Thoughts on the Monteverdi-Artusi Controversy." *Journal of the American Musicological Society* 46 (1993):1-25.

———. "On a Lesbian Relationship with Music: A Serious Effort Not to Think Straight." *Queering the Pitch: Gay and Lesbian.* Ed. Philip Brett, Elizabeth Wood, Gary C. Thomas, 67-83. New York: Routledge, 1994.

Dalglish. "The Origin of the Hocket." *Journal of the American Musicological Society* 31 (1978): 3-20.

Davidson, Audrey Ekdahl. "Music and Performance: Hildegard of Bingen's "*Ordo virtutum.*" In *The Ordo virtutum of Hildegard of Bingen: Critical Studies.* Ed. Audrey Ekdahl Davidson, 1-29. Kalamazoo, MI: Medieval Institute Publications, 1992.

Davies, Stephen. *Musical Meaning and Expression.* Ithaca: Cornell University Press, 1994.

Delatte, A. "Les harmonies dans l'embryologie hippocratique." In *Mélanges Paul Thomas.* Bruges, 1930: 160-72.

Dillard, Annie. *Pilgrim at Tinker Creek*. New York: Harper's Magazine Press, 1974.

Douglas, Mary. *Purity and Danger: An Analysis of Concepts of Pollution and Taboo*. London: Routledge & Kegan Paul, 1966.

Dronke, Peter. *Women Writers in the Middle Ages: A Critical Study of Texts from Perpetua to Marguerite Porete*. Cambridge: Cambridge University Press, 1984.

Eagleton, Terry. *The Ideology of the Aesthetic*. Oxford: Blackwell, 1990.

Edwards, J. Michele. "Women in Music to ca. 1450." In *Women and Music: A History*. Ed. Karin Pendle, 8-30. Bloomington: Indiana University Press, 1991.

Epstein, Dena J. *Sinful Tunes and Spirituals: Black Folk Music to the Civil War*. Urbana: University of Illinois, 1977.

Epstein, Heidi. "Immanence as Music Incarnate: Prelude to a Feminist Theology of Music." In *The Annual Review of Women in World Religions*. Vol. 5. Ed. Arvind Sharma and Katherine Young, 90-116. New York: State University of New York Press, 1999.

———. "Re-Vamping the Cross: Galas's Musical Mnemonic of Promiscuity." *Theology and Sexuality* 15 (2001): 57-77.

Fassler, Margot. "Composer and Dramatist: Melodious Singing and the Freshness of Remorse." In *Voices of the Living Light: Hildegard of Bingen and Her World*. Ed. Barbara Newman, 149-75. Berkeley: University of California Press, 1998.

Floyd, Samuel A., Jr. *The Power of Black Music: Interpreting Its History from Africa to the United States*. New York: Oxford University Press, 1995.

Gehr, Richard. "Mourning in America: Diamanda Galas." *Artforum* (May 1989): 116-18.

Grant, Jacquelyn, *White Women's Christ and Black Women's Jesus: Feminist Christology and Womanist Response*. Atlanta: Scholar's Press, 1989.

Greenblatt, Stephen Jay. *Shakespearean Negotiations: The Circulation of Social Energy in Renaissance England*. Oxford: Clarendon Press, 1988.

Grosz, Elizabeth. "Kristeva, Julia." In *Feminism and Psychoanalysis: A Critical Dictionary*. Ed. Elizabeth Wright, 194-200. Oxford: Blackwell, 1992.

———. *Sexual Subversions: Three French Feminists*. Boston: Allen & Unwin, 1989.

Herbert, George. *Herbert: The Laurel Poetry Series*. Ed. Dudley Fitts. New York: Dell, 1962.

Hildegard of Bingen. *Symphony of the Harmony of Celestial Revelations*. 2nd ed. Trans. and ed. Barbara Newman. Ithaca: Cornell University Press, 1998.

Hollander, John. *The Untuning of the Sky: Ideas of Music in English Poetry, 1500-1700*. Princeton: Princeton University Press, 1961.

Hollywood, Amy. *The Soul as Virgin-Wife*. South Bend, IN: University of Notre Dame Press, 1995.

———. "Transcending Bodies." *Religious Studies Review* 25/1 (1999): 13-18.

Holsinger, Bruce W. "The Flesh of the Voice: Embodiment and the Homoerotics of Devotion in the Music of Hildegard of Bingen (1098-1179)." *Signs: Journal of Women in Culture and Society* 19/1 (1993): 92-123.

———. *Music, Body, and Desire in Medieval Culture: Hildegard of Bingen to Chaucer*. Stanford: Stanford University Press, 2001.

hooks, bell. *Teaching to Transgress: Education as the Practice of Freedom*. New York: Routledge, 1994.

Hoppin, Richard. *Medieval Music*. New York: W. W. Norton, 1978.

Horne, B. L. "A *Civitas* of Sound: On Luther and Music." *Theology* 88/1 (1985): 21-28.

Irwin, Joyce. "German Pietists and Church Music in the Baroque Age." *Church History* 54/2 (1985): 29-40.

———. "Shifting Alliances: The Struggle for a Lutheran Theology of Music." In *Sacred Sound: Music in Religious Thought and Practice*. Ed. Joyce Irwin, 55-68. Journal of the American Academy of Religion Thematic Studies 50/1. Chico, CA: Scholars; Press, 1982.

Johnson, Mark. *The Body in the Mind: The Bodily Basis of Meaning, Imagination, and Reason*. Chicago: University of Chicago Press, 1987.

Jones, LeRoi. *Blues People: Negro Music in White America*. New York: William Morrow and Co., 1963.

Kaufman, Gordon D. *In Face of Mystery: A Constructive Theology*. Cambridge: Harvard University Press, 1993.

Kazarow, Patricia A. "Text and Context in Hildegard of Bingen's *Ordo virtutum*." In Wiethaus, 127-51.

Keller, Evelyn Fox. *Reflections on Gender and Science*. New Haven: Yale University Press, 1985.

Kendrick, Robert. *Celestial Sirens: Nuns' Music in Early Modern Milan*. New York: Oxford University Press, 1996.

Kierkegaard, Søren. *Either/Or: A Fragment of Life*. Trans. Alastair Hannay. London: Penguin, 1992.

Köhler, Joachim. *Nietzsche and Wagner: A Lesson in Subjugation*. Trans. Ronald Taylor. New Haven: Yale University Press, 1998.

Koskoff, Ellen. Introduction to *Women and Music in Cross-Cultural Perspective*. Ed. Ellen Koskoff. Westport, CT: Greenwood Press, 1987.

Kraege, Jean-Denis. "Luther: Théologien de la Musique." *Etudes théologiques et religieuses* 58/4 (1983): 449-63.

Kristeva, Julia. *Desire in Language: A Semiotic Approach to Literature and Art*. Trans. Thomas Gora, Alice Jardine, and Leon S. Roudiez. Ed. Leon S. Roudiez. New York: Columbia University Press, 1980.

———. *Powers of Horror: An Essay on Abjection*. Trans. Leon S. Roudiez. New York: Columbia University Press, 1982.

Küng, Hans. *Mozart: Traces of Transcendence*. Trans. John Bowden. Grand Rapids: Eerdmans, 1992.

Lambropoulou, Voula. "Some Pythagorean Female Virtues." In *Women in Antiquity: New Assessments*. Ed. Richard Hanley and Barbara Levick, 122-34. New York: Routledge, 1995.

Lanier, Sidney. *Selected Poems of Sidney Lanier*. New York: C. Scribner's Sons, 1947.

Léon, Céline, and Sylvia Walsh, eds. *Feminist Interpretations of Søren Kierkegaard*. University Park PA: Pennsylvania State University Press, 1997.

Leonardi, Susan J., and Rebecca A. Pope. *The Diva's Mouth: Body, Voice, Prima Donna Politics*. New Brunswick, NJ: Rutgers University Press, 1996.

Lippman, Edward, ed. *Musical Aesthetics: A Historical Reader*, vol. 1. New York: Pendragon Press, 1986.

———. *Musical Thought in Ancient Greece*. New York: Columbia University Press, 1964.

Lloyd, Genevieve. *The Man of Reason: "Male" and "Female" in Western Philosophy*. Minneapolis: University of Minnesota Press, 1984.

Lochrie, Karma. *Margery Kempe and Translations of the Flesh*. Philadelphia: University of Pennsylvania Press, 1991.

Lorde, Audre. *Sister Outsider: Essays and Speeches*. Trumansburg NY: Crossing Press, 1984.

Matter, E. Ann. "Interior Maps of an Eternal External." In Wiethaus, 60-73.

McKinnon, James, ed. *Music in Early Christian Literature*. Cambridge: Cambridge University Press, 1987.

McClary, Susan. "The Blasphemy of Talking Politics during Bach Year," In *Music and Society: The Politics of Composition, Performance and Reception*. Ed. Richard Leppert and Susan McClary, 13-62. Cambridge: Cambridge University Press, 1987.

———. *Feminine Endings: Music, Gender, and Sexuality*. Minneapolis: University of Minnesota Press, 1991.

———. "A Musical Dialectic from the Enlightenment: Mozart's Piano Concerto in G Major, K.453, Movement 2." *Cultural Critique* 4/4 (1986): 129-70.

———. "Music, The Pythagoreans, and the Body." In *Choreographing History*. Ed. Susan Leigh Foster, 82-104. Bloomington: Indiana University Press, 1995.

———. "Paradigm Dissonances: Music Theory, Cultural Studies, Feminist Criticism." *Perspectives of New Music* 32/1 (1994): 68-85.

———. "Pitches, Expression, Ideology: An Exercise in Mediation." *Enclitic* 7/1 (1983): 76-86.

McFague, Sallie. *Metaphorical Theology: Models of God in Religious Language*. Philadelphia: Fortress Press, 1982.

———. *Models of God: Theology for an Ecological, Nuclear Age*. Philadelphia: Fortress Press, 1987.

McGinn, Bernard. *The Flowering of Mysticism: Men and Women in the New Mysticism—1200-1350*. Volume 2 of *The Presence of God: A History of Western Christian Mysticism*. New York: Crossroad, 1996.

McNamara Jo Ann. "The Rhetoric of Orthodoxy: Clerical Authority and Female Innovation in the Struggle with Heresy." In Wiethaus, 9-27.

Meyer Baer, Kathi. "Nicholas of Cusa on the Meaning of Music." *Journal of Aesthetics* 5 (1947): 301-8.

———. "Psychologic and Ontologic Ideas in Augustine's *De musica*." *Journal of Aesthetics* 11 (1953): 224-30.

Meyers, Carol. "The Drum, Dance, Song-Ensemble." In *Rediscovering the Muses: Women's Musical Traditions*. Ed. Kimberley Marshall, 49-67. Boston: Northeastern University Press, 1993.

Miles, Margaret. *Carnal Knowing: Female Nakedness and Religious Meaning in the Christian West*. New York: Vintage Books, 1991.

———. *Desire and Delight: A New Reading of Augustine's Confessions*. New York: Crossroad, 1992.

———. *Fullness of Life: Historical Foundations for a New Asceticism*. Philadelphia: Westminster Press, 1981.

———. *Practicing Christianity: Critical Perspectives for an Embodied Spirituality*. New York: Crossroad, 1990.

Miller, Clement A. "Erasmus on Music." *Musical Quarterly* 52 (1966): 332-49.

Monson, Craig. *Disembodied Voices: Music and Culture in an Early Modern Italian Convent*. Berkeley: University of California Press, 1995.

Newcomb, Anthony. "Sound and Feeling." *Critical Inquiry* 10 (June 1984): 614-43.

———."Courtesans, Muses, or Musicians? Professional Women Musicians in Sixteenth-Century Italy." In *Women Making Music: The Western Art Tradition, 1150-1950*. Ed. Jane Bowers and Judith Tick, 90-115. Urbana: University of Illinois, 1986.

Newman, Barbara. Introduction to *Symphony of the Harmony of Celestial Revelations* by Hildegard of Bingen. 2nd ed. Trans. and ed. Barbara Newman. Ithaca: Cornell University Press, 1998.

———. *Sister of Wisdom: St. Hildegard's Theology of the Feminine*. Berkeley: University of California Press, 1987.

Nicholas of Cusa. *De ludo globi: The Game of the Spheres*. Trans. Pauline Moffitt Watts. New York: Abaris Books, 1986.

———. *Idiota de mente: The Layman*. Trans. Clyde Lee Miller. New York: Abaris Books, 1979.

———. *On Learned Ignorance*. Trans. Jasper Hopkins. Minneapolis: A. J. Banning Press, 1981.

Nietzsche, Friedrich. *The Birth of Tragedy* and The *Genealogy of Morals*. Trans. Francis Golffing. New York: Doubleday, 1956.

Oliver, Kelly. *Reading Kristeva: Unraveling the Double Bind*. Bloomington: Indiana University Press, 1993.

Oliver, Paul. "Blues," *The New Grove Dictionary of Music and Musicians*. 2nd ed. Ed. Stanley Sadie, 812-19. New York: Groves Dictionaries, 1980.

Nietzsche, Friedrich. *Joyful Wisdom*. Trans. Thomas Common. London; Allen and Unwin, 1910.

Page, Christopher. *The Owl and the Nightingale: Musical Life and Ideas in France, 1100-1300*. Berkeley: University of California Press, 1989.

Pelikan, Jaroslav. *Bach among the Theologians*. Philadelphia: Fortress Press, 1986.

Pickstock, Catherine. "Music: Soul, City and Cosmos after Augustine." *Radical Orthodoxy: A New Theology*. Ed. John Milbank et al., 243-77. New York: Routledge, 1999.

Plato. *The Collected Dialogues*. Ed. Edith Hamilton and Huntington Cairns. Princeton: Princeton University Press, 1961.

———. *Philebus*. Trans. Dorothea Frede. Indianapolis: Hackett, 1993

———. *Symposium*. Trans. Alexander Nehemas and Paul Woodruff. Indianapolis: Hackett, 1989.

Quasten, Johannes. *Music and Worship in Pagan and Christian Antiquity*. Trans. Boniface Romey. Washington DC: National Association of Pastoral Musicians, 1973.

Rich, Adrienne. "Transcendental Etude." In *The Dream of a Common Language: Poems 1974-44*, 72-77. New York: W. W. Norton, 1978.

Ross, Ellen. "She Wept and Cried Right Loud for Sorrow," in Wiethaus, 45-59.

Samuel, Claude. *Conversations with Olivier Messiaen*. Trans. Felix Aprahamian. London: Stainer and Bell, 1976.

Sands, Kathleen M. *Escape From Paradise: Evil and Tragedy in Feminist Theology*. Minneapolis: Fortress Press, 1994.

Scholtz, Gunter. *Schleiermachers Musikphilosophie*. Göttingen: Vandenhoeck & Ruprecht, 1981.

Schüssler Fiorenza, Elisabeth. *Bread Not Stone: The Challenge of Feminist Biblical Interpretation*. Boston: Beacon Press, 1984.

———. *In Memory of Her: A Feminist Reconstruction of Christian Origins*. 10th Anniversary Edition. New York: Crossroad, 1994.

———. *Jesus: Miriam's Child, Sophia's Prophet*. New York: Continuum, 1994.

Skeris, Robert A. *Chroma Theou: On the Origins and Theological Interpretation of the Musical Imagery Used by the Ecclesiastical Writers of the First Three Centuries, with Special Reference to the Image of Orpheus*. Altötting: Verlag Alfred Coppenrath, 1976.

Smith, Ruth. *Handel's Oratorios and Eighteenth-Century Thought*. New York: Cambridge University Press, 1995.

Söhngen, Oskar. "Music and Theology: A Systematic Approach." Trans. Joyce Irwin. In *Sacred Sound: Music in Religious Thought and Practice*. Ed. Joyce Irwin, 1-19. Journal of the American Academy of Religion Thematic Studies 50/1. Chico, CA: Scholars; Press, 1982.

———. *Theologie der Musik*. Kassel: Stadtsverlag, 1967.

Spencer, Jon Michael. *The Blues and Evil*. Nashville: University of Tennessee Press, 1993.

———. *Theological Music: Introduction to Theomusicology*. Westport, CT: Greenwood Press, 1991.

Spencer, Jon Michael, ed. *Sacred Music of the Secular City: From Blues to Rap*. Special Issue of *Black Sacred Music: A Journal of Theomusicology* 6/1 (1992).

Spivak, Gayatri Chakratovy. "Displacement and the Discourse of Woman." In *Displacement: Derrida and After*. Ed. Mark Krupnick, 169-94. Bloomington: Indiana University Press, 1983.

Squire, Russell N. *Church Music: Musical and Hymnological Developments in Western Christianity.* St. Louis: Bethany Press, 1962.

Stevens, John, and Dennis Libby. "Carol." *The New Grove Dictionary of Music and Musicians.* 2nd ed. Ed. Stanley Sadie, 802-13. New York: Groves Dictionaries,1980.

Strunk, Oliver, ed. *Source Readings in Music History: From Classical Antiquity through the Romantic Era.* 1st ed. New York: Norton, 1950.

Strunk, Oliver, and Leo Treitler, eds. *Source Readings in Music History.* Rev. ed. New York: Norton, 1998.

Stuckey, Priscilla. "Light Dispels Darkness: Gender, Ritual, and Society in Mozart's *The Magic Flute," Journal of Feminist Studies in Religion* 11 (Spring 1995): 5-39.

Surtz, Ronald E. *The Guitar of God: Gender, Power, and Authority in the Visionary World of Mother Juana de la Cruz (1481-1534).* Philadelphia: University of Pennsylvania Press, 1990.

Temperley, "Wesley, John." In *The New Grove Dictionary of Music and Musicians.* 2nd ed. Ed. Stanley Sadie. New York: Groves Dictionaries, 1980.

TeSelle, Eugene. *Augustine the Theologian.* New York: Herder and Herder, 1970.

Thornton, Bruce S. *Eros: The Myth of Ancient Greek Sexuality.* Boulder, CO: Westview Press, 1997.

Tracy, David. *The Analogical Imagination: Christian Theology and the Culture of Pluralism.* New York: Crossroad, 1981.

Van der Leeuw, Gerardus. *Sacred and Profane Beauty: The Holy in Art.* Trans. David E. Green. Nashville: Abingdon Press, 1963.

Waits, James L., Wilson Yates, and Nancy Merrill, eds. *Sacred Imagination: The Arts and Theological Education.* Special Issue of *Theological Education* 31/1 (1994).

Weinberg, Steven. "Reflections of a Working Scientist." *Daedalus* 103/3 (1974): 33-45.

White, Deborah G. *Ar'n't I a Woman?: Female Slaves in the Plantation South.* New York: Norton, 1985.

Wiethaus, Ulrike, ed. *Maps of Flesh and Light: The Religious Experience of Mediaeval Women Mystics.* New York: Syracuse University Press, 1993.

Willett, Cynthia. *Maternal Ethics and Other Slave Moralities.* London: Routledge, 1995.

Wilson-Dickson, Andrew. *The Story of Christian Music; From Gregorian Chant to Black Gospel: An Authoritative Illustrated Guide to all the Major Traditions of Music for Worship.* Minneapolis: Fortress Press, 1996.

Winn, James Anderson. *Unsuspected Eloquence: A History of the Relations between Poetry and Music.* New Haven: Yale University Press, 1981.

Ziegler, Joanna E. "Reality as Imitation: The Role of Religious Imagery Among the Beguines of the Low Countries," in Wiethaus, 112-26.

Zuckerkandl, Victor. *Sound and Symbol.* Trans. Willard R. Trask and Norbert Guterman. 2 vols. New York: Pantheon Books, 1956-73.

Index